Effective Business and Professional Writing

From Problem to Proposal

Third Edition

William Magrino

Michael Goeller

Nicole Reda

RUTGERS, THE STATE UNIVERSITY OF NEW JERSEY

Kendall Hunt
publishing company

www.kendallhunt.com
Send all inquiries to:
4050 Westmark Drive
Dubuque, IA 52004-1840

Copyright © 2009, 2012, 2016 by William Magrino, Michael Goeller and Nicole Reda

ISBN 978-1-4652-7737-4

Kendall Hunt Publishing Company has the exclusive rights to reproduce this work, to prepare derivative works from this work, to publicly distribute this work, to publicly perform this work and to publicly display this work.

All rights reserved. No part of this publication may be reproduced, stored in a retrieval system, or transmitted, in any form or by any means, electronic, mechanical, photocopying, recording, or otherwise, without the prior written permission of the copyright owner.

Printed in the United States of America

Contents

Preface to Instructors vii

Chapter One: The Project Proposal From the Ground Up 1
    The Six Parts of the Project Proposal 1
    The Interdependence of the Six P's 4
    The Six P's in Action 5
    Works Cited 6
    Newspaper Exercise 7
    Six P's Exercise 9

Chapter Two: Readings in Business and Professional Writing 15
    Authors' Introduction and Works Cited 16
    Defining a Paradigm 17
        Questions for Discussion 23
    Making It 25
        Questions for Discussion 31
    Humanism in Business—Towards a Paradigm Shift? 33
        Questions for Discussion 47
    Teaching Leadership Critically: New Directions for Leadership Pedagogy 49
        Questions for Discussion 73
    "I'm Ambivalent about It": The Dilemmas of PowerPoint 75
        Questions for Discussion 91
    The 5 R's: An Emerging Bold Standard for Conducting Relevant Research in a Changing World 93
        Questions for Discussion 105
    Organizing Data in Tables and Charts: Different Criteria for Different Tasks 107
        Questions for Discussion 113

The Missing Link: The Lack of Citations and Copyright Notices in
Multimedia Presentations   115
    Questions for Discussion   123

Chapter Three: The Cover Letter and Résumé   125

The Assignment   125
Sample Job Descriptions, Cover Letters, and Résumés   126
Cover Letter and Résumé Peer Review Workshop   133

Chapter Four: Researching Your Topic   139

Primary and Secondary Sources   139
Scholarly, Professional, and Popular: Evaluating Secondary Sources   140
Researching the Patron, Problem, and Paradigm   141
Searching for a Theoretical Frame   144
Searching for Models of Success   144
Merging Theory and Practice   144
White Paper Assignment   145
Sample White Papers   146
Finding Books, Journal Articles, and Other Sources at the Library   152
Some Advice on Searching the Internet   152
A Brief Guide to Using MLA Style   153
Sample Annotated Bibliographies   155
Works Cited   156
Annotated Bibliography Peer Review Workshop   163

Chapter Five: The Initial Sales Letter   169

The Assignment   169
Requirements   169
Purpose   170
Typical Pitfalls and Problems   170
Some General Advice, or "14 Steps to a Strong Sales Letter"   170
Sample Initial Sales Letters   173
Initial Sales Letter Peer Review Workshop   185

Chapter Six: The Oral Presentation   191

The Assignment   191
The Basic Parts of the Presentation   192
How to Prepare   192
The Question of Delivery   193
Advice on Using PowerPoint Slides   194
Some PowerPoint Slide "Don'ts"   196
Final Words of Advice   196

    Using Presentation Software to Develop a Presentation   198
    Graphic Aids Assignment   200
    Sample Oral Presentation Slides   201
    Oral Presentation Evaluation   209

Chapter Seven: The Project Proposal   211
    The Assignment   211
    The Parts of the Proposal   212
    Sample Project Proposals   217
    Project Proposal Peer Review Workshop I   253
    Project Proposal Peer Review Workshop II   259
    Project Proposal Peer Review Workshop III   265
    Project Proposal Peer Review Workshop IV   271
    Project Proposal Evaluation   277

Index   279

Preface to Instructors

This is the third edition of a text built around a single concept—that students learn professional writing through ownership of their ideas. The composition of this book, and its evolution through subsequent editions, coincided with the development of the course it was intended to serve as the main instructional resource at the Business & Technical Writing division of the Writing Program at Rutgers, The State University of New Jersey. At this time, this text is the primary resource for one of our most popular upper-level writing courses, Writing for Business and the Professions.

The first chapter is an introduction to the text and the course that it serves. First and foremost, this is a proposal writing text. In line with our learner-centered philosophy, this text assists students in building a proposal, in a very real way, from the ground up. The development of their proposals is based on a heuristic we constructed, known as the *Six P's*. This is a concept that students put into practice very early in the proposal writing process, and carry with them throughout the rest of the course. For each sequential assignment, leading up to the project proposal, the development of the Six P's assists each student in understanding the information accumulated up to a given point and, more importantly, where he or she needs to go next in the research process. The evolution of the Six P's mirrors the development of the project proposal, from its inception at the White Paper and Annotated Bibliography, though the Initial Sales Letter and Oral Presentation, until reaching the point of the Project Proposal.

In chapter 2, we offer a number of readings to help acclimate students to the idea of working within paradigms and how these paradigms help inform our ideas in the business and professional fields. As in the previous editions, we begin this series of readings with a selection from Joel Arthur Barker's *Paradigms: The Business of Discovering the Future*. The concept of *paradigm* discussed by Barker, as identified by Thomas Kuhn in *The Structure of Scientific Revolutions*, serves as the foundation for our text and the series of assignments that it supports. For this edition, six out of the eight readings are new. We provide both essays and articles that illustrate the influence of Kuhn's ideas concerning *paradigms*, as well as a number of pieces that show how this use of paradigms inform the fields of business and professional writing and, specifically, the assignments our students will be developing as they use this text. Each reading is followed by a number of discussion questions, to allow for vigorous class debate, as well as consideration of the significant links between the concepts in the readings to the students' project ideas.

Frequently, other authors of professional writing texts present the *job search* chapter toward the end of their books. We feature ours much earlier, in preparation for subsequent, and less familiar, assignments. Chapter 3 discusses a foundational task in any business and professional writing course—the cover letter and résumé assignment. However, in keeping with the real-world setting of this text, the entire assignment is a product of the student's independent research, in light of what the he or she personally brings to the individual job search. This is one of the most practical ways to get a student engaged in the process of professional writing. The cover letter and résumé assignment functions on a number of related levels: Foremost, this is an assignment that every student at this point in his or her college career will find valuable either immediately or in the near future. Similarly, this is an opportunity for a student to write for a professional audience in a way that he or she will have at least some familiarity. In addition, since these job-search documents are persuasive, in which the student is selling his or her unique skills and experiences to a potential employer, it relates directly to the discourse that guides the future assignments in which ideas are addressed to a specific funding source. As with each new edition, all of the student samples are new. For the first time, in this third edition, we are following two actual students through every assignment. In keeping with the learner-centered theme of this text and course upon which it is based, you will find the first of a series of peer review workshop exercises for a number of the key assignments. It is our belief that as students work through the assignments, routine, and guided, peer review will help them acquire an expertise in the assignment criteria and, in turn, become better proofreaders of their own work. We offer a number of duplicate peer review forms in each chapter, which can be removed from the text, for in-class group evaluation.

Chapter 4 discusses the type of research students will need to do in the process of developing the project proposal, as well as the assignments that precede it. There is a detailed discussion of the secondary, including scholarly, research that must be done throughout the proposal writing process. In addition, there is significant discussion of the primary *fieldwork* that normally needs to be completed to help document and quantify the first three P's. This chapter also introduces students to MLA style, which is the citation and bibliographic format that must be used for the research-based assignments. As with the cover letter and résumé assignment, you will find respective student samples and peer review workshop forms in this chapter. At this point, we introduce students to the White Paper, the first of a series of assignments designed to assist them in their work toward the project proposal, and the Annotated Bibliography, which will help them collate and describe the relevance of their sources as they identify their first three P's and begin to develop their paradigms.

In chapter 5, we discuss the document that signifies the first contact that must be made with a potential funding source, which we refer to as the Initial Sales Letter. This is the first assignment that requires a significant amount of scholarly research, cited in-text, and accompanied by a list of works cited. At this point in the proposal writing process, awareness of the role of the patron takes the forefront. Within the real-world milieu of the course, this assignment marks the first level of communication with the funding source. Assuming the patron's interest is piqued, this letter will be followed by their presence at the oral presentation, which will culminate, hopefully, in a review of the full proposal. Although the initial sales letter, in light of the point in which the students are engaged in the research process, will focus more heavily on the first three P's, all of the P's should be represented in some way. As a result, this is where scholarly research should be presented and analyzed in support of an emerging paradigm. In this chapter, we present a detailed description of the sales letter, as well as samples from the students who produced the previous assignments and the corresponding peer review forms.

Chapter 6 addresses the Oral Presentation. This chapter includes a number of resources to assist students in developing an oral presentation in support of their proposals. Chronologically speaking, within the context of this course, the funding source has received and read the initial sales letter and this document has generated enough interest for the patron to attend a presentation in support of a potential project proposal. In accord with the precepts of the course for which this text has been developed, each student is responsible to deliver an oral presentation to his or her respective patron. The instructor and classmates normally play the part of the funding source, especially during the question and answer period. The chapter concludes with an evaluation form to assist in measuring the level of success for each presentation.

The final chapter of the text, chapter 7, examines the complete project proposal and the many interdependent parts that compose it. Each of the fourteen parts of the proposal are delineated and described. Here, the paradigm, as a justification for a specific course of action, takes center-stage. As in the real-world professional fields, this proposal will succeed or fail in large part upon the quality and level of analysis of current, peer-reviewed research. At this point, the higher-level proposals will showcase the theoretical framework that guides the thinking, as well as the models of success that inform the detailed plan. Again, sample assignments are included from the students we have been following throughout the proposal writing process. The peer review workshop materials in this chapter are divided into three sections to allow for a thorough review of the entire proposal. In addition, a final evaluation form with a condensed view of the criteria is provided.

I hope your students will find this text as valuable as mine have. From its inception, our goal has been to equip students with the real-world skills that today's employers seek. It is incredibly gratifying when a student from a previous semester contacts me following graduation to tell me about how this text and course helped him or her transition into the workplace, in terms of writing and communication. It's even more exciting when a student returns to my office to tell me about a research proposal developed in our course that was ultimately funded and put into action.

William Magrino
July 2016

The Project Proposal From the Ground Up

Chapter 1

Someone once said, "those who know *how* will always have a job, but those who know *why* will lead the way." When you write a project proposal, you need to answer two critical *why* questions: "why do this?" and "why *this way* as opposed to some *other* way?" A key premise of this text is that you can only answer those *why* questions through research. Without research, you will not have knowledge (or, at least, you will not be able to persuade other people that you have knowledge), and without knowledge you cannot answer "why" in a way that persuades people to follow you.

We live in a society where knowledge is at the heart of the decision-making process. In this *knowledge society,* as Peter Drucker has called it, *knowledge workers* need many complex skills and abilities to get things done. They need to be able to:

- guide their own learning to master new knowledge and skills,
- analyze new situations, assess information needs, and locate that information,
- understand and digest both factual and theoretical material,
- think creatively to combine or improve available ideas,
- harness knowledge to justify a plan,
- develop and explain complex plans of action to others, and
- manage people and resources by putting information into action.

Knowledge workers need to be prepared for the creative challenge of solving problems through research, and they need practice in communicating their research to others. Having the experience of writing a project proposal where they use research to rationalize a plan of action can be a great first step toward professional competence. This book is designed to help you through the process of writing such a proposal.

The Six Parts of the Project Proposal

Though formats differ from organization to organization, there are always six basic parts to any strong project proposal:

- Patron (the person who will fund your proposal)
- Population (the people who will benefit from it)

- Problem (the need or opportunity that your proposal addresses)
- Paradigm (the research rationale for your plan)
- Plan (the way you will address the problem)
- Price (the budget to implement your plan)

A good project proposal will always help a specific *population* to address a *problem* by developing a *paradigm*-based *plan* of action that stays within the *price* that your *patron* is willing to pay. Though formats will differ from place to place, all strong proposals will have these six basic elements. The difficult part of developing a strong proposal is having all of the parts fit together into a coherent whole.

The *Six P Formula* can be used to organize both your written product and your writing process. The ideal process will follow the Six P's in order, more or less, focusing first on identifying a population to assist, a problem to solve, and a patron who would be willing to fund; then developing a paradigm through research that will help you design a well-justified plan of action; and once you have your plan you can develop your budget. Until you have a firm grasp on the first three P's, you will not be able to deal adequately with the last three. The first three help direct you to the right research to justify your plan and the last three present that research and use it to advance a coherent plan of action.

Patron

Who will fund your project? This is the person to whom you will literally address your proposal, and therefore the person whose name will be on your cover letter or memo. He or she will be your chief audience or reader. This is the person you most need to persuade. The patron could be your boss, the people at headquarters, a government group, or any public or private foundation. Like the *patrons* of the arts who paid for public and private projects during the Renaissance, your patron is the person whose hand controls the purse. The interests of your patron will ultimately influence the proposal. If you choose a funding source that is most compatible with your approach, you will have fewer problems justifying your plan to them.

Population

Who will benefit from your project? These are the people who will directly or indirectly be affected by your proposal. This must be a significant, measurable number of people. In a business setting, they may be your customers or people in your organization. In the case of a scientific project, the population should be thought of as both the people in your field who want certain questions answered and the people in the world who might benefit from your research. In any case, a persuasive project proposal will have a well-thought-out human dimension. After all, why should a proposal be funded if no one but you will benefit from it?

Sometimes students choose a project proposal (such as any reform at their college) where they themselves are part of the population to be served. If you do that, it is especially important for you to remain objective. No one wants to fund a self-serving project, and until you can imagine other beneficiaries for your work (the larger population of students to be served, for example) you will not be able to make a persuasive case for funding.

Problem

What instigates your project? This could be a theoretical question (in the case of scientific research), or an opportunity not to be missed (in the case of an entrepreneurial endeavor), or a persistent issue that needs remedying (in the narrowest sense of problem). All good proposals begin with a problem. If you find yourself beginning with a plan of action, then you have really jumped to conclusions. Before anyone should consider acting, after all, they need to be convinced that the problem is objectively real and that it needs to be addressed. You must first define and quantify your problem so that your patron can understand its scale, scope, and significance. In the case of a theoretical question, you will need to show how this question arose in prior research. In a business proposal, you will typically need to quantify the problem so that your patron can weigh the costs and benefits of action and inaction. Why does the problem even need to be addressed? Ultimately, you need to provide evidence to answer that question. You are not advancing a course of action just *because it sounds like a good idea.* If there is no problem, then there is no need to write a proposal.

Paradigm

Why is your plan of action the best one available for addressing the problem? To answer *why* you need a research-based rationale that answers these two questions: *How do you know* that your plan will solve the problem? And *why* try to solve the problem *this way* rather than any number of other ways? A good research-based rationale will show that you have a consensus within your field that justifies your approach. It might also show that the plan you want to implement has strong precedents to suggest that it will succeed. This is basically what we mean by a *paradigm*.

The way we use the term *paradigm* today has been greatly influenced by the work of Thomas Kuhn. In Kuhn's view, experiments form the basis of scientific knowledge by being what he called *exemplars*, or models of how problems can be solved. The larger theory that explains why the models work, which he called the *disciplinary matrix,* often comes much later. But the part and the whole are mutually dependent. When there is a consensus within a field of endeavor that this model and this matrix agree with each other, you have a paradigm. In terms of writing a persuasive project proposal, a paradigm can be either a model of success (or benchmark) that you think should be imitated or it can be a theoretical framework for understanding why your plan should succeed. The ideal paradigm will feature both an exemplar and a disciplinary matrix: it will have both a model of success and a theory of why that model succeeds. It will have both the part and the whole.

Paradigms describe the rhetorical and conceptual spaces that practitioners of any discipline generally follow. In the sciences and some areas of social research, paradigms are so commonly shared that a shorthand has developed for describing them, so that many paradigms can be summed up in a phrase that names a theory within a specific discipline: *integrated pest management* in agriculture, or *experiential learning* in education, or *ecological risk assessment* in environmental planning, or *the broken windows theory* in sociology or law enforcement. These terms grew out of exemplary practices that became common knowledge within a field of endeavor.

If you want to develop a paradigm for your project, you might ask these questions: How have other people solved this problem or addressed this question in the past? What models of successful practice are available to give me ideas and help justify a plan or experiment? What theories or ideas might help me to develop a logical approach to this problem or to develop experimental procedures? How might language from my discipline help describe and understand the problem?

Once you have a paradigm, you will be able to construct your plan based on research. Without a paradigm you will be inventing your plan out of whole cloth with nothing but your own ethos to justify it, and that is not likely to take you very far with your patron.

Plan

Your plan might be a construction project, a training or education program, an experiment to test a hypothesis, a study to determine what course of action is best, or some other specific initiative. Since a good plan will have to grow organically out of the people, problem, and paradigm, it is generally not the first thing you will work on for the project. It has to be responsive to your research findings.

How you present your plan will depend upon your project, but you should strive to be as explicit as possible about all that will be involved. If you can find a way to visually organize this part of your proposal, it will help your reader to understand it better. If the project will take place in a series of steps, you might be able to set up a calendar showing the sequence of events. If the plan requires construction, you will probably want to draw a diagram of the thing you are going to build. But a good plan needs to look back at its problem and paradigm: it should detail the specific ways you are going to address the problem and suggest how it follows logically from your models and theoretical research.

Price

Once you have your plan in place, you will need to calculate a budget. Often, your budget is restricted before you begin your project, and you should recognize the ways that price can have a strong influence over choices you make in dealing with the other five P's. If you are making a case for overall long-term savings from your project, you may want to include those in your calculations. If the materials for your project can be broken down and detailed, then do so. Find out the price of the materials you need, either by contacting suppliers or looking up prices online. Talk to people who have done this sort of work before if you can. Use your judgment if you are not certain of costs, but try to be as realistic as possible.

Other Considerations

The Six P's are not an exhaustive list, but they should handle the critical issues you need to cover in any good proposal. We could add some other P's here, and I would like to mention two more, since they often come up: partners and politics.

By *partners* I mean the people who will help you achieve your goals yet who will not necessarily be benefiting from the project or providing funding for it. They might be other organizations or other people in your company. They can sometimes be very important to discuss in your proposal, since mentioning their support will show that you already have convinced other people that you have a good project idea.

By *politics* I mean the larger cultural, economic, legal, or political situation that may impact your proposal. As we know, projects that might gain support at one time or in one place will not gain support in another time or place. If your project runs counter to prevailing ideology, you may have a problem on your hands. For example, it would be politically difficult to get backing to promote the medical use of illegal drugs in a state with tough anti-drug laws; it would be difficult to organize a deer hunt to address a deer overpopulation issue in a community that is anti-hunting; it might be foolhardy to propose new accounting tricks in the wake of accounting scandals like Enron's; and costly projects will not be well received during times of fiscal difficulty. At the very least, you may need to give special attention to your rhetorical frame (that is, how you argue for your project) or you may need to adjust some of your assumptions to make your proposal more feasible given current realities (or *politics*).

The Interdependence of the Six P's

You should imagine the Six P's spatially, as the parts of a coherent project that might come together in any temporal order. Making the Six P's fit together can sometimes feel like building a structure with six interlocking parts. As previously stated, the last three P's rely upon your command of the first three. The Six P's are completely interdependent entities, so choices in one area impact choices in other areas. You need to be open to revising the different parts of your project as it develops. How will decisions about the funding source (the addressee for your proposal) affect the way you approach the problem? How will the population to be served by the project impact the approach you might take?

For example, suppose your lab has expanded beyond its present capacity to give experimental space to all who need it. The people in charge of finding a solution to this problem will begin by asking themselves a number of questions:

- Patron: Where might we get money to solve this problem?
- Population: Who is most affected by the problem?
- Problem: What are some of the causes of the problem? What is its scope? What nonsubjective evidence do we have that there really is a problem?
- Paradigm: How have other labs succeeded in solving this problem? What innovative approaches (such as time sharing) have they used? What areas of knowledge can be brought to bear on the problem?
- Plan: What plans are feasible given current fiscal and political realities?
- Price: How much do you think you might be able to raise to fund your project? How much have similar projects cost?

If you find a patron willing to give you whatever money you need, then that will make it possible to build additional space. However, if your funds are limited and you need to make do with the space available, then that will clearly change your approach. In the case of limited funds, you may need to make decisions about which researchers should have priority over others, and that will create a narrower population that needs extra assistance. At each step of your project you should recognize how your choices can have cascading effects down the line.

The Six P's in Action

Because you are likely to make changes in your proposal at each step of its development, you should be prepared to revise your project as you go in order to make it more coherent. While not every project develops in a coherent step-by-step process following the order of the Six P's, they all need to put the Six P's together in a way that meshes. The order in which they are discussed here, however, is the order in which they will appear in the project proposal. Some projects begin logically but then require extensive revision to resolve conflicts between various areas of the Six P's (such as when the patron doesn't like the price).

A computer science student taking a professional writing course—let's call her Sandy—wanted to build a web page for a restaurant where she worked, but she didn't see how that web page could be used to improve business. She had begun with the plan (*I want to build a website*), and her dilemma was that she didn't see the problem to be solved or the paradigm to solve it. As a result, she had to go back to the beginning and ask some of the questions that had been skipped over in leaping to the plan of action. This is why you should avoid *working backward* and find the best research before identifying a course of action. You do not want to advocate for a plan for which there is no justification.

Sandy already knew the funding source: the restaurant owners would pay to develop a good website. But she had not yet thought about the people to be served (Who are our customers? What are their needs?), or the problem (How could a website improve business? What opportunities are we missing out on by not having one?), or the paradigm to guide her (What principles or models of success might give us ideas?). Without answers to these questions, the website could very well become a waste of resources. She had to work on the Six P's from the beginning.

A good project always depends on good research. And what Sandy most needed was a paradigm to guide her research. Always remember that the success of a proposal is dependent upon the quality of the paradigm research—not the ambition of the plan.

In her initial writings about the project, Sandy had made the textbook distinction between *target marketing*, which seeks to attract new consumers from a specific group, and *relationship marketing*, which involves improving loyalty among the base of consumers who already use your product or service. She suggested that the Internet was probably more useful for relationship marketing than for target marketing because of how expensive and difficult it is to reach consumers who haven't already heard of your business. In fact, she recognized it might be easier to attract people to the website by using the restaurant than to attract people to the restaurant by using the website.

What Sandy did not recognize right away was that the term *relationship marketing* describes a researchable concept, literally a marketing paradigm. Sandy had stumbled upon the term in her initial research, but because she was not a marketing major (she was a computer science major, after all) it had not occurred to her that she could explore that concept further through more focused research and reading. To do that, she needed to look at resources in the marketing field and examples of relationship marketing in action. A brief stop at the library index *Business Source Premier* (which indexes business sources and even offers full-text versions online) showed her that there was a wealth of source material within easy reach. A single search turned up almost 500 potential sources on *relationship marketing* alone. Though she found no examples of restaurants using the concept, she did discover quite a few service-sector models for using a website to build relationships with loyal customers. One of the best examples she found, described at length in one article, was of a dry cleaner that used a sophisticated website not only to communicate with customers but also to offer other services that helped to develop a sense of community around the establishment. The site even had a singles meeting page that allowed people going to this dry cleaner to connect with local singles, many of whom would post their pictures both online and in the lobby of the establishment.

You might say that Sandy's paradigm was supported by both the exemplar (or example) of the dry cleaner and the disciplinary matrix (or theory) of *relationship marketing*, two things she knew nothing about when she began her research. There were other approaches she could have explored (for example, there is a large body of research on building a *virtual community*, a term coined by Howard Rheingold). But the approach she found gave her what she needed to begin developing a paradigm for a workable plan. The idea Sandy ended up developing was quite creative and went beyond the things she had learned as a computer science major. In many ways, the project helped her to understand the human dimensions of her field.

After looking at how a number of other companies used their websites to develop relationships with customers, Sandy was able to synthesize an original yet proven plan for her workplace. She decided to work on developing a sense of community around the restaurant, so that even when customers were not there they could participate in the social life of the institution, developing a relationship with it like the patrons of the television bar *Cheers*. To entice current customers of the restaurant to visit the website, she would offer them online coupons, based upon the models offered by a number of other establishments. Customers visiting the site could find out more about the staff, e-mail suggestions directly to the chef, check out the calendar of upcoming events, join the restaurant "listserv" to receive announcements and advertisements, or check out what was going on at one of the live chat rooms. In a business built on loyal customers, a website that helped build loyalty was a concept worth implementing.

It took research to lead the way.

Works Cited

Drucker, Peter F. "The Age of Social Transformation." *The Atlantic Monthly*, 274.5, Nov. 1994, pp. 53–80.

Kuhn, Thomas. *The Structure of Scientific Revolutions*. University of Chicago Press, 1970.

Newspaper Exercise

Preparation

To participate in this exercise, you should read several newspapers and choose **one** article that could be the basis for a project proposal. The best articles will suggest a problem that you can imagine trying to address. The purpose of this exercise is *not* to get you to choose the topic that you will actually work on for this class (though it is possible that some of you might stumble upon your topic this way). Rather, this exercise is intended to get you to practice the process of project development. After reading chapter one, take notes on the Six P's that you could imagine developing from the article you have chosen. This may be collected and used in class discussions.

In Class

Get into small groups, and do the following:

1. Each of you, in turn, should present your article to the other group members. Describe the article and explain how this might make a good project idea. (About 10 minutes)

2. After the individual presentations, decide, as a group, which of them would make the most interesting basis for a project. (About 5 minutes)

3. Elect a group leader. This person does not have to be the one whose article was chosen, but he or she should present your ideas to the class. (About 5 minutes)

4. Once you have elected a group leader, begin developing a project idea based upon the article and on your own general knowledge. Obviously, to develop a strong project you would have to do a significant amount of research, but do the best you can with the information provided in the article. Use the following questions as a guide to discussion: (About 20 minutes)

    - Patron: Who might fund your idea? Why would they want to fund it?

    - Population: Who is affected by this problem? What specific population will your project serve?

    - Problem: What is the basic problem or need your project will address? Why is it a problem? How could you illustrate the extent of this problem? What are the tangible effects of this issue upon the population?

    - Paradigm: What disciplines (e.g., marketing, education, nutrition, medicine, etc.) might be useful in addressing this problem? What specific types of research would help?

    - Plan: How might you address the problem you have identified? What is your plan of action? Who will carry out this plan?

    - Price: What resources or assistance will you need? How much do you think your project might cost?

5. Present your ideas to the class and answer any questions. (5 minutes for each group)

Name: _____ Date: _____

Chapter 1 ■ The Project Proposal From the Ground Up

Six P's Exercise

Use the following form in a class exercise as directed by your instructor to analyze your project idea or the idea of someone else in your class.

Patron

Who would be willing to fund this project? Why would they want to fund it?

Population

Who does the problem affect? That is, who has a stake in seeing that there is a solution to the problem? Does your population have the same interests as the patron?

Problem

What are the main problems that need to be addressed? How could research shed light on these problems to emphasize their scale, scope, and significance? What sources of information about the problem would the patron find most persuasive?

Paradigm

What disciplines (e.g., computer science, marketing, education, psychology, etc.) might be useful in developing a disciplinary matrix for providing a rationale for action? Where might models of success be found to help shape the plan? What specific types of research would help?

Plan

What possible plans of action can you already imagine at this point? What plans are politically feasible? What would you need to know in order to develop a logical plan?

Price

How might your budget be limited? How much do you think the project might cost? How can that spending be justified?

Name: _____ Date: _____

Chapter 1 ■ The Project Proposal From the Ground Up

Six P's Exercise

Use the following form in a class exercise as directed by your instructor to analyze your project idea or the idea of someone else in your class.

Patron

Who would be willing to fund this project? Why would they want to fund it?

Population

Who does the problem affect? That is, who has a stake in seeing that there is a solution to the problem? Does your population have the same interests as the patron?

Problem

What are the main problems that need to be addressed? How could research shed light on these problems to emphasize their scale, scope, and significance? What sources of information about the problem would the patron find most persuasive?

Paradigm

What disciplines (e.g., computer science, marketing, education, psychology, etc.) might be useful in developing a disciplinary matrix for providing a rationale for action? Where might models of success be found to help shape the plan? What specific types of research would help?

Plan

What possible plans of action can you already imagine at this point? What plans are politically feasible? What would you need to know in order to develop a logical plan?

Price

How might your budget be limited? How much do you think the project might cost? How can that spending be justified?

Name: _____ Date: _____

Chapter 1 ▪ The Project Proposal From the Ground Up

Six P's Exercise

Use the following form in a class exercise as directed by your instructor to analyze your project idea or the idea of someone else in your class.

Patron

Who would be willing to fund this project? Why would they want to fund it?

Population

Who does the problem affect? That is, who has a stake in seeing that there is a solution to the problem? Does your population have the same interests as the patron?

Problem

What are the main problems that need to be addressed? How could research shed light on these problems to emphasize their scale, scope, and significance? What sources of information about the problem would the patron find most persuasive?

Paradigm

What disciplines (e.g., computer science, marketing, education, psychology, etc.) might be useful in developing a disciplinary matrix for providing a rationale for action? Where might models of success be found to help shape the plan? What specific types of research would help?

Plan

What possible plans of action can you already imagine at this point? What plans are politically feasible? What would you need to know in order to develop a logical plan?

Price

How might your budget be limited? How much do you think the project might cost? How can that spending be justified?

Readings in Business and Professional Writing

Chapter

A large part of your success in developing a project proposal depends upon understanding some important concepts, including culture, paradigm, and leadership. These concepts are best grasped in the context of discussing readings that offer commentary on the social situation of writing, descriptions of the paradigm concept, and examples of paradigms and paradigm shifts in action.

Each reading is chosen to help reinforce a major facet of professional communication. Joel Arthur Barker's discussion of paradigms in our opening reading, for example, offers an accessible representation of Thomas Kuhn's ideas. Without understanding the paradigm concept, you may have trouble conducting your research and successfully supporting your argument. You will also have difficulty envisioning ways of making change within an organization, which often depends less on what Kuhn calls *normal science* than on what he calls a *paradigm shift*.

Evgeny Morozov's essay from *The New Yorker* examines the paradigms that have guided the "Maker" movement and their possible implications in the digital era. Michael A. Pirson and Paul R. Lawrence's discussion of management theory helps us see how a paradigm—in this case humanism—shapes professional practice and may address some of the current challenges facing the corporate world. As Kuhn illustrates, when the old rules no longer apply, a *paradigm shift* may occur. Importing paradigms from one field into another, as Pirson and Lawrence advocate, is one way to bring about change within a field of study or an organization. David Collinson and Dennis Tourish's article on leadership education, and the paradigms that have historically informed it, helps us understand the larger consequences of fostering change within a given area of inquiry.

We have also included a number of readings that will help you understand how the notion of paradigm, as well as the other key concepts featured in this text, relates to the required assignments. Andrea Hill, et al.'s article discusses how the paradigms that shape a given subject area can affect pedagogical practices, such the use of as PowerPoint, within that field of study. Peek, et al. talk about how changes in health care fields affects how research needs to be conducted. Jane E. Miller demonstrates how organization and order of numeric data must work in conjunction with a given author's intentions concerning how that data is to be used. In the final reading, Stephanie Huffman discusses how we need to change our views about citation in the technological age.

Paradigms, which are the product of consensus, are ultimately social products, and as such they are rarely without critics, because they can dramatically affect people's lives. Paradigms make winners and losers: those whose work is funded and those whose work is not, for example. Being able to situate your work within such traditions and use them to innovate is the key to being a strong research writer in the business and professional fields. We hope that you find these essays worthwhile both in this course and in your future careers.

Works Cited

Barker, Joel A. *Defining a Paradigm.* Harper Business, 1993, pp. 30–41.

Collinson, David, and Dennis Tourish. "Teaching Leadership Critically: New Directions for Leadership Pedagogy." *Academy of Management from Academy of Management Learning and Education,* vol. 14, no. 4, 2015, pp. 576–594.

Hill, Andrea, et al. "I Am Ambivalent About It: The Dilemmas of Powerpoint." *Teaching Sociology. American Sociological Association,* vol. 40 no. 3, 2012, pp. 242–256.

Huffman, Stephanie. "The Missing Link: The Lack of Citations and Copyright Notices in Multimedia Presentations." *Springer Science+Business Media: Tech Trends,* vol. 54, no. 3, 2010, pp. 38–44.

Miller, Jane E. "Organizing Data in Tables and Charts: Different Criteria for Different Tasks." *Teaching Statistics,* vol. 29, no. 3, Aug. 2007, pp. 98–101.

Morozov, Evgeny. "Making It." *The New Yorker* by Condé Nast, 2014.

Peek, C. J., et al. "The 5 R's: An Emerging Bold Standard for Conducting Relevant Research in a Changing World." *Annals of Family Medicine,* vol. 12, no. 5, Sept./Oct. 2014, pp. 447–455.

Pirson, Michael S. and Paul Lawrence. "Humanism in Business—Towards a Paradigm Shift?" *Springer Science+Business Media: Tech Trends,* vol. 93, no. 4, 2009, pp. 553–565

Defining a Paradigm
"It's Twenty Cents, Isn't it?"

Joel Arthur Barker

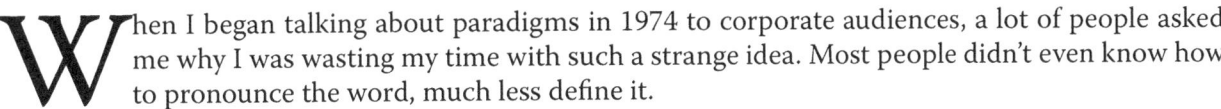

When I began talking about paradigms in 1974 to corporate audiences, a lot of people asked me why I was wasting my time with such a strange idea. Most people didn't even know how to pronounce the word, much less define it.

Most of the changes [in the business environment] were driven by a special phenomenon—a switch in paradigms (pronounced pair-a-dimes). And, in the jargon of futurists, they would be called "paradigm shifts."

The concept of paradigms and paradigm shifts can help you better understand the nature of those unexpected changes [in the business environment]. Being able to understand what caused them will give you a better chance to anticipate other paradigm shifts.

Today, "paradigm" is a buzzword and people use it loosely. But it is not a loose idea.

What is a paradigm? If you look up the word in the dictionary, you discover that it comes from the Greek *paradeigma,* which means "model, pattern, example."

Let me give you some definitions that have appeared in various books since 1962. Thomas S. Kuhn, a scientific historian, and author of *The Structure of Scientific Revolutions,* brought the concept of the paradigm to the scientific world. Kuhn wrote that scientific paradigms are "excepted examples of actual scientific practice, examples which include law, theory, application, and instrumentation together—[that] provide models from which spring particular coherent traditions of scientific research." He adds: "Men whose research is based on shared paradigms are committed to the same rules and standards for scientific practice" (page 10).

Adam Smith's definition, in his *Powers of the Mind,* is: "A shared set of assumptions. The paradigm is the way we perceive the world; water to the fish. The paradigm explains the world to us and helps us to predict its behavior." Smith's point about prediction is important. We will see that most of the time we do not predict things with our paradigms. But paradigms do give us the added advantage of being able to create a valid set of expectations about what will probably occur in the world based on our shared set of assumptions. "When we are in the middle of the paradigm," Smith concludes, "it is hard to imagine any other paradigm" (page 19).

In *An Incomplete Guide to the Future,* Willis Harmon, who was one of the key leaders of the Stanford Research Institute, writes that a paradigm is "the basic way of perceiving, thinking, valuing, and doing associated with a particular vision of reality. A dominant paradigm is seldom if ever stated explicitly; it exists as unquestioned, tacit understanding that is transmitted through culture and to succeeding generations through direct experience rather than being taught."

From Paradigms: *The Business of Discovering the Future* by Joel Barker. Copyright © 1993 by Joel Barker. Reprinted by permission of the author.

In *The Aquarian Conspiracy*, Marilyn Ferguson, who first made her name as editor and publisher of the *New Sense Bulletin*, writes: "A paradigm is a framework of thought . . . a scheme for understanding and explaining certain aspects of reality" (page 26).

Let me offer my definition:

A paradigm is a set of rules and regulations (written or unwritten) that does two things: (1) it establishes or defines boundaries; and (2) it tells you how to behave inside the boundaries in order to be successful.

And how do you measure success?

For most situations success is really measured by your ability to solve problems, problems from trivial to profound. If you think about that definition, you should immediately get a sense of how widely it could be applied. For example: Based on my definition, is the game of tennis a paradigm? If you think about it for a minute, you'll discover that it is. Does the game of tennis have boundaries? Of course, that's the easy part. The tricky part has to do with success and problem solving. What is the problem in tennis? It's the ball coming over the net. And you must solve that problem according to the rules of tennis.

You must hit the problem with the tennis racket; not a baseball bat or your hand or your foot. And if you hit it back over the net so that it drops inside the boundaries on the other side, you have solved the problem. And your successful solution becomes your opponent's problem. In a very real sense, you and your opponent exchange problems until one of you offers the other a problem that he or she cannot solve. Tennis is a paradigm. All games are paradigms. The beauty of games is that the boundaries are so clearly defined and the requirements for winning—problem solving—are so specific. Games allow for clear winners and losers. It is that aspect that generates much of any game's attraction. It is also that aspect that greatly disconnects them from reality.

Let us look at more important paradigms. Like your field of expertise. Almost everyone has one, either at work or at home. You may be an engineer, or a salesperson, or a chef or a carpenter or a nurse or an economist. Are these paradigms?

Again, let us apply the test. What does the word "field" suggest? Boundaries. How do you feel when you are outside your field? Not competent, right? Not competent to do what? Solve problems. Why do people come to you? To receive help from you in solving problems in your field. That sounds like paradigms, doesn't it?

Do artists have paradigms? I used to tease and say artists were just wild and crazy folks. Then I got straightened out by an artist. She came up after one of my speeches and said, "I'm a sculptor. What do you think the piece of marble I work with is?" I saw that it was her "field" and then realized she was going to work "inside the field" by chiseling into that block of marble.

"Okay," I said to her, "but you can do anything you want with that piece of marble."

"Not if I want to be judged successful," she retorted. And then she told me of the rules of "texture" and "form" and "balance' and "content" that she had to follow in order to be considered successful.

Since that encounter, I have begun to listen to artist's talk, especially about the "problems" they have solved in their work, whether it is a problem of perspective, or of color, or of tonality, or of character development. Artists have paradigms.

In a sense, I am constructing a hierarchy. At the top sits science and technology. That's where Thomas Kuhn focused. Science and technology deserve top billing because they are so careful with their paradigms, in terms of writing them down, and of developing measurement devices of increasing precision to tell whether they have solved a particular problem.

And, once a scientist has performed a successful experiment, it is expected that he or she should be able to hand the notes and the apparatus to another scientist who should then be able to replicate that experiment, getting the same results.

We would never expect a tennis player to be able to "replicate" Boris Becker's serve by just reading his notes and using the same tennis racket. Or someone to replicate an artist's work by being given the same pigments, paintbrushes, and canvas. The requirement of reproducibility constitutes a very important difference between science and all other fields. It results in science and its technologies having much more power to manipulate reality. But, even though they are more powerful, if you apply the definition I offered to science and technology, you will see that it holds true.

Over the years, I have collected words that represent subsets of the paradigm concept. Below they are ordered on a spectrum ranging from challengeable to unchallengeable. You may disagree with my arrangement, but take a look at the words and think about the boundaries and rules and regulations for success that is implicit in them.

1. **Theory**
2. **Model**
3. **Methodology**
4. **Principles**
5. **Standards**
6. **Protocol**
7. **Routines**
8. **Assumptions**
9. **Conventions**
10. **Patterns**
11. **Habits**
12. **Common Sense**
13. **Conventional Wisdom**
14. **Mind-set**
15. **Values**
16. **Frames of Reference**
17. **Traditions**
18. **Customs**
19. **Prejudices**
20. **Ideology**
21. **Inhibitions**
22. **Superstitions**
23. **Rituals**
24. **Compulsions**
25. **Addictions**
26. **Doctrine**
27. **Dogma**

Please note that nowhere in the list do the words "culture," "worldview," "organization," or "business" appear. That is because cultures, worldviews, organizations, and businesses are **forests of paradigms.** IBM is not one paradigm; it is a collection of many. That is true for any business. Large or small, they have management paradigms, sales paradigms, recruitment paradigms, marketing paradigms, research and development paradigms, human resource development paradigms. It goes on but I am sure you get the point. And there are even more paradigms in our cultural life: how we raise our children; how we deal with sex; how we define honesty; the food we eat; the music we listen to.

And the interrelationship of all these paradigms is crucial to the success and longevity of any culture or organization. That is captured in the word "forest"—a highly interdependent structure. As we know from the environmental paradigm, when one thing in the forest is altered, it affects everything else there. So when someone within your organization starts messing with their paradigm and says, "Don't worry, it's got nothing to do with you," start worrying. It is never just one paradigm that is changed.

A paradigm, in a sense, tells you that there is a game, what the game is, and how to play it successfully. The idea of a game is a very appropriate metaphor for paradigms because it reflects the need for borders and directions on how to perform correctly. A paradigm tells you how to play the game according to the rules.

A paradigm shift, then, is a change to a new game, a new set of rules.

It is my belief that changes in paradigms are behind much of society's turbulence during the last thirty years. We had sets of rules we knew well, then someone changed the rules. We understood the old boundaries, then we had to learn new boundaries. And those changes dramatically upset our world.

In *Megatrends*, the best-seller of 1982, John Naisbitt reflects in an indirect way how important paradigm shifts are. Naisbitt suggested that there were ten important new trends that would generate profound changes in our society in the next fifteen to thirty years.

I believe that if you look for what initiated those trends, you will find a paradigm shift. What Naisbitt identifies for us in Megatrends is important, because he shows us a pathway of change that we can follow through time to measure how we are getting more of something or less of something.

But even more important than the pathway is our understanding of what instigated that change in the first place. We almost always find that at the beginning of the trend, someone created a new set of rules. The trend toward decentralization is an excellent example of a paradigm shift. The old rules, the old game, required that we "centralize the organization and make the hierarchy complex." But the game ultimately created big problems. Then somebody discovered that there was a different way to deal with the problems, which was to decentralize the organization and simplify the structure; in other words, to change the rules. The result was a paradigm shift.

So if you want to improve your ability to anticipate the future, don't wait for the trends to develop. Instead, **watch for people messing with the rules, because that is the earliest sign of significant change.**

Four Questions

One of the difficulties I have with Thomas Kuhn's *Structure of Scientific Revolutions* is his insistence that paradigms exist only in science. In his afterword, Kuhn takes great pains to talk about all the other disciplines as being "preparadigmatic" because they do not have the exactness of science. And yet, again and again I saw the phenomena he writes about in nonscientific settings and situations. Then I realized that a key element in one of his most powerful examples was not scientific but cultural—a simple deck of cards. The cards were used in a scientific experiment to prove that people have great difficulty perceiving "red" spades and "black" hearts when they are intermixed with standard cards and flashed very quickly to an observer. But even though the experiment was scientific, the objects of the experiment, the cards, are cultural artifacts. And the expectations about the correct colors are cultural expectations, not scientific expectations.

So the experiment was actually a measure of the power of a simple cultural paradigm—the card-deck paradigm—to set up boundaries that dramatically influenced the way the subjects of the experiment saw the anomalous cards.

I am convinced that what Thomas Kuhn discovered about paradigms is a description not just of science but of the human condition.

When we look back to the 1960's, we see nonscientific paradigm shifts: Parents responded so violently to drugs and long hair on their children because these things represented a cultural paradigm shift; we missed the OPEC revolution because of an economic paradigm shift. Our country's inability to understand the Iranian revolution had to do with religious paradigms. Much of the confusion we have about the future is because of changes in paradigms.

These paradigm changes are especially important for all of us because, whether it is in business or education or politics or our personal lives, a paradigm change, by definition, alters the basic rules of the game.

And, when the rules change, the whole world can change.

The points that Kuhn makes about scientific paradigm shifts are true for any situation where strongly held rules and regulations exist.

I should also add the following disclaimer: I doubt very much if Kuhn appreciates the extent to which I, and others, have generalized his concepts. In his book he states that only in science, where the rules and examples and measures are precise, can paradigms exist. He also contends that only with the subtlety and accuracy possessed by science can changes in paradigms be measured so as to trigger the search for a new paradigm. I accept the obligation imposed by Kuhn's own careful qualification. In spite of his argument to the contrary, I still believe that his observations can be applied in a broader sense with great utility. I hope you will find this true as well.

To frame this broader discussion, we will ask four questions about paradigms:

1. **When do new paradigms appear?** This question is all about timing. If we can know when the new rules are going to show up, then we can anticipate our future with much greater accuracy. Timing may not be everything, but it's a great place to start.

2. **What kind of person is a paradigm shifter?** It is as important to understand who are the paradigm shifters, the people who change the rules, as it is to know when they show up. Of the four kinds of paradigm shifters that will be described, three are already inside your organization. But typically, we do not understand how to use them to our advantage. In fact, we usually are very hard on these people.

3. **Who are the early followers of the paradigm shifters and why do they follow them?** I call these people paradigm pioneers. Without them, paradigm shifts take much longer. Paradigm pioneers bring the critical mass of brainpower and effort and key resources necessary to drive the new rules into reality. Very few of us can be paradigm shifters; many more of us, if we understand our roles, can be paradigm pioneers.

4. **How does a paradigm shift affect those who go through it?** It is crucial to answer this last question if we are going to understand why there is so much resistance to new paradigms. It also explains the great gulf between old and new paradigm practitioners.

When we have answered these four questions, we will have identified the Paradigm Principles.

Name: _____ Date: _____

Chapter 2 ■ Defining a Paradigm

Questions for Discussion

1. Barker says of the term *paradigm* that "people use it loosely... but it is not a loose idea." Yet he goes on to list 27 loosely equivalent terms, suggesting that the definition is not so set in stone. Does Barker finally settle on a definition? What is it? Based on your reading of Barker, how would you define a paradigm in your own words?

2. As part of the process of developing a definition, get into groups of three and try to draw a picture of a paradigm. Of course, the word describes an abstract concept so there can be no actual picture of a paradigm. But in drawing a picture you will be able to objectify it and thus make it easier to describe in your own words. Give it a try. What does a paradigm look like? How might you describe it metaphorically?

3a. Students often say that they are prevented from being original by the requirement that they use research to provide a rationale for their plan. After all, they ask, where is the room for pure invention if everything needs to be supported by research into what other people have done? How can new ideas come out of old ones?

3b. How might Barker respond to these questions? Can tradition actually *support* original work? Can the fact that fields outside of science do not have the same reproducibility introduce an element of creativity? Or does creativity get introduced through the concept of paradigm shifts?

4. How do you research a paradigm? Think of a common problem and the paradigm that governs that specific area of inquiry. Where would you begin your research? What would you look for?

Making It

Pick up a spot welder and join the revolution.

Evgeny Morozov

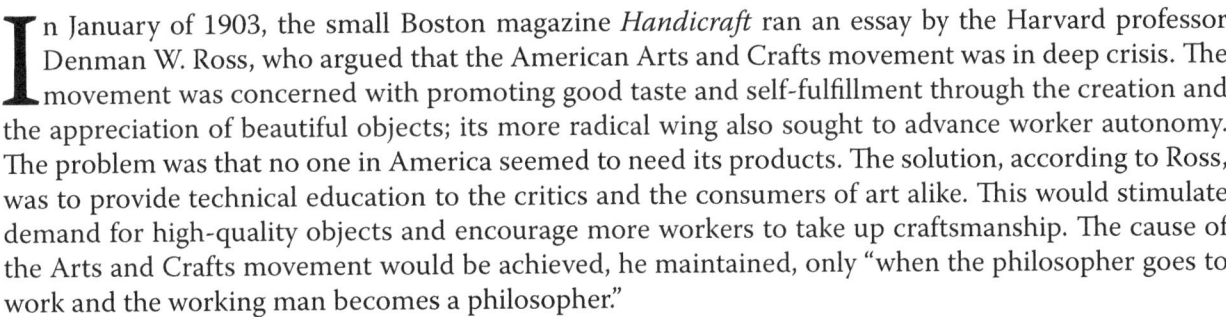

In January of 1903, the small Boston magazine *Handicraft* ran an essay by the Harvard professor Denman W. Ross, who argued that the American Arts and Crafts movement was in deep crisis. The movement was concerned with promoting good taste and self-fulfillment through the creation and the appreciation of beautiful objects; its more radical wing also sought to advance worker autonomy. The problem was that no one in America seemed to need its products. The solution, according to Ross, was to provide technical education to the critics and the consumers of art alike. This would stimulate demand for high-quality objects and encourage more workers to take up craftsmanship. The cause of the Arts and Crafts movement would be achieved, he maintained, only "when the philosopher goes to work and the working man becomes a philosopher."

In a long rebuttal, Mary Dennett, who later became an important advocate for women's rights, pointed out that the roots of the problem were economic and moral. Reforming the school curriculum wouldn't do much to change the structural conditions that made craftsmanship impossible. The Arts and Crafts movement was spending far too much time on "rag-rugs, baskets, and . . . exhibitions of work chiefly by amateurs," rather than asking the most basic questions about inequality. "The employed craftsman can almost never use in his own home things similar to those he works on every day," she observed, because those things were simply unaffordable. Economics, not aesthetics, explained the movement's failures. "The modern man, who should be a craftsman, but who, in most cases, is compelled by force of circumstances to be a mill operative, has no freedom," she wrote earlier. "He must make what his machine is geared to make."

Dennett's tireless social activism bore fruit in other realms, but she lost this fight to aesthetes like Ross. As the historian Jackson Lears describes it in "No Place of Grace" (1981), the Arts and Crafts movement no longer represented a radical alternative to the alienated labor of the factories. Instead, it provided yet another therapeutic escape from it, turning into a "revivifying hobby for the affluent." Lears concluded, "The craft impulse has become dispersed in millions of do-it-yourself projects and basement workshops, where men and women have sought the wholeness, the autonomy, and the joy they cannot find on the job or in domestic drudgery."

Although the Arts and Crafts movement was dead by the First World War, the sentiment behind it lingered. It resurfaced in the counterculture of the nineteen-sixties, with its celebration of simplicity, its back-to-the-land sloganeering, and, especially, its endorsement of savvy consumerism as a form of political activism. The publisher and sage Stewart Brand was the chief proponent of such views. "The consumer has more power for good or ill than the voter," he announced in the pages of his "Whole Earth Catalog," which debuted in 1968 and was geared to communalists and others who sought to drop out of the mainstream.

Inspired by the technophilia of his intellectual hero Buckminster Fuller, Brand played a key role in celebrating the personal computer as the ultimate tool of emancipation. He convinced the consumers he celebrated that they were actually far more radical than the student rebels who were being beaten up by the police. At a recent conference, Brand drew a contrast between "what happened around Berkeley

From The New Yorker, *January 13, 2014 by Evgeny Morozov. Copyright © 2014 by Condé Nast. Reprinted by permission.*

in the sixties and what happened around Stanford in the sixties," a contrast that captures the fate of activism in America more broadly:

> Around Berkeley, it was Free Speech Movement, "power to the people." Around Stanford, it was "Whole Earth Catalog," Steve Wozniak, Steve Jobs, people like that, and they were just power to people. They just wanted to power anybody who was interested, not "the people." Well, it turns out there is no, probably, "the people." So the political blind alley that Berkeley went down was interesting, we were all taking the same drugs, the same length of hair, but the stuff came out of the Stanford area, I think because it took a Buckminster Fuller access-to-tools angle on things.

To convince consumers that they were rebels, Brand first convinced them that they were "hackers," a slang term that was already in use in places like M.I.T. but that Brand went on to popularize and infuse with much wider meaning. In 1972, he published "Spacewar," a long and much read article in *Rolling Stone* about Stanford's Artificial Intelligence Laboratory He distinguished the hackers from the planners, those rigid and unimaginative technocrats, noting that "when computers become available to everybody, the hackers take over." For Brand, hackers were "a mobile new-found elite." He seemed to have had a transcendental experience in that lab: "Those magnificent men with their flying machines, scouting a leading edge of technology which has an odd softness to it; outlaw country, where rules are not decree or routine so much as the starker demands of what's possible." Computers were the new drugs—without any of the side effects.

In a later edition of the "Whole Earth Catalog," Brand reminisced about its mid-seventies heyday, when it recommended two products: the Vermont Castings Defiant woodstove and the Apple personal computer. The odd juxtaposition made sense to Brand. "Both cost a few hundred dollars, both were made by and for revolutionaries who wanted to de-institutionalize society and empower the individual." Yet, while the Defiant woodstove ran into trouble, Apple prospered—because it was in the business of manipulating information, not heat. With information now intruding into every field, Brand held, there was considerably more scope for hacking. And the country was ready for it. His subscribers were more likely to be office workers than factory workers; few were forced to be mill operatives, as in Dennett's day. But the transition to "cognitive capitalism" (as some labor theorists would put it) didn't make the workplace less alienating. Brand's remedy was hacking of a particular kind: "With over half of the American workforce now managing information for a living, any apparent drone drudging away on mainstream information chores might be recruited, via some handy outlaw techniques or tool, into the holy disorder of hackerdom. A hacker takes nothing as given, everything as worth creatively fiddling with, and the variety which proceeds from that enricheth the adaptivity, resilience, and delight of us all."

For all the talk of the "de-institutionalization of society" enabled by the personal computer, Brand was brutally honest about the kinds of emancipation that he had to offer. The way to join the holy disorder of hackerdom was by, say, playing Tetris—and, on weekends, going home and hacking rubber stamps, postcards, and whatever else one had ordered from the "Whole Earth Catalog."

Is Brand's hacking revolutionary, or counter-revolutionary? The plentiful recent books that preach hacking as a way of life—"Reality Hacking," "Hacking Your Education," "Hacking Happiness"—express devotion at least to the rhetoric of revolt. "Hacking Work," a business book published in 2010, announces that "you were born to hack" and suggests ways in which one could "hack" work to achieve *"morebetterfaster results."* As in most of these books, our hackers aren't smashing the system; they're fiddling with it so that they can get more work done. In this vision, it's up to individuals to accommodate themselves to the system rather than to try to reform it. The shrinking of political imagination that accompanies such attempts at doing more with less usually goes unremarked.

> *"I guess you could say I was a little distracted."*

That hacking has come to mean two very different aspirations became evident when Barack Obama belittled Edward Snowden as "a twenty-nine-year-old hacker" only a few weeks after the White House endorsed the first National Day of Civic Hacking. In Britain, the Metropolitan Police might be busy finding hackers like Snowden, but in April it helped organize "Hack the Police"—a so-called "hackathon," where software developers and designers were encouraged to bring their "unique talents to the fight against crime." In contrast to jabbering, feckless politicians, hackers offer hope for the most hopeless endeavors. "I'd like to see the spirit of hackerdom improve peace in the Middle East," the influential technology publisher and investor Tim O'Reilly proclaimed a couple of years ago.

Inevitably, hacking itself had to get hacked. When, in November, Brand was asked about who carries the flag of counterculture today, he pointed to the maker movement. The makers, Brand said, "take whatever we're not supposed to take the back off of, rip the back of and get our fingers in there and mess around. That's the old impulse of basically defying authority and of doing it your way." Makers, in other words, are the new hackers.

There are already plenty of intellectual entrepreneurs eager to capitalize on the new counterculture. Kevin Kelly—who used to work with Brand on his many magazines—has revived the "Whole Earth Catalog" tradition with his new catalogue-like publication, "Cool Tools." It features product tips for the true reality hacker—from "quick-refreshing underwear for travel" to the "luxurious, squirting WC seat" (thermostatically warmed, and yours for just eight hundred dollars). "A third industrial revolution is stirring the Maker era," Kelly writes in the introduction to "Cool Tools." "The skills for this accelerated era lean toward the agile and decentralized. Therefore tools recommended here are aimed at small groups, decentralized communities, the do-it-yourselfer, and the self-educated. . . . These possibilities cataloged here will help makers become better makers." In his world, the main thing it takes to be a maker is a credit card.

The maker era might not be upon us yet, but the maker movement has arrived. Just who are these people? Like the Arts and Crafts movement—a mélange of back-to-the-land simplifiers, socialists, anarchists, and tweedy art connoisseurs—the makers are a diverse bunch. They include 3-D-printing enthusiasts who like making their own toys, instruments, and weapons; tinkerers and mechanics who like to customize household objects by outfitting them with sensors and Internet connectivity; and appreciators of craft who prefer to design their own objects and then have them manufactured on demand.

Each of these subgroups has its own history. What turns them into a movement is the intellectual infrastructure that allows makers to reflect on what it means to be a maker. Makers interested in honing their skills can take classes in well-equipped "makerspaces," where they can also design and manufacture their wares. Makers have their own widely read publication—the magazine *Make*—a cheerleader for "technology on your time." Then there are Maker Faires—exhibitions dedicated to the celebration of the D.I.Y. mind-set which were pioneered by *Make* and have quickly spread across the country and far beyond, including a Maker Faire Africa. And, as befits a contemporary movement, the makers want respect: a Maker's Bill of Rights has been drafted. Kelly isn't jesting when he identifies the rise of makers with a third industrial revolution: many promoters of the maker movement believe that personal manufacturing will undermine the clout of large corporations. It might even liberate labor in a way that the Arts and Crafts radicals hadn't anticipated, with office workers abandoning their jobs in pursuit of meaningful self-employment amid sensors and 3-D printers. Meanwhile, the prospect of being able to print guns, drug paraphernalia, and other regulated objects appeals to libertarians.

A proper movement requires more than newsletters and magazines; it also needs manifestos. Chris Anderson, the *Wired* editor-in-chief who quit his job to become the C.E.O. of 3D Robotics, a company that develops personal drones, published one such manifesto, "Makers," in 2012. More recently, Mark Hatch, the C.E.O. of TechShop, a chain of makerspaces across the country, published "The Maker Movement Manifesto." Both books promise a revolution.

Anderson defines "making" so expansively that all of us seem to qualify, at least once a day. "If you love to plant, you're a garden Maker. Knitting and sewing, scrap-booking, beading, and cross-stitching—all Making." There's nothing in this book about mythmaking, but that surely qualifies as well. For someone who spent more than a decade at the helm of *Wired,* Anderson sounds surprisingly unhappy with the virtual turn that our lives have taken. He repeatedly blames screens and personal computers for our lack of contact with physical objects. "The digital natives are starting to hunger for life beyond the screen," he writes. "Making something that starts virtual but quickly becomes tactile and usable in the everyday world is satisfying in a way that pure pixels are not." Many aesthetes in the early Arts and Crafts debates complained about machines, rather than about the economic conditions under which they were used. Anderson, likewise, sees "pure pixels" as the source of discontent, as opposed to the uses to which those pixels are put (the boring spreadsheet, the senseless PowerPoint deck).

For Anderson, it's the democratization of invention—anyone can become an app mogul these days—that defines the past two decades of Internet history. Owing to the maker movement, he thinks, the same thing might happen to manufacturing: "Three guys with laptops' used to describe a Web startup. Now it describes a hardware company, too." Every inventor can become an entrepreneur. Indeed, he anticipates a Web-like future for the maker movement: "ever-accelerating entrepreneurship and innovation with everdropping barriers to entry."

The kind of Internet metaphysics that informs Anderson's account sees ingrained traits of technology where others might see a cascade of decisions made by businessmen and policymakers. (Would "the history of the Web" be the same if the National Science Foundation hadn't relinquished control of the Internet to the private sector in 1995?) This is why Anderson starts by confusing the history of the Web with the history of capitalism and ends by speculating about the future of the maker movement, which, on closer examination, is actually speculation on the future of capitalism. What Anderson envisages—more of the same but with greater diversity and competition—may come to pass. But to set the threshold for the third industrial revolution so low just because someone somewhere forgot to regulate A.T. &T (or Google) seems rather unambitious.

In the absence of a savvy political strategy, the maker movement could have even weaker political and social impact than Anderson foresees. One worrying sign appeared in the fall of 2012, when MakerBot, a pioneer in open-source 3-D printing, embraced a controlled, closed model. Then MakerBot was acquired by Stratasys, a big, established manufacturer of 3-D printers—a company that is the opposite of what MakerBot once aspired to be. 3-D printing is raising challenges with respect to copyright and trademark law, and regulatory backlash is inevitable. Some corporations will target the many intermediaries involved in the process, from the manufacturers of 3-D printers to sites hosting the files that users download in order to print an object. Other companies are developing software that would prevent printers from creating components that could be used to assemble a gun. Such a mechanism might control the printing of other artifacts, like the ones that litigious, patent-holding corporations claim a property interest in.

Then there are the temptations facing the movement. Two years ago, DARPA—the research arm of the Department of Defense—announced a ten-million-dollar grant to promote the maker movement among high-school students. DARPA also gave three and a half million dollars to TechShop to establish new makerspaces that could help the agency with its "innovation agenda." As a senior DARPA official told *Bloomberg BusinessWeek,* "We are pretty in tune with the maker movement. We want to reach out to a much broader section of society, a much broader collection of brains." The Chinese government, too, seems to have embraced the makers with open arms. Authorities in Shanghai have announced plans to launch a hundred makerspaces, while the Communist Youth League has been active in recruiting visitors to Maker Faires—or Maker Carnivals, as they are known in China. One of the co-founders of MakerBot has left New York for Shenzhen. Makers, it appears, are not necessarily troublemakers.

"I suppose you realize you're ruining my Tai Chi session."

Mark Hatch, for one, shows no concern that proximity to power might compromise his movement's revolutionary potential. "Now, with the tools available at a makerspace, anyone can change the world," he writes in "The Maker Movement Manifesto." "Every revolution needs an army.... My objective with this book is to *radicalize* you and get you to become a soldier in this army." How radical is Hatch's project? At the start of the acknowledgments that open the book, he thanks Autodesk, Ford, DARPA, the V.A., Lowe's, and G.E. His talk of becoming an army soldier may not be a metaphor.

TechShop charges a monthly membership fee, which provides access to facilities equipped with everything from oxyacetylene welders to the latest design software. TechShop's support staffers are called Dream Consultants, and the book is peppered with yarns about desperate souls—laid off, poor, depressed, sleeping in their cars right next to the makerspace—who have been transformed by the experience of making. (Describing a woman who became a vender on Etsy after visiting TechShop, Hatch writes, "An accidental entrepreneur was born. And what was Tina's background? She was a labor organizer.") Like Anderson, Hatch emphasizes how we are all born makers but are everywhere in ready-made chains. We must abandon the virtual and embrace the physical—preferably at Hatch's TechShop.

Hatch and Anderson alike invoke Marx and argue that the success of the maker movement shows that the means of production can be made affordable to workers even under capitalism. Now that money can be raised on sites such as Kickstarter, even largescale investors have become unnecessary. But both overlook one key development: in a world where everyone is an entrepreneur, it's hard work getting others excited about funding your project. Money goes to those who know how to attract attention.

Simply put, if you need to raise money on Kickstarter, it helps to have fifty thousand Twitter followers, not fifty. It helps enormously if Google puts your product on the first page of search results, and making sure it stays there might require an investment in search-engine optimization. Some would view this new kind of immaterial labor as "virtual craftsmanship"; others as vulgar hustling. The good news is that now you don't have to worry about getting fired; the bad news is that you have to worry about getting downgraded by Google.

Hatch assumes that online platforms are ruled by equality of opportunity. But they aren't. Inequality here is not just a matter of who owns and runs the means of physical production but also of who owns and runs the means of intellectual production—the so-called "attention economy" (or what the German writer Hans Magnus Enzensberger, in the early sixties, called the "consciousness industry"). All of this suggests that there's more politicking, and politics—to be done here than enthusiasts like Anderson or Hatch are willing to acknowledge.

A comparison to the world of original hackers—the folks that Brand profiled in his *Rolling Stone* article, not the "reality hackers" of later decades—may be illuminating. It's a comparison that the makers are fond of. The subtitle of Hatch's book, tellingly, is "Rules for Innovation in the New World of Crafters, Hackers, and Tinkerers." Anderson pays homage to the Homebrew Computer Club—a small hobbyist group that, starting in 1975, brought together computer enthusiasts from the Bay Area, including Steve Wozniak and Steve Jobs. For Anderson, such innovation is the prelude to a great business: when hobbyists cluster together to work on obscure technologies, someone eventually gets rich. But it's misleading to view the Homebrew Computer Club solely through the prism of innovation and entrepreneurship. It also had, at least at first, a political vision.

One of the leaders of the Homebrew Computer Club was Lee Felsenstein. A veteran of the Free Speech Movement in Berkeley, he wanted to build communication infrastructure that would allow citizens to swap information in a decentralized manner, bypassing the mistrusted traditional media. In the early nineteen-seventies, he helped launch Community Memory—a handful of computer terminals installed in public spaces in Berkeley and San Francisco which allowed local residents to communicate anonymously. It was the first true "social media."

Felsenstein got his inspiration from reading Ivan Illich's "Tools for Conviviality," which called for devices and machines that would be easy to understand, learn, and repair, thus making experts and institutions unnecessary. "Convivial tools rule out certain levels of power, compulsion, and programming, which are precisely those features that now tend to make all governments look more or less alike," Illich wrote. He had little faith in traditional politics. Whereas Stewart Brand wanted citizens to replace politics with savvy shopping, Illich wanted to "retool" society so that traditional politics, with its penchant for endless talk, becomes unnecessary.

Felsenstein took Illich's advice to heart, not least because it resembled his own experience with ham radios, which were easy to understand and fiddle with. If the computer were to assist ordinary folks in their political struggles, the computer needed a ham-radio-like community of hobbyists. Such a club would help counter the power of I.B.M., then the dominant manufacturer of large and expensive computers, and make computers smaller, cheaper, and more useful in political struggles.

Then Steve Jobs showed up. Felsenstein's political project, of building computers that would undermine institutions and allow citizens to share information and organize, was recast as an aesthetic project of self-reliance and personal empowerment. For Jobs, who saw computers as "a bicycle for our minds," it was of only secondary importance whether one could peek inside or program them.

Jobs had his share of sins, but the naïveté of Illich and his followers shouldn't be underestimated. Seeking salvation through tools alone is no more viable as a political strategy than addressing the ills of capitalism by cultivating a public appreciation of arts and crafts. Society is always in flux, and the designer can't predict how various political, social, and economic systems will come to blunt, augment, or redirect the power of the tool that is being designed. Instead of deinstitutionalizing society, the radicals would have done better to advocate reinstitutionalizing it: pushing for political and legal reforms to secure the transparency and decentralization of power they associated with their favorite technology.

One thinker who saw through the naïveté of Illich, the Homebrewers, and the Whole Earthers was the libertarian socialist Murray Bookchin. Back in the late sixties, he published a fiery essay called "Towards a Liberatory Technology," arguing that technology is not an enemy of craftsmanship and personal freedom. Unlike Brand, though, Bookchin never thought that such liberation could occur just by getting more technology into everyone's hands; the nature of the political community mattered. In his book "The Ecology of Freedom" (1982), he couldn't hide his frustration with the "access-to-tools" mentality. Bookchin's critique of the counterculture's turn to tools parallels Dennett's critique of the aesthetes' turn to education eighty years earlier. It didn't make sense to speak of "convivial tools," he argued, without taking a close look at the political and social structures in which they were embedded.

A reluctance to talk about institutions and political change doomed the Arts and Crafts movement, channeling the spirit of labor reform into consumerism and D.I.Y. tinkering. The same thing is happening to the movement's successors. Our tech imagination, to judge from catalogues like "Cool Tools," is at its zenith. (Never before have so many had access to thermostatically warmed toilet seats.) But our institutional imagination has stalled, and with it the democratizing potential of radical technologies. We carry personal computers in our pockets—nothing could be more decentralized than this!—but have surrendered control of our data, which is stored on centralized servers, far away from our pockets. The hackers won their fight against I.B.M.—only to lose it to Facebook and Google. And the spooks at the National Security Agency must be surprised to learn that gadgets were supposed to usher in the "de-institutionalization of society."

The lure of the technological sublime has ruined more than one social movement, and, in this respect, even Mary Dennett fared no better than Felsenstein. For all her sensitivity to questions of inequality, she also believed that, once "cheap electric power" is "at every village door," the "emancipation of the craftsman and the unchaining of art" would naturally follow. What electric company would disagree?

Name: _____ Date: _____

Chapter 2 ■ Making It

Questions for Discussion

1. As Morozov recounts, Harvard professor Denman W. Ross maintains in his 1903 essay, "The cause of the Arts and Crafts movement would be achieved . . . only 'when the philosopher goes to work and the working man becomes a philosopher.'" Discuss with a partner: What did Ross mean by this? Is this idea still applicable today? If so, how? If not, how can we update this statement to make it more relevant to the present day?

2. Morozov explains, "Although the Arts and Crafts movement was dead by the First World War, the sentiment behind it lingered. It resurfaced in the counterculture of the nineteen-sixties, with its celebration of simplicity, its back-to-the-land sloganeering, and, especially, its endorsement of savvy consumerism as a form of political activism." As researchers, what can we learn from this "less is more" approach? What does it mean to be a "savvy" consumer in a world where a plethora of technology exists to make our daily lives easier? Explain.

3. "Hacking" is a term used frequently in this article. Stewart Brand, as cited by Morozov, states, "A hacker takes nothing as given, everything as worth creatively fiddling with, and the variety which proceeds from that enricheth the adaptivity, resilience, and delight of us all." How can paradigms be "hacked" so that there is a clear blueprint of what has worked before, but also so that there is room for creativity and innovation?

4. As Morozov tells us, Chris Anderson, former editor-in-chief of *Wired* Magazine, "defines 'making' so expansively that all of us seem to qualify, at least once a day. 'If you love to plant, you're a garden Maker. Knitting and sewing, scrap-booking, beading, and cross-stitching—all Making.'" Does the attitude that everyone is a "Maker" take away from the recognition that inventors, businesspeople, and others should receive for doing great work in their respective fields? Or, does it allow for more individuals to be applauded for their ideas, thus resulting in more successful networking and innovation?

5. Morozov highlights the irony of some statements made by Mark Hatch, the author of "The Maker Movement Manifesto." In it, Hatch enthusiastically explains that "Every revolution needs an army . . . my objective with this book is to *radicalize* you and get you to become a soldier in this army," painting himself as the leader of this movement. However, he opens his book with list all of the corporations that have helped him become a "Maker." Is it acceptable to take what someone else has introduced to you and taught you, rebrand it, and "sell" it as if it is your own idea? If not, how can we justify using paradigms as such a large part of our research proposals?

6. Introduce your proposal idea to your class or a small group. Explain how the perspective that everyone is a "Maker" could potentially help or harm your proposal. Has your research presented paradigms that are mostly similar, or do you have a good amount of differentiation when it comes to your research? Is there room for a few "Makers" in the discipline(s) you're working within?

Humanism in Business—Towards a Paradigm Shift?

Michael A. Pirson and Paul R. Lawrence

Abstract

Management theory and practice are facing unprecedented challenges. The lack of sustainability, the increasing inequity, and the continuous decline in societal trust pose a threat to 'business as usual' (Jackson and Nelson, 2004). Capitalism is at a crossroad and scholars, practitioners, and policy makers are called to rethink business strategy in light of major external changes (Arena, 2004; Hart, 2005). In the following, we review an alternative view of human beings that is based on a renewed Darwinian theory developed by Lawrence and Nohria (2002). We label this alternative view 'humanistic' and draw distinctions to current 'econotnistic' conceptions. We then develop the consequences that this humanistic view has for business organizations, examining business strategy, governance structures, leadership forms, and organizational culture. Afterward, we outline the influences of humanism on management in the past and the present, and suggest options for humanism to shape the future of management. In this manner, we will contribute to the discussion of alternative management paradigms that help solve the current crises.

Key Words

humanism, economism, management paradigms, sustainability, management theory, business strategy

Introduction

Management theory and practice are facing unprecedented challenges. The lack of sustainability, the increasing inequity, and the continuous decline in societal trust pose a threat to 'business as usual' (Jackson and Nelson, 2004). Capitalism is at a crossroad and scholars, practitioners, and policy makers are called to rethink business strategy in light of major external changes (Arena, 2004; Hart, 2005). As current management theory is largely informed by economics, it draws substantively from neoclassical theories of human beings (Ghoshal, 2005).

Accordingly, humans are materialistic utility maximizers that value individual benefit over group and societal benefit. A 'homo economicus' engages with others only in a transactional manner to fulfill his or her interests. He/she is amoral, values short term gratification, and often acts opportunistically to further personal gain. This theory of human behavior has drawn support from the highly popular interpretation of Darwinian theory of evolution as favoring the survival of the toughest over the weak, as Spencer proposed, instead of the survival of the most adaptive as Darwin intended.

Business strategy and organizational design are largely based on the mistaken assumptions about Darwinism, and, in turn, are blamed by others for creating negative externalities. Argyris (1973), for example, claims that organizational mechanisms based on principal-agent theory create opportunistic and

Journal of Business Ethics, "Humanism in Business—Towards a Paradigm Shift?" Volume 93 (4), 2009, by Michael A. Pirson. Copyright © 2009 Springer Science+Business Media B.V. With permission of Springer.

short-term gain oriented actors in a self-fulfilling prophecy (see also Davis et al., 1997). Other critical scholars argue that management theory needs to be rethought based on psychological insights rather than theoretical assumptions (Ghoshal, 2005; Tyler, 2006). Tyler (2006) finds overwhelming evidence that people look for respect, acceptance, communion, and shared values instead of short-sighted personal utility increases. Diener and Seligman (2004) find that 'Leading a meaningful life' is more important to most people than money, power, and status. De Cremer and Blader (2005) underline the importance of a sense of belongingness, which is contradictory to the individualization aspects of economic theory. We hence suggest that we need a broader way of understanding humans on which we can prescribe a renewed theory of leadership and management, to design our organizations and to formulate business strategy.

In the following, we will review an alternative view of human beings that is based on a renewed Darwinian theory developed by Lawrence and Nohria (2002). We label this alternative view of human beings as a 'humanistic' theory and draw distinctions to the current 'economistic' conceptions. We then develop the consequences that this humanistic view has for business organizations, examining business strategy, governance structures, leadership forms, and organizational culture. Afterward, we outline the influences of humanism on management in the past and the present, and suggest options for humanism to shape the future of management. In this manner, we will contribute to the discussion of alternative management paradigms that help solve the current crises.

Economism and Humanism—Competing Paradigms

A Common Background but then a Divergence

Following Nida-Ruemelin (2009), the discipline of economics originated from Scottish moral philosophy during the European Enlightenment. In contrast to prevailing philosophy that focused on deity, Scottish moral philosophy centered on the human individual. It emphasized the human ability to reason and was therefore hostile to collectivist and naturalistic anthropologies. Classical economic theory was similar in that regard and also closely bound to utilitarianism. Bentham (1789), one of the founding fathers of utilitarianism, tried to create rational normative criteria for good legislation, where every single person was considered equal, independent from social status and origin. John Stuart Mill, one of the leading economic theoreticians, was both a utilitarian and an ethicist at the same time. However, while economics and ethics were originally closely linked, they gradually became disconnected (Table 1).

Following Nida-Ruemelin's (2009) analysis, utilitarianism has several flaws that eventually led to the de-ethicalization (or de-moralization) of economics. Despite being liberal, universalist and rationalist origins utilitarian principles can, in fact, be used to justify collectivist practices: "To maximize the total sum of happiness efficiently can include the instrumentalization of one person for the sake of one or several others. Under certain conditions, even slavery can be justified by utilitarian principles" (p. 10). In addition, utilitarianism does not provide an understanding of unalienable individual rights and thus enables instrumentalization of human beings. Integrity and morality are not considered intrinsic to human beings. "No project that might be essential for leading an upright and coherent life will survive if the duty to maximize the total sum of happiness has priority in each moment of the agent's life" (p. 10).

Despite many popular misconceptions, humanism as a philosophic tradition, and utilitarian economism have very similar roots. Humanistic philosophy also takes the human individual as its starting point and emphasizes the human capacity of reasoning. It is therefore equally hostile to any form of collectivism.[1] In contrast to economism, however, humanism assumes that human nature is not entirely a given, that it can be refined, through education and learning. In addition, the ethical component remains a cornerstone in humanism in that it attributes unalienable rights to everybody, independent from ethnicity, nationality, social status or gender. Humanism addresses everybody and is universal in its outreach.

The Comparative Views of the Individual

As stated before, economism views the human being as a fixed entity, predetermined by its utility function which is stable. This economic man (homo oeconomicus) is utterly self-serving and only interested in maximizing his immediate utility. Economic man is therefore only engaging in transactional, short-term oriented encounters with others. His engagements are interest based and other people are a means to an end. He acts opportunistically and is mainly motivated by the lower level needs in Maslow's hierarchy of needs (physiological and safety needs). His actions are not evaluated for universal applicability, and hence he is amoral (Dierksmeier and Pirson, 2008).[2]

The philosophy of humanism in contrast views the individual as a zoon politikon, a relational man. Someone, who materializes his freedom through value-based social interactions. People he or she engages with are means but also an end in themselves. Human beings in the humanistic view are guided by universally applicable principles and aim at long-term relationships. They are intrinsically motivated to self-actualize and serve humanity through what they do. They do not have fixed preconceived utility functions, but their interests, needs, and wants take shape through discourse and continuous exchange with the outside world. As such human beings are not maximizing their own utility, but balancing the interests of themselves and people around themselves in accordance with general moral principles (Dierksmeier and Pirson, 2008).

Paradigm	Economism	Humanism
Individual level		
Model	Homo oeconomicus	Zoon politikon
Motivation	Two drive motivated	Four drive motivated
	Drive to acquire	Drive to acquire
	Drive to defend	Drive to bond
		Drive to comprehend
		Drive to defend
Goal	Maximization of utility	Balance of interests
Disposition	Transactional	Relational
View of other	Means to an end	Means and end
Organizational level		
Organization	Nexus of contracts	Social community
Governance	Shareholder oriented	Stakeholder oriented
Model in management theory	Agent	Steward
Leadership style	Transactional	Transformational
Goal setting	Command and control based	Discourse based
Goal	Profit maximization	Financial, social, and environmental sustainability
Incentives	Geared to 1st and 2nd need (Maslow)	Geared to 3rd 4th order needs (Maslow)
	Drive to acquire	Drive to acquire
	Drive to defend	Drive to bond
		Drive to comprehend
		Drive to defend
Culture	Mechanistic	Organic
Time frame	Short term	Long term
System level		
State orientation to business	Laissez faire	Subsidiary actor
State-managerial responsibility	Financial value creation	Supporting a balanced society

Table 1 Economism and Humanism.

The Perspective of the Renewed Darwinian Theory of Human Beings

Both views have their traditions, but so far, no real test of these theoretical assumptions was possible. Lawrence and Nohria (2002), however, took up the task of evaluating recent findings from neuroscience, behavioral economics, and evolutionary psychology and developed a theory that allows viewing human beings in a more complete fashion. Lawrence (2007a) in his most recent follow-up work calls it a renewed Darwinian theory (RD Theory) of human beings, referring to Darwin's groundbreaking insights on human behavior that are often overlooked or misunderstood. In essence, RD theory illuminates how the human brain has developed via natural selection and also through sex and group selection mechanisms to make complex decisions regarding all aspects of life (personal, communal, and societal). It posits *four basic drives,* ultimate motives that underlie all human decisions. There are two ancient drives which are shared by all animals with some capacity to sense and evaluate its surroundings; *the drive to acquire* (dA) life-sustaining resources, and *the drive to defend* (dD) from all lifethreatening entities. The two newer drives, that evolved to an independent status in humans, are *the drive to bond* (dB) in long-term mutually caring relationships with other humans, and *the drive to comprehend* (dC), to make sense of the world around us in terms of its multifaceted relations to ourselves.

Darwin (1909) observed the drive to bond in humans, when describing: "Every one will admit that man is a social being. We see this in his dislike of solitude and in his wish for society beyond that of his own family. Solitary confinement is one of the severest punishments which can be inflicted" (p. 110) or, "Under circumstances of extreme peril, as during a fire, when a man endeavors to save a fellow-creature without a moment's hesitation, he can hardly feel pleasure; and still less has he time to reflect on the dissatisfaction which he might subsequently experience if he did not make the attempt. Should he afterward reflect over his own conduct, he would feel that there lies within him an impulsive power widely different from a search after pleasure or happiness; and this seems to be the deeply planted social instinct" (p. 122).

Similarly, Darwin describes the drive to comprehend in the following words. "As soon as the important faculties of the imagination, wonder, and curiosity, together with some power of reasoning, had become partially developed, man would naturally crave to understand what was passing around him, and could have vaguely speculated on his own existence" (p. 95).

The "independent status" of these two drives means that they are treated as ends themselves and rewarded by the brain and nervous system in the same manner as the dA or dD. Unsurprisingly, the four independent drives are frequently in conflict with each other in everyday life as we struggle to decide how to behave, how to adaptively respond to the immediate circumstances we face. This condition of drive-conflict brings the pre-frontal cortex into action. This part of the brain is uniquely complex in humans. This is the part of the brain that, when faced with drive-conflict, has the capacity to call on all the resources of the rest of the cortex (long-term memory, skills, etc.) to search for a response that satisfies all four drives and can be expected to optimize only in a holistic four drive manner.

The concept of economic man however assumes (in RD terms) that humans are exclusively motivated by the *drive to acquire* and the *drive to defend*. In effect, therefore, the drive to bond with fellow humans and the drive to comprehend, and make sense of the world only exist as secondary drives to fulfill the former two. In contrast, the RD theory supports a humanistic view in that we have four independent underlying natural drives that need to be continually balanced. While the drives to acquire and to defend still remain viable and important factors in determining human behavior, the drive to bond with fellow humans and the drive to comprehend are also strong independent forces. Thus RD theory provides a humanistic understanding of behavior. It is also able to provide higher level insight with regard to organizational principles and decision making. Furthermore, it can be rigorously tested by natural science. Below, we will examine what the implications of this humanistic paradigm (based on RD theory) paradigm are for organizations and societies.

View of the Business Organization

In a purely economistic view organizations are not needed, as the market would suffice to coordinate individuals in their maximization of fixed utility functions. Utilitarianism fails to explain why and how cooperation is needed, as economic men with similar preconceived utility functions only need coordination (Nida-Ruemelin, 2009). Nevertheless, based on some additional assumptions, namely transaction costs and bounded rationality, humans are thought to engage in cooperation only when the market provides suboptimally efficient results.

Business Strategy

The organizations that are based on the notions of homo oeconomicus are designed to fit the maximization imperative. Decisions in the economistic paradigm are aiming at maximizing one overarching drive (drive to acquire in RD terms) to fulfill utility needs. Organizations in the economistic mold are hence built to maximize the utility in terms of wealth, and need to profit maximize. An optimal way to ensure utility maximization is for organizational leadership to focus on the shareholder interest only. In his refutation of stakeholder theory, Jensen (2002) argues that there has to be a single objective for the firm otherwise one could not purposefully manage it. He bases this claim on assumptions of economic theory, which posit that maximization strategies are required in situations where there are no externalities. "Two hundred years of work in economics and finance implies that in the absence of externalities and monopoly (and when all goods are priced), social welfare is maximized when each firm in an economy maximizes its total market value" (p. 2).

Externalities, however, are very real, negative, drastic, and persistent, as can be witnessed in the environmental crisis as well as the social inequity crisis. Monopolies are also very real without aggressive antitrust enforcement, so it is clear that the economistic setup is suboptimal. The humanistic view of organizations (Mele, 2009, p. 15), in contrast, is that they are much more than mere set of contracts or mechanisms for profit creation. Humanism views organizations as a social phenomenon essential for the relational nature of human beings. Since humans, following RD theory, have a drive for friendly and cooperative relationships, humanistic organizations embrace a balance of qualitatively desirable outcomes. Discourse based social processes are central to the notion of organizing and supporting the creation of mutual goals. The aim of these processes is to achieve a balance and therefore any imperative for maximization of one single objective is rejected. The universal ambition of humanism requires that multiple objectives are integrated and *harmonized*. Shared value creation processes are theoretically and practically imperative; a balance between multiple stakeholders and between short and long-term interests is essential. At best humanistic organizing endorses a satisfying or holistic optimizing strategy (Frederick et al., 1988; Simon, 1979, 1982).

Governance

The different philosophical approaches have consequences for the top-level governance structures in organizations. The governance notions in the economistic setting are largely informed by agency theory. In order to maintain total control in the hands of ownership, agency theory governance mechanisms focus on creating an environment where opportunistic, self-serving managerial agents are in check to not harm the fulfillment of whatever goal the owners intend to fulfill. In contrast, humanistic governance theories such as stewardship theory focus on reinforcing the other-regarding positive aspects of human nature. According to Davis et al. (1997), stewardship theory assumes intrinsically motivated human beings that are mainly driven by higher-order needs such as social and self-actualization needs (Maslow, 1954). Stewards are guided by the intention to serve all stakeholders, demonstrate a high level of commitment to total value creation, to focus on long-term results, and an equitable distribution of rewards to all stakeholders. As such, governance mechanisms focus on strategic support for the steward and less on hierarchical control. Economistic types of top-down control (such as time clocks, monitoring systems, etc.) are thus deemed detrimental to the motivation and performance of stakeholders (Donaldson and Davis, 1991; Macus, 2002; Muth and Donaldson, 1998). While top-down control mechanisms are essential to the governance structure of economistic organizations, (some organizational theorists call them "remnants of feudalism"), checks and balance systems are essential in humanistic organizational structures so that power abuse can be prevented. Lawrence (2007a, b) argues that checks and balance arrangements parallel the function of the prefrontal cortex in the human brain rather than the hierarchical control. That is why he argues that checks and balance systems (such as instituted in the U.S. Constitution) are better able to fulfill the role of representing all major stakeholders in strategic decisions. Akin to democratic institutions, humanistic organizations can use different stakeholder councils (e.g., worker councils) to prevent decisions that favor one group over the other in the long term. These internal checks and balances will mutually reinforce each other to serve various stakeholder needs in a balanced form (see also Gratton, 2004).

Structures

Structures in the economistic paradigm have to serve the maximization strategy and are efficiency oriented. To that end, the organizational structure is centered on hierarchies and top-down decision making. Humanistic organizational structures on the contrary center on human capabilities and effectiveness. While economistic structures rely on a large number of authority levels, humanistic structures reduce authority levels in the organization. In humanistic organizations, decision rights are spread throughout the entire organization in a way that utilizes the expertise of all employees and provides them with the opportunity to fulfill their drive to comprehend at work (dC).

To further use the capabilities of employees humanistic organizations employ integrative mechanisms that cut across the vertical lines of control: i.e., product or project managers, task forces, matrix elements, innovative information management systems. Such structural elements help to keep the focus on over-all organizational goals, but also provide opportunities for employees to put meaning into their work and fulfill their drive to comprehend (dC) and extend their bonded network of trust (dD).

In economistic organizations, incentive systems are central. They are an important structural element to align diverging interests and the only way to deal with opportunistic agents effectively. These economistic incentives are mainly monetary in nature (such as financial bonuses), target the individual, and address the drive to acquire (dA). The incentives are also short-term oriented because they are mostly based on yearly financial results. In humanistic organizations, incentive systems include both monetary and symbolic incentives. These incentives are tied to holistic organizational goals, reward not only the individual but also the team and are primarily tied to long-term organizational goals. These methods prevent an over-stimulation of competitive (dA) drives compared to collaborative drives (dB).

Leadership

In the economistic view, the organization is generally seen as a nexus of contracts that is continuously negotiated. The role of the leader requires being involved in a constant negotiation process and the task is to clarify goals and desired outcomes with followers. Bass and Avolio (1994) call the economistic type of leader a transactional leader. The transactional leader is primarily involved in ensuring compliance and setting incentives so that the followers deliver. Nurturing quality long-term relationships is rather irrelevant and oftentimes hindering (hiring and firing, e.g., is a capacity that requires leaders to be emotionally disconnected from followers). Followers are mainly considered as human resources (not human beings), and a skillful transactional leader is one that is efficiency maximizing. The organization is therefore set up in a linear way to support efficiency maximization, which in turn renders the culture rather mechanistic.

What Bass and Avolio (1994) term transformational leadership, fits well with a humanistic view of leadership. Transformational leaders are actively balancing their personal four drives and also engage their followers to do so. Based on moral values, transformational leaders inspire followers, stimulate them intellectually and engage them emotionally with the organizational tasks. They base their influence on the power of the argument rather than hierarchy and demonstrate care for the individual follower and his personal development. Transformational, humanistic or four-drive leaders are able to create a climate in which people clearly understand cognitively and embrace emotionally the purpose of the organization (drive to comprehend), are able to maintain very positive long-term relationships with each other (drive to bond), create financial value (drive to acquire), and can count on their collective strength to weather the storms of competition (drive to defend).

But humanistic leaders do not only stop acting and influencing within their own organization. They are able and compelled by their active four drives to contribute to a society that is balancing the four drives as well. Lawrence (2007a, b) therefore argues for a much more active role of business leaders in the public policy process, not as is currently seen in terms of a laser focus on firm profitability (dA), but rather in terms of creating a balance in society among all four drives.

Culture

The different paradigm, unsurprisingly, also contributes to the creation of distinctive organizational cultures. Economistic organizations support cultures and organizational identities that are oriented mostly towards the individual (Brickson, 2007). These cultures are also often described as transactional in nature (Bass and Avolio, 1994). As a consequence, economistic organizations are following rather linear, mechanistic, and closed-loop thought and interaction processes. As Collier and Esteban (1999) argue, mechanistic organizations attempt to transform the environment "adversarially and competitively rather than seek to respond to it" (p. 176). Uncontrolled change is viewed as a threat, because it interferes with the optimal implementation of the maximization paradigm. In addition, the domination of the drives to acquire (dA) and to defend (dD) translate into a need to control the outside, and to manage and manipulate the environment, particularly government, in order to support firm profitability (Dierksmeier and Pirson, 2008). Economistic cultures are two-drive cultures.

Humanistic organizations, in contrast, support cultures that are more transformational in nature and create organizational identities based on inter-human relations (relational) inclusive of a larger group (communal) (Brickson, 2007). They are driven by all four human drives and are creating balanced cultures. The humanistic organizational culture is organic, circular, constantly changing and evolving, and engages with outside forces as parameters of internal action. Said culture is open, flexible, participative, and value-based. As it thrives from the exchange with the outside, it fosters constant dialog amongst and with its stakeholders and is guided by a dialogically generated set of values (Dierksmeier and Pirson, 2008). It not only balances the four drives of internal stakeholder groups, but also aims at contributing to a balance of the four drives for external stakeholders. Google, Nucor, Medtronics, or the Grameen Bank can be seen as typical organizations with four-drive cultures.

View of the Societal System

These different paradigms also influence the view of the systemic environment and the responsibilities towards it. In an economistic view, the main function of the corporation is to accumulate wealth, and heed the drive to acquire, while the main function of the state is to provide safety and cater to the drive to defend. In this division of labor, the state is creating rules to coordinate organizations and organizational leadership's main responsibility is to obey those rules while maximizing profits. These rules, however, are based on "laissez faire" assumptions so that individuals and organizations can follow their respective utility functions. Any further commitment to societal causes is incompatible with the individual and organizational level utility maximization. Talk of responsibilities is generally viewed as systematic interference with liberty. Calls for corporate responsibility and sustainability are only heeded when they are compulsory and part of the legal infrastructure. Voluntary engagement for societal issues such as equity and intergenerational justice do not fit with the economistic view unless they make strategic sense in terms of increasing material wealth (Dierksmeier and Pirson, 2008).

In the humanistic perspective, individuals, organizations, and the state all play important roles in balancing the four drives. As there needs to be a balance on each level, respectively, there is no real division of labor in terms of fulfilling the four basic drives. Rather, there is cooperation in terms of ensuring that the checks and balances enable an optimal balance of the four drives on all levels. In the humanistic view, personal morality is connected with responsibility for the systemic consequences. Business leaders accept and assume responsibility for consequences of their actions both on the systemic level and the individual level. As such, organizations engage with the outside and view responsibility to stakeholders as elementary for conducting business. Liberty is contingent on morality; individual and organizational freedom materialize through care and concern for the other. Sustainability and corporate responsibility are endorsed parameters in the humanistic view of business; attempts to alleviate social problems through business are an imperative. Only in that mutual responsibility for individuals, organizations and the wider system is a balance of the four drives possible.

Humanism and Economism in Business—Past, Present and Future

Historical Development and Current Tendencies

As demonstrated, the two paradigms have a long historical background, but they have enjoyed fluctuating support in management thinking. In fairly recent history, economistic thinking has come to dominate the managerial practices. But its persistent catering to the drive to acquire has already created a serious imbalance regarding the satisfaction of the four intrinsic human drives. As a consequence, we witness the social and ecological crises discussed in the introduction.

Historically, economistic thinking has been the most obvious in the development of 'scientific management' in the early 20th century. Frederick Taylor and Henry Ford brought unprecedented productivity with their functional view of management. However, soon after, the shortcomings of their technical management styles became obvious. Elton Mayo and the Hawthorne experiments unveiled the importance of psychological effects and the drive to bond on human productivity. As a result, a more human-centered approach to management was called for. This humanistic management or "human relations" movement stressed the importance of human needs and motivations for organizational success (see Maslow, 1954; Mayo, 1933, 1946). Significant contributions by Argyris (1957), McGregor (1960), and Herzberg (1976) pointed at the significance of motivational factors outside of the monetary realm, such as the importance of a meaningful job (drive to comprehend). Overall, they underscored that successful organizations are able to cater to all four drives. But because the early literature held that this humanistic approach could also lead to more efficient and effective organizations (dA), Mele (2009), among others, questioned whether this first wave of humanism in business was not a masked form of economism. Citing examples where psychological techniques were used only to increase productivity, he argued that these ideas were only an extension of an economistic two-drive paradigm. Without the scientific tools to prove their ideas and in the face of a resurgent economistic thinking in the form of Agency theory, the "human relations" model faded in importance. However, there have been several very recent developments that reconnect to the long tradition of humanistic thought in business practice. There are several humanistic tendencies in current business that are complementing and challenging economistic approaches, which demonstrate how the paradigms are again shifting in influence (Mele, 2008). Among these tendencies are (1) the focus on the individual for highly specialized business activities, (2) the focus on high performance cultures, and (3) the focus on moral values.

Focus on the Individual for Highly Specialized Business Activities

During early economistic forms of management (Taylorism, Fordism), individuals were considered as human machines. To better deal with psychological needs, businesses employed job enlargement and job rotation. To increase motivation, many businesses also restructured their work so jobs fit better with employee capabilities, aspirations and values. Job enrichment and a focus on person-job fit put the individual center stage. Today, with increased needs for specialized knowledge workers, many organizations also focus on creating optimal person-organization fits. They hence spend a lot of energy on matching needs, desires, or preferences of employees and employer (Buckingham and Coffman, 1999; Cable and Judge, 1994; Chatman, 1989; Judge and Bretz, 1992). Both, "job redesign" and concern for "person-organization fit" underline respect for the individual and try to view humans in a more holistic fashion. Management is often guided by the idea that every person is different and therefore should be treated in accordance with his or her qualities and personality (Mele, 2009). Even though these concepts are mainly applied to the elite at this point, it is likely that consideration for individual differences becomes a key to future business success, and thus humanistic approaches are complementing economistic ones.

Focus on High Performance Cultures

As discussed above, in the economistic view companies are considered as mere sets of contracts. The purpose of the corporation is to enrich their owners and employees are motivated by pay for performance. Management's role is to enforce contracts and coordinate employees using command and control mechanisms. Scholars found that purely economistic cultures are continuously outperformed by organizations with humanistic cultures. Collins and Porras (2002) argue that organizations which pursue a purpose greater than wealth maximization are better able to motivate employees and other stakeholders. Pfeffer and Veiga (1999) point out that high involvement and high commitment practices lead to enormous economic returns. As such there is substantial evidence that humanistic organizational cultures lead to better performance. However, "trends in actual management practice are, in many instances, moving in a direction exactly opposite to what this growing body of evidence prescribes" (Pfeffer and Veiga, 1999, p. 37). Mele argues that brutal downsizing, delocalization of plants with scarce consideration for the laid-off employees, and other practices demonstrate the continuing power of the economistic paradigms.

Focus on Moral Values

A third humanistic tendency in business is the increased discourse about values and ethics. Values-based management approaches are increasingly discussed and many companies have institutionalized ethics by way of ethical codes, ethical offices, and ethical training. However, as Anderson points out, "despite discussion in the popular and academic press, the connection between value judgments and economic success is still unclear in the minds of many executives" (1997, p. 25). Despite these tensions, it is clear that the amoral character of business and the pure focus on increasing wealth are increasingly disputed. The discourse on corporate social responsibility opens doors for humanistic argumentation that was previously unthinkable.

Overall, there are several tendencies towards a more humanistic approach to business. While most of these trends are manifest in public discourse, business behavior remains more often than not unchanged. In the following, we will focus on the obstacles and look at what an organization could look like if it actually follows through with a humanistic approach to business.

Humanistic Business Concepts for the Future

If we start at the very basics and consider Darwin's insights seriously, we need to aim at the creation of organizations that satisfy all four independent human drives in a balanced way. Creating such four-drive business organizations (or what we interchangeably call humanistic organizations) requires different thinking, different objective functions, different incentive structures, as well as a different institutional support system.

Milton Friedman's paradigm of 'the business of business is business', meaning creating the highest shareholder value, can only hold when financial value creation will not create negative externalities. The current sustainability crisis, however, calls for business to actively create positive externalities, what we would call sustainability plus. As such the economistic paradigm needs to be replaced by a business paradigm that includes, a positive concern for the environment and social problems. To reconnect business with its humanistic roots, we need new concepts. Nobel laureate Yunus (2009) claims that the separation of economic and social dimensions has always been nonsensical and even the managing partner of McKinsey & Co, Ian Davis, agrees that the continued separation of the social and the economic is strategically unsustainable for big business (Nicholls, 2006, p. 24). Good businesses understand that a proactive approach to the sustainability, inequity, and trust crises is also a good strategy (Jackson and Nelson, 2004; Porter and Kramer, 2006). Hence, businesses need to increasingly combine financial and social value creation (Sharp Paine, 2003).

Strategic Corporate Social Responsibility

In recent years, initiatives that make profit seekers aware of social responsibilities while maintaining their profit-maximizing objective have gained momentum. These sometimes take the form of self-imposed restrictions on activities and/or of the creation of a philanthropic window with some profit.

Many businesses spin off a foundation to deal with social and environmental value creation. They consciously and carefully keep financial value and social value creation separate. Oftentimes foundations have nothing in common with the fonder except for the name, e.g., Ford Foundation, Alcoa foundation, etc. Fewer businesses look at corporate profit responsibility and social responsibility as a joint opportunity for sustainable business success. Porter and Kramer (2006) argue that business should not outsource social or environmental value creation, but instead look at how they can combine their current resources and capabilities to create products and services that create social, environmental, and financial value. They call this approach as strategic corporate social responsibility. It starts with the premise that current social and environmental problems are strategic opportunities. Businesses should evaluate problems strategically to select business situations where they can most effectively contribute on both fronts simultaneously.

In this context, social and environmental problems can be solved in a business context, providing direct financial support. The approaches might well not maximize shareholder value in the short term, but will be able to satisfy shareholders who are focused on more sustainable long-term profits. The current strategy of General Electric seems to be testing this hypothesis (Tichy and Bennis, 2007).

Social Entrepreneurship as the Solution?

While to a great extent business has been and still is treated as responsible only for financial value creation and NGO's or the government for social value creation, social entrepreneurship allows the conceptualization of blended value models. These shared-value creation concepts escape traditional business logic and represent a further step forward in humanistic business development. Muhammad Yunus, recipient of the 2006 Nobel Peace prize, argues that our current economic system is flawed because it only caters to the limited set of investors/people who only want to enrich themselves: "the market is the exclusive playground of the personal gain seekers, overwhelmingly ignoring the common interest of the people and the planet" (Yunus, 2009, p. 3). He finds, however, that many people want to serve others and enjoy contributing to something larger than mere wealth creation (himself included). He calls these people social entrepreneurs. These people are driven to make a difference in the world and to give people a better chance in life. "They want to achieve their objectives by creating and supporting a special kind of enterprise. Such businesses may or may not earn profit, but like any other business, they must not incur losses. We could describe this new class of businesses as 'non-loss' businesses" (p. 2). He therefore argues that we must reinterpret capitalism to account for those investors/people who are in one way or the other interested in social value creation. "Once we have recognized social entrepreneurs, the supportive institutions, policies, regulations, norms, and rules can be developed to help them enter the mainstream" (p. 2).

Social entrepreneurship is a wider concept than strategic corporate social responsibility, because it allows for all blended value propositions, from profit making plus social value creation to social value creation models where capital requirements are funded through non-earned income strategies.

Models of Social Entrepreneurship

Social enterprises are defined by their dual objectives—the depth and breadth of social and environmental values to be realized, and the expected amount of money to be earned. In the social enterprise, money and mission are very closely aligned. Even though a wide range of social enterprises have emerged, Alter (2006) suggests that there are three main categories defined by the emphasis and priority given to its financial and social objectives: external, integrated, and embedded social enterprises (cf: Alter, 2006). All of these can be models for the reform of current financially driven businesses.

External social enterprise. In external social enterprises, social programs are distinct from profit-oriented business activities. The business enterprise activities are 'external' from the organization's social operations and programs. Businesses can partner with not-for-profit organizations to create external enterprises that fund respective social programs and/or operating costs. This stage represents an incremental change towards a more humanistic organization. Examples for external social enterprises are partnership programs such as Product Red or licensing partnerships with the WWF. In these partnerships, an organization capitalizes on the motivational benefits of a worthy cause and strengthens it through financial and operational capacities. The relationship between the business activities and social programs is supportive, oftentimes providing financial and nonfinancial resources to the external program. That way the traditional two-drive culture of business (dA, dD) is complemented with the two drives (dB, dC) the culture of the social value partner is offering. Many businesses already capture the motivational energy such partnerships can create (see the alliance of Timberland and City Year), but there seems to be much more potential.

Integrated social enterprises. In integrated social enterprises, social programs overlap with business activities, but are not synonymous. Social and financial programs often share costs, assets, and program attributes. The social enterprise activities are thus 'integrated' even as they are separate from the organization's profit-oriented operations. This type of social enterprise often leverages organizational assets such as expertise, content, relationships, brand, or infrastructure as the foundation for its business (Alter, 2006). The Aravind Eye Hospital in Madurai, India is an example of an integrated social enterprise. It serves cataract patients in a main hospital, where wealthy patients pay a market fee for their surgery. The profit surplus created by these fees is then used to pay for the surgery of poor patients in the free hospital (Rangan, 1993). The relationship between the business activities and the social programs is hence synergistic, adding financial and social value to one another. These mixed or shared value models have largely been unexplored by traditional businesses, but could serve well as a blueprint for future shared value creation.

Embedded social enterprise. In the embedded social enterprise, business activities and social programs are synonymous. Social programs are self-financed through enterprise revenues and thus, the embedded social enterprise can also be a stand-alone sustainable program. The relationship between business activities and social programs is comprehensive; financial and social benefits are achieved simultaneously. The Grameen Bank model of micro-loans serves as an example for an embedded social enterprise. In this model, micro-loans are paid back by the borrowers with a somewhat high interest rate, but still serve the poorest of the poor who do not have access to normal credit, as they are lacking collateral. Other models that serve the Bottom of the Pyramid (see Prahalad, 2005) such as Grameen

Phone or BracNet could also be valid approaches. But even traditional publicly traded businesses can successfully merge social, environmental, and financial value creation. Google and Medtronics serve as interesting examples, even though they are operating within a strong dA driven environment.

Conclusion

If we want to solve the current crises, we need to go back to the fundamentals. We need to question the understanding of how we view ourselves as human beings and how we build organizations based upon that understanding. We need to understand the current paradigm and be able to supplant it with a new one. We propose a humanistic paradigm for the sustainable development of business in the future. The Renewed Darwinian theory of human beings brings much needed scientific support for how the brain actually works and shows the way to the future of sustainable organizing. The emergence of blended value models is indicative of a paradigm shift. Blended value models show how the economic system can be reconnected to its humanistic roots.

While there are several obstacles, it seems that there are tendencies within and outside of business that support humanistic business development. As such it can be argued that that the humanistic view of the economy is gaining strength, but a lot of groundwork to restructure economistic institutions remains to be done.

Notes

1. Collectivism here is defined as the theory and practice that makes some sort of group rather than the individual, the fundamental unit of political, social, and economic concern. In theory, collectivists insist that the claims of groups, associations, or the state must normally supersede the claims of individuals.

2. We are aware that the notion of economic man has been enlarged and adapted. Most notably, Jensen and Meckling promote the model of REMM as a better fit version of economic man (one who is not only maximizing money). However, the main postulates of limitless needs (wants) and of maximization remain.

References

Alter, S. K.: 2006, 'Social Enterprise Models and Their Mission and Money Relationships', in A. Nicholls (ed.), *Social Entrepreneurship–New Models for Sustainable Social Change* (Oxford, Oxford University Press).

Anderson, C.: 1997, 'Values-Based Management', *Academy of Management Executive* **11**(4), 25–46.

Arena, C.: 2004, *Cause for Success: 10 Companies That Put Profit Second and Came in First* (New World Library, Novato).

Argyris, C.: 1957, *Personality and Organization. The Conflict Between System and Individual* (Harper, New York).

Argyris, C.: 1973, 'Some Limits of Rational Man Organizational Theory', *Public Administration Review* **33**, 253–267.

Bass, B. M. and B. J. Avolio: 1994, 'Transformational Leadership and Organizational Culture', *International Journal of Public Administration* **17**(3/4), 541–554.

Bentham, J.: 1789, *Introduction to the Principles of Morals and Legislation* (Payne, London).

Brickson, S. L.: 2007, 'Organizational Identity Orientation: The Genesis of the Role of the Firm and Distinct Forms of Social Value', *Academy of Management Review* **32**(3), 864–888.

Buckingham, M. and C. Coffman: 1999, *First Break All the Rules* (Simon and Schuster, New York).

Cable, D. M. and T. A. Judge: 1994, 'Pay Preferences and Job Search Decisions: A Person-Organization Perspective', *Personnel Psychology* **47**(2), 317–348.

Chatman, J. A.: 1989, 'Improving Interactional Organizational Research: A Model of Person-Organization Fit', *Academy of Management Review* **14**(1), 333–349.

Collier, J. and R. Esteban: 1999, 'Governance in the Participative Organisation: Freedom, Creativity and Ethics', *Journal of Business Ethics* **21**(2–3), 173–188.

Collins, J. and J. Porras: 2002, *Built to Last* (HarperCollins, New York).

Darwin, C.: 1909, *The Descent of Man and Selection in Relation to Sex* (Appleton and Company, New York).

Davis, J. H. and F. D. Schoorman, et al.: 1997, 'Toward a Stewardship Theory of Management', *Academy of Management Review* **22**(1), 20–47.

De Cremer, D. and S. Blader: 2005, 'Why Do People Care About Procedural Fairness? The Importance of Belongingness in Responding and Attending to Procedures', *European Journal of Social Psychology* **36**(2), 211–228.

Diener, E. and M. E. P. Seligman: 2004, 'Beyond Money: Toward and Economy of Well-Being', *Psychological Science in the Public Interest* **5**, 1–31.

Dierksmeier, C. and M. Pirson: 2008, *Freedom and the Modern Corporation* (ISBEE, Capetown, SA).

Donaldson, L. and J. H. Davis: 1991, 'Stewardship Theory or Agency Theory: CEO Governance and Shareholder Returns', *Australian Journal of Management* **16**(1), 49–66.

Frederick, W. C. and K. Davis, et al.: 1988, *Business and Society: Corporate Strategy, Public Policy, Ethics* (McGraw-Hill, New York).

Ghoshal, S.: 2005, 'Bad Management Theories are Destroying Good Management Practices', *Academy of Management Learning and Education* **4**(1), 75–91.

Gratton, L.: 2004, *The Democratic Enterprise: Liberating Your Business with Freedom, Flexibility and Commitment* (Financial Times, London).

Hart, S.: 2005, *Capitalism at the Crossroads: The Unlimited Business Opportunities in Solving the World's Most Difficult Problems* (Wharton School Publishing, Philadelphia).

Herzberg, F.: 1976, *The Managerial Choice: To be Efficient and to be Human* (Dow Jones-Irwin, Homewood).

Jackson, I. and J. Nelson: 2004, *Profits with Principles--Seven Strategies for Delivering Value with Values* (Currency Doubleday, New York).

Jensen, M. C.: 2002, 'Value Maximization, Stakeholder Theory and the Corporate Objective Function', *Business Ethics Quarterly* **12**(2), 235–257.

Judge, T. A. and R. D. J. Bretz: 1992, 'Effects of Work Values on Job Choice Decisions', *Journal of Applied Psychology* **77**(3), 261–271.

Lawrence, P.: 2007a, *Being Human--A Renewed Darwinian Theory of Human Behavior* (Cambridge, MA). www.prlawrence.com.

Lawrence, P.: 2007b, 'Organizational Logic--Institutionalizing Wisdom in Organizations', in E. H. Kessler and J. R. Bailey (eds.), *Handbook of Organizational and Managerial Wisdom* (Sage, Thousand Oaks, CA), Chap. 3.

Lawrence, P. and N. Nokia: 2002, *Driven: How Human Nature Shapes Our Choices* (Jossey-Bass, San Francisco).

Macus, M.: 2002, *Towards a Comprehensive Theory of Boards--Conceptual Development and Empirical Exploration* (HSG, St. Gallen), pp. 1–37.

Maslow, A. H.: 1954, *Motivation and Personality* (Harper & Brothers, New York).

Mayo, E.: 1933, *The Human Problems of an Industrial Civilization* (Macmillan, New York).

Mayo, E.: 1946, *The Social Problems of an Industrial Civilization* (Cambridge University Press, Cambridge, UK).

McGregor, D. V.: 1960, *The Human Side of Enterprise* (McGraw-Hill, New York).

Mele, D.: 2009, 'Current Trends of Humanism in Business', in H. Spitzeck, M. Pirson, W. Amann, S. Khan and E. von Kimakowitz (eds.), *Humanism in Business: Perspectives on the Development of a Responsible Business Society* (Cambridge University Press, Cambridge, UK).

Muth, M. M. and L. Donaldson: 1998, 'Stewardship Theory and Board Structure: A Contingency Approach', *Corporate Governance: An International Review* **6**(1), 5–29.

Nicholls, A.: 2006, 'Introduction', in A. Nicholls (ed.), *Social Entrepreneurship--New Models of Sustainable Social Change* (Oxford University Press, Oxford).

Nida-Ruemelin, J.: 2009, 'Philosophical Grounds of Humanism in Economics', in H. Spitzeck, M. Pirson, W. Amann, S. Khan and E. von Kimakowitz (eds.), *Humanism in Business: Perspectives on the Development of a Responsible Business Society* (Cambridge University Press, Cambridge, UK).

Pfeffer, J. and J. F. Veiga: 1999, 'Putting People First for Organizational Success', *Academy of Management Executive* **13**(2), 37–48.

Porter, M. and M. Kramer: 2006, 'Strategy and Society: The Link Between Competitive Advantage and Corporate Social Responsibility', *Harvard Business Review* **84**(12), 78–92.

Prahalad, C. K.: 2005, *The Fortune at the Bottom of the Pyramid: Eradicating Poverty Through Profits* (Wharton School Publishing, Upper Saddle River).

Rangan, K.: 1993, The Aravind Eye Hospital, Madurai, India: In Service for Sight. H. c. 9-593-098. Harvard Business School Publishing.

Sharp Paine, L.: 2003, *Value Shift: Why Companies Must Merge Social and Financial Imperatives to Achieve Superior Performance* (McGraw Hill, New York).

Simon, H. A.: 1979, 'Rational Decision Making in Business Organizations', *American Economic Review* **69**, 493–513.

Simon, H. A.: 1982, *Models of Bounded Rationality* (MIT Press, Cambridge, MA).

Tichy, N. and W. Bennis: 2007, *Judgment: How Winning Leaders Make Great Calls* (Penguin Group, New York).

Tyler, T. R.: 2006, *Social Justice Research*. S. f. S. o. Justice. Cambridge, MA.

Yunus, M.: 2009, 'Social Entrepreneurs are the Solution', in H. Spitzeck, M. Pirson, W. Amann, S. Khan and E. von Kimakowitz (eds.), *Humanism in Business: Perspectives on the Development of a Responsible Business Society* (Cambridge University Press, Cambridge, UK).

Name: _____ Date: _____

Chapter 2 ■ Humanism in Business—Towards a Paradigm Shift?

Questions for Discussion

1. Pirson and Lawrence explain, "As current management theory is largely informed by economics, it draws substantively from neoclassical theories of human beings." Discuss the term "neoclassicism." Specifically, what theoretical traditions, according to the authors, are informing management today? Why might sticking with these ideals become problematic for a business in the 21st century? How might it be beneficial?

2. This article contends that "humanism assumes that human nature is not entirely a given, that it can be refined, through education and learning. In addition, the ethical component remains a cornerstone in humanism in that it attributes unalienable rights to everybody, independent from ethnicity, nationality, social status or gender." Conduct research to find a company that is based on humanistic beliefs. Outline their business model, hiring policies, and any other guidelines put in place to ensure that everyone is given an equal opportunity to work for this organization. Be prepared to present this to your group and/or the class as a whole.

3. The authors present the following as an alternative to humanism:

    . . . economism views the human being as a fixed entity, predetermined by its utility function which is stable. This economic man (homo oeconomicus) is utterly self-serving and only interested in maximizing his immediate utility. Economic man is therefore only engaging in transactional, short-term oriented encounters with others. His engagements are interest based and other people are a means to an end. He acts opportunistically and is mainly motivated by the lower level needs in Maslow's hierarchy of needs (physiological and safety needs).

    Research Maslow's hierarchy of needs and consider how they could be related to business. Take note of what each category entails. Then, as though you are creating a hierarchy for your own business, give a concrete example of a measure you would implement within each category.

4. Analyze Table 1: Economism and Humanism. In a small group, examine the elements of each column. Discuss the following:

    a. Which school of thought is more beneficial to a business? Why?
    b. Can the two schools of thought coexist in one workplace? Why or why not?
    c. How might a company blend the two perspectives in an effort to achieve optimal success?

5. Pirson and Lawrence explain, according to renewed Darwinian (RD) theory, humans have four separate drives: "*the drive to acquire (dA)* life-sustaining resources, *the drive to defend (dD)* from all life-threatening entities . . . *the drive to bond (dB)* in long-term mutually caring relationships with other humans, and *the drive to comprehend (dC),* to make sense of the world around us in terms of its multifaceted relations to ourselves." They go on to explain that "the four independent drives are frequently in conflict with each other in everyday life as we struggle to decide how to behave, how to adaptively respond to the immediate circumstances we face." What factors in the workplace could affect the relationship among these four drives? What specific hurdles might one face that could tip the balance?

6. Incentives are vital in ensuring that employees do their jobs well. As outlined in the article, "In economic organizations, incentive systems are central . . . These economist incentives are mainly monetary in nature (such as financial bonuses), target the individual, and address the drive to acquire (dA)." On the other hand, "In humanistic organizations, incentive systems include both monetary and symbolic incentives. These incentives are tied to holistic organizational goals, reward not only the individual but also the team and are primarily tied to long-term organizational goals. These methods prevent an over-stimulation of competitive (dA) drives compared to collaborative drives (dB)." How can companies get their employees to buy into rewards that aren't so individualized? What input should employees have when it comes to determining the rewards received? Should employers introduce job requirements that necessitate a certain amount of collaboration within companies? Discuss.

7. We chose this article in part because it offers a good model of the type of reading you might find valuable as you write your own proposals. How is this piece different from more popular sources, such as newspaper and magazine articles? Do you think the article is persuasive? What factors contribute to its credibility? How might you use a source like this to develop the paradigm in your proposal?

Teaching Leadership Critically: New Directions for Leadership Pedagogy

David Collinson and Dennis Tourish

Conventional approaches to teaching leadership in business schools have overrelied on transformational models that stress the role of charismatic individuals, usually white men, in setting compelling visions to which all organizational actors are expected to subscribe. Such approaches pay insufficient attention to the dynamics of power, the influence of context, and the significance of follower dissent and resistance. This article examines the pedagogical potential of critical leadership studies: an emergent, alternative paradigm questioning deepseated assumptions that power and agency should be vested in the hands of a few leaders and exploring the dysfunctional consequences of such power dynamics for individuals, organizations, and societies. It also recognizes that follower compliance and conformity, as well as resistance and dissent, are important features of leadership dynamics. Informed by our own experience of trying to teach leadership more critically, this essay highlights a number of guiding principles that we have used in the classroom to encourage a more questioning approach from our students in their study of leadership

Over the past 50 years or so, leadership has been one of the most widely taught subjects in business schools around the world. In recent times the importance and influence of leadership studies in business school curricula has increased even further. Just as there is no single way to enact or study leadership, so there is considerable diversity in the ways that leadership is conceived and taught. Scholars in different business schools emphasize different theories, approaches, and themes, often informed by their own research interests and concerns. They also utilize a diversity of teaching methods including in-class lectures, leader speaker programs, case studies, experiential and action learning, coaching, feedback sessions, team projects, simulations and self-analysis (Murphy & Johnson, 2011). However, despite this diversity, most leadership courses adhere to a rather narrow set of psychological assumptions and approaches that, in privileging the role of powerful individuals, are highly "leader-centered" (Jackson & Parry, 2011).

In their primary focus on developing leaders' abilities and skills, mainstream courses typically draw on a familiar list of theories, such as "great man"–trait, styles–skills, situational–contingency, charisma, transformational–transactional, leader–member exchange, servant, and more recently, spiritual and authentic leadership. Many leadership programs informed by these perspectives promise to turn students into inspirational leaders capable of impacting powerfully and positively on the world (Tourish, Craig, & Amernic, 2010). Yet, in practice, these high expectations are rarely achieved. Disappointment with this state of affairs is evident in the growing criticism of business schools (e.g., Pfeffer & Fong, 2002; Khurana, 2007; Alajoutsijarvi, Juusola, & Siltaoja, 2014), and which has partly inspired this forum.

Thanks to the anonymous referees and the special issue acting editor, Ken Parry, for helpful feedback on earlier versions of this article.

Republished with permission of Academy of Management from *Academy of Management Learning and Education*, Volume 14 (4), © 2015, by David Collinson and Dennis Tourish. Permission conveyed through Copyright Clearance Center, Inc.

While acknowledging that elements of more critical thinking are evident in a number of business school courses,[1] we first highlight the continued predominance of mainstream leadership teaching in elite, "top-ranked" schools, and the limits of this perspective. Second, we explore the potential value of teaching leadership more critically. This alternative approach draws on the emergent field of critical leadership studies (CLS) to rethink and revitalize leadership pedagogy. CLS holds that leadership is fundamentally about the effective or ineffective exercise of power, authority, and influence.[2] Arguing that conventional approaches to teaching leadership in business schools pay insufficient attention to situated power relationships,[3] critical pedagogies caution against depictions of leaders as miracle workers who do and should have absolute power, and of followers as people who should unquestioningly commit to the causes espoused by leaders. There are important recurrent tensions and dilemmas in these complex organizational and social dynamics that are central concerns of critical leadership courses.

Proposing a more nuanced approach to leader and follower power, influence, and agency, critical courses reconceptualize leadership as a coconstructed, asymmetrical, and shifting dynamic characterized by complex situated and mutually reinforcing relations between leaders and followers. Informed by our own experience of teaching leadership critically, we highlight three illustrative principles that, we argue, have the potential to reshape and enrich leadership pedagogies in business schools: critiquing romanticism, foregrounding power, and rethinking followership. Addressing these themes, critical leadership courses can, we contend, more adequately prepare students for careers in contemporary workplaces. The article concludes by emphasizing the emancipatory potential of critical pedagogies for leadership teaching in business schools.

Business Schools and the Myths of Heroic Leadership

The assumptions, theories, methodologies, and findings of mainstream studies have had an enormous influence on the design and delivery of leadership courses in business schools. These predominantly psychological approaches tend to privilege and romanticize individual leaders while also underestimating the dynamics of power, the influence of context, and the significance of follower dissent and resistance. They tend to assume that the interests of leaders and followers automatically coalesce, that leadership is an uncontested form of top-down influence, follower consent is its relatively unproblematic outcome, and that resistance is abnormal or irrational. This is particularly evident in the teaching of courses on leading change, where the idea of "change" is usually held to be a "good" thing, irrespective of its content (Ford, Ford, & D'Amelio, 2008). Opposition is explained in terms of "misunderstanding" and "self-interested political behavior" (e.g., Kotter & Schlesinger, 1979), rather than as a form of useful feedback. The job of leaders is defined in terms of creating and communicating a vision for change in ways that secure employee buy-in (Kotter, 2012). From this perspective, any dissent that occurs can be overcome by the adoption of this or that technique, since the "vision" comes from the insights of the leader rather than through a process of co-construction between leaders and followers. This message leaves business students unprepared for the challenges that they will face when they encounter active, questioning, and dissenting employees, or when they themselves might be faced with a decision about whether to disagree with their boss on an important issue.

As an example, the Judge Business School of Cambridge University offers an open executive education course on transformational leadership. Its premise is that the course will help turn participants into transformational leaders capable of "breaching resistance to change." They will be able to motivate "employees beyond monetary incentives" and provide "inspirational leadership and result-oriented management."[4] Employees, it seems, bring little to the table other than a capacity for resistance, and are sufficiently lacking in nonpecuniary motivation that it must be generated for them by others. The downsides of entrusting a select few with such power are side-lined in favor of extravagant promises about what the program will accomplish. Firmly rooted in functionalist traditions, these approaches neglect the power dynamics through which leadership and followership are enacted in specific conditions, often producing unintended and contradictory consequences.

Rather than address such issues, mainstream approaches tend to emphasize the importance of leaders as charismatic visionaries, often with minimal to no evidence that their claimed impact on organizational performance has actually occurred (Meindl, Ehrlich, & Dukerich, 1985). For example, Spector (2014) argues that the portrayal of Iaccoca in the 1980s as a transformer of Chrysler was unsubstantiated, but also foundational to early conceptualizations in the literature of transformational leadership and its subsequent popularization in the business school curriculum (Bass, 1990; Bass & Riggio, 2006). Thus, leaders are routinely depicted as "change masters" (e.g., Kanter, 1985); heroes and saviors (see Hatch, Kostera, & Kozminski, 2005); and miracle workers (see Slater, 1999).

Some leadership scholars adopt more nuanced positions. For example, Zacher, Pearce, Rooney, and McKenna (2014) suggest that leaders' personal wisdom can sometimes offset the potentially harmful effects of narcissistic transformational leaders since it increases positive forms of individualized consideration.[5] But this is not common. More typical is the position of influential U.S. leadership scholar Warren Bennis, who decried the prevalence of different factions and interests in organizations and politics and concluded that "[p]eople in authority must develop the vision and authority to call the shots" (Bennis, 1989: 144). There is no explicit consideration of any downsides to entrusting those with formal authority to "call the shots," presumably with minimal input from the factions and subgroups over which they preside. Dissent is here equated with subversion and dysfunction, rather than regarded as a possible source of strength to be encouraged.

Leader-centered teaching influenced by such heroic perspectives focuses on identifying those traits, behaviors, and competencies that are most correlated with effectiveness. For business students, one of the messages of this approach is that leadership is a relatively stable construct that is amenable to observation with the correct tools, which in turn will provide leaders with the techniques they need to reliably influence others (e.g., Antonakis, Fenley, & Liechti, 2011). Yet, there is little evidence that human behavior can be rendered pliable and predictable in this manner (Grey, 2013). Business school graduates taught to expect otherwise are likely to find the world of work much more frustrating than the simplistic prescriptions of leadership textbooks have led them to expect. In particular, the idea that leadership is socially constructed and interpreted and that "it" could mean very different things to different actors in different situations is largely ignored.[6]

Linking Leadership Theory to Context and Practice

Most research into transformational leadership seeks to identify "gaps" in incidental aspects of the theory, while taking its fundamental postulates for granted. It proposes more and more mediating factors that attempt to explain core relationships and moderating factors that establish boundary conditions. In principle, this can be an important part of theory building (Colquitt & Zapata-Phelan, 2007). Here, however, we suggest that the theory of transformational leadership has grown so complex and diffuse that its theoretical foundations, practical utility, and pedagogical value have been undermined.[7] For example, van Knippenberg and Sitkin's (2013) exhaustive review identified 58 moderating variables in the literature that purportedly have relationships with 37 dependent variables. They also found 52 mediators predicting 38 different outcomes. This ensures that negative results can be hypothesized as due to the presence of still-to-be identified moderating or mediating variables. Finding them requires "more research." This Sisyphean task conveniently banishes the prospect of falsification. Despite a proliferation of theories, one major review of theory development in leadership studies concluded that new waves of theorization had not displaced their predecessors (Glynn & Raffaelli, 2010). This allows both "strong" and "weak" forms of theory to thrive—at least as measured by the amount of research and number of publications they attract. The cost is that it becomes progressively more difficult to integrate such a multitude of variables into a coherent and internally consistent theoretical model with which students can critically engage.

Leaders and would-be leaders can only pay attention to so many issues. Theories that essentially require them to take account of everything are unlikely to be fully implemented. Nor could educators accommodate such complexity in their time-limited classroom delivery. Students are inclined to prefer simple prescriptions for leadership (Mumford & Fried, 2014). These considerations widen the gulf between what theorists understand by transformational leadership and what students take it to be. The practice of leadership in real organizations, torn between theory and expediency, becomes more fissiparous, and so even harder to study. But, as we now argue, such tensions and paradoxes are often unacknowledged in business school curricula.

Business School Pedagogy and the Perils of Hubris

Despite these difficulties, business schools around the world remain keen to embrace the idea of "leadership." A survey of 48 MBA program directors in U.S. universities found that all but one confirmed "their business school was committed to developing leadership in their curriculum" (Klimiski & Amos, 2012: 694). Murphy and Johnson (2011) found that all of the top-10 business schools in the United States (based on *U.S. News and World Report's* rankings) offered at least one course in leadership (see also, Doh, 2003; Navarro, 2008). Kellerman (2012) reports that at Harvard *all* professional schools (i.e, those concerned with teaching such occupational groups as managers, dentists, lawyers, and doctors) now stress the development of leaders as crucial to their overall mission. Business schools also increasingly suggest to potential students that by studying leadership they will become exceptional leaders, able to exercise extraordinary influence over others.

Illustrating this, De Rue, Sitkin, and Podolny, (2011: 369) took a sample of mission statements from leading business schools. Typical of many, Harvard promises to "educate leaders who make a difference in the world;" Stanford seeks to "develop innovative, principled, and insightful leaders who change the world;" and, not to be outdone, Duke University's business school wants to "develop smart and real leaders of consequence, who are looking to make their mark and effect positive change in the world."[8] This flattering prospectus has more marketing appeal than, for example, suggestions that they will be primarily taught to "first, do no harm," even if this is more in line with what business schools can actually deliver. The impact of promoting such seductive images of leadership and overoptimistic predictions of future capability is likely to be considerable (Sinclair, 2009; Gagnon, & Collinson 2014).

Hype and Hubris

Underlying such dynamics are the twin perils of hype and hubris. We argue that these temptations should be resisted rather than embraced. Business schools have tended to overstate what they can offer in terms of developing the leadership potential of their students. Podolny (2009), a former Stanford and Harvard professor and a dean at Apple University, identifies the pressure to climb up institutional rankings as a driver of such behavior, since it incentivizes schools to compete ferociously for the "best" students. This in turn encourages a tendency to stress the image of a "heroic" leader changing the world, since its lure to potential students is obvious—a key reason why mainstream leadership pedagogies have acquired such traction. Moreover, practices by "elite" schools are then likely to be copied by others who assume that imitation will improve their own prospects of moving up rankings that are increasingly valued (Starkey & Tiratsoo, 2007). But such heroic approaches rarely suggest that leaders should listen to and learn from others, including their followers. Recognition of the potential benefits of humility, dissent, or follower input is also conspicuously absent. Rather, the preponderant assumption is that those who emerge from a business school education will unidirectionally influence the behaviors of others. These are messages that seem tailor-made to encourage hubris—arguably one of the chief perils confronting leaders in large corporations (Claxton, Owen, & Sadler-Smith, 2015).

Developing this critique, we suggest that theories privileging the agency of those who hold formal, hierarchically based leadership positions above that of other organizational actors will likely have an intuitive appeal for many business students. In turn, the theory and the practice of leadership can become mutually constitutive. The theory finds traction because it legitimizes dominant power relations and status hierarchies, which is appealing to those who either hold power or covet it, and those relations in turn further legitimize and promote a theory which appears simply to describe "what is," and that therefore (surely?) must lie beyond interrogation. A form of discursive closure develops, in which alternatives are not only ignored, but in an Orwellian sense become unthinkable. The dominant focus on leadership in business schools can render unimaginable the notion of communities of people jointly participating in decision making. This further sustains mainstream approaches to leadership teaching, since it reproduces a world view that is often congenial to its target audiences. In turn, students can develop an exaggerated impression of their ability to determine organizational and societal outcomes. The assumption is one in which the views of a powerful leader hold sway over those of others, and in which there is little need for leaders to take into account critical or dissenting perspectives when making decisions.

Business School Curricula

It is therefore not surprising that the fascination with powerful, transformational, "top-down" leadership has gone beyond the marketing materials of business schools and entered into their curricula (Doh, 2003). The predominant approach seems to be based on the cardinal assumptions that all members of organizations have an overwhelming common interest (even if growing differentials of power, status, and remuneration suggest the contrary) and that senior managers are best equipped to articulate a compelling vision to capture this interest. In addition to their unitarist assumptions, mainstream pedagogies assume that the practice of leadership is an extraordinary phenomenon, which can only be mastered by a "new breed of change agents" (Morrison, 2003: 4). Typically, there is little mention of misjudgment, greed, narcissism, shame, duplicity, stupidity, hubris, soaring CEO salaries, power, and lack of democracy or employee involvement: that is, there is no mention of many of the emotional and political issues that frequently preoccupy real people in real organizations. Rather, power is depicted as a neutral resource to be deployed for relatively unproblematic ends.

The job of theorists and business school instructors is thereby defined in terms of identifying those tools (such as emphasizing one's similarity to powerful others) that may help students to secure more power for themselves (Pfeffer, 2013). This perspective transforms leadership courses into finishing schools in ingratiation and flattery in the pursuit of short-term career advancement. The exercise of power is also naturalized, with no consideration of context or its potentially harmful effects on those in subordinated positions (Willmott, 2013a). Accordingly, leadership courses are often designed to improve students' ability to direct the efforts of others, rather than reflexively to consider power's potential for productive use, while simultaneously registering the perils of hubris (Nirenberg, 1998). The job of educators is then to instill the "skills" and "competencies," such as "charisma," that will enable future leaders to influence others—a technocratic bias that divorces leadership from purpose and means from ends.

By contrast, critical pedagogies draw attention to the socially constructed—and hence contested—nature of knowledge, since action is rooted in powersaturated organizational contexts characterized by conflicts of interest. This is not to say that actors have no interests in common. But placing excessive emphasis on where they converge leaves students unprepared for the world of work. We argue here that in the interests of both business students and the organizations they may eventually lead, more critical and reflective perspectives can enhance the teaching of leadership. Below we explore some of the key assumptions that can helpfully inform the teaching of more critical approaches to studying leadership.

Rethinking Leadership Teaching

Like mainstream courses, critical leadership teaching takes a variety of forms. Drawing on philosophical perspectives, Cunliffe (2009) encouraged U.S. MBA students to become "philosophical leaders" who, through dialogue and discussion, would learn to think more critically and reflexively about leadership, organizations, and themselves. Informed by psychoanalytic, psychodynamic and feminist perspectives, Sinclair (2007a) encouraged Australian MBA students to rethink their assumptions and experiment with alternative ways of "doing" leadership through "practical reflexivity." By working experientially as well as critically, she was able to raise challenging leadership issues in classroom dynamics about gender, emotions, the effects of structure, collusion, and dominance, and flights into fantasy. Both Cunliffe (2009) and Sinclair's (2007a) studies focus on MBA executive classes where participants are likely to be particularly enmeshed in prevailing managerial ideologies, structures, and control systems.

Our focus here is on teaching leadership critically to final-year undergraduate and specialist masters' students. We have been teaching critical leadership courses for a number of years in our respective U.K. universities. Students typically begin our courses holding taken-for-granted assumptions, particularly about the value of heroic leaders (often defined in terms of charisma); the positive nature of follower conformity (often defined in terms of "loyalty"); and the problematic or negative nature of follower dissent and resistance (often defined in terms of "troublemaking"). In our experience, students typically tend to romanticize leaders, which continues to pervade their everyday thinking and is often evident in the popular, practitioner, and business press. Many also expect the course to focus primarily on prescribing "tools" and "techniques" on how to be a "good" leader: that is, one who sets a direction for others, influences and persuades them to support a corporate vision, and overcomes "resistance."[9]

Against this background, our interdisciplinary critical courses challenge students to think more deeply and reflexively about leadership dynamics, and to be more proactive in their reading, writing, and classroom interactions. In seminars students are required to undertake research on specified leadership topics and make small-group presentations based on their work. The seminar program is designed to involve students proactively in the learning process in the belief that participation generates real, rather than parrot-fashion knowledge. As part of the process of increasing participation, students are encouraged to draw on their experiences of leadership and followership dynamics in schools, workplaces, and families. Through this and other methods, we encourage them to become proactive co-constructors of leadership knowledge through group discussion and debate. Informed by our own teaching experiences, the following sections now outline three guiding principles that underpin the design and delivery of our critical leadership courses:

(1) critiquing romanticism, (2) foregrounding power, and (3) rethinking followership. Intended to be illustrative, rather than exhaustive of possible ways to teach leadership critically, these three principles have proved relatively effective in encouraging our students to adopt more questioning approaches to leadership studies.

Critiquing Romanticism

After outlining mainstream leadership theories, our critical courses introduce students to debates on leadership romanticism (e.g., Meindl et al., 1985). They are encouraged to recognize the tendency to credit responsibility for organizational success to the supposedly superior insights of formal leaders, such as CEOs, as well as apportion most blame to these same people when organizations fail. This means directing students' attention to the complexities of organizational life; the role of accident and coincidence in determining the outcomes of leader decisions; and the need to distinguish more clearly between correlation (the presence of Leader A when Organization B succeeds or fails) and causation. Challenging simplistic attributions engages students in a much deeper dialogue about the role of powerful individuals and the possibilities and limits of their agency. It also surfaces the gendered and racialized assumptions that typically inform the heroic leader identity underpinning romanticism.

Equally, it urges students to question conventional ideas around the ascription of charisma to individual leaders, and the assumption that such leaders must be exceptional people who hold their position of authority because they possess powerful personalities and unique capabilities. Through this inquiry, critical courses encourage students to recognize how organizational success can be (over)attributed to leadership in general, and to the CEO in particular (Rosenzweig, 2007). Equally, the converse tendency, to overattribute blame for failure to individual leaders can also be examined (see Amar, Hentrich, Bastani, & Hlupic, 2012). When performance dips, hero leaders of yesterday are suddenly blamed for the decline. Accordingly, assumptions of either Messianic leadership or its Satanic antithesis (as the prime determinants of organizational performance) can be critically interrogated.

Recent illustrations of leadership romanticism are used to encourage students' critical reflection. For example, Finkelstein's list of "best" and "worst" CEOs of 2013 (*Business world*, 2013) named Amazon's CEO, Jeff Bezos, as "CEO of the year." A tone of hyperbole is evident in Finkelstein's[10] observation that "Bezos is building a huge talent pipeline via MBA hires and his recent use of the drone delivery story as a PR coup just before Cyber Monday was a stroke of genius. Jeff Bezos is the new Steve Jobs of business." This is not to say that the actions of CEOs are inconsequential or make no difference. But puffery of this kind places excessive credit or blame on their shoulders. It depicts leadership in terms of great men performing miraculous deeds, whose behavior the rest of us are encouraged to emulate unreflexively. The complexities of the business environment are reduced to the innate wisdom or clumsy misjudgments of a single individual. Hindsight also affords commentators the luxury of judging the quality of their decisions without confronting the elements of uncertainty that existed when they were made.

> *"The complexities of the business environment are reduced to the innate wisdom or clumsy misjudgments of a single individual. Hindsight also affords commentators the luxury of judging the quality of their decisions without confronting the elements of uncertainty that existed when they were made."*

Critical courses also encourage students to consider the ethical dilemmas of leadership practice in much greater depth than is normal in mainstream approaches (Ciulla, 2004). In the case of Bezos, for example, this means going beyond an evaluation based on Amazon's balance sheet to ask how well the organization treats its workforce. As Friedell (2013) noted, Amazon's initial warehouses largely neglected to install air conditioning on the assumption that it was cheaper to place private ambulances outside to treat those employees who collapsed from heat exhaustion. Huge efforts are made to prevent employees organizing in trade unions, normally considered a basic democratic right (Stone, 2013). McClelland's (2012) in-depth account of working in an Amazon distribution center paints a bleak picture of training regimes that resemble indoctrination, exhausted employees, poor pay, excessive performance goals, and relentless monitoring to ensure that goals are met and exceeded. Such issues do not seem to have been considered by Finkelstein when evaluating Bezos's performance.

But even if we grant that Bezos and other business leaders deserve such accolades, other questions arise for students of leadership to consider. For example, did Bezos deliver all that he is being credited for by himself, or was he assisted by the 109,000 people that Amazon now employs? What evidence is there that the decisions being singled out for praise even originated with him? Did group processes influence decision making at Amazon? More important, can someone's performance in a complex environment be meaningfully evaluated, and causal links identified, over a 12-month time frame? Perhaps if Amazon falters slightly in the year ahead, Finkelstein will then conclude that Bezos neglected to develop internal talent, and brought in outsiders who undermined the culture that made it successful in the first place. Through such examples, students begin to learn that behaviors depicted as "positive" in a context of success can just as readily be redefined as "negative" in conditions of failure. In either case, the leadership attribution being made is linked to knowledge of the outcome, which tends to undermine the validity of the causal attributions being claimed.

Similarly, the *Harvard Business Review* regularly seeks to identify "the best performing CEOs in the world."[11] Typically, such articles attempt to identify "which global CEOs actually delivered solid results over the long run" (e.g., Ignatius, 2014: 47). In this instance, the metric of "solid results" was shareholder return and market capitalization. The point is not whether, or to what extent, leadership makes a difference to organizational performance, however narrowly such performance is defined. Rather, total agency is here invested in the leader whose stewardship is depicted as the primary causal factor behind organizational success or failure. Can this really be an accurate account of organizational dynamics? However brilliant a leader may be, whatever they are attempting to achieve requires a great deal of help from others. Publications such as these illustrate the extent to which romanticism continues to pervade leadership theory and practice. Critical courses, in contrast, explore alternative perspectives that view leadership as more distributed, relational, situated, and contested.

Critical courses also question the often interrelated essentialist assumption that there is one best way to lead, regardless of context. While we challenge the depiction of individual leaders as paragons of effectiveness, to be admired and emulated uncritically, we do not question the value of business leaders addressing students, as they often do, or of treating their views with respect. But we do question the tendency to introduce them as "rock stars" and "legends." This is typical of how Jack Welch, among others, has been introduced to students at prominent institutions, including MIT and Stanford (Tourish, 2013). The implication is that the academy can do little more than learn lessons from what such leaders have done, as though their behavior is bereft of error, self-interest, or self-aggrandizement. Our courses encourage a more critical attitude to the flattering interviews and hagiographies that appear in such outlets as *Harvard Business Review,* and in which the voices of employees are largely silent—a drama with only leading parts, but without a supporting cast. We sometimes ask the simple question: "If you were an employee of this organization, is this a picture of how it works that you would recognize?" And we add a corollary: "Is there evidence in this article or book that gives you any insight into what employees think?"[12] By encouraging students to question the self-proclaimed (and sometimes self-aggrandizing) stories of leaders, critical pedagogies seek to explore the purposes of leadership and question who is most likely to benefit from the attainment of leader-declared goals (Sinclair, 2007b). One valuable means of developing this critique of essentialist assumptions is to explore the influence and diversity of contexts, cultures, and countries on leadership dynamics.[13] Historically, the perceived significance of contexts in relation to leadership has shifted back and forth, but the general tendency has been to privilege "heroic" leaders and downplay contexts. Exploring the impact of context on leaders is anathema to heroic perspectives, since, if "great men" make "his-tory," then it is (male) leaders, not contexts, that should be the primary focus of study.

The Importance of Contexts and Cultures

More recently, there has been growing recognition that organizational (Bligh, 2006) and national cultural contexts significantly shape leadership dynamics (Jepson, 2009). The multiple cultures, values, and identities of leaders and followers in diverse societies significantly impact on the possibilities and limits of leadership (Hartog & Dickson, 2004; Dickson, Castano, Magomaeva, & Hartog, 2012). Globalization processes also crucially shape contemporary leadership dynamics. Rapid changes in political, economic, social, and technological landscapes are transforming the modus operandi of organizations around the world. Research also demonstrates that many global business ventures fail because of the mismanagement of intercultural differences (Wibbeke & McArthur, 2014).

Exploring these transnational and intercultural meanings in the classroom opens up new ways of thinking about leadership and followership. It also helps students to appreciate how contexts can significantly shape leadership practices in important ways. For example, local labor markets, product markets, supply chains, and cultures and histories all facilitate and constrain leadership dynamics. Equally, contexts are often contested and competitive, frequently characterized by intersecting inequalities based, for example, on class, gender, ethnicity, age, religion, and so forth. Highlighting the importance of context encourages the voices of those students from non-North American backgrounds to raise cultural issues about leadership assumptions and practices in their own countries and regions.

This critical appreciation of the importance of contexts may also be explored with students through a focus on alternative organizations (Parker et al., 2014). Beyond the not-for-profit and voluntary sectors, these include worker cooperatives, communes and indigenous communities, social change movements, and families. For example, research into social movement organizations explores how participants prohibit people from assuming permanent leadership roles and seek to distribute power and responsibility as widely as possible. However, the absence of formal leaders does not mean the absence of leadership (Sutherland, Land, & Bohm, 2014). Studies have also revealed profound patterns of leadership dysfunctionality in some radical social-change organizations, where the systems of domination often evident in more conventional organizations have been faithfully reproduced, sometimes in an even more extreme form (Tourish, 2013). Alternative organizations are useful sites for exploring leadership dynamics and bringing different perspectives into the classroom. In this way, the benefits and limits of participative forms of leadership, and the emancipatory ideologies that often underpin them, can be brought into sharper relief. This approach also demonstrates what businesses can learn from alternative organizations, rather than assuming that the flow of learning is always from business to other sectors. To facilitate this kind of reflection, we encourage the systematic study of leadership practices in noncorporate settings.

Contexts are also important in relation to the conditions in which knowledge about leadership is produced. As most studies are conducted by U.S. researchers in U.S. companies about U.S. employees, informed by U.S. perspectives and methods, it is perhaps not surprising that leadership research articulates primarily U.S. values. Similarly, most textbooks on which leadership courses are built tend to be U.S. in origin and orientation. CLS perspectives suggest that the Western, white male-dominated paradigm of transformational leadership is the new colonial model, with global leadership development programs often shaped by the cultural history of the United States with its masculine mythical heroes, from "John Wayne" cowboy figures to charismatic business entrepreneurs (Jones, 2006). This U.S. cultural affinity with heroic individualism informs the tendency to privilege individual leaders (Lipman-Blumen, 2000).[14]

In sum, by highlighting the considerable influence of contexts and cultures on leadership dynamics, critical courses challenge romanticized views of leaders and the essentialist assumptions that frequently underpin them. Encouraging students to reflect on leadership romanticism and its detrimental effects has valuable learning outcomes. The cultural-specificity of leadership also brings to students' attention how U.S. values have shaped leadership studies, and how many other ways of understanding and enacting leadership are possible. Accordingly, topic areas such as cross-cultural and indigenous perspectives on leadership, organizational or national cultures, and Eastern ethical systems (e.g., Confucianism), help to enhance students' cultural intelligence and understanding of global leadership dynamics.

Foregrounding Power

Critical leadership courses view an understanding of power dynamics as fundamental to the examination of leadership (Collinson, 2005, 2011; Alvesson & Spicer, 2012; Tourish, 2013). They recognize that, for good or ill, leaders exert significant power and influence over contemporary organizational processes. While the exercise of power and authority is sometimes necessary and may deliver desirable ends, CLS also addresses the dangers of concentrating control in the hands of a few. Finkelstein (2003: 43) noted that "[b]eing CEO of a sizeable corporation is probably the closest thing in today's world to being king of your own country."[15] CLS encourages students to question the view that such extreme power imbalances in corporations are both desirable and immutable features of organizations.

Viewing leadership in terms of the effective or ineffective exercise of power, authority, and influence, CLS examines the situated power relations through which leadership discursive practices are socially constructed, frequently rationalized, sometimes resisted, and occasionally transformed. It challenges mainstream assumptions that power relations are unproblematic and that white male leaders are the people in charge who create visions, make decisions, and transmit orders, while followers are an undifferentiated collective who carry out orders from "above." In our courses we seek to illustrate how leaders' power can take many structural and interpersonal economic, political, ideological, discursive, and psychological forms. CLS suggest that leaders control key decisions. They typically construct strategic visions and agendas, shape structures and cultures, hire and fire, monitor work and performance, provide promotions and rewards, and apply sanctions. Through this and other means they can define situations and "manage meanings" (Smircich & Morgan, 1982) in ways that suit their purposes, and which may or may not meet the needs of other organizational actors.[16] Rather than viewing power as simply a functional resource, critical leadership courses explore how organizations may be saturated with power dynamics and how leaders' control can be exercised through coercion, manipulation, and domination, as well as through more inspirational means.

> "CLS examines the situated power relations through which leadership discursive practices are socially constructed, frequently rationalized, sometimes resisted, and occasionally transformed."

Critical leadership courses also reveal how the exercise of power can be disguised, for example through ideologies that seek to rationalize sectional as universal interests, through discourses that construct excessively positive definitions of reality, and by leaders "distancing" themselves from particular local practices. One of the important learning objectives of critical leadership courses is therefore to render transparent and explicit such disguised dynamics of power and control. Critical courses seek to denaturalize leadership, question taken-for-granted relationships, and explore how leadership dynamics are the product of an ongoing process of social construction between myriad organizational actors within particular cultural contexts. This approach involves going "beyond the affirmation and reconstitution of the familiar world to recognize other possibilities" (Calhoun, 1995: 2).

The study of power in this way encourages a focus on dysfunctional leadership and its paradoxical and sometimes unintended effects. We acknowledge that many leadership programs now feature Enron and Royal Bank of Scotland (RBS), among others, in a sort of "rogue's gallery" of leadership practice gone wrong. However, in our critical courses, these examples are used as part of a wider study of dysfunctional, toxic, or bad leadership that goes beyond a focus on individual character traits and locates these failings in a more systematic study of how the concentration of power in the hands of a few has an innate potential to move in such directions.

Put bluntly, the teaching of leadership needs to go beyond a "rotten apple" theory of dysfunctionality and corruption to examine the barrel within which the apples have soured. The "bad apple" theory often avoids the fundamental questions of power dynamics in leadership practices, particularly around issues of organizational politics, social justice, exploitation, discrimination, and intimidation. These downsides of organizational life are common to most people's experiences of work. They need greater recognition in any serious study of leadership. There is much to learn from leadership dysfunctionality and the strategic mistakes that it produces.

> "Put bluntly, the teaching of leadership needs to go beyond a 'rotten apple' theory of dysfunctionality and corruption to examine the barrel within which the apples have soured."

The Banking Crisis and CLS Pedagogy

In line with this, we encourage students to examine the behavior of banking leaders in the run-up to the recent financial crisis that precipitated the Great Recession. Equally, we explore how dominant leadership theories contributed to the banking crisis, rather than maintain what Board (2010: 275) has described as a "deafening silence" on the issue. The few studies that have addressed the leadership behaviors implicated in the crash explore how bankers became an "elite field" detached from their own organizations (Kerr & Robinson, 2011); how power was concentrated in the hands of a few people, with deleterious effects on the quality of their decisions and their ability to manage risk (Martin, 2013); the development of grotesque systems of privilege and reward that facilitated hubris and narcissism (Fraser, 2014); the dominance of excessively positive discourses that silenced dissent (Collinson, 2012); and how banking leaders have subsequently produced accounts that systematically downplay their responsibility for the Great Financial Crash (Tourish & Hargie, 2012). We encourage students to appreciate how such accounts can damage banking leaders' ability, and that of others, to learn from failure. Thus, critical pedagogies analyze the discursive strategies employed by key banking actors to build trust in business practices that proved to be self-serving and disastrous (e.g., Bourne & Edwards, 2012).

Central here is the extent to which critical leadership courses move on from an analysis of *individual failings* to challenge leadership models that encourage overdependency on the wisdom or otherwise of designated leaders through a close analysis of how leader power is institutionalized and used to stifle critical voices. For example, Fraser (2014) reports that under Fred Goodwin the Royal Bank of Scotland imported "rank and yank" into its appraisal process. This system of forced curve measurement required RBS managers to classify employees into three categories: those that performed well, and who received huge rewards; a middle group who were deemed to be satisfactory; and a "bottom" group alleged to be underperforming and who were targeted for dismissal. This CLS approach was used within Enron (Tourish & Vatcha, 2005) and its effects at RBS were similar. A culture of fear that discouraged dissent took root. High sales targets were set and became the ultimate criteria for promotion and bonuses. Numerous side effects proliferated, including attempts to poach customers who were often poor credit risks in need of further loans that their existing banks would not provide. Persuading these risky customers to switch enabled bank employees to meet high targets for new business, and so prosper under the system in place.[17] Self-interest overrode the wider institutional interest that regulators erroneously assumed would act as a safeguard against what became collectively irrational behavior. The discursive framework and ideological assumptions that justified such behavior fed institutional isomorphism, with short-term success breeding copycat behavior on a wide scale (McKenna & Rooney, 2012).

Moreover, the lionization of business leaders and the absence of critical analysis that we have highlighted here, and which certainly characterized much dialogue about banking leaders before the crash, legitimizes and encourages excessive executive pay (Koehn, 2014). This, in turn, can feed a narcissistic mind-set that encourages the quest for even higher levels of remuneration and wider differentials between those at the top and the rest in their organizations (O'Reilly, Doerr, Caldwell, & Chatman, 2014). The effects have been damaging. A key role of critical pedagogy is to bring these varied interests and paradoxical processes to the fore in classroom discussion, thereby challenging the notion of more or less homogenous organizational interests and "the assumed rationality of the economic individual" (Roberts & Ng, 2012: 101).

Thus, a critical pedagogy challenges the tendency among many students to assume that large organizations invariably have a sound rationale for their strategies and practices. It denaturalizes such practices as rank and yank and encourages students to consider the intended and unintended consequences for employee conformity and dissent, the quality of leader decision making, the consolidation of power in elite hands, and organizational efficacy. Such critical interrogations of leadership practice offer lessons for understanding power, authority, and control far beyond the banking sector. For example, Padilla, Hogan, and Kaiser (2007) and Einarsen, Aasland, and Skogstad, (2007) identify various features of destructive leadership that include dominance, coercion, and manipulation, and locate these within a dynamic whereby the inclinations of destructive leaders interact with susceptible followers and conducive environments to produce unwelcome outcomes. Thus, the failures at organizations such as Enron are not seen as purely the products of the individual pathologies of individual leaders. Rather, they are the outcome of leader predisposition, environmental context, and the active role of followers, whether as questioning or conforming subjects of power in their own right. CLS acknowledges the need to explore these issues, rather than focus relentlessly on the positive aspects of leadership, but also to "account for the difficult balancing act between leadership as a productive source of power and a destructive one" (Alvesson & Spicer, 2012: 382). Such critical thinking means examining truth claims, the alleged evidence base behind theories, and being skeptical of conventional wisdom. In the context of leadership, it means encouraging students to question leader claims for agency, and problematizing the dominant leadership theories of the past 30 years that have tended to take such claims at face value.

Reconceptualizing Power in Leadership Studies

Power can be (re)conceptualized in multiple structural and interpersonal ways. For example, a recent review of the literature (Sturm & Antonakis, 2015: 139) defines (interpersonal) power in terms of "having the discretion and means to asymmetrically enforce one's will over others." Power in all its diverse forms and embeddedness in structures, cultures, and practices is a central concern of critical studies of organization and management (Fleming & Spicer, 2014). Critiquing rhetoric, tradition, authority, and objectivity, Critical management studies (CMS) in particular opens up new ways of thinking about alternative forms of management (Mingers, 2000). Comprising a variety of approaches, CLS often draws on the more established field of CMS which, in turn is informed by a plurality of perspectives, from structuralism and labor-process theory, to feminism, poststructuralism, postcolonial theory, environmentalism, and psychoanalysis. Critical feminist and postcolonial scholars, for example, show how power is also exercised in gendered and racialized ways (as well as through other sources of diversity and inequality).

CLS differs from CMS by emphasizing that leaders and leadership dynamics (not just managers and management) exercise significant power and influence over contemporary organizational processes. While CMS concentrates primarily on management (and neglects leadership[18]), the emergent field of CLS suggests that power is also a central feature of leadership dynamics (Gordon, 2002). This issue is now attracting greater, and much needed, attention. For example, a study of the neglected area of corruption (Bendahan, Zehnder, Pralong, & Antonakis, 2015) highlights power and testosterone as key determinants of leader malfeasance. It shows that even the possession of a small amount of power increases people's willingness to engage in corrupt practices—a challenge to leadership models that suggest leaders should have greater power rather than less.

Above we suggested how CLS perspectives approach the banking crisis by emphasizing systemic institutional practices rather than the individual frailties of banking leaders. The consideration of power, utilizing the above-cited studies and others, is a further apposite illustration. Following Foucault, Hardy and Clegg (2006) discuss the disciplinary nature of power, and how this is manifest through surveillance, routinization, and cultural practices, all of which seek to codify and control employee behavior. In this view, power is not a neutral resource to be used for unproblematic organizational ends as determined by its formal leaders (e.g., Pfeffer, 2013). Rather, it serves variegated interests, and while inviting compliance, it often generates resistance. Drawing on these insights, we explore the disciplinary role of the "rank and yank" systems in place within organizations such as RBS. By monitoring employees through measurement and ranking, they seek to promote an ideal, conformist self in their employees, where leader decisions are assumed to be beyond critical interrogation. We challenge students to think through the intended effects of such systems, which in themselves can be questioned, but also to consider their unintended consequences, and how these can produce dysfunctional organizational outcomes. Both implicitly and explicitly, this kind of dialogue creates a space in which conventional assumptions about the role of heroic leaders can be critically evaluated.

It also creates opportunities to consider the dysfunctional consequences for individual leaders themselves. Harding (2014) draws attention to the toll that leadership often places on leaders. In assuming greater power, they find themselves dealing with multiple, competing demands, which can be very difficult to manage. She suggests that leaders are therefore simultaneously powerful and powerless. They hold decision-making power over more and more issues, about which they often know less and less. They lead people whom they must trust to deliver, while simultaneously managing systems of surveillance that implicitly assume subordinates cannot be trusted. Thus, it is clear that in many instances, banking leaders had a minimal grasp of the complex environment within which they operated, and of the likely consequences of their own decisions. This runs counter to the image of powerful leaders found in mainstream approaches, and which rarely considers the possibility that leaders may have less knowledge and power than is imagined, or that would be needed to deliver a "transformational" agenda. Critical courses open up such considerations of power and explore the paradoxical and often unwanted effects of having a great deal of it. Rather than prescribing a new or morally superior view of the world and the place of leadership within it, critical courses seek to encourage a greater sensitivity to the limits of power, to draw attention to its institutional manifestations in appraisal and ranking systems, and to highlight the problems that it often creates.

Flowing from this understanding, we emphasize to students that although leadership power dynamics are important, they are rarely, if ever, so asymmetrical that they are invariably one-way, all-determining, or necessarily effective. Exploring the dialectical nature of leadership power dynamics, CLS highlights the fundamental tensions, dilemmas, paradoxes, and contradictions that can also characterize the ways leadership power is enacted (Collinson, 2005). These tensions and contradictions are based on opposing but interdependent forces that produce conflict and change, "a dynamic knot of contradictions, a ceaseless interplay between contrary or opposing tendencies" (Baxter & Montgomery, 1996: 3). This means acknowledging that in certain contexts leaders act in contradictory ways. For example, while leaders' excessive optimism may have short-term motivational effects, in the longer term it often leaves organizations ill-prepared to deal with unexpected and problematic changes (Collinson, 2012). It may also encourage leaders to escalate their commitment to already failed courses of action (Staw, 1976). Such optimism is evident in forecasting discourses within the banking sector that are inherently predisposed to play down or exclude elements of uncertainty in favor of overly precise "fictions" about the state of the world that encourage complacency in the face of difficulty (Svetlova, 2012). Critical courses subject such discourses to rigorous interrogation and challenge the widespread preference for discursive closure over open-ended inquiry. Conversely, excessive forms of coercive control, surveillance, and micromanagement can alienate subordinates who subsequently feel that trust and respect have been eroded and compromised. In a further manifestation of the law of unintended consequences, follower alienation can lead to disaffection, demoralization, and a reduction in commitment: the very opposite outcomes to those intended. This in turn is likely to generate follower resistance, as the next section now elaborates.

Rethinking Followership

We argue that an important component of any critical leadership course is a reconceptualization of the importance of followers' agency, knowledgability, and proactivity. CLS courses focus more fully on what constitutes "effective" follower behaviors, examining the impact of followers on leaders and vice versa (Chaleff, 2009).[19] There is now a growing literature on followership (e.g., Uhl-Bien, Riggio, Lowe, & Carsten, 2014) that highlights the systematic neglect of followers in leader-centric perspectives. In our experience, insights about followers' knowledgeable agency and their latent potential resonate with many students in ways that facilitate their reappraisal of leadership dynamics. This deeper understanding also encourages students to appreciate the importance of follower diversity, expressed for example, in multiple possible meanings of the term (from disciples and supporters to employees) and in various embodied follower identities related to gender, ethnicity, class, age, religion, and so forth.

Yet many followership studies continue to adopt a functionalist framework, underestimating or taking power differentials for granted (Crossman & Crossman, 2011). Accordingly, "[f]ollowership is a relational role in which followers have the ability to influence leaders and contribute to the improvement and attainment of group and organizational objectives. It is primarily a hierarchically upwards influence" (Carsten, Uhl-Bien, West, Patera, & McGregor, 2010: 559). Here, it is simply assumed that "group" and "organizational," as opposed to sectional, objectives exist, and that leaders are the prime arbiters of what they should be—albeit while remaining open to an unspecified degree of influence. Moreover, followership is viewed as being what assists in the "improvement" and "attainment" of such objectives, rather than what might fundamentally interrogate them.

Functionalist approaches of this kind tend to presume that (a) follower conformity is an inherently positive feature of leadership dynamics, and (b) resistance is incompatible with the notion of "good" followership. Rather, "good" followers are those "to whom a leader can safely delegate responsibility, people who anticipate needs at their own level of competence and authority" (Kelley, 1988: 144).[20] Not only do they follow instructions from powerful others, they have sufficiently advanced mindreading skills to determine what these might be in advance. Followers therefore "display competences that mirror those of their leaders" (Cunha, Rego, Clegg, & Neves, 2013: 87), rather than develop contrary competences, values, or objectives of their own. Critical leadership courses challenge functionalist theories and practices of followership. In addition to highlighting followers' proactivity and knowledgeability, critical pedagogies emphasize how followership is implicated in the reproduction of asymmetrical power relations and identity dynamics.

Rather than view follower conformity as inherently positive, critical leadership courses problematize its conditions, the processes through which it is enacted, and its consequences. In particular, they show how conformity produces paradoxical and unintended consequences both for followers and for organizations. Equally, our courses encourage students to rethink followership in relation to its potential for dissent (Banks 2008), whether explicit (e.g., strikes) or disguised (e.g., output restriction). They illustrate how followers can express resistance in multiple ways, for example through working to rule, output restriction, working the system, and sabotage (Ackroyd & Thompson, 1999). The countercultures which emerge in some organizations can invert dominant values and hierarchies, as Bakhtin outlined in relation to the carnival and Willis (1977) described in relation to the highly masculine working class countercultures he found on the shop floor. To illustrate resistance, studies such as that by Ezzamel, Willmott, and Worthington (2001) can be used, which examine management's failed attempts to introduce what they saw as progressive working practices into a factory that were met with individual and collective resistance from employees and their trade unions. The profound differences in attitudes between senior managers and employees led to conflict and stalemate. Followers may also just "switch off," distancing themselves physically or mentally. By disengaging, employees ascribe primary significance to life outside work, dividing their identity between the "indifferent me at work" and the "real me" outside (Collinson, 2003). The discursive processes whereby leaders and nonleaders seek to make sense of each other's world, with varying degrees of success, are central issues in such studies (Fairhurst, 2007, 2009). These dynamics offer a far richer insight into the potential and limits of leader agency than can be found in most mainstream accounts.

Conventional perspectives tend to promote the idea that leaders can unproblematically shape followers' attitudes, identities, and behaviors, and secure their compliance with centrally sanctioned goals (Collinson, 2006). There is little focus on the potential benefits of follower dissent, which is often dismissed as an inherently negative organizational feature that needs to be overcome, rather than viewed as potentially useful feedback (Tourish & Robson, 2006). Thus, frank, open, and honest feedback from followers to leaders is frequently absent in organizations. Critical courses give more emphasis to critical upward communication and its potential to create a dynamic in which employees feel empowered to highlight the internal contradictions and problems that beset their organizations. While many top U.S. business schools, such as Harvard, Stanford, and MIT have sessions billed as "the view from the top," in which "celebrity" CEOs share their insights with students, very few courses offer a "view from below," in which rank-and-file employees (i.e., "followers") of large organizations are given the opportunity to share their perspective on leadership dynamics. In terms of pedagogy, we see no good reason for this. An important message here is that followers (and students of leadership) have considerable insight and experience about both leadership and followership (Kouzes & Posner, 2012; Collinson & Collinson, 2009).

In line with this pedagogical approach, we also suggest that critical courses rethink the case study method, originally derived from Harvard Business School (HBS). The primary sources for material included in these studies are usually drawn from the leaders and managers of the organizations being studied (Starkey & Tiratsoo, 2007). The hyperbolic content of these "studies" can be inferred from their titles, which include "Enron's transformation: From gas pipeline to New Economy Powerhouse." Starkey and Tiratsoo (2007) report that one study was written by a faculty member who was simultaneously earning $50,000 a year for serving on Enron's board of advisors. No wonder that Enron was happy to cross market them on their website. No wonder that HBS published 11 (now unobtainable) case studies on Enron before it imploded. HBS also produced a case on the Royal Bank of Scotland entitled "masters of integration," before it too fell into bankruptcy and disgrace. In these accounts followers are rendered largely mute, their perspectives subordinated to those of leaders. This bias against offering a much needed critique of leadership practice is intensified, as we suggested above in relation to Enron, by the cozy consulting relationships that many faculty often develop with "top" companies (Butler et al., 2015). If case studies are to be of any real value, and break from what can only be described as a culture of sycophancy, then they need to reflect a much wider variety of organizational perspectives. They need, in any event, to avoid conveying the message to students that leaders can produce definitive strategies based on minimal information and with no exposure at all to actual organizational contexts. Again, this kind of critical analysis highlights the dangers of leadership hubris: a fundamental message of critical leadership courses.

Conclusion

Our essay has explored the potential of critical leadership courses to offer a different teaching design and agenda from that which remains dominant in elite business schools. There are many ways to teach leadership critically. The approach outlined above discussed a number of illustrative guiding principles that seek to encourage students to question the taken-for-granted and to rethink leadership dynamics in new and innovative ways. In terms of design, critical courses strongly encourage student participation and dialogue in their learning. In terms of content, critical courses go beyond the romanticized assumptions of mainstream perspectives to highlight the importance of power in leadership practices; the multiple contexts and cultures through which leadership dynamics are reproduced; the potential of follower agency and dissent; the paradoxes and unintended effects of leaders' practices, and the negative consequences of certain leadership dynamics. Critical courses also investigate the damaging effects of overconformity to destructive behavioral norms, the promotion of monocultures that can stifle critical feedback, and the extent and dangers of "executive hubris" (Picone, Dagnino, & Mina, 2014).

By raising these often underexplored issues, critical leadership courses have a significant educational benefit and are more consistent with the inquiring and independent role of the university in society. There is a stronger recognition in critical leadership courses of the possible tensions, paradoxes, and contradictions that power dynamics can engender, as well as of the need for researchers systematically to explore how these (often unacknowledged) contradictions are typically embedded in extant theories of leadership. We commented earlier that students often want simple prescriptions on leadership. The lionization of business leaders such as Jeff Bezos and Jack Welch certainly offers such simplicity, and it evidently has considerable appeal to many students. But a critical pedagogy challenges such leader-centric accounts of business success and urges students to dig deeper, however uncomfortable that may sometimes feel.

This poses its own dilemmas and problems. Challenging deeply held views, and the student preferences that come with them, sometimes takes students out of their "comfort zones." This can lead to critical feedback (or "resistance"). Faced with this, we suggest that educators should avoid the temptation to replace one orthodoxy with another, by insisting that a more "correct" perspective on leadership must be uncritically accepted by students. Conformity of this kind would itself be oppressive. Rather than present definite answers and new established truths, our approach can be defined as a dialogic one, in which multiple perspectives are presented and debated, without an expectation that they will be fully resolved. Our goal is to promote openness rather than closure. To achieve this, those teaching leadership critically should themselves be reflexive about their purpose, values, assumptions, and classroom practices.

In that spirit of on-going inquiry, we encourage business school educators to avoid reproducing myths that purport to chronicle how powerful and charismatic male leaders routinely "rescue" organizations from the precipice of failure. Few CEOs are women. Even fewer are "Supermen." They share the same foibles, weaknesses, doubts, dilemmas, and worries as the rest of us. Suggesting otherwise encourages business students to develop inflated notions of their own leadership potential and future role, to invoke leadership theories that overstate the directive role of leaders, and to underestimate the potential impact of proactive followers. Similarly, a wide variety of stakeholders have a legitimate interest in the outcomes of leader action, and the purposes for which it is deployed. Critical leadership education in general challenges the suggestion that various leadership skills can be taught as if they are neutral vehicles for achieving unproblematic ends. This means foregrounding a wider stakeholder view of who business schools need to serve.

It also means developing the knowledge base of critical leadership studies—an area of research that is still in its infancy. There is a need for more critical studies that examine, for example, leadership power dynamics, the ways in which white men and specific masculinities continue to pervade leadership decision making, the conditions and consequences of leader hubris, the downsides of follower conformity, the processes and consequences of follower resistance, and the ethical and emotional dynamics of leadership and followership. There is also a particular need to extend our knowledge of global leadership processes and the many forms that leadership takes in different international contexts and cultures.

Suffice it to say here that heroic models of leadership have legitimized the overconcentration of power, encouraged hubris rather than humility, helped to disempower employees, and played a significant part in business scandals. Neither society nor its organizations have benefitted. It is time to rethink. We propose that business schools adopt approaches to leadership education and research that are more critical, questioning, relational, reflective, and reflexive. CLS can make a significant contribution to that effort. It challenges students to think differently about leadership, organizations, societies, and themselves both as leaders and as followers. CLS argues that leadership is about the exercise of power, whether effective or ineffective, productive or destructive, emancipatory or oppressive. The critical courses we deliver to our students seek to explore, not only the problematic dynamics that can occur in leadership processes, but also the potential for more effective, relational, ethical and inclusive ways of exercising power and authority. This might be the prelude to different, more empowering forms of leadership and followership action from which we would all benefit.

Notes

1. Although contemporary leadership courses may question the way that women, ethnic minorities, or other subordinated groups are excluded from senior positions, they may still neglect underlying power relations and intersecting inequalities. As a consequence, these courses can remain confined within the mainstream leader-centric paradigm.

2. We do not intend here to rehearse the now ageing debate about the extent to which "management" and "leadership" are distinct entities. Our view is that while it makes sense to see management as somewhat more concerned with day-to-day operational activities than leadership, the difference has been overblown. Many management activities have been relabeled as leadership seemingly in a quest to imbue them with the greater sense of grandiosity associated with transformational leadership theories. Nevertheless, the term leadership has heuristic value in that it captures the approach, perceptions, and interactional dynamics of varied organizational actors when they encounter uncertain environments, powerful others, and complex strategic dilemmas, and in which the salience of leadership issues is therefore heightened. However, attempts to establish absolutist distinctions between them can be viewed as another example of the "dichotomizing tendency" in leadership studies—such as leaders/followers; transformational/ transactional, and leaders/contexts (Collinson, 2014). Discussion of these issues, and the value of conventional distinctions between management and leadership, is also a useful issue in more critically oriented leadership courses.

3. Burns' (1978) influential text illustrates the tendency in mainstream leadership studies to eschew any critical analysis of power. Differentiating between "leaders" (who successfully engage and satisfy followers' motives) and "power holders" (who use followers for their own purposes, and utilize "naked" and "brute" power to achieve their ends), Burns asserted that "power-wielders" were not leaders. For example, he argued that Hitler was not a leader but a tyrant, "an absolute wielder of brutal power" who crushed all opposition: "A leader and a tyrant are polar opposites" (1978: 3). This approach sanitizes the concept of leadership to such an extent that brutal dictators and autocrats are no longer considered to be leaders at all. Since the publication of Burns's highly influential text, this tendency to "purify" leadership of questions related to power has become increasingly embedded in mainstream business school teaching and research on leadership (Collinson, 2014).

4. See the program's website at http://www.jbs.cam.ac.uk/programmes/execed/open-programmes/transformational-leadership/. Accessed 15 October 2014.

5. Rarely utilized by leadership scholars, research on wisdom challenges overly heroic notions of leaders (McKenna, Rooney, & Kenworthy, 2013; Shotter & Tsoukas, 2014). It recognizes that if excessive agency is invested in leaders there is little need for anyone else to take much responsibility for ensuring organizational success. There is also little need for leaders to pay serious attention to followers' input, if any is offered.

6. The notion that while subjective experiences of phenomena overlap between actors, there are also variations from person to person is commonplace to philosophers and cognitive scientists who study consciousness. The word "qualia" is used to denote the way that the quality of subjective experiences differs from the "objective" properties of outside stimuli, and how the same stimuli and external environment is often interpreted differently by each person (Dennett, 1993).

7. Transformational leadership theories are not alone in suffering from this problem. For example, Spears (1995) suggested that servant leadership had 10 major characteristics. But a more recent review indicates that this has grown to 44 (van Dierendonck, 2011). These include courage, vision, the ability to exercise transforming influence (while empowering others), and humility. This clearly poses implementation challenges. Attending to 44 characteristics in one's daily leadership practice would require levels of sagacity rarely found outside Mount Olympus.

8. The U.S. universities of Harvard, Stanford, and Duke are named after wealthy benefactors who provided substantial donations. This naming process is very common in North American business schools. The benefactors' association with the study of business tends to reinforce the "great man" theory of leadership. A number of U.S. business schools are also named after "leadership gurus." For example, in 2006, Sacred Heart University, a Catholic university in Connecticut, announced that it had renamed its college of business the John F. Welch College of Business. It would be "committed to educating students in the leadership tradition and legacy of Jack Welch," who is described on the university's website as "legendary," adding "he made the corporation [GE] into a global powerhouse, and his leadership style has been analyzed and imitated the world over." His early incarnation as "Neutron Jack," famous for laying off thousands of employees, is not mentioned. Outside North America, it is much less common for business and management schools to be named after a "generous benefactor" or "a leadership guru" or indeed to receive such donations (Cambridge and Oxford are the exceptions that prove this general rule). Typically, non-North American business and management schools tend to be named after their university and geographical location.

9. During the opening session of a recent course, one student announced that she wanted to learn how to "influence" employees without them being aware that such influence was taking place or of the means by which it was being accomplished. The ethical problems posed by this had not occurred to her.

10. Finkelstein is based at The Tuck School of Business, which is named after Amos Tuck—the father of Edward Tuck (1842–1938)—who was an international financier and philanthropist. Critical courses can explore how this naming process tends to inscribe leader romanticism into organizational identity (which in turn encourages an excessive reverence toward business leaders on the part of students).

11. HBR is recommended reading on most MBA leadership courses. It therefore has a particularly direct impact on how leadership is taught and on the mind-sets of students.

12. Grey (2013) offers an interesting example of this absence in relation to Semco, a Brazilian company whose seemingly participative and democratic approach has been popularized by its CEO (Semler, 1993)—or, as he prefers to be termed, its "counsellor." Semler's book has been influential and led to invitations to speak at many leading business schools, including MIT. Grey's point is that "we hear nothing at all of the voice and experience of those who actually work there. We are simply invited to take on trust the organization as refracted through Semler's lens" (p. 83). Note that we are not suggesting Semler's account is necessarily a distortion. But we are pointing out that in the absence of evidence that brings other organizational voices to the fore we have no way of knowing either way.

13 Rosenzweig (2007) provides a particularly incisive critique of such promises, and shows how similar strategies and behaviors produce radically different outcomes depending on context.

14. Equally influential in U.S. leadership studies are the positivist methodologies that underpin mainstream perspectives. Positivism seeks to produce "objective," primarily quantitative findings, that try to separate "fact" from "value," and "science" from "common-sense." Many social scientists have argued that positivism is fundamentally flawed, not least because the distinctive nature of human beings requires more interpretive and qualitative research methodologies and because all observation is in fact "theory-laden." Suffice it to say here that the quest to discover universal laws of leadership encourages researchers to privilege leaders' agency as the primary causal factor. Equally, the pressure to generalize and measure marginalizes complex context specificities, which are especially difficult to quantify given their shifting and unpredictable nature.

15. Finkelstein discusses major problems with how many leaders exercise authority over others. But, consistent with mainstream approaches to leadership, he does so purely from the perspective of identifying toxic personal habits and traits of particular leaders, such as John DeLorean, and does not problematize wider, systemic power relationships.

16. CLS also recognizes that leadership is often distributed. Leaders can emerge informally in more junior positions and dispersed locations, as well as in oppositional organizations, such as trade unions (Knowles, 2007) and in revolutionary movements (Rejai, 1979).

17. Fraser (2014) discusses one individual who was highly rated by this system, and who was named business manager of the year three times. Unfortunately, he also embezzled £21 million from RBS. In mitigation, his defense cited the pressure he was under from RBS to meet sky high sales targets.

18. Despite their concern to examine the exercise of power and control, many CMS writers ignore the study of leadership (Collinson, 2011, 2014). An index of this neglect is the influential *Oxford Handbook of Critical Management Studies,* edited by some of the key names in CMS (Alvesson et al., 2009). There is no chapter on leadership. "Leadership" attracts just three mentions in the book's index. All are from a chapter dealing with gender and diversity, which discusses leadership briefly (Ashcraft, 2009).

19. For example, they explore questions such as how might some of the command and control mechanisms that flow from agency theory impede effective follower behaviors, thus distorting the leadership function? How can they be dismantled? What stops many leaders from implementing even elementary mechanisms to institute follower involvement, such as suggestion schemes? In an inversion of normal protocols, we might conceive the follower as a teacher to the leader, rather than the other way round.

20. Kelley et al.'s article was published in *Harvard Business Review*. Above its title appeared the caption: "Not all corporate success is due to leaders." The clear implication is that although followers could claim some credit for success, most could still be attributed to leaders.

References

Ackroyd, S., & Thompson, P. 1999. *Organizational misbehaviour*. London: SAGE.

Alajoutsijarvi, K., Juusola, K., & Siltaoja, M. 2014. The legitimacy paradox of business schools: losing by gaining? *Academy of Management Learning & Education*: 277–291.

Alvesson, M., Bridgman, T., & Willmott, H. (Eds.). 2009. *The Oxford handbook of critical management studies*. Oxford: Oxford University Press.

Alvesson, M., & Spicer, A. 2012. Critical leadership studies: The case for critical performativity. *Human Relations*, 65: 367–390.

Amar, A., Hentrich, C., Bastani, B., & Hlupic, V. 2012. How managers succeed by letting employees lead. *Organizational Dynamics*, 41: 62–71.

Antonakis, J., Fenley, M., & Liechti, S. 2011. Can charisma be taught? Tests of two interventions. *Academy of Management Learning & Education*, 10: 374–396.

Ashcraft, K. 2009. Gender and diversity: Other ways to "make a difference." In M. Alvesson, T. Bridgman, & H. Willmott, H. (Eds.), *The Oxford handbook of critical management studies*: 304–327. Oxford: Oxford University Press.

Banks, S. 2008. *Dissent and the failure of leadership*. Cheltenham: Edward Elgar.

Bass, B. 1990. From transactional to transformational leadership: Learning to share the vision. *Organizational Dynamics*, 18: 19–31.

Bass, B., & Riggio, R. 2006. *Transformational leadership*, (2nd ed.), New Jersey: Lawrence Erlbaum.

Baxter, L. A., & Montgomery, B. M. 1996. *Relating: Dialogues and dialectics*. New York: Guildford Press.

Bendahan, S., Zehnder, C., Pralong, F., & Antonakis, J. 2015. Leader corruption depends on power and testosterone. *Leadership Quarterly*, 26(2): 101–122.

Bennis, W. 1989. *Why leaders can't lead*. San Francisco: Jossey-Bass.

Bligh, M. 2006. Surviving post-merger culture clash: Can cultural leadership lessen the casualties? *Leadership*, 2(4): 395–426.

Board, D. 2010. Leadership: The ghost at the trillion dollar crash? *European Management Journal*, 28: 269–277.

Bourne, C., & Edwards, L. 2012. Producing trust, knowledge and expertise in financial markets: The global hedge fund industry 're-presents' itself. *Culture and Organization*, 18: 107–122.

Burns, J. M. 1978. *Leadership*. New York: Harper Row.

Butler, N., Delaney, H., & Spoelstra, S. 2015. Problematizing relevance in the business school: The case of leadership studies. *British Journal of Management*, DOI: 10.1111/1467-8551.12121.

Businessworld 14 December, 2013. Finkelstein's best & worst CEOs of 2013. Available online at *http://www.businessworld.in/news/economy/finkelstein-s-best-&-worst-ceos-of-2013/ 1186665/page-1.html*, Retrieved 11 January 2014.

Calhoun, C. 1995. *Critical social theory: Culture, history and the challenge of difference.* Oxford: Blackwell.

Carsten, M., Uhl-Bien, M., West, B., Patera, J., & McGregor, R. 2010. Exploring social constructions of followership: A qualitative study. *Leadership Quarterly,* 21: 543–562.

Chaleff, I. 2009. *The courageous follower,* (3rd ed.), San Francisco: Berrett-Koehler.

Ciulla, J. B. 2004. *Ethics, The heart of leadership.* (2nd ed.). Westport, CT: Praeger.

Claxton, G., Owen, D., & Sadler-Smith, E. 2015. Hubris in leadership: A peril of unbridled intuition? *Leadership,* 11: 57–78.

Collinson, D. 2003. Identities and insecurities: Selves at work. *Organization,* 10: 527–547.

Collinson, D. 2005. Dialectics of leadership. *Human Relations,* 58: 1419–1442.

Collinson, D. 2006. Rethinking followership: A post-structuralist analysis of follower identities. *Leadership Quarterly,* 17: 179–189.

Collinson, D. 2011. Critical leadership studies. In A. Bryman, D. Collinson, K. Grint, B. Jackson, & M. Uhl-Bien (Eds.), *The SAGE handbook of leadership:* 179–192. London: SAGE.

Collinson, D. 2012. Prozac leadership and the limits of positive thinking. *Leadership,* 8: 87–107.

Collinson, D. 2014. Dichotomies, dialectics and dilemmas: New directions for critical leadership studies. *Leadership,* 10: 36–55.

Collinson, D., & Collinson, M. 2009. Blended leadership: Employee perspectives on effective leadership in the UK further education sector. *Leadership,* 5: 365–380.

Colquitt, J., & Zapata-Phelan, C. 2007. Trends in theory building and theory testing: A five-decade study of the Academy of Management Journal. *Academy of Management Journal,* 50: 1281–1303.

Crossman, B., & Crossman, J. 2011. Conceptualising followership–A review of the literature. *Leadership,* 7: 481–497.

Cunha, M., Rego, A., Clegg, S., & Neves, P. 2013. The case for transcendent followership. *Leadership,* 9: 87–106.

Cunliffe, A. 2009. The philosopher leader: On relationism, ethics and reflexivity—A critical perspective to teaching leadership. *Management Learning,* 40: 87–101.

Dickson, M., Castano, N., Magomaeva, A., & Hartog, D. 2012. Conceptualizing leadership across cultures. *Journal of World Business,* 47: 483–492.

Dennett, D. 1993. *Consciousness explained.* London: Penguin Books.

De Rue, D., Sitkin, S., & Podolny, J. 2011. From the guest editors: Teaching leadership—Issues and insights. *Academy of Management Learning & Education,* 10: 369–372.

Doh, J. 2003. Can leadership be taught? Perspectives from management educators. *Academy of Management Learning & Education,* 2: 54–67.

Ezzamel, M., Willmott, H., & Worthington, F. 2001. Power, control and resistance in 'the factory that time forgot.' *Journal of Management Studies,* 38: 1053–1079.

Einarsen, S., Aasland, M., & Skogstad, A. 2007. Destructive leadership behaviour: A definition and conceptual model. *Leadership Quarterly,* 18: 207–216.

Fairhust, G. 2009. Considering context in discursive leadership research. *Human Relations*, 62(11): 1607–1633.

Fairhurst, G. 2007. Discursive leadership. *Conversation With Leadership Psychology.* London: SAGE.

Finkelstein, S. 2003. Seven habits of spectacularly unsuccessful people. *Business Strategy Review*, 14: 39–50.

Fleming, P., & Spicer, A. 2014. Organizational power in management and organization science. *Academy of Management Annals*, 8: 237–298.

Ford, J., Ford, L., & D'Amelio, A. 2008. Resistance to change: The rest of the story. *Academy of Management Review*, 33: 362–377.

Fraser, I. 2014. *Shredded: Inside RBS, the bank that broke Britain.* Edinburgh: Birlinn.

Friedell, D. December, 2013. Review of "The Everything Store: Jeff Bezos and the age of Amazon," *London Review of Books*, 17–19.

Gagnon, S., & Collinson, D. 2014. Rethinking global leadership development programmes: The interrelated significance of power, context and identity. *Organization Studies*, 35: 1–26.

Glynn, M., & Raffaelli, R. 2010. Uncovering mechanisms of theory development in an academic field: Lessons from leadership research. *Academy of Management Annals*, 4: 359–401.

Gordon, R. 2002. Conceptualising leadership with respect to its historical-contextual antecedents to power. *The Leadership Quarterly*, 13(2): 151–167.

Grey, C. 2013. *A very short, fairly interesting and reasonably cheap book about studying organizations*, (3rd ed.), London: SAGE.

Harding, N. 2014. Reading leadership through Hegel's master/ slave dialectic: Towards a theory of the powerlessness of the powerful. *Leadership*, 14: 391–411.

Hardy, C., & Clegg, S. 2006. Some dare call it power. In S. Clegg, C. Hardy, T. Lawrence, & W. Nord (Eds.). *The SAGE handbook of organization studies (2nd Ed.)*: 754–775. London: SAGE.

Hartog, D. D., & Dickson, M. W. 2004. Leadership and culture. In J. Antonakis, A. T. Cianciolo, and R. J. Sternberg (Eds.), *The nature of leadership*: 249–278. London: SAGE.

Hatch, M. J., Kostera, M., & Kozminski, A. 2005. *The three faces of leadership: Manager, artist, priest.* Oxford: Blackwell.

Ignatius, A. 2014. The best performing CEOs in the world. *Harvard Business Review*, 92: 47–56.

Jackson, B., & Parry, K. 2011. *A very short, fairly interesting and reasonably cheap book about studying leadership*, (2nd Ed.), London: Sage.

Jepson, D. 2009. Studying leadership at cross-country level: A critical analysis. *Leadership*, 5(1): 61–80.

Jones, A. M. 2006. Developing what? An anthropological look at the leadership development process across cultures. *Leadership*, 2(4): 481–498.

Kanter, R. 1985. *The change masters.* London: Jossey Bass Wiley.

Kellerman, B. 2012. *The end of leadership.* New York: Harper Collins.

Kelley, R. 1988. In praise of followers. *Harvard Business Review*, 66: 142–148.

Kerr, R., & Robinson, S. 2011. Leadership as an elite field: Scottish banking leaders and the crisis of 2007–2009. *Leadership*, 7: 151–173.

Knowles, H. 2007. Trade union leadership: Biography and the role of historical context. *Leadership*, 3: 191–209.

Koehn, N. 12 June, 2014. Great Men, great pay? Why CEO compensation is sky high. *The Washington Post*, Available online at http://www.washingtonpost.com/opinions/great-men-great-pay-why-ceo-compensation-is-sky-high/2014/06/12/6e49d796-d227-11e3-9e25-188ebe1fa93b_story.html, Accessed 19 June 2014.

Kouzes, J., & Posner, B. 2012. *The leadership challenge*, (5th Ed.), Hoboken, NJ: Jossey Bass.

Khurana, R. 2007. *From higher aims to hired hands: The social transformation of American business schools and the unfulfilled promise of management as a profession.* Princeton, NJ: Princeton University Press.

Kotter, J. 2012. How the most innovative companies capitalise on today's rapid-fire strategic challenges – and still make their numbers. *Harvard Business Review*, 90: 44–58.

Kotter, J., & Schlesinger, L. 1979. Choosing strategies to change. *Harvard Business Review*, 57: 106–114.

Lipman-Blumen, J. 2000. *Connective leadership.* Oxford: Oxford University Press.

Martin, I. 2013. *Making it happen: Fred Goodwin, RBS and the men who blew up the British economy.* New York: Simon and Schuster.

McClelland, M. March-April, 2012. I was a warehouse wage slave. *Mother Jones.* Available online at http://www.motherjones.com/politics/2012/02/mac-mcclelland-free-online-shipping-warehouses-labor?page-4, Accessed 24 June 2014.

McKenna, B., & Rooney, D. 2012. Making sense of irrealis in the Global Financial Crisis. *Culture and Organization*, 18: 123–137.

McKenna, B., Rooney, D., & Kenworthy, A. 2013. Introduction: Wisdom and management—A guest-edited special collection of resource reviews for management educators. *Academy of Management Learning & Education*, 12: 306–311.

Meindl, J., Ehrlich, S., & Dukerich, J. 1985. The romance of leadership. *Administrative Science Quarterly*, 30: 78–102.

Mingers, J. 2000. What is it to be critical? Teaching a critical approach to management undergraduates. *Management Learning*, 31: 219–237.

Morrison, J. 2003. Leadership is our business. *Journal of Education for Business*, (September/October): 4–5.

Mumford, M., & Fried, Y. 2014. Give them what they want or give them what they need? Ideology in the study of leadership. *Journal of Organizational Behavior*, 35, 622–634.

Murphy, S. E., & Johnson, S. K. 2011. Leadership research and education: How business schools approach the concept of leadership. In M. Harvey & R. E. Riggio (Eds.). *Leadership studies: The dialogue of disciplines:* 129–148. Cheltenham: Edward Elgar.

Nirenberg, J. 1998. Myths we teach, realities we ignore: Leadership education in business schools. *Journal of Leadership Studies*, 5: 82–99.

Navarro, P. 2008. The MBA core curricula of top-ranked business schools: A study in failure? *Academy of Management Learning and Education*, 7: 108–123.

O'Reilly, C., Doerr, B., Caldwell, D., & Chatman, J. 2014. Narcissistic CEOs and executive compensation. *Leadership Quarterly*, 25: 218–231.

Padilla, A., Hogan, R., & Kaiser, R. 2007. The toxic triangle: Destructive leaders, susceptible followers, and conducive environments. *The Leadership Quarterly*, 18: 176–194.

Parker, M., Cheney, G., Fournier, V., & Land, C. (Eds.). 2014. *The Routledge companion to alternative organization.* London: Routledge.

Pfeffer, J. 2013. You're still the same: Why theories of power hold over time and across contexts. *Academy of Management Perspectives,* 27: 269–280.

Pfeffer, J., & Fong, C. 2002. The end of the business schools? Less success than meets the eye. *Academy of Management Learning & Education,* 1: 78–95.

Picone, P., Dagnino, G., & Mina, A. 2014. The origin of failure: A multidisciplinary appraisal of the hubris hypothesis and proposed research agenda. *Academy of Management Perspectives,* 28: 447–468.

Podolny, J. 2009. The buck stops (and starts) at business school. *Harvard Business Review,* 87: 62–67.

Rejai, M. 1979. *Leaders of revolution.* London: Sage.

Roberts, J., & Ng, W. 2012. Against economic (mis)conceptions of the individual: Constructing financial agency in the credit crisis. *Culture and Organization,* 18: 91–105.

Rosenzweig, P. 2007. *The halo effect... and the eight other business delusions that deceive managers.* New York: Free Press.

Sacred Heart University. 2014. "Sacred_Heart_University_names_ college_of_business_for_legendary_ GE_Chairman_Jack_Welch".

Semler, R. 1993. *Maverick.* New York: Random House.

Shotter, J., & Tsoukas, H. 2014. In search of phronesis: Leadership and the art of judgment. *Academy of Management Learning & Education,* 13: 224–243.

Sinclair, A. 2007a. Teaching leadership critically to MBAs: Experiences from heaven and hell. *Management Learning,* 38(4): 458–472.

Sinclair, A. 2007b. *Leadership for the disillusioned: Moving beyond myths and heroes to leading that liberates.* Crows Nest, NSW: Allen and Unwin.

Sinclair, A. 2009. Seducing leadership: Stories of leadership development. *Gender, Work and Organization,* 16: 266–284.

Slater, R. 1999. *Jack Welch and the GE way.* New York: McGraw-Hill.

Smircich, L., & Morgan, G. 1982. Leadership: the management of meaning. *The Journal of Applied Behavioral Science,* 18(3): 257–273.

Spears, L. 1995. *Reflections on leadership: How Robert K. Greenleaf's theory of leadership influenced today's top management thinkers.* New York: John Wiley.

Spector, B. 2014. Flawed from the "get-go": Lee Iacocca and the origins of transformational leadership. *Leadership,* 10: 361–379.

Starkey, K., & Tiratsoo, N. 2007. *The business school and the bottom line.* Cambridge: Cambridge University Press.

Staw, B. 1976. Knee-deep in the big muddy: A study of escalating commitment to a chosen course of action. *Organizational Behavior and Human Performance,* 16: 27–44.

Stone, B. 2013. *The everything store: Jeff Bezos and the age of amazon.* New York: Bantam Press.

Sturm, R., & Antonakis, J. 2015. Interpersonal power: A review, critique, and research agenda. *Journal of Management,* 41: 136–163.

Sutherland, N., Land, C., & Bohm, S. 2014. Anti-leadership in social movement organizations: The case of autonomous grassroots groups. *Organization,* 21: 759–781.

Svetlova, E. 2012. Talking about the crisis: Performance of forecasting in financial markets. *Culture and Organization,* 18: 155–169.

Tourish, D. 2013. *The dark side of transformational leadership: A critical perspective.* London: Routledge.

Tourish, D., Craig, R., & Amernic, J. 2010. Transformational leadership education and agency perspectives in business school pedagogy: A marriage of inconvenience? *British Journal of Management,* 21: S40–S59.

Tourish, D., & Hargie, O. 2012. Metaphors of failure and the failures of metaphor: A critical study of metaphors used by bankers in explaining the banking crisis. *Organization Studies,* 33: 1044–1069.

Tourish, D., & Robson, P. 2006. Sensemaking and the distortion of critical upward communication in organizations. *Journal of Management Studies,* 43: 711–730.

Tourish, D., & Vatcha, N. 2005. Charismatic leadership and corporate cultism at Enron: The elimination of dissent, the promotion of conformity and organizational collapse. *Leadership,* 1: 455–480.

Uhl-Bien, M., Riggio, R. E., Lowe, K. B., & Carsten, M. 2014. Followership theory: A review and research agenda. *Leadership Quarterly,* 25(1): 83–104.

van Dierendonck, D. 2011. Servant leadership: A review and synthesis. *Journal of Management,* 37: 1228–1261.

van Knippenberg, D., & Sitkin, S. 2013. A critical assessment of charismatic-transformational leadership research: Back to the drawing board? *Academy of Management Annals,* 7: 1–60.

Wibbeke, E., & McArthur, S. 2014. *Global Business Leadership,* (2nd Ed.), Abingdon: Routledge.

Willis, P. 1977. *Learning to labour.* London: Saxon House.

Willmott, H. 2013. Reflections on the darker side of conventional power analytics. *Academy of Management Perspectives,* 27: 281–286.

Willmott, H. 2013b. The substitution of one piece of nonsense for another: Reflections on resistance, gaming, and subjugation. *Journal of Management Studies,* 50: 443–473.

Zacher, H., Pearce, L., Rooney, D., & McKenna, B. 2014. Leaders' personal wisdom and leader-member exchange quality: The role of individualised consideration. *Journal of Business Ethics,* 121: 171–187.

Bios

David Collinson is professor of Leadership and Organisation at Lancaster University Management School. He is the founding coeditor of the journal, *Leadership,* and founding coorganiser of The International Conference on Studying Leadership. Collinson's publications focus on critical approaches to leadership, organization, and management. His articles have appeared in many leading journals including *Organization Studies, Human Relations, Journal of Management Studies, Leadership Quarterly,* and *Organization.* d.collinson@lancaster.ac.uk

Dennis Tourish is professor of Leadership and Organization Studies at Royal Holloway, University of London. Tourish is editor of the journal *Leadership,* and a fellow of the Leadership Trust Foundation and the Lancaster Leadership Centre. His research interests focus on developing critical approaches to leadership. His most recent book is *The Dark Side of Transformational Leadership: A Critical Perspective* (2013). Dennis.Tourish@rhul.ac.uk

Name: _____ Date: _____

Chapter 2 ■ Teaching Leadership Critically: New Directions for Leadership Pedagogy

Questions for Discussion

1. In preparation for a class discussion, look up the following leadership theories and provide an example for each:

    a. "great-man"-trait theory
    b. styles-skills theory
    c. situational-contingency theory
    d. transformational-transactional theory

2. Collinson and Tourish assert, "'change' is usually held to be a 'good' thing, irrespective of its content." Discuss with your group: When can change be problematic? Give a concrete business scenario in which implementing change might do more harm than good.

3. Collinson and Tourish discuss how leadership instruction in business schools leave students "unprepared for the challenges that they will face when they encounter active, questioning, and dissenting employees, or when they themselves might be faced with a decision about whether to disagree with their boss on an important issue." What changes might business schools implement to help better equip students to be able to deal with "real world" situations? How could coursework be modified to send a more appropriate message? Give specific examples.

4. According to the authors, business schools "increasingly suggest to potential students that by studying leadership they will become exceptional leaders, able to exercise extraordinary influence over others." At the same time, many of these schools state that their goal is to "develop smart and real leaders of consequence, who are looking to make their mark and effect positive change in the world." After reading these statements, consider the following: Is there room in business for this many individuals to become exceptional leaders with significant power over others? If yes, how? If not, why not?

5. This article touches upon the selectivity of business pedagogy, stating: "Typically there is little mention of misjudgment, greed, narcissism, shame, duplicity, stupidity, hubris, soaring CEO salaries, power, and lack of democracy or employee involvement: that is, there is no mention of many of the emotional and political issues that frequently preoccupy real people in real organizations. Rather, power is depicted as a neutral resource to be deployed for relatively unproblematic ends." Why might business schools choose to shy away from covering such topics? In what ways are they doing a disservice to their students by ignoring these truths? How can schools integrate this information in a way that is helpful and cautionary rather than off-putting?

6. With a group, look back at the mission statements of the various business schools mentioned in this article. After examining the approaches of each statement, work together to come up with a mission statement for a business school you'll "create" together. Be sure to think about what you want the overall goal of your business program to be. Write down the courses, experiences, internships, etc. you would like the students to participate in before graduating. Take all of this into account in order to create a cohesive and concise mission statement to share with the class.

"I'm Ambivalent about It": The Dilemmas of PowerPoint

Andrea Hill[1], Tammi Arford[1], Amy Lubitow[2], and Leandra M. Smollin[1]

Abstract

The increasing ubiquity of PowerPoint in the university classroom raises complex questions about pedagogy and the creation of dynamic and effective learning environments. Though much of the sociological teaching literature has focused on engagement and active learning, very little of this work has addressed the presence of PowerPoint in sociology classrooms. Teaching sociology requires discussion, critical thinking, and debate—characteristics many critics argue are at odds with PowerPoint's unique presentation style. Utilizing survey data from faculty and students at a private university, this research explores PowerPoint usage and the many ways it influences the learning environment of the sociology classroom.

Keywords

technology, student engagement, active learning

Since its introduction in 1987, PowerPoint presentation software has become almost inescapable. Found on over 250 million computers worldwide, it is estimated that over 1 million PowerPoint presentations take place each hour (Mahin 2004; Parker 2001). While long present in corporate boardrooms, in recent years the technology has become entrenched in the academy. From accounting to geology, it is now a common feature of academic instruction (Cyphert 2004; Mackiewicz 2008). The increasing ubiquity of PowerPoint in the university has been accompanied by mounting concern over the ways it shapes learning environments. Though the matter has been addressed by other disciplines, sociological exploration of PowerPoint's influence on classroom culture has been sparse (Benson et al. 2002; Reinhardt 1999; Stoner 2007). This silence is particularly surprising because much of the sociological teaching literature is concerned with critical pedagogy—a goal seen as directly threatened by slide technology. It is essential for sociologists to concern themselves with "the culture, customs, and behavior that are dragged along with PowerPoint and how they affect the way we think" (Craig and Amernic 2006:158). Recognizing this need, our research explores PowerPoint and its implications for pedagogy and learning environments.

[1]Northeastern University, Boston, MA, USA
[2]Portland State University, Portland, OR, USA

From *Teaching Sociology*, Volume 40 (3), April 2015 by Andrea Hill, Tammi Arford, Amy Lubitow, and Leandra M. Smollin. Copyright © 2012 SAGE Publications. Reprinted by permission of SAGE Publications, Inc.

Previous Research

PowerPoint and Learning Outcomes

Most of the sociological empirical work on technology in the classroom has been concerned with a variety of technologies, including Web sites, statistical software, Internet discussion groups, Blackboard, and other multimedia (Persell 1992; Susman 1988). This research has most often explored PowerPoint in combination with other instructional technologies. Hence, though these works have commonly concluded that technology in the classroom "makes possible and calls forth from students increased response to and interaction with the instructor and the course" (Koeber 2005:298), these assertions cannot be attributed to PowerPoint alone. In fact, research focused solely on the slide technology has produced decidedly mixed conclusions.

Most studies have found PowerPoint to have no measurable influence on course performance and a minimal effect on grades—concluding, as Levasseur and Sawyer (2006:111) do, the technology brings "no significant change in learning outcomes when instructors augment their lectures with computer-generated slides" (see also Dietz 2002; Howard 2005; Kunkel 2004; Susskind 2005). In the studies that found an association between slide usage and higher exam scores, students were exposed to slides during lecture and were also either given printed versions of slides prior to class or were able to access slides via the Internet. Thus, access to instructor-prepared, thorough class notes, in combination with PowerPoint, was the crucial factor in improving student performance (Levasseur and Sawyer 2006).

While its effect on student *performance* remains largely unclear, several studies have found that PowerPoint has a measurable influence on student *perception*. These works, which explore software and course experiences, find that students greatly enjoy slide technology. In their review of the research on reactions to PowerPoint in the classroom, Levasseur and Sawyer (2006) found that the majority of empirical research concludes that students view slide usage positively. For example, despite the fact that PowerPoint made relatively little difference in their grade outcomes, Susskind's (2005) students reported that PowerPoint positively impacted their learning, organization, and note taking. Similarly, Wilmoth and Wybraniec's (1998) social statistics classes had favorable perceptions of PowerPoint's ability to increase their interest in course material, promote learning, and improve their exam performance. Time and again, studies show that students favor slides over chalkboards or overhead projectors and feel that computer-generated slides improve course organization and note taking and make classes more interesting (Bartsch and Cobern 2003; Pippert and Moore 1999; Young 2004). Students also perceive PowerPoint-using instructors as more effective and are more likely to give these instructors favorable evaluations (Koeber 2005; Susskind 2005; Weinraub 1998). To date, there has been little research exploring the dynamics of PowerPoint classrooms and pedagogy, and most existing treatments of the subject are primarily theoretical. Despite a lack of empirical foundation, however, these treatments raise important debates regarding the ways that slide software shapes learning

PowerPoint and Learning Environments

Critics observe that PowerPoint, which was created for business environments, has a style that is naturally suited for marketing and counterproductive for educating (Knoblauch 2008; Tufte 2003a, 2003b). According to Tufte (2003a:26), the software's best recognized and most vociferous detractor, it has a "definite, well-enforced, and widely-practiced cognitive style that is contrary to serious thinking." There is little question that slide software uses simplification to enable efficient and straightforward information dissemination. Though simplification is important for learning, when it becomes oversimplification, it can discourage and even derail critical thinking. Slide settings, which provide limited space for words, cultivate "oversimplification by asking presenters to summarize key concepts in as few words as possible" (Simons 2005:5). Critics charge that presentations transform content into overly simple snippets or buzz phrases that elide intricacy and nuance. This maximization of brevity trivializes and homogenizes knowledge (Adams 2006; Fendrich 2010; Norvig 2003). Further, critics note that minimally worded bullet-pointed content forced into outline form neglects context and fails to explore the multiple and complex relationships between concepts. The loss of breadth, depth, and complexity results in the transmission of material that is at best deficient and at worst so simple it belies the nature of course content.

PowerPoint's detractors also maintain that it is an impediment to fostering engaged student participants and active classrooms, noting that slides encourage students to passively consume information and make it possible to acquire knowledge at little cognitive expense. These critics charge that PowerPoint cheapens learning experiences by structuring the lecture hall in ways that discourage discussing, engaging, and interacting with instructors and peers. For example, they note that classroom lighting must be at least partially dimmed and seats must be arranged so that the projected images may be seen clearly by all. In essence, the screen becomes the focal point of the class, making the physical setup of a PowerPoint classroom much like that of a theater. Such a unidirectional environment is set up for one-way knowledge transmission rather than knowledge exchange and establishes "a dominance relationship between speaker and audience" (Adams 2006; Creed 1997; Tufte 2003a:13). The environment of the PowerPoint lecture hall creates "spectators rather than participants, in a classroom where the professor 'orchestrates' a multimedia presentation" (Reinhardt 1999:49). Critics argue that instead of a supplementing the educational experience, slideshows become a substitute for the lecturer.

Many also decry software's influence on pedagogy, noting that the PowerPoint-using instructor tends to proceed through class by following the pre-determined path established by slides. This pre-planned organization inhibits instructor digressions, anecdotes, and creativity—moments that often inspire student questions that are so vitally important for effective learning (Norvig 2003; Simons 2005). PowerPoint discourages teaching improvisation and in turn student questions, because "the slides tend to impel the lecture conversation along a pre-set unidirectional course, disregarding and sometimes blind to . . . the unbidden: the unsolicited question or unexpected comment" (Adams 2006:404). Thus, though the technology enables well-planned lectures, order may come at the cost of student engagement and instructor spontaneity. Rather than critically engaging with the meaning and context of materials, students simply copy the information they see in front of them each time they are presented with a new slide. As such, critics note that engagement with course content ends when projected information has been successfully copied into learners' notes.

While existing studies have been useful for understanding some aspects of the student PowerPoint relationship, they fail to address the nature of PowerPoint classroom environments. In turn, those works that do address behavior and interaction in slide-using classrooms tend to be somewhat speculative and lack empirical grounding. As Benson et al. (2002:145) note, "We need research that reveals how students use digital technology in a classroom setting and the extent to which this use affects learning in both planned and unplanned ways." In addition, there are no studies that explore how sociology instructors view the technology and its influence on learning environments (Koeber 2005; Pippert and Moore 1999). Recognizing these needs, we explore student and instructor perceptions of slide technology and classroom dynamics.

Method

To explore PowerPoint classroom culture, we administered surveys to undergraduates enrolled in sociology courses and instructors from the sociology and anthropology department at a mediumsized private university in New England. The university's institutional review board (IRB) approved the study and the survey instruments prior to distribution. We chose to focus on PowerPoint because the overwhelming majority of presentations in higher education utilize the Microsoft software. Alternative presentation programs have emerged in recent years—one of the most commonly used alternative programs is Prezi, a software package with an interactive style that allows users to create nonlinear, nonhierarchical shows and manipulate projected content to move, flow, and connect. Although this and other similar technologies may combat many of the challenges posed by static slideware, existing critiques suggest that *all* presentational software is problematic for teaching and learning (Cooper 2009; Gries and Brooke 2010; Stryker 2010). Admittedly, the choice to limit our study to PowerPoint may neglect important developments that alternative programs have brought to the small number of classes in which they are used. However, our work will usefully inform much-needed future research on Prezi and other similar programs.

Undergraduate and Instructor Surveys

Our undergraduate sample consisted of students enrolled in one of eight sociology classes during the summer and fall semesters of 2010. We distributed paper surveys to those enrolled in two sections of Introduction to Sociology and one section each of Deviant Behavior and Social Control, Drugs and Society, Family Violence, American Society, Environmental Sociology, and Social Theory. The sampled classes ranged in size from 9 to 113 students—five of the courses had more than 50 undergraduates and three had fewer than 30. In order to build understanding of how the average student enrolled in a sociology course experiences slide software, we did not restrict survey participation to sociology majors or minors. Although the 9 participants from the Social Theory class included in the study were primarily juniorand senior-level sociology majors, the other courses surveyed did not require prerequisites and thus contained a wide variety of majors and grade levels. The undergraduate survey consisted of 10 questions adapted from previous research on student perceptions of technology use in the classroom (Burke and James 2008; Nowaczyk, Santos, and Patton 1998). In addition to 9 fixed-choice questions regarding frequency and purpose of use, preferences, and impressions of the technology's effectiveness, the survey also included an open-response question that asked students to explain what they most like and dislike about instructional PowerPoint (contact authors for complete survey). A total of 384 students (approximately 87 percent of the sample) completed the survey.

Sociology instructors, including full-time faculty, graduate student instructors (teaching as adjunct lecturers or funded graduate instructors), and adjunct lecturers, were also surveyed. We administered questionnaires to graduate student and adjunct instructors through an online platform and distributed paper copies of the instrument to faculty during a department meeting. The nine-question survey administered to instructors included three fixed-choice questions assessing rank, teaching experience, and course load and a further three fixed-choice questions regarding frequency and purpose of instructional PowerPoint use. This survey also included three open-response questions that asked instructors to reflect on their perceptions of how students feel about PowerPoint and their personal impressions of its effects on the classroom environment and their own pedagogy (contact authors for complete survey). A total of 33 instructors (approximately 72 percent of sampled population) completed the survey.

Data Analysis

After compiling and quantitatively analyzing responses to the fixed-choice questions for both the undergraduate and instructor surveys, we then inductively coded answers to the open-ended questions and analyzed them for recurrent themes and concepts. Using a multistep process of constant comparison to analyze the qualitative responses, the authors (1) read through the written survey answers to develop a series of thematic categories, (2) sorted the written data into emergent categories, (3) compared observations to confirm or disconfirm trends in the data, and (4) reviewed data to verify the accuracy and relevance of themes (Bogdan and Biklen 2007; Glaser and Strauss 1967; Strauss and Corbin 2008). We chose to use both open-response and fixed-choice survey questions to elicit quantitative and qualitative data and thus better explore students' and instructors' perceptions of PowerPoint.

Findings

Prevalence, Frequency, and Purpose of Use

We found PowerPoint to be a prevalent feature of undergraduate classes: 67 percent of students reported that all or most of their instructors use the software, and 23 percent reported that at least half of their instructors use it. According to respondents, not only are slide presentations present in the majority of their courses; they are also present in most individual class meetings: 95 percent of students reported that PowerPoint-using instructors use the software in all or most class meetings.

Sociology instructors reported similar usage prevalence: Approximately 91 percent use PowerPoint at least some of the time in their courses—76 percent of instructors use it in between one quarter and three quarters of their class meetings, while 55 percent use it in at least three quarters of their classes. Frequency of use differs by professional rank (see Table 1). Twenty percent of full professors report using PowerPoint frequently (more than three quarters of classes) or always, while 60 percent of associate and 50 percent of assistant professors use it that often. Graduate student instructors are the most frequent users of the technology—69 percent reported using slides frequently or always. Instructors' *lack* of PowerPoint use also differs by rank: 63 percent of full professors reported that they do not use it at all or do so in less than a quarter of class meetings, while no graduate student instructors gave that reply. Though our findings indicate that prevalence and frequency of use is significantly higher among graduate student instructors, we did not find a consistent rank/use relationship across the sample. Given the limitations posed by the size and nature of the sample, the relatively large dichotomy between the most (full professors) and least (graduate student) experienced instructors cannot be interpreted as anything more than a suggestive avenue for future research.

We also explored the purposes for which slideware is used. All PowerPoint-using instructors reported using slides to project lecture notes, charts, definitions, and explanations. Just over half (54 percent) of those surveyed also embed video clips in presentations, and 41 percent use slides to display discussion questions. Undergraduate answers confirmed that PowerPoint most often serves as a tool of information display; when asked what their instructors typically use PowerPoint for (e.g., to show pictures, play video clips, or project lecture notes), 95 percent answered that their instructors use slides for lecture notes most of the time.

Student Perceptions

Undergraduates reported PowerPoint is a useful feature of classroom instruction that improves learning. When asked which of the software's functions they found most helpful, a small number of students chose "showing pictures" (16 percent) or "showing video clips" (4 percent) while the vast majority—approximately 80 percent—reported that slideware is most useful when it is used to outline lecture notes and information. Students' answers to the open-ended question, "What do you like most about PowerPoint?" support this finding (see Table 2): Over half (52 percent) of the responses to this query mentioned liking the software for its ability to outline lectures and point to important information.

	Grad Student	Assistant Professor	Associate Professor	Full Professor	All Instructors
Always/frequently	68.7	50.0	60.0	20.0	54.5
Moderately	31.3	0.0	20.0	12.5	21.2
Infrequently/never	0.0	50.0	20.0	62.5	24.2
Total	100	100	100	100	100

Table 1 Instructor Frequency of PowerPoint Use by Percentage.

Note: Frequency of PowerPoint use was measured using the following scale: never, infrequently (less than 25 percent of class meetings); moderately infrequently (25 percent to less than 50 percent of class meetings); moderately frequently (50 percent to less than 75 percent of class meetings); frequently (75 percent to almost every class meeting); and always.

What do you like most about PowerPoint?

Outlines lectures and points to what is important (52 percent)

"how it shows you the information and makes it easier to outline what we will be learning that day and makes it easier to follow along."

"I like how it hits the key points our professors want us to know. And it gives a general outline of the reading."

"I like that I can focus more on what the professor is saying because I can add what the professor says in class but also already have the major points I need written down (because of the slides)."

"It shortens main points up and makes them easier to understand."

Makes class interesting/keeps me awake (30 percent)

"How it keeps my attention and makes lecture easy to follow."

"When there are pictures it helps to keep my attention."

"Keeps me interested by giving me something to look at and focus on."

Good for visual learners (10 percent)

"Because I am a visual learner, it makes it easier for me to comprehend material."

"I am a visual learner, so I like to see outlines as well as pictures and video clips. If I miss what the teacher says I can see it up on the slide."

What do you dislike most about PowerPoint?

Instructor reads verbatim off of slides (32 percent)

"I wish some professors wouldn't just read the Power Point word for word, I wish there was more discussion."

"How it encourages me at times to not come to class since some professors read directly from the PowerPoint and posts them online to easily access."

"When my professor reads directly off a slide, I would rather them not use it. It makes me feel as if class is optional."

Lecturing too fast, not enough time to read/take notes (24 percent)

"Teachers switch too fast and can't copy everything. Sometimes just copy the PowerPoint and not what the teacher talks about."

"When a teacher puts too many words on the slides and you can't write everything down before they move to the next slide."

"If a professor doesn't give out the PowerPoint you have to keep up and try to copy the slides and still copy or listen to what the professor says."

Discourages discussion (12 percent)

"It distracts from actual discussions . . . people are so busy trying to take down notes, no one's really paying attention."

"It monopolizes the class and leaves little opportunity for discussion or interaction. It also can be an excuse to not take notes and not pay attention as it can be accessed online whenever it is convenient for me."

"It encourages passive rather than active learning."

Table 2 Students' PowerPoint Likes and Dislikes.

As one student wrote, slideware is helpful because "it shows you the information and makes it easier to outline what we will be learning that day." This appreciation is manifest in students' self-reported classroom behavior, as the vast majority said that they regularly copy information from slides—82 percent report that they "always," "almost always," or "usually" do so, while only 5 percent answered that they "almost never" or "never" copy words from slides.

When evaluating PowerPoint's utility for improving several components of learning, students reported that it is "almost always" or "always" effective for aiding exam preparation (56 percent), enhancing comprehension of course material (52 percent), and improving attention in class (38 percent). Though

	Exam Preparation	Paper Writing	Comprehension of Material	Paying Attention in Class	Engaging Discussion
Always/almost always	56.1	25.3	52.3	38.1	24.5
Often/usually	38.1	50.5	43.7	49.6	55.4
Sometimes	1.6	14.6	3.2	9.9	17.9
Almost never/never	4.2	9.6	0.8	2.4	2.2
Total percent	100	100	100	100	100

Table 3 Student Perceptions of PowerPoint effectiveness for Learning Tasks by . . .

they found the software somewhat less useful for paper writing and engaging discussion (25 percent answered that it is "almost always" or "always" effective for both), only a minority of students (fewer than 10 percent) answered it was "almost never" or "never" effective for any of the learning tasks they evaluated (Table 3).

Written responses to the open-ended questions "What do you most like/dislike about PowerPoint?" support these findings. After projection of lecture outlines, the second most commonly mentioned advantage of slideware was its ability to make class more interesting. Approximately 30 percent of answers to the "like" question were a variation of one student's comment that PowerPoint "keeps me interested by giving me something to look at and focus on." Further, responses to the open-ended "dislike" question correspond to the previously mentioned finding that PowerPoint is less effective for encouraging discussion than it is for any other learning task. In discussing what they most disliked about the software, many students found fault with its tendency to discourage discussion—approximately 12 percent of these responses expressed sentiments along the lines of one student's observation that "[PowerPoint] monopolizes the class and leaves little opportunity for discussion or interaction." In addition, the more commonly cited failings—32 percent most disliked instructors reading from slides and 24 percent felt slides cause instructors to lecture too fast—are undoubtedly implicated in suppressing discussion, as one response illustrates: "I wish some professors wouldn't just read the PowerPoint word for word, I wish there was more discussion."

Given their perceptions of its usefulness, it is unsurprising that the undergraduates surveyed greatly enjoy classroom PowerPoint. Eighty-four percent of students agreed that the technology improves their overall classroom experience, and only a small minority (9 percent) reported that it does nothing to enhance their learning (Figure 1). Fully 69 percent of students expressed a preference for PowerPoint classes, while only 10 percent answered that they prefer classes without the technology.

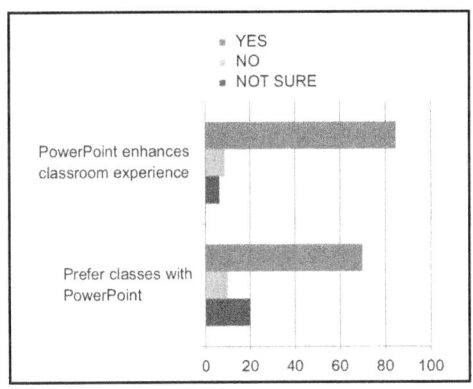

Figure 1 Percentage of students who believe PowerPoint enhances classroom experience and prefer classes with PowerPoint

Instructor Perceptions

PowerPoint's popularity among undergraduates was not lost on sociology instructors, whose responses to the open-ended question, "What are your perceptions of students' expectations regarding PowerPoint?" reflected an awareness that students expect and greatly enjoy slide-supplemented lectures. While some instructors (30 percent) answered that they felt that at least some students dislike it, more than twice as many (65 percent) disagreed, reporting that students expect and/or like slides. As one explained, "Some of our students had PowerPoint in high school and have come to expect it." Instructors revealed a commonly shared explanation of why undergraduates favor slideware: Approximately 70 percent commented that students enjoy the technology because it simplifies information and makes class easier.

Responses to the question, "What are your reasons for using/not using PowerPoint?" indicated that instructors use the software for two primary reasons—to provide clarity for students and to improve their own teaching performances. Approximately 70 percent of responses to this question explained that slides are used because they help students by organizing information. As one instructor commented, "[they] can be helpful as a 'carry-all' for information that students can look back on while they study." In addition, 60 percent of the instructors who answered this question noted that they use slideware because it improves their teaching performance and helps them manage class. This, the second most commonly reported reason for using PowerPoint, was illustrated by one instructor's explanation that using it "allows me to move away from feeling like I'm reading from my lecture notes, but rather am able to have a more natural flow prompted by slides." Of those who answered that they rarely or never use it, 75 percent commented that they do not use slideware because it discourages student discussion—as one explained, slides put "students into passive 'audience' mode."

Answers to the open-response survey question, "Do you think that PowerPoint affects your teaching performance?" revealed that instructors recognize a significant relationship between the technology and pedagogy (Table 4). Every instructor who answered this question agreed that slideware has an impact on the way they teach. The majority—86 percent—noted that slides improve their organization and pacing by ordering lectures and keeping them on track, a function they greatly appreciate. In addition, approximately one third of instructors noted that PowerPoint alleviates performance anxiety, as one explained, it "gives me confidence, and gives me something to refer to if I have a moment of panic." Although instructors largely shared favorable impressions of the technology, a sizeable portion acknowledged that PowerPoint could negatively influence instruction. In fact, 43 percent of responses to this question mentioned that preset slideware can constrain teaching and limit interaction.

Discussion: The Dilemmas of Instructional PowerPoint

PowerPoint is hailed as a tool for delivering information in an entertaining, quick, and efficient manner; the Microsoft Web site boasts: "Get your class to sit up and take notice! You can easily transform your presentation from boring lists and blocks of text to a vibrant and engaging slide show with images and video to underscore your main points" (Microsoft Corporation 2012). While the technology's core purposes and strongest selling points—simplifying information and making learning entertaining—are highly valued by students and instructors alike, they also pose serious dilemmas for educators. Our research revealed that the software's strengths are also sources of potentially detrimental influences on classroom environments. According to responses to open-ended survey questions, instructional use of PowerPoint raises three serious dilemmas: First, while students and instructors appreciated the technology's manifest function of clarification, their comments revealed anxiety regarding the software's latent tendency to oversimplify. In addition, although respondents reported that the software captures attention, some students and most instructors also acknowledged that it may often result in passivity and disengaged entertainment. Finally, sociology instructors' responses uncovered a tension between pragmatic career concerns and personal pedagogical philosophies. These dilemmas shed much-needed light on the complex experiential realities of PowerPoint in the sociology classroom.

Clarification and Oversimplification

Survey responses indicate that instructional PowerPoint gives rise to a tension between clarification and oversimplification. The majority of undergraduates agreed that slides are most useful when they outline lectures, and their written comments repeatedly cited the technology's ability to organize and simplify course material as its greatest advantage. One student commented that PowerPoint "shortens up main points and makes them easier to understand," and another noted that it serves to "outline material so students know what info is important and what they can forget." In essence, the software allows learners to cut through complexity and focus on—as several put it—"only the important material." Instructors shared this appreciation for simplification—several noted that the technology

What are your perceptions of students' expectations regarding PowerPoint?

Students think it simplifies information and/or makes class easier (70 percent)

"I think that students want an outline. They don't want every word the professor says. They want it before class so they know what to expect and can print it out and use the lecture to fill in the notes."

"That it simplified what they have to know for exams."

"Students like PowerPoint because it is a crutch."

Students like or expect it (65 percent)

"The students expect instructors to use PowerPoint."

"Some of our students had PowerPoint in high school and have come to expect it."

"They like it."

Some or most students dislike it (30 percent)

"I find that students are used to most of their sociology classes using PowerPoint, but are very divided about whether they like it or not."

"[Students] probably think it is boring and tedious."

What are your reasons for using, or not using, PowerPoint?

Organization and clarity for students (88 percent)

"It can provide a path for the lecture to take which can be easily followed."

"PowerPoint helps to clearly follow the lecture use. It summarizes the lecture points."

"PowerPoint can be helpful as a 'carry-all' for information that students can look back on while they study."

"Helps to organize material."

Improve teaching performance and classroom management (60 percent)

"Allows me to move away from feeling like I'm reading from my lecture notes, but rather am able to have a more natural flow prompted by slides."

"I do think PowerPoint can be helpful in that I don't waste class time writing down extensive notes on the blackboard."

"It seems like a way to avoid my anxiety about teaching, particularly since I use it every day."

Provide visuals and media (50 percent)

"I find that it helps provide a visual guide for students who may be visual learners or who may benefit from seeing the outline of a lecture laid out."

"I also enjoy using PP to show my class various pictures and graphs to illustrate what I am lecturing about."

"Also to show images, maps, links to YouTube, etc."

Reasons for not using: hampers discussion (75 percent of nonusers)

"It oversimplifies complex info and puts students into passive 'audience' mode."

"I believe in the power of the presentation and class interactions. PowerPoint detracts."

Do you feel that using PowerPoint affects your performance? If so, how?

Organization and pacing (86 percent)

"It does help with the organization and making sure that I and the students get the main points."

"Overall, I think it makes me more effective—keeps me on point, keeps the lecture structured and clear."

Works to constrain performance and/or interaction (43 percent)

"I am wary of being too tied to the slides, and therefore unwilling to veer from the presentation if the class wants to."

"[O]ccasionally, I discuss topics in a different order than I originally planned, which makes more sense in the context of a class discussion or a student question. That can be difficult to coordinate with the PowerPoint. Sometimes I feel like I have to 'teach to the PowerPoint.'"

Relieves performance anxiety (33 percent)

"It allows me to move away from feeling like I'm reading from my lecture notes, but rather am able to have a more natural flow prompted by slides."

"I think that PowerPoint makes me more effective in the sense that it gives me confidence, and gives me something to refer to if I have a moment of panic."

Table 4 Instructor Perceptions of PowerPoint.

Note: Percentages are calculated from the number of responses to each open-ended question. Some respondents left one or more of the open-ended questions unanswered.

increases learning by "breaking down" course material and helping "students to clearly follow the lecture."

Instructors enjoyed that slides enable them to "communicate key points to students." This appreciation, however, was tinged by uneasiness with what they see as PowerPoint's tendency to dilute knowledge, and their explanations of their slide usage revealed tension between the value of clarification and the problem of oversimplification. Instructors were aware that students desire presentations with, as one explained, "not too much text on each slide," and most reported they use PowerPoint for overviews and outlines. Though distillation illuminates basic information, it may do so by oversimplifying complex material. Half of the instructors who praised clarity also worried that slideware breaks down information too much and were concerned that excessive parsimony could deter learning. They mentioned that slides can present information as misleadingly simple and uniform—one instructor wrote, "I sometimes have a concern that students will think that the takeaway from the content of the lecture can be distilled into the slides." Another frequent user expressed this tension:

> PowerPoint simplifies and dumbs down the info for them into neat little bullet points. The reality of our social world is often messier and more complicated than that which can be expressed by neat little bullet points. Because the info is already synthesized for them in PP slides, the students are less responsible for (and increasingly less capable of) picking out the crucial elements of a lecture, as they always have the slides to fall back on.

Of the majority who cited improved clarity as their primary reason for use, a significant portion also expressed concern that PowerPoint's inherent tendency to oversimplify could threaten learning.

Education and Entertainment

According to survey responses, instructional PowerPoint gives rise to a second dilemma—a tension between entertaining and educating. Although the technology successfully captures learners' attention, some students and many instructors reported that this might prove to be more diversion than useful tool. The learning goals in sociological education typically extend far beyond knowledge transmission—in fact, because the discipline has a particularly powerful ability to inspire critical thinking, "teaching *only* the content of [the] discipline may do students a real disservice" (Fobes and Kaufman 2008; Roberts 2002:2). Thus, sociological learning objectives commonly include developing analytical reasoning abilities, inspiring creativity, and establishing the foundations necessary for critical intellectual growth—all vital parts of the sociological imagination. Learning experts maintain that these goals are best achieved through active learning that requires students to expend cognitive energy to reach understanding. Key features of active learning—discussions and exchanges, questions, improvisations, and off-the-map developments—ensure that learners actively participate in knowledge creation rather than simply passively consume information. When students reflectively engage by talking about what they know, questioning what they don't, and interacting with instructors and peers, they develop the ability to understand and apply what they have learned. In contrast, learning that consists of information consumption and little else may be more entertainment than education. Classrooms in which students take notes instead of actively engaging with material are little different from movie theaters—both are arenas of passive entertainment rather than active knowledge construction.

This education/entertainment dilemma plainly was apparent in survey responses. Students overwhelmingly reported that slideshow presentations capture their interest—most agreed that slides help them pay attention (Table 2), and 30 percent commented that they feel PowerPoint helps them, as several students put it, "stay awake" in class. One undergraduate explained that presentations are useful because "they give me something to look at so I don't get distracted by other things." Although slideware does the important job of capturing students' attention, it could discourage in-depth, reflective engagement. Responses from the undergraduate survey indicated that the technology is less useful for engaging discussion than for any other task. Students' written comments further illuminated this: Several noted that although graphics help them focus, they sorely missed the active discussions that they felt slideshows discouraged. According to one respondent, PowerPoint "monopolizes the class and leaves little opportunity for discussion or interaction."

Students frequently mentioned that PowerPoint "makes class less exciting" because it compels them to replicate what they see on slides, a task that they feel consumes their classroom experience. Indeed, the overwhelming majority of students (82 percent) answered that they focus on copying projected words into their notes. Although transcribing information requires students to focus to a certain degree, this type of attention can be mindless, unreflective, and even counterproductive. Many students were aware of this problem and admitted that copying slides negatively affects their learning, as one student explained:

> I frequently write down blindly anything that is written on the Power Point without absorbing it until studying for the test. Also, when I'm copying down the Power Point words I'm not usually listening to the instructor. Power Point minimizes the engagement I have with a class and instead condenses it into a few slides with bullet points.

Some undergraduates reported that focusing on copying projected words distracts them from the meaning and context of the topics being discussed; as another student commented, slides make it "easy to lose focus on the topic and JUST copy PowerPoints without engaging in the topic." These critiques make it clear that although slides capture notice, thoughtful engagement and attention are not one in the same.

The worry over entertainment and education was more troubling to sociology instructors. Their open-ended comments revealed a deep and broadly shared concern that PowerPoint distracts and fosters passivity among students. Those who never or infrequently use the software were most critical of the ways it shapes classroom dynamic; as one infrequent user noted, the technology "often makes class discussions less engaging. Students focus on 'writing notes'... instead of engaging in critical thought and discussion." In fact, passivity was the most cited reason that non and infrequent users rejected slideware. Regular users of the technology were less critical, but did express anxiety over the disengaged, entertainment-like nature of slideshows. Many instructors expressed suspicion that students' copying of projected information may inhibit discussion, as one commented, "I do worry that they may become too reliant on [slides] (rather than paying close attention to the lecture and taking their own notes)."

Instructors were also highly critical of PowerPoint's influence on pedagogy—all agreed that the technology shapes instruction, and most commented that it does so in ways that inhibit engaged, interactive teaching. Again, non and infrequent users were most critical of PowerPoint instruction. One non-using faculty member noted that it "has nothing to do with teaching and learning," and another remarked that it is "not as effective as raw teaching." While frequent users were most likely to report that slides improve teaching, many also conceded that streamlined lectures can sometimes make classes more like "entertainment" or a "show" and less interactive and spontaneous. These instructors worried that slides may create distance between themselves and their students. One reflected, "I feel PowerPoint lowers my engagement with students," and another admitted, "it takes away some of the spontaneous nature of class discussions, [and] limits students' active participation sometimes." Slide using instructors also mentioned that PowerPoint can constrict creativity, as one explained, "[it] puts me in lecture mode [and is] less interactive." The majority of users noted that slides make ad hoc interactions and off-the-cuff examples a challenge, as another explained:

> Occasionally, I discuss topics in a different order than I originally planned, which makes more sense in the context of a class discussion or a student question. That can be difficult to coordinate with the PowerPoint. Sometimes I feel like I have to "teach to the PowerPoint."

Thus, on one hand, most students and instructors agree that slideware aids learning by capturing attention and organizing teaching. On the other, however, reports of disengaged teaching and learning behaviors indicate that the technology may be passively entertaining rather than actively educating learners.

Career Pragmatism and Pedagogical Commitment

Finally, instructors' reflections unveiled a third dilemma brought forth by instructional PowerPoint—there exists a significant tension between career pragmatism and pedagogical commitments. Though the majority of sociology instructors expressed at least some unease regarding the technology's pedagogical merit, most use it regularly. Many instructors explained that they continue to use slideware in spite of their concerns because they know students expect and desire it, as one noted: "I think that students want an outline. They don't want every word the professor says." Awareness of and compliance with this expectation was most prevalent among graduate student instructors, as one explained:

> The first time I taught, I didn't use PowerPoint for the first half of the semester, and on my mid-semester evaluation (that I hand out to see how things are going generally for the students), there was such a big request for PowerPoint that I used it in every class after that.

Instructors' discussions of student expectations were marked by hesitation and concern over the true educational value of the technology. One commented, "I think unfortunately [students] expect it.... Also—it is contributing, sadly, to [an] atmosphere of each class meeting as a drop-in experience and really more like distance learning." Another instructor agreed that the student-PowerPoint relationship has become "a hugely problematic expectation" because "there are numerous situations in which... their education would be better served by digesting data in a less formalized or summarized manner."

Slideware-using instructors were conflicted over their decision to integrate PowerPoint into their classes. While many recognized the importance of teaching in ways that students enjoy, they also noted that slides might not always be best for learning. Instructors indicated that student preference for slide-augmented lectures had become so prevalent that it was now an expectation they felt pressured to conform to. A full professor with over 20 years of teaching experience demonstrated the strong pull of PowerPoint culture, remarking, "I believe in the power of the presentation and class interactions. PowerPoint detracts. Having said that, I will move toward PowerPoint in a major way next year, and use it quite a bit." For some instructors, when student expectations and teaching ideology are at odds, demand trumps philosophy.

Several of those most conflicted by this dilemma noted that the institutional pressure to receive positive student evaluations of teaching lay at the heart of their compromise. Teaching evaluations play a major role in career success—they are often the primary means by which schools evaluate teaching and are routinely used for hiring and promotion decisions (Delucchi and Smith 1997; Kulik 2001; Sojka, Gupta, and Deeter-Schmelz 2002). Given that instructors who meet student expectations receive better evaluations and that today's students expect PowerPoint, it is not surprising that instructors incorporate the technology to boost their evaluations (Greenwald and Gillmore 1997; Williams and Ceci 1997). In fact, this approach has proven rewarding, as "many lecturers, to their delight, discovered that teaching scores and student satisfaction improved with the use of PowerPoint" (Gabriel 2008:257; see also Delucchi 2000; Delucchi and Korgen 2002; Titus 2008).

The lure of tailoring teaching to meet student preferences is directly related to pragmatic concerns about career success. This may be even more powerful for newer instructors who do not have the security of tenure and are often adjunct or contingent lecturers. Indeed, we found graduate students were most vocal about the dilemma of pedagogical commitment and career pragmatism, as one noted:

> I am still inclined to use PowerPoint because my future career is dependent upon good teaching evals, which only happen when the students are happy with the class. They like and expect their profs to use PowerPoint.... Unfortunately, I also perpetuate the overuse of PowerPoint out of fear of being unfavorably compared to my colleagues who all use Power-

> Point and post the slides online. I'm troubled by the fact that I often decide to use and post PP slides because my teaching evals would suffer if I didn't, not because I think PP is always the best thing for their intellectual development or understanding of the subject matter.

The software's ubiquity, popularity with students, and instructors' perceptions of student expectations speak to a growing PowerPoint culture in the university—it has become a normative feature of academic instruction. It is important to recognize that this norm carries several potentially problematic implications. While students enjoy slides and instructors continue to use them, both users and consumers recognize that PowerPoint can shape learning environments and experiences in positive and negative ways.

Conclusion

The sociology instructor who concluded "I am ambivalent about PowerPoint. Sometimes it helps the quality of discussion tremendously and sometimes it is distracting" perhaps best summarizes our study. While the technology has a great many advantages, these advantages may also have negative consequences for lasting learning. The dilemmas identified by our research contribute to an ongoing debate in the academic scholarship surrounding PowerPoint pedagogy. While many have concluded that PowerPoint should be used in academia, others have expressed concerns about how it has transformed teaching and learning. Our exploration of the issues surrounding PowerPoint in the university provides support for both advocates and critics of the software. We found that undergraduates expect and enjoy instructional use of PowerPoint, and sociology instructors who use the software often find it to be a useful teaching tool. We also found that classroom slideshows may negatively influence-earning by encouraging mindless copying and discouraging questions and participation.

Future research comparing classroom dynamics and long-term learning outcomes of students in PowerPoint and non-PowerPoint courses would be useful for identifying the mechanics of how this technology influences learning. In addition, studies with larger and more diverse samples could answer important questions regarding the possible impact of class size (Are slideshows appreciated more in larger classes than smaller classes?), student demographics (Do factors such as student major, gender, or other characteristics influence how learners feel about the technology?), and course content (Are intro students more apt to enjoy slideware than upper-level students?). Finally, empirical evaluation of the various strategies instructors employ to make slides a tool for engaged learning would be enlightening for practice.

It would be a mistake to "overlook the over-whelming influence of this software presentation tool on today's educational culture, particularly in redefining what a lecture looks like, consists of, and how it is experienced" (Adams 2006:408). Whether one agrees that the technology is a tool for conveying information in a clear and engaging way or sees that even thoughtful use cannot escape an inexorable cognitive style that oversimplifies material and fosters passivity, it is impossible to deny that slide software has had transformative repercussions for education. Reflexively considering the costs and benefits of PowerPoint is essential for educators concerned with creating effective learning environments that inspire and nurture developing sociological imaginations.

Note

Reviewers for this manuscript were, in alphabetical order, Anne F. Eisenberg and Karl R. Kunkel.

References

Adams, Catherine. 2006. "PowerPoint, Habits of Mind, and Classroom Culture." *Journal of Curriculum Studies* 38(4):389–411.

Bartsch, Robert A. and Kristi M. Cobern. 2003. "Effectiveness of PowerPoint Presentations in Lectures." *Computers and Education* 41(1):77–86.

Benson, Denzel E., Wava Haney, Tracy E. Ore, Caroline Hodges Persell, Aileen Schulte, James Steele, and Idee Winfield. 2002. "Digital Technologies and the Scholarship of Teaching and Learning in Sociology." *Teaching Sociology* 30(2):140–57.

Bogdan, Robert and Sari Knoop Biklen. 2007. *Qualitative Research for Education*. Boston: Allyn and Bacon.

Burke, Lisa A. and Karen E. James. 2008. "PowerPoint-based Lectures in Business Education: An Empirical Investigation of Student-perceived Novelty and Effectiveness." *Business Communication Quarterly* 71(3):277–96.

Cooper, Elizabeth. 2009. "Overloading on Slides: Cognitive Load Theory and Microsoft's Slide Program PowerPoint." *Association for the Advancement of Computing in Education Journal* 17(2):127–35.

Craig, Russell J. and Joel H. Amernic. 2006. "PowerPoint Presentation Technology and the Dynamics of Teaching." *Innovative Higher Education* 31(3):147–60.

Creed, Tom. 1997. "PowerPoint, No! Cyberspace, Yes." *The National Teaching and Learning Forum*. Retrieved July 26, 2010 (http://www.ntlf.com/html/sf/cyberspace.htm).

Cyphert, Dale. 2004. "The Problem of PowerPoint: Visual Aid or Visual Rhetoric?" *Business Communication Quarterly* 67(1):80–84.

Delucchi, Michael. 2000. "Don't Worry, Be Happy: Instructor Likeability, Student Perceptions of Learning, and Teacher Ratings in Upper-level Sociology Courses." *Teaching Sociology* 22(3):220–31.

Delucchi, Michael and Kathleen Korgen. 2002. "'We're the Customer—We Pay the Tuition': Student Consumerism among Undergraduate Sociology Majors." *Teaching Sociology* 30(1):100–07.

Delucchi, Michael and William L. Smith. 1997. "Satisfied Customers versus Pedagogic Responsibility: Further Thoughts on Student Consumerism." *Teaching Sociology* 25(4):336–37.

Dietz, Tracy L. 2002. "Predictors of Success in Large Enrollment Introductory Courses: An Examination of the Impact of Learning Communities and Virtual Learning Resources on Student Success in an Introductory Level Sociology Course." *Teaching Sociology* 30(1):80–88.

Fendrich, Laurie. 2010. "PowerlessPoint." *The Chronicle of Higher Education*, April 27. Retrieved July 27, 2010 (http://chronicle.com/blogs/brainstorm/powerlesspoint).

Fobes, Catherine and Peter Kaufman. 2008. "Critical Pedagogy in the Sociology Classroom: Challenges and Concerns." *Teaching Sociology* 36(1):26–33.

Gabriel, Yiannis. 2008. "Against the Tyranny of PowerPoint: Technology-in-use and Technology Abuse." *Organization Studies* 29(2):255–76.

Glaser, Barney and Anslem Strauss. 1967. *The Discovery of Grounded Theory: Strategies for Qualitative Research*. Chicago: Aldine.

Greenwald, Anthony G. and Gerald M. Gillmore. 1997. "No Pain, No Gain? The Importance of Measuring Course Workload in Student Ratings of Instruction." *Journal of Educational Psychology* 89(4):743–51.

Gries Laurie Ellen and Collin Gifford Brooke. 2010. "An Inconvenient Tool: Rethinking the Role of Slideware in the Writing Classroom." *Composition Studies* 38(1):9–26.

Howard, Jay R. 2005. "An Examination of Student Learning in Introductory Sociology at a Commuter Campus." *Teaching Sociology* 33(2):195–205.

Knoblauch, Hubert. 2008. "The Performance of Knowledge: Pointing and Knowledge in Powerpoint Presentations." *Cultural Sociology* 2(1):75–97.

Koeber, Charles. 2005. "Introducing Multimedia Presentations and a Course Website to an Introductory Sociology Course: How Technology Affects Student Perceptions of Teaching Effectiveness." *Teaching Sociology* 33(3):285–300.

Kulik, James A. 2001. "Student Ratings: Validity, Utility, and Controversy." Pp. 9–25 in *The Student Ratings Debate: Are They Valid? How Can We Best Use Them?*, edited by M. Theall, P. C. Abrami, and L. A. Mets. San Francisco: Jossey-Bass.

Kunkel, Karl R. 2004. "A Research Note Assessing the Benefit of Presentation Software in Two Different Lecture Courses." *Teaching Sociology* 32(2):188–96.

Levasseur, David G. and J. Kanan Sawyer. 2006. "Pedagogy Meets PowerPoint: A Research Review of the Effects of Computer-generated Slides in the Classroom." *The Review of Communication* 6(1/2):101–23.

Mackiewicz, Jo. 2008. "Comparing PowerPoint Experts' and University Students' Opinions about PowerPoint Presentations." *Journal of Technical Writing and Communication* 38(2):149–65.

Mahin, Linda. 2004. "PowerPoint Pedagogy." *Business Communication Quarterly* 67(2):219–22.

Microsoft Corporation. 2012. "Make Over a Presentation with PowerPoint 2010." Retrieved February 6, 2012 (http://office.microsoft.com/en-us/makeovers/microsoft-powerpoint-2010-class-presentation-makeover-FX102237806.aspx).

Norvig, Peter. 2003. "PowerPoint: Shot with Its Own Bullets." *The Lancet* 362(9381):343–44.

Nowaczyk, Ronald H., Lyndee T. Santos, and Chad Patton. 1998. "Student Perception of Multimedia in the Undergraduate Classroom." *International Journal of Instructional Media* 25(1):367–68.

Parker, Ian. 2001. "Absolute PowerPoint." *The New Yorker*, May 28. Retrieved July 28, 2010 (http://www.newyorker.com/archive/2001/05/28/010528fa_fact_parker).

Persell, Caroline Hodges. 1992. "Bringing PCs into Introductory Sociology Courses: First Steps, Missteps, and Future Prospects." *Teaching Sociology* 20(2):91–103.

Pippert, Timothy and Helen A. Moore. 1999. "Multiple Perspectives on Multimedia in the Large Lecture Classroom." *Teaching Sociology* 37(2):92–103.

Reinhardt, Linda. 1999. "Confessions of a 'Techno-teacher.'" *College Teaching* 47(2):48–50.

Roberts, Keith A. 2002. "Ironies of Effective Teaching: Deep Structure Learning and Constructions of the Classroom." *Teaching Sociology* 30(1):1–25.

Simons, Tad. 2005. "Does PowerPoint Make You Stupid?" *Presentations*. Retrieved July 26, 2010 (http://www.sociablemedia.com/PDF/press_presentations_magazine_03_01_04.pdf).

Sojka, Jane, Ashok K. Gupta, and Dawn R. Deeter-Schmelz. 2002. "Student and Faculty Perceptions of Student Evaluations of Teaching: A Study of Similarities and Differences." *College Teaching* 50(2):44–49.

Stoner, Mark K. 2007. "PowerPoint in a New Key." *Communication Education* 56(3):365–81.

Strauss, Anselm and Juliet Corbin. 2008. *Basics of Qualitative Research: Techniques and Procedures for Developing Grounded Theory*. 3rd ed. Thousand Oaks, CA: Sage.

Stryker, Christian. 2010. "Slideware Strategies for Mathematics Educators." *Journal of Mathematics Education at Teachers College* 1:46–50.

Susman, Mary Beth. 1988. "Developing Computer-based Education and Self-pacing for Introductory Sociology: A Teacher's Perspective." *Teaching Sociology* 16(1):74–77.

Susskind, Joshua E. 2005. "PowerPoint's Power in the Classroom: Enhancing Students' Self-efficacy and Attitudes." *Computers and Education* 45(2):203–15.

Titus, Jordan J. 2008. "Student Ratings in a Consumerist Academy: Leveraging Pedagogical Control and Authority." *Sociological Perspectives* 51(2):397–422.

Tufte, Edward. 2003a. *The Cognitive Style of PowerPoint*. Cheshire, CT: Graphics Press.

Tufte, Edward. 2003b. "PowerPoint Is Evil." *Wired Magazine*. Retrieved April 21, 2010 (http://www.wired.com/wired/archive/11.09/ppt2.html).

Weinraub, Herbert J. 1998. "Using Multimedia Authoring Software: The Effects on Student Learning Perceptions and Performance." *Financial Practice and Education* 8(2):88–92.

Williams, Wendy M. and Stephen J. Ceci. 1997. "'How'm I Doing?' Problems with Student Ratings of Instructors and Courses." *Change* 29(5):12–23.

Wilmoth, Janet and John Wybraniec. 1998. "Profits and Pitfalls: Thoughts on Using a Laptop Computer and Presentation Software to Teach Introductory Social Statistics." *Teaching Sociology* 26(3):166–78.

Young, Jeffrey R. 2004. "When Good Technology Means Bad Teaching." *Chronicle of Higher Education* 51(12):31–36.

Bios

Andrea Hill is a PhD candidate at Northeastern University, where she teaches courses such as Research Methods in Sociology, Social Theory, and Introduction to Sociology. Her research interests include the cultural dynamics of neoliberalism and the ways it is lived and felt in the daily lives of U.S. workers. She is currently researching the relationship between economic crisis and neoliberal ideologies and practices.

Tammi Arford is a PhD candidate at Northeastern University, where she teaches courses such as Deviant Behavior and Social Control and Drugs and Society. Her research interests include punishment and social control, deviance, criminology, and social theory.

Amy Lubitow is an assistant professor of sociology at Portland State University, where she teaches courses related to environmental sociology, social movements, health, and gender. Her research focuses on the environmental health movement and public policy efforts to regulate toxic chemicals.

Leandra Smollin is a PhD candidate at Northeastern University, where she teaches courses in the Sociology and Women, Gender, and Sexuality Studies programs. She is also a lecturer at Tufts University, where she teaches about gender-based social inequalities and social change. Her research interests focus on the intersections of race, class, gender, and sexuality; health and violence; and feminist theory and methodologies.

Name: _____ Date: _____

Chapter 2 ■ "I'm Ambivalent about It": The Dilemmas of PowerPoint

Questions for Discussion

1. As mentioned in the article, some educators argue that "Slide settings, which provide limited space for words, cultivate 'oversimplification by asking presenters to summarize key concepts in as few words as possible'" and that "presentations transform content into overly simple snippets or buzz phrases that elide intricacy and nuance." As researchers, how can outlining key concepts and focusing on buzz phrases serve to lure your patron into following up with you for more information? How might it be beneficial for you to not give away all of your information in your presentation? How can you use your presentation as a jumping off point for a meaningful discussion?

2. The article outlines how some educators feel as though the classroom is transformed into a theater-like setting when using PowerPoint. Although some educators feel as though "Such a unidirectional environment is set up for one-way knowledge transmission rather than knowledge exchange and establishes 'a dominance relationship between speaker and audience,'" how might treating your presentation as a performance make the endeavor more successful? In what ways might this technique elicit more interest from your patron?

3. Another criticism of PowerPoint is that "pre-planned organization inhibits instructor digressions, anecdotes, and creativity—moments that often inspire student questions that are so vitally important for effective learning." As a presenter, how can you plan out meaningful pauses in your presentation where your audience might be able to ask a relevant question or share a personal anecdote? How can you strike a balance between reading from your prepared slides and adding information and/or personal stories as you go along? What potential pitfalls could you run into by not pre-planning enough for your presentation?

4. Hill, et al. explain that "In discussing what they most disliked about the software, many students found fault with its tendency to discourage discussion—approximately 12 percent of these responses expressed sentiments along the lines of one student's observation that '[PowerPoint] monopolizes the class and leaves little opportunity for discussion or interaction.'" Discuss with a partner: How can you build small moments in your presentation when your audience can react to what you are saying? What questions might you include in your slides that prompt the audience to turn to a neighbor and discuss the information? What other techniques might you use to get the audience more involved in the presentation?

5. Many students explained that they found PowerPoint useful because it "shortens up main points and makes them easier to understand" and has the ability to "outline material so students know what info is important and what they can forget." How can you strike a balance between disseminating only the most important information while still prompting your audience to think deeply about the information that may come up later on in the research process? How might you be selective in choosing to share information that is both necessary **and** thought-provoking?

6. One critic of PowerPoint cited in the article argues, in reference to students, "there are numerous situations in which . . . their education would be better served by digesting data in a less formalized or summarized matter." Discuss with a group: Is it important to have your presentation "feel" formal in order for your patron to take your work seriously? How can you be creative while still maintaining a professional tone? What activities might you be able to add into your presentation to make the process less passive?

The 5 R's: An Emerging Bold Standard for Conducting Relevant Research in a Changing World

C. J. Peek, PhD[1], Russell E. Glasgow, PhD[2], Kurt C. Stange, MD, PhD[3], Lisa M. Klesges, PhD[4], E. Peyton Purcell, MPH[5], and Rodger S. Kessler, PhD, ABPP[6]

Abstract

Research often fails to find its way into practice or policy in a timely way, if at all. Given the current pressure and pace of health care change, many authors have recommended different approaches to make health care research more relevant and rapid. An emerging standard for research, the "5 R's" is a synthesis of recommendations for care delivery research that (1) is relevant to stakeholders; (2) is rapid and recursive in application; (3) redefines rigor; (4) reports on resources required; and (5) is replicable. *Relevance* flows from substantive ongoing participation by stakeholders. *Rapidity and recursiveness* occur through accelerated design and peer reviews followed by short learning/implementation cycles through which questions and answers evolve over time. *Rigor* is the disciplined conduct of shared learning within the specific changing situations in diverse settings. *Resource reporting* includes costs of interventions. *Replicability* involves designing for the factors that may affect subsequent implementation of an intervention or program in different contexts. These R's of the research process are mutually reinforcing and can be supported by training that fosters collaborative and reciprocal relationships among researchers, implementers, and other stakeholders. In sum, a standard is emerging for research that is both rigorous and relevant. Consistent and bold application will increase the value, timeliness, and applicability of the research enterprise.

Ann Fam Med 2014;12:447-455. doi:10.1370/afm.1688.

The Need For Relevant Research In A Rapidly Changing Health Care World

Accelerated pressure for change in health care creates an exploding need for relevant and rapidly generated new information. A growing volume of care delivery experiments around the country pose questions that research can help answer: Which interventions or system changes improve care, access, safety, or quality—and for which populations, under what conditions? Which system changes reduce underuse, overuse, or misuse? Which approaches are implementable and engaging to clinicians and patients—and can be done at reasonable cost?[1,2]

From *Annals of Family Medicine*, Volume 12 (5), September/October 2014. Copyright © 2014 by the Annals of Family Medicine, Inc. Reprinted by permission.

[1] Department of Family Medicine and Community Health, University of Minnesota Medical School, Minneapolis, Minnesota
[2] Department of Family Medicine and Colorado Health Outcomes Program, University of Colorado, Denver, Colorado
[3] Department of Family Medicine & Community Health, Department of Epidemiology & Biostatistics, and Department of Sociology, Case Comprehensive Cancer Center, Cleveland Clinical & Translational Science Collaborative, Case Western Reserve University, Cleveland, Ohio
[4] School of Public Health, University of Memphis, Memphis, Tennessee
[5] Clinical Research Directorate/CMRP, SAIC-Frederick, Inc, Frederick National Laboratory for Cancer Research, Frederick, Maryland
[6] Department of Family Medicine and the Center for Clinical and Translational Science, University of Vermont College of Medicine, Burlington, Vermont

Evolving clinical, organizational, and business models for health care, such as patient-centered medical homes[3] and accountable care organizations[4] need rapidly generated research evidence in real-world experiments for multiple stakeholders: implementers who want to improve their practices; purchasers who want to pay for value; health plans that administer benefits and take risks for care provided; policy makers who are being asked to change "the rules of the game" to support new approaches; patients who wish to know their care is effective, safe, and worth their effort and money; and public health, community groups, and agencies who wish to see improved health at a societal level.[5,6]

The current research approach is not up to this challenge. Most recent research is slow to influence practice, does so only in pockets, or does not address practical needs for decision making.[7-9] Innovative ideas to remedy this situation have been proposed and some implemented. Yet the overall problem remains. It is time to pull together and implement changes in research paradigms and habits to better meet the research needs of changing health care delivery.[10-14]

The threads of a fresh research paradigm are already apparent, having been suggested separately in many publications,[15-17] but need to be woven together to form a picture—the whole cloth with which to tailor research to answer the important stakeholder questions. This article weaves those threads together in the form of an integrated set of "5 R's" to guide research.

The 5 R's of Health Care Delivery Research

Below we articulate the issues and how they can be addressed through the 5 R's to generate health care research that (1) is relevant to stakeholders; (2) is rapid and recursive in application; (3) redefines rigor; (4) reports on resources required; and (5) is replicable. *Relevance* flows from substantive ongoing participation by stakeholders. *Rapidity and recursiveness* occur through accelerated design and grant reviews followed by short learning/implementation cycles through which questions and answers evolve over time. *Rigor* is the disciplined conduct of shared learning within the specific changing situations in diverse settings. *Resource reporting* includes costs of interventions and likely cost of replication in other settings. *Replicability* involves designing for the factors that may affect subsequent implementation of an intervention or program in different contexts.

Relevant to Stakeholders

What Is the Issue?

Perceived lack of relevance is cited as the primary reason practitioners do not use research.[18-21] Research must generate setting-based evidence designed to flow into practice realities and meet stakeholder needs; as has been stated, "If we want more evidence-based practice, we need more practice-based evidence."[22]

How Can It Be Addressed?

Involve end users meaningfully and continuously from the outset in forming research questions and selecting outcomes.[2,5,15,16,18,21-24] Research agendas should have origins in need on the ground[16]—with stakeholders being not only customers for research, but also producers of meaningful questions. Questions come from implementers, policy makers, health plans, purchasers, and patients—with researchers who listen and translate different user concerns into researchable questions.[5,24] Such participatory, practiceor community-based "partnership research"[15] extends to all phases of research: question generation, designs and measures, implementation, interpretation, presentation, and application of results.

Build an ultimate use perspective into all stages of the research process. If research waits too long before considering sustainable real-world implementation, investment in the preceding research may prematurely "freeze" the intervention in ways not compatible with later use. Engaging stakeholders in how to implement at earlier phases may help avoid retooling and reduce the time to real-world application.

Seek continuation, not only translation. Health care practitioners are arguably more likely to apply and sustain what is learned from research in their own practices.[25] The question becomes not, "how do we translate this to our practice?" but, "how do we continue, adapt, and spread what we just learned in our practice?" If done widely, this continuation could make research relevant and make knowledge generation part of the fabric of practice.

Rapid and Recursive in Application

What Is the Issue?

It is not acceptable that it takes 17 years on average for a 14% uptake of funded research into practice.[7] In a rapidly changing environment, we need to find ways to accelerate the research enterprise.

How Can It Be Addressed?

Engage stakeholders in rapid-learning research systems. In "rapid-learning health care," "routinely collected real-time clinical data drive the process of scientific discovery, which becomes a natural outgrowth of patient care."[26] Components may include databases or registries organized by populations, electronic health records, guidelines and clinical decision support, patient engagement, and multiple sponsors or research networks.[26,27] In "rapid-learning research systems"[21] researchers, funders, implementers, health systems, and community partners are brought together to develop questions, answer them, and then ask new questions of practical importance.

Streamline review processes. The health care delivery world moves on with new partners, questions, and technology, whereas traditional grant application and review often takes a long time.[21] Rapid review processes[26] that shorten the time from conception of a study to its approval, funding, and start can help keep studies timely and relevant.

Pose research questions to multiple networked practices. Practice-based research networks (PBRNs) are practices that work together to answer health care questions and translate findings into practice. PBRNs can generate relevant questions from stakeholders, design research, and collect data that result in rapid answers from large data sets, including deidentified data from clinical and financial records stored in electronic health records from natural experiments happening in real time, such as data for complex patients treated under real-world conditions by real-world clinicians. Some of these practice settings, as well as public health system research networks,[28] are becoming true "learning organizations"[27] where quality improvement research is included with, not separated from, more experimental findings.

Allow discoveries within a study to influence the study. Discoveries, sometimes unexpected, can modify subsequent data collection and measurement. Data collection is no longer only at fixed points, using static measures. Implementation or study processes are continuously improved along the way. This is a recursive and rapid learning situation.[27] When discoveries in a study begin to appear, they may reshape stakeholder questions or begin to answer others. The next set of questions may begin to emerge, along with energy for answering those reshaped or more insightful questions. As discoveries roll in, stakeholders, in partnership with researchers, guide these iterations.

Redefines Rigor

What Is the Issue?

Scientific rigor is essential, but common conceptions of rigor may limit the range of real-world situations that can be studied—and methods, settings, and populations with which to do so. The hallmark of rigor has been the "gold standard" efficacy randomized controlled trial (RCT) emphasizing internal validity.

How Can It Be Addressed?

We suggest a modified version of rigor suited to broader questions meaningful to multiple stakeholders and answered in heterogeneous populations and settings with attention to transportability and sustainable implementation.

Regard rigor as a property of a series of decisions, observations, and relationships rather than of techniques.[29] Rigorous research (1) is systematic and organized about concepts, tools, data collection, measures, procedures, and analyses; (2) checks for superfluous connections and confounding variables; (3) has controls and conclusions justified by standards of evidence; and (4) uses transparent descriptions of what was done. Rigor is not defined as a list of certain techniques and exclusion of others. Particular experimental designs, data collection, or analysis techniques are not always considered more rigorous than others or that any one is the optimal design for all questions and all situations. Others have commented, "If techniques are tools in a researcher's toolbox, then this is like saying that 'A saw is better than a hammer because it is sharper.'"[29] Stated as a principle, "Research agenda determines the research methods rather than methods determine the research agenda."[16]

Give attention to both external and internal validity. Most methods developed to assess research quality focus predominantly or exclusively on internal validity. Rigor also implies attention to transparent reporting on issues related to generalizability.[16,30]

Reporting on Resources

What Is the Issue?

Use of health care resources is a major concern when a priority is to bend the cost curve. Stakeholders are making decisions among alternative care approaches based on the cost of interventions as well as on clinical effectiveness. Information on resources used to conduct or replicate interventions can be helpful in larger economic analysis, but is seldom well reported.[31]

How Can It Be Addressed?

Use a consistent vocabulary for reporting. For example, measuring cost includes money, but also clinician and staff time and energy, plus intervention systems, infrastructure, or training costs. There are start-up costs, ongoing costs, and opportunity costs. There are costs of doing a study intervention, and likely costs of recreating it in another setting. Costs incurred in one place or to one stakeholder may save costs in some other place or for another stakeholder.

Report on as many of the relevant costs of different interventions as possible and do so in a standard manner.[14,32,33] For example, what did the program in question cost to promote and implement, and what are estimates of what it would cost to replicate a similar program under different conditions or settings? Such estimates do not require researchers to do complex economic or cost-benefit analyses, but reporting on resources is important to those who pay attention to *value* in health care. Although value may mean many things to many people, it is being defined and becoming part of efforts to be rigorous, transparent, and relevant to stakeholders,[34] including patients who have their own perspective on value.[35]

Replicability

What Is the Issue?

Research design can help address questions regarding how an innovation will perform in a new system with different contextual influences.[36] Replication of findings is increasingly recognized[37] as a major challenge across the translation spectrum from basic discovery (eg, genomewide association studies) to community interventions. The conditions under which a finding can be replicated are central to understanding robust effects that can be reasonably expected under various conditions. Hence, researchers must design for replicability and report results needed for reproducibility—either under the same or different conditions in which the findings are likely to be applied.

How Can It Be Addressed?

Design for sustainable implementation from the start. This approach is arguably more efficient and effective if it saves rework for real-world application. We recommend asking 3 questions: (1) is the study designed to inform implementation—and re-invention in different settings? (2) is the "how" reported as well as the "what" of interventions, and to what extent are procedures replicable in similar or diverse settings? and (3) are contextual factors reported that are important to understanding what happened and why—for example, relevant policies, and inclusion and exclusion criteria for settings and staff as well as patients?

These strategies can go a long way toward making findings replicable, realizing that not every study can be transported to other settings. But such data will allow others to make reasonable judgments about what aspects to retain and what to change for replication or reinvention in a different time and place, using relevant domains for contextual factors.[38]

Examples

Some of the 5 R's have found their way into research studies, networks, and tools. Table 1 describes a few examples. Readers can likely cite other examples or see other R's in these. The 5 R's are emerging not as a response to a *completed* record of implementation in full scope, but as a logical (and promising) *challenge* to package in application the separate elements already abundantly demonstrated in the literature, but not yet combined to full effect in more than a few examples. What is "bold" is the proposal to routinely apply the 5 R's as a package and to take on the substantial challenges of practical implementation and evolution. For inspiration, consider McDonnell Douglas' bold integration of 5 existing technologies for the first time in 1 airplane (the 1935 DC-3), the innovation that swept away the competition and opened the era of commercial air travel, when a plane with 4 of those technologies failed commercially the previous year.[51]

Conclusions

Health care transformation needs the full benefit of research to inform decision making and discover new options. The research community owes it to its "customers" and the public to evolve its standards and methods for health care research. The 5 R's are offered as a next step in the developmental trajectory of an evolving field—a framework for a much needed discussion and adjustment of criteria for what is considered high-quality research.

Example: Study/Project/ Resource Title and Relevant R's	Study/Project/Resource Details
Particular studies and programs	
DIAMOND (Depression Improvement Across Minnesota–Offering a New Direction) 1. Relevant to stakeholders 2. Redefines rigor 3. Replicability	The DIAMOND initiative for depression in primary care was a statewide collaborative of practices and health plans accompanied by a separately funded NIMH research study using a stepped wedge/phased intervention design.[15,25,39,40] Practices launched the DIAMOND care process in cohorts, 6 months apart, with baseline data collected for all. Outcomes that mattered to different stakeholders were compared before and after launch across the many practices launching at different times. Outcomes were tracked using both quantitative and qualitative measures, including clinical outcomes, health plan claims data, patient surveys, and practice leader surveys regarding implementation. An explicit balance of fidelity and adaptation to local situations—specifics that practices had to tailor for themselves (eg, choice of discipline for care managers, specific workflow for PHQ-9, type of data tracking system)—helped practices implement the DIAMOND intervention.[41,42]
P4H (Prescription for Health) 1. Relevant to stakeholders 2. Recursive 3. Redefines rigor 4. Reports on resources	P4H was an initiative of The Robert Wood Johnson Foundation (RWJF) with the Agency for Healthcare Research and Quality (AHRQ) to fund a collaboration of 17 PBRNs that developed and evaluated strategies to improve health behavior changes for multiple behaviors through linkage to community resources.[43] Practices worked with researchers, and teams of researchers, and PBRN leaders worked with each other and with a cross-cutting research group to share evolving learning, and develop common measures and an evolving research agenda.[44] Using mixed quantitative and qualitative methods (including researcher diary data and interviews)[45] and cost analyses, P4H showed that primary care practices have the ability to develop their linkages to connect patients with community resources[46] to improve practice processes,[47] health behavior counseling, and patient behavior change.[48]
¡Viva Bien! 1. Relevant to stakeholders 2. Reports on resources 3. Replicability	¡Viva Bien![32,33] was a randomized trial that provided a clear description of methods, implementation costs for a diabetes self-management program, and estimates of costs to replicate the program under different conditions, calculating incremental costs per behavioral, biologic, and quality-of-life change. It discussed how to separate the costs of development and research from implementation, and how to conduct relatively straight-forward sensitivity analyses to estimate costs of replicating a program or policy under different conditions.
MOHR (My Own Health Report) 1. Relevant to stakeholders 2. Rapid and recursive 3. Redefines rigor 4. Reports on resources 5. Replicability	MOHR[23,49] is a pragmatic participatory trial in which diverse primary care practices implement the collection of patient-reported information and provide patients advice, goal setting, and counseling in response—with deliberate diversity of settings and populations to ensure greater generalizability of results. Practices, patients, funding agencies, and content experts were engaged throughout the study to take into account local resources and characteristics in design, implementation, evaluation, and dissemination. Core elements of the study protocol were identified, with local tailoring to ensure implementation was relevant to local culture and practice on issues such as workflows, eligible patients, when and where assessment would be completed, whether electronic or paper, and how clinicians would receive the feedback. The trial used mixed methods, including cost analyses.
Research networks across studies	
PRC (Prevention Research Centers) of the Centers for Disease Control and Prevention 1. Relevant to stakeholders 2. Recursive 3. Replicability	PRC directs a national network of 37 academic research centers at public health or medical schools with a preventive medicine residency program, translating research results into policy and public health practice. Centers have capacity for community-based, participatory prevention research needed to drive community changes to prevent and control chronic disease. Research involves collaboration among partners bringing different expertise to the table, identifies research needs of partners, conducts research that builds on previous evidence for promising interventions, and recommends how interventions can be packaged for replication and adoption (http://www.cdc.gov/prc/index.htm).
QUERI (Quality Enhancement Research Initiative) 1. Relevant to stakeholders 2. Rapid and recursive 3. Redefines rigor 4. Replicability	QUERI is a Veterans Affairs initiative that brings together operations with research staff to address key gaps in quality and outcomes. It has contributed to remarkable and rapid improvements in the quality of care received by veterans across 10 conditions deemed high-risk or highly prevalent. This initiative uses a 6-step process to spot gaps in performance and to identify and implement interventions. QUERI studies and facilitates adoption of new treatments, tests, and models of care into routine clinical practice—feasibility, implementation, adoption, and impact (http://www.queri.research.va.gov/default.cfm).
Research application tools and resources	
RTIPs (Research Tested Intervention Programs) 1. Relevant to stakeholders 2. Reports on resources 3. Replicability	RTIPs is a resource of the National Cancer Institute that provides information on the specific conditions under which each of their tested interventions has been evaluated and tools for addressing issues about applicability (http://rtips.cancer.gov/rtips). New features related to external validity using the RE-AIM framework are included to help users better determine the likely public health impact of a given program if replicated in their setting. RTIPs also reports on the resources required to implement these programs.
PRECIS (Pragmatic Explanatory Continuum Indicator Summary) 1. Relevant to stakeholders 2. Redefines rigor 3. Replicability	PRECIS[50] is a graphic representation of the extent to which a study is pragmatic (testing effect in usual conditions) vs explanatory (testing effect in ideal conditions) on 10 key dimensions. If used consistently, this tool could greatly help practitioners decide whether a study is likely to be reproducible in their setting and researchers to investigate the dimensions along which similarity is more vs less critical for replication.

Table 1 Examples of Projects Illustrating the R's.

NIMH = National Institute of Mental Health; PBRN = practice-based research network; PHQ-9 = 9-item Patient Health Questionnaire; RE-AIM = Reach Effectiveness–Adoption Implementation Maintenance.

Routinely Apply the Complete Package of 5 R's

As is the case for other models—for example, the Reach Effectiveness–Adoption Implementation Maintenance (RE-AIM) evaluation model,[52,53] the Chronic Care Model,[54] and the Institute of Medicine 6 quality aims[55]—the effect of the 5 R's model comes not from doing separate R's or even 2 or 3 of them, but from doing them all in an integrated fashion whereby each reinforces the others. The 5 R's are proposed to work together across stages of the research and dissemination process. Table 2 shows a research "preflight" checklist.

Bold Standard 5 R's

Stage of Research	Relevant to Stakeholders	Rapid and Recursive	Refines Rigor	Report on Resources	Replicability
Design	End users of this research identified? Stakeholders who need to be involved identified? Plan in place to engage their perspectives? Plan in place to gather stakeholder questions and what is important to them?	Rapid cycle measurement and assessment built into the design? How? Approach in place to allow early discoveries to shape the study?	How is study systematic and pragmatic about concepts, measures, data collection procedures, and analysis plan? Multiple methods used? How? Internal and external validity balanced? How?	Intervention costs (monetary and other) measured? How? A standard vocabulary for reporting on resources in place? What?	Study designed to inform implementation and reinvention in different settings? How? Likely relevant settings for this research identified?
Implementation	Stakeholders involved in ongoing refinement? How? Changes they suggested along the way recorded? Changes suggested implemented? Which ones?	Short cycle learning taking place to refine design and measurement? Is learning influencing the study? How?	Systematic approach being followed to concepts, tools, data collection, measures, procedures, analyses? Checks for bias and superfluous connections in place? Clear description of what is being done recorded?	Cost data gathered on an ongoing basis? Using a consistent vocabulary for different kinds of costs?	Contextual factors documented that are important to understanding what happened (and why) in the study setting?
Reporting	Diverse stakeholders involved in interpreting and reporting findings? Their different interpretations reported?	Emergent findings shared on an ongoing basis throughout the study? Have adaptations made been reported?	Study methods reported transparently and thoroughly? Reported how study checked for potential biases and superfluous connections? Reported how conclusions are justified by standards of evidence?	Study reports useful cost data using a defined vocabulary for different kinds of costs? Estimates made for costs under different conditions?	Contextual factors relevant to reinvention in new settings reported, including variation across settings or within settings?
Dissemination	Target audiences, stakeholders, or likely users involved in next steps? Findings expressed in language and context that mean something to different stakeholders?	Guidelines provided for adaption and customization/tailoring for future use?	Description included for how internal and external validity findings support wider use?	Intervention cost data discussed as a factor in dissemination?	Data-supported suggestions included about the contexts for which program or intervention is relevant or reproducible?

Table 2 Questions to Apply the 5 R's at Each Stage of the Research and Dissemination Process.

Overcome the Practical Challenges of Implementing the R's

There is little doubt that implementing the 5 R's on a meaningful scale will require continued changes in thinking and infrastructure pointed out in literature on the separate R's. Table 3 summarizes such changes.

Although many of these changes are under way in different places in different ways, considerable challenges remain. We believe that emerging stakeholder interests align well with the 5 R's and will drive such change. For example, the 2014 Academy Health report on improving the evidence base for Medicare policy making[56] interviewed leaders in health policy and care delivery for their most pressing health services research needs over the next 3 to 5 years; it was research that (1) aims at understanding the performance of new organizational forms such as accountable care organizations and Medicare Advantage plans; (2) uses comparable data sets for performance of physician practices and new organizational arrangements; (3) engages with the promises and pitfalls of electronic data, rapid cycle research, and comparative effectiveness research; (4) understands how the politics of evidence and policy affect research relevance and usefulness; and (5) builds relationships between researchers and policy makers, with study findings available at the time decisions were made—even if "best available" rather than "best" evidence. Although this study was focused on Medicare, we believe its lessons can be much more broadly taken.

In addition, we solicited feedback from a convenience sample of 8 stakeholders on the importance of research for practical decision making and on the 5 R's. Participants were balanced across practitioners, other implementers, and administrators. Responses indicated that *relevant* was the most important R, with *rapid* a close second, followed by other R's—none of which were considered unimportant. The most important role for research in practical decisions was testing viability of approaches in their own settings and available resources. Suggested reasons why research is often not useful were lack of relevance, rapidity, or good relationships with researchers. The 2 facets identified as making research more helpful were "faster turnaround" and building better relationships between researchers and clinicians; as one clinician put it, "Relationship is so important, you should put a 6th R in there!"

Recognize the Wide Range of Application for the 5 R's

Admittedly aspirational, we do not expect every study to comprehensively address all 5 R's. We do not expect, for example, all epidemiologic research or basic mechanism studies to address all of them. Studies having as their long-term goal achieving translation to real-world settings or making a population impact, however, would benefit from considering each R, reporting on those most relevant, and discussing implications for the others. Examining the implications of all 5 R's should be useful in the vast majority of research studies, from efficacy to effectiveness to implementation and dissemination, not just for a few community translational "T4" studies, which are investigations of practice intervention effects on population health. This strategy would help align the pipeline of potential interventions with real-world pragmatic requirements.

Build Better Relationships Using the 5 R's

Practitioners often experience research as interfering with practical procedures or believe that researchers just want study participants to address their own questions and further their careers. On the other hand, researchers often experience clinicians as not interested in research, resistant to research protocols, or not being ready to implement evidence-based findings. This is not a perceived relationship between researchers and practitioners or other stakeholders that will carry us into a successful future. The 5 R's proposed embody the terms of a new and more transparent win-win partnership between researchers and stakeholders with important questions that research can help answer.

Challenges	Changes to Address Challenges
Accelerating the pace and iterative nature of the research enterprise Decision-maker needs outpace current speed of review cycles: grant review; funding decision; IRB approval and modification processes Study implementation time frames Publication cycles not amenable to "just in time" decisions; slow review and release of findings (see more below on dissemination) Low priority assigned to designs that can speed research	Harness stakeholder interest in timeliness to drive a cultural shift to shorten what is considered "rapid" or "timely" compared with present custom Implement a variety of technical changes to research processes already suggested in literature[19,21,26,27,54] Use rapid-cycle testing of hypotheses, allowing ineffective ideas to "fail fast" and successful innovations to spread quickly Link social media with traditional communications vehicles
Expanding limited concepts of rigor (eg, preference for, confidence in, or insistence on certain designs such as RCTs) by: Funding agencies offering calls for proposals Grant application reviewers Researchers "Customers" of research (stakeholders who use the findings)	Among all parties, build awareness of and comfort with a broader "palette" of research designs, so that research design is driven by the questions, rather than research questions driven by designs Use professional meetings/training events to more clearly articulate features, pros/cons of different designs—their appropriate or promising scope of application
Ensuring a blend of research team skills and interests Skill and interest in stakeholder involvement in generating questions, articulating ultimate use of study findings, study design, implementation, reporting, and dissemination Awareness of and respect for political as well as scientific concerns of stake- holders such as policy makers Skill and comfort in building relationships with clinicians and clinics—consultative, cooperative, problem solving Experience and confidence with the broader "palette" of research designs, including rapid learning in real-world experiments	Propose an enhanced "job description" for research teams—a checklist of skills, interests, and relationships required for specific studies Beyond essential methodologic, data-gathering, and analytic skills, include "softer" skills and methods such as shown in left column Build up those skills through examples, conferences, and training among both existing and new researchers
Increasing clinician familiarity with being active research partners Negative experiences or preconceptions about feasibility or practical value of doing research in the practice Few or no current relationships with researchers Unfamiliarity of working with researchers to turn practice concerns and curiosity into researchable questions Unfamiliarity with building research data gathering into routine clinic systems rather than being an effortful "add on" Not connecting research with more familiar quality improvement, rapid- cycle learning	Provide examples and assistance through professional venues and practice facilitation or technical assistance that help clinicians and researchers adjust mindset, methods, and interactions to create practical research partnerships along the lines described in the literature[15,16,25]
Raising priority on collection and reporting on context and resources Limited researcher and reviewer expectation that data on resource use of interventions or on context information relevant to transportability or reinvention in new settings be gathered systematically or reported Space limitations and/or customary priorities in journals that reduce additional context and resource data reporting	Adjust research announcements and grant review guidelines to ask for greater reporting on context and resources required; accompany by explanation of why For publication in limited space, consider other methods such as web supplements to access detailed context and resource use data if not in standard published article
More powerfully bringing publication and dissemination to practical decision making Limited readiness to publish replications of key findings in original or new contexts or to publish negative results of replication Reaching those stakeholders who want to make research-based decisions at the time and place decisions are made Limited dissemination in publications or forms in which stakeholders are already engaged, knowing that different forms of publication/dissemination reach different stakeholders	Publish replications (successful or not) in places where stakeholders will find them Reward researchers via funding and career paths for key replications, not only for new positive results Create a stakeholder map—which stakeholders need what information from the study, in what form, and where it is most likely to be read Create stakeholder-specific versions of core journal publications to increase reach of the information

Table 3 Challenges and Changes for Routine Implementation of 5 R's.
IRB= institutional review board; RCT= randomized controlled trial.

Teach to This New Standard

This new standard (and its implicit partnership between stakeholders and researchers) is especially important for students and those early in their careers, whether clinicians, researchers, policy makers, or others wishing to develop or use research evidence. The 5 R's are offered as teaching tools as well as research tools—helping all stakeholders wear constructive "hats" with each other when addressing important questions. Over time, this approach may lead to an improved relationship between the research and health care enterprises—on behalf of the public they both serve.

References

1. Smith JM, Topol E. A call to action: lowering the cost of health care. *Am J Prev Med.* 2013;44(1)(Suppl 1):S54–S57.

2. Patient-Centered Outcomes Research Institute (PCORI). Funding announcement: Improving healthcare systems. May 22, 2012. http://www.pcori.org/assets/PFA-Improving-Healthcare-Systems-05222012.pdf. Accessed Jul 15, 2013.

3. Nutting PA, Crabtree BF, Miller WL, Stange KC, Stewart E, Jaén C. Transforming physician practices to patient-centered medical homes: lessons from the national demonstration project. *Health Aff (Millwood).* 2011;30(3):439–445.

4. Fisher ES, Shortell SM. Accountable care organizations: accountable for what, to whom, and how. *JAMA.* 2010;304(15):1715–1716.

5. Selby JV, Beal AC, Frank L. The Patient-Centered Outcomes Research Institute (PCORI) national priorities for research and initial research agenda. *JAMA.* 2012;307(15):1583–1584.

6. Stange KC. Refocusing knowledge generation, application, and education: raising our gaze to promote health across boundaries. *Am J Prev Med.* 2011;41(4)(Suppl 3):S164–S169.

7. Balas EBS. *Managing Clinical Knowledge for Health Care Improvement. Yearbook of Medical Informatics.* Stuttgart, Germany: Schattauer; 2000.

8. Brownson RC, Colditz GA, Proctor EK, eds. *Dissemination and Implementation Research in Health: Translating Science to Practice.* 1st ed. New York, NY: Oxford University Press, Inc; 2012.

9. Kessler R, Glasgow RE. A proposal to speed translation of healthcare research into practice: dramatic change is needed. *Am J Prev Med.* 2011;40(6):637–644.

10. Moher D, Hopewell S, Schulz KF, et al; Consolidated Standards of Reporting Trials Group. CONSORT 2010 Explanation and Elaboration: Updated guidelines for reporting parallel group randomised trials. *J Clin Epidemiol.* 2010;63(8):e1–e37.

11. Schulz KF, Altman DG, Moher D, CONSORT Group. CONSORT 2010 statement: updated guidelines for reporting parallel group randomised trials. *BMC Med.* 2010;340:c332.

12. Higgins J, Green S. Cochrane Handbook for Systematic Reviews of Interventions. Updated 2011. http://www.cochrane-handbook.org. Accessed Jul 16, 2013.

13. Equator Network. Library for Health Research Reporting. EQUATOR Network Resource Center website. Updated 2013. http://www.equator-network.org/resource-centre/library-of-health-research-reporting. Accessed Jul 16, 2013.

14. Gold M, Siegel J, Russell L, Weinstein M. *Cost Effectiveness in Health and Medicine.* New York, NY: Oxford University Press; 2003.

15. Solberg LI, Glasgow RE, Unützer J, et al. Partnership research: a practical trial design for evaluation of a natural experiment to improve depression care. *Med Care.* 2010;48(7):576–582.

16. Kottke TE, Solberg LI, Nelson AF, et al. Optimizing practice through research: a new perspective to solve an old problem. *Ann Fam Med.* 2008;6(5):459–462.

17. Berwick DM. Broadening the view of evidence-based medicine. *Qual Saf Health Care.* 2005;14(5):315–316.

18. Rothwell PM. External validity of randomised controlled trials: "to whom do the results of this trial apply?" *Lancet.* 2005;365(9453): 82–93.

19. Glasgow RE, Chambers D. Developing robust, sustainable, implementation systems using rigorous, rapid and relevant science. *Clin Transl Sci.* 2012;5(1):48–55.

20. Kessler RS. The patient centered medical home: a great opportunity to move beyond brilliant and irrelevant. *Transl Behav Med.* 2012;2(3):311–312.

21. Riley WT, Glasgow RE, Etheredge L, Abernethy AP. Rapid, responsive, relevant (R3) research: a call for a rapid learning health research enterprise. *Clin Transl Med.* 2013;2(1):10.

22. Green LW. Making research relevant: if it is an evidence-based practice, where's the practice-based evidence? *Fam Pract.* 2008; 25(Suppl 1):i20–i24.

23. Krist AH, Glenn BA, Glasgow RE, et al. Designing a valid randomized pragmatic primary care implementation trial: the My Own Health Report (MOHR) project. *Implement Sci.* 2013;8:73.

24. Tunis SR, Stryer DB, Clancy CM. Practical clinical trials: increasing the value of clinical research for decision making in clinical and health policy. *JAMA.* 2003;290(12):1624–1632.

25. Solberg LI, Crain AL, Jaeckels N, et al. The DIAMOND initiative: implementing collaborative care for depression in 75 primary care clinics. *Implement Sci.* 2013;8(1):135.

26. Abernethy AP, Etheredge LM, Ganz PA, et al. Rapid-learning system for cancer care. *J Clin Oncol.* 2010;28(27):4268–4274.

27. Etheredge LM. A rapid-learning health system. *Health Aff (Millwood).* 2007;26(2):w107–w118.

28. Mays GP, Hogg RA. Expanding delivery system research in public health settings: lessons from practice-based research networks. *J Public Health Manag Pract.* 2012;18(6):485–498.

29. Ryan B. Data management and analysis methods. In: Denzin N, Lincoln Y, eds. *Handbook of Qualitative Research.* 2nd ed. Thousand Oaks, CA: Sage Publications; 2000:769–802.

30. Green LW, Glasgow RE. Evaluating the relevance, generalization, and applicability of research: issues in external validation and translation methodology. *Eval Health Prof.* 2006;29(1):126–153.

31. Glasgow RE, Klesges LM, Dzewaltowski DA, Bull SS, Estabrooks P. The future of health behavior change research: what is needed to improve translation of research into health promotion practice? *Ann Behav Med.* 2004;27(1):3–12.

32. Ritzwoller DP, Sukhanova A, Gaglio B, Glasgow RE. Costing behavioral interventions: a practical guide to enhance translation. *Ann Behav Med.* 2009;37(2):218–227.

33. Ritzwoller DP, Sukhanova AS, Glasgow RE, et al. Intervention costs and cost-effectiveness for a multiple-risk-factor diabetes self-management trial for Latinas: economic analysis of Viva bien! *Transl Behav Med.* 2011;1(3):427–435.

34. Porter ME. What is value in health care? *N Engl J Med.* 2010;363(26): 2477–2481.

35. deBronkart D. How the e-patient community helped save my life: an essay by Dave deBronkart. *BMJ.* 2013;346:f1990.

36. Cohn S, Clinch M, Bunn C, Stronge P. Entangled complexity: why complex interventions are just not complicated enough. *J Health Serv Res Policy.* 2013;18(1):40–43.

37. Ioannidis JP. Effect of the statistical significance of results on the time to completion and publication of randomized efficacy trials. *JAMA.* 1998;279(4):281–286.

38. Tomoaia-Cotisel A, Scammon DL, Waitzman NJ, et al. Context matters: the experience of 14 research teams in systematically reporting contextual factors important for practice change. *Ann Fam Med.* 2013;11(Suppl 1):S115–S123.

39. Crain AL, Solberg LI, Unützer J, et al. Designing and implementing research on a statewide quality improvement initiative: the DIAMOND study and initiative. *Med Care.* 2013;51(9):e58–e66.

40. Glasgow RE, Magid DJ, Beck A, Ritzwoller D, Estabrooks PA. Practical clinical trials for translating research to practice: design and measurement recommendations. *Med Care.* 2005;43(6):551–557.

41. Cohen D, McDaniel RR Jr, Crabtree BF, et al. A practice change model for quality improvement in primary care practice. *J Healthc Manag.* 2004;49(3):155–168, discussion 169–170.

42. Allen J, Linnan L, Emmons K. Fidelity and its relationship to implementation effectiveness, adaptation and dissemination. In: Brownson R, Colditz G, Proctor E, eds. *Dissemination and Implementation Research in Health: Translating Science to Practice.* 1st ed. New York, NY: Oxford University Press; 2012:281–303.

43. Cohen DJ, Tallia AF, Crabtree BF, Young DM. Implementing health behavior change in primary care: lessons from prescription for health. *Ann Fam Med.* 2005;3(Suppl 2):S12–S19.

44. Cohen DJ, Crabtree BF, Etz RS, et al. Fidelity versus flexibility: translating evidence-based research into practice. *Am J Prev Med.* 2008;35(5)(Suppl):S381–S389.

45. Cohen D, Leviton L, Isaacson N, Tallia A, Crabtree B. Online diaries for qualitative evaluation: gaining real-time insights. *Am J Eval.* 2006;27(2):1–22.

46. Etz RS, Cohen DJ, Woolf SH, et al. Bridging primary care practices and communities to promote healthy behaviors. *Am J Prev Med.* 2008;35(5)(Suppl):S390–S397.

47. Balasubramanian BA, Cohen DJ, Clark EC, et al. Practice-level approaches for behavioral counseling and patient health behaviors. *Am J Prev Med.* 2008;35(5)(Suppl):S407–S413.

48. Cohen DJ, Balasubramanian BA, Isaacson NF, Clark EC, Etz RS, Crabtree BF. Coordination of health behavior counseling in primary care. *Ann Fam Med.* 2011;9(5):406–415.

49. Glasgow R, Kessler R, Ory M, et al. Conducting rapid, relevant research: lessons learned from the My Own Health Report (MOHR) project. *Am J Prev Med.* 2014;47(2):212–219.

50. Thorpe KE, Zwarenstein M, Oxman AD, et al. A pragmatic-explanatory continuum indicator summary (PRECIS): a tool to help trial designers. *J Clin Epidemiol.* 2009;62(5):464–475.

51. Senge PM. *Fifth Discipline: Mastering the Five Practices of the Learning Organization.* New York, NY: Doubleday & Co; 1990.

52. Gaglio B, Shoup JA, Glasgow RE. The RE-AIM framework: a systematic review of use over time. *Am J Public Health.* 2013;103(6):e38–e46.

53. Kessler RS, Purcell EP, Glasgow RE, Klesges LM, Benkeser RM, Peek CJ. What does it mean to "employ" the RE-AIM model? *Eval Health Prof.* 2013;36(1):44–66.

54. Wagner EH. Academia, chronic care, and the future of primary care. *J Gen Intern Med.* 2010;25(Suppl 4):S636–S638.

55. Committee on Quality of Health Care in America. *Crossing the Quality Chasm: A New Health System for the 21st Century.* Washington, DC: National Academy Press; 2001.

56. Gluck ME, Radomski L. The AcademyHealth Listening Project Report: Improving the Evidence Base for Medicare Policymaking. Academy-Health. Updated February 2014. http://academyhealth.org/files/publications/listeningprojectmedicare.pdf. Accessed Apr 4, 2014.

Name: _____ Date: _____

Chapter 2 ■ The 5 R's: An Emerging Bold Standard for Conducting Relevant Research in a Changing World

Questions for Discussion

1. How do the 5 R's help you maintain a clear focus on the 6 P's as you conduct your research? Explain the connection using a few sentences, a diagram, or an illustration.

2. How can you use your paradigms as a model to help you make a plan for how your research track and scope might change over the course of the semester?

3. Based on the definition given in "Redefines Rigor," give two examples of external validity that you might find useful when choosing paradigms for your own research proposal.

4. Work with a partner or small group to analyze Table 2. Add one question per section that is relevant to your own research (Design, Implementation, Reporting, Dissemination). Be prepared to explain to the class a) why you added each question and b) how it relates to your research.

5. Map out how you can address all 5 R's in your own research. Then, list them in order of relevance. Are there any R's that do not specifically apply to your proposal? If not, why?

Organizing Data in Tables and Charts: Different Criteria for Different Tasks

Jane E. Miller

Introduction

Tables and charts are efficient tools for organizing numbers. Too often, however, students and quantitative analysts do not give much consideration to the order in which they present data in tables or charts. This lack of thought means that the sequence of items may not be compatible with the author's objectives, whether testing a hypothesis, describing a pattern or reporting data for others' use. The appropriate criteria for arranging data in tables or charts often differ depending on whether they are to be used primarily with or without a prose description. Tables or charts intended to pre-sent numbers as evidence to address a specific question or to accompany a description of a pattern are usually best organized so that they coordinate with the associated narrative. On the other hand, tables intended to present data for reference use such as periodic series from the Bureau of Labour Statistics or a national census might work better if structured so that readers can find the numbers of interest to them with little written guidance. These two broad objectives suggest very different considerations for organizing variables or response categories.

No one of these purposes is inherently more important than the other, but in many cases a particular objective can be identified for reporting numbers in a given type of document. For example, numbers presented in a science laboratory report or a history essay are usually being applied as evidence for a particular hypothesis or to illustrate a trend or other pattern. In such cases, empirical or theoretical criteria are frequently a sensible basis for arranging the data because that is how they will be discussed in the accompanying prose. In contrast, detailed reference data on population or income for each of a dozen or more dates or places might not come with a written description, so using a self-guiding convention is well-suited to such tasks. This article uses data from the U.S. Consumer Expenditure Survey to illustrate four approaches to organizing data within tables and charts, discussing the situations for which each approach might be preferred.

Table 1 presents data on major categories of expenditures from the 2002 Consumer Expenditure Survey (CEX). The CEX is conducted annually by the Bureau of Labor Statistics (BLS) using a diary survey form to collect detailed information on expenditures (U.S. Department of Labor 2004a). The information is then coded into the

Item	Expenditures ($)
Average annual expenditures	42,557
Food	5612
Alcoholic beverages	415
Housing	13,481
Apparel and services	1872
Transportation	7984
Health care	2410
Entertainment	2167
Personal care products and services	562
Reading	145
Education	771
Tobacco products and supplies	334
Miscellaneous	846
Cash contributions	1366
Personal insurance and pensions	4593

Table 1 Average annual expenditures by major expenditure category, a U.S. Consumer Expenditure Survey, 2002.

Source: U.S. Department of Labor, Bureau of Labor Statistics, 2004a. Table 1.

[a] For all households with complete income reporting.

From *Teaching Statistics*, Volume 29 (3), August 2007, pp. 98–101. Copyright © 2007 John Wiley and Sons. Reprinted by permission.

standard categories shown in Table 1, which retains the original order of major expenditure categories from a standard BLS report (U.S. Department of Labor 2004b).

Organizing Data to Accompany a Prose Description

When testing hypotheses or portraying trends or other patterns, it is helpful to organize your data in tables or charts in the order you will describe them. For such purposes, alphabetical order and the sequence of items from the original data source are poor organizing principles because they rarely correspond to substantively interesting or empirically relevant patterns. Consider Figure 1, which presents the information from Table 1 in chart form, again preserving the order of expenditure categories from the BLS report. The heights of the bars and the conceptual content of adjacent categories vary erratically, requiring readers to zigzag back and forth across the axes to identify the rank order of expenditure categories by dollar amount or to compare categories of necessities to one another or to non-necessities.

For similar reasons, Figure 2—which sequences the expenditure categories alphabetically—would also be a poor choice to accompany a description of empirical rankings or a discussion of necessities versus non-necessities.

Instead, to complement a prose description of a pattern, it is often sensible to arrange your data so that the audience can easily follow the associated narrative using the well-established conventions of tracking left-to-right and top-to-bottom within the table or chart. Before creating the table or chart or writing the associated prose, consider which of the organizing principles described below best matches the main point you wish to make. Arrange the rows and columns (or axes and legend) accordingly, and then describe the numbers in the same order as they appear in the table or chart.

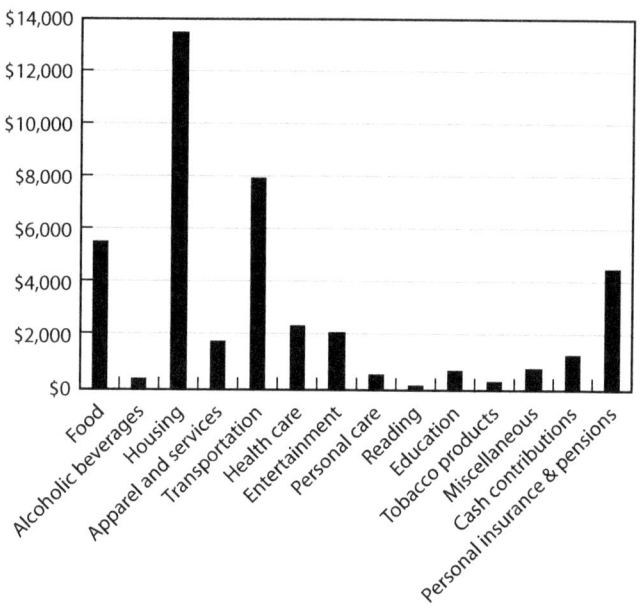

Figure 1 Major categories of expenditures, BLS ordering, 2002 U.S. Consumer Expenditure Survey.

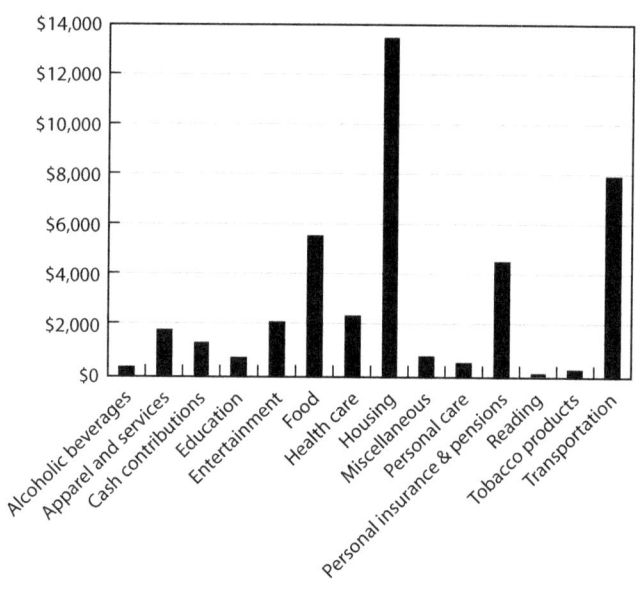

Figure 2 Major categories of expenditures, alphabetical order, 2002 U.S. Consumer Expenditure Survey.

Which organizing criterion to use depends largely on the type of variables in question. When reporting results for ordinal variables such as age group or income quintile, the sequence of items in rows, columns or axes will be obvious. Likewise, it makes sense to follow the natural order of values for interval or ratio variables such as date, age in years or income in dollars or pounds.

For tables or charts that present nominal variables such as favourite flavour of ice cream, or items such as categories of consumer expenditures, the categories or variables lack an inherent order. In those instances, either empirical criteria or theoretical principles usually provide a good basis for deciding how to organize them.

Empirical Ordering

For many tables or charts presenting distributions or associations, an important aim is to show which items have the highest and the lowest values and where other categories fall relative to those extremes. If this is your main point, it is often suitable to organize the categories in ascending or descending order of frequency or value. For example, Figure 3 shows major categories of consumer expenditures in descending order of dollar value.

Theoretical Grouping

Arranging items into conceptually related sets can be very effective. For example, Duly (2003) reports statistics on consumer expenditures for necessities, which she defines as housing (including shelter and utilities but excluding other categories of housing-related expenses), food and apparel. To present the associated numbers, Figure 4 groups the expenditure categories into necessities on the left-hand side of the x-axis and non-necessities on the right-hand side, with axis titles to identify those classifications. A table version would comprise separate panels for necessities and non-necessities, each with rows reporting the respective component categories. The accompanying description could then contrast the relative shares of necessities and non-necessities without requiring the audience to meander all over the table or chart to find the pertinent numbers.

Using Multiple Organizing Criteria

For tables or charts that present more than a few variables, a combination of approaches is often useful. For instance, consider grouping items theoretically and then arranging them within those groups in order of descending frequency or other empirical consideration. Figure 4 divides categories of consumer expenditures into necessities and non-necessities, and then organizes them in descending order of dollar value within each of those classifications, providing a useful structure for pointing out key patterns in the data.

Sometimes it makes sense to apply the same criterion sequentially, such as identifying major theoretical groupings and then minor topic groupings within them. Among the necessity categories of consumer expenditures are items related to housing, food and apparel, each with a major heading. Within each of those major categories would be minor categories and subcategories, such as shelter and utilities as subcategories under housing.

For charts or tables organized into several theoretically or empirically similar groups of items, alphabetical order can be a logical way to sequence items within those groups. For example, data on all the nations of the world might be grouped by continents, and then listed alphabetically within each continent. Alphabetizing within conceptual or empirical groupings also works well if several items have the same value of the statistics reported in the table (e.g., mean value or frequency).

Writing a Narrative to Accompany the Table or Chart

Having created a table or chart that presents data in empirical or theoretical order, it is usually helpful to write the narrative to coordinate with that pattern, mentioning the organizing principle as you refer to the associated table or chart. For example, to describe the empirical pattern across categories of consumer expenditures, you might write:

> Figure 3 presents average consumer expenditures for the United States in 2002 in descending order of dollar value. Housing was the highest single highest expenditure category, followed by transportation, food and personal expenditures and pensions...

An analysis that compares necessities and non-necessities could read:

> Figure 4 shows average consumer expenditures for necessities and non-necessities in the U.S. in 2002. Among necessities, shelter was the highest. . . . Among non-necessities, transportation . . .

Organizing Data for Reference Use

Reference documents typically include little if any prose description, so using a familiar convention or standard sequence is a sensible way to help readers find specific information quickly.

Alphabetical Order

Alphabetical order is a widely understood organizing principle, commonly used in a variety of settings. For example, the daily stock market report of opening, closing, high and low prices effectively organizes thousands of numbers in a predictable format that readers can use without guidance.

Order of Items from a Standard Document

Reference data from periodic surveys, censuses or surveillance systems are frequently best organized using the order of items from the original data collection instrument or following a standard coding or reporting scheme for that data source. People wishing to use those data often locate the variables

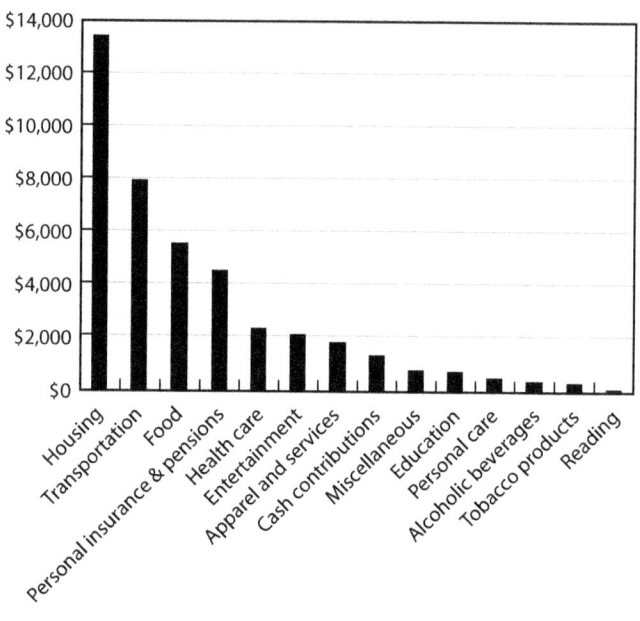

Figure 3 Major categories of expenditures, descending dollar value, 2002 U.S. Consumer Expenditure Survey.

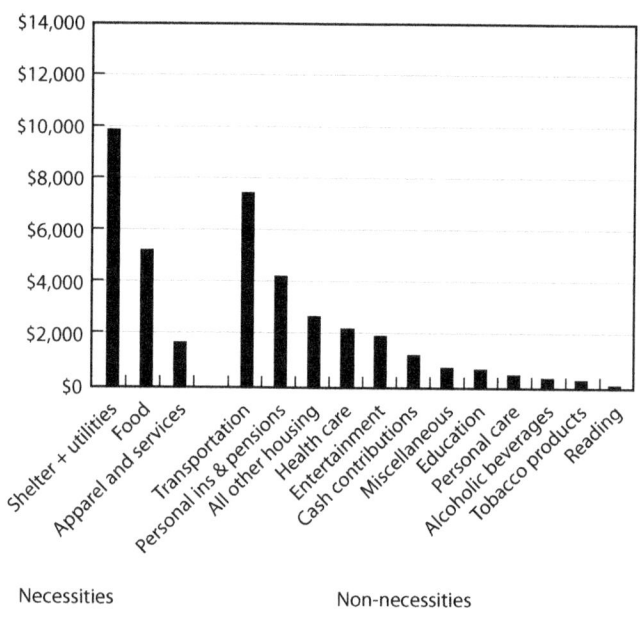

Figure 4 Descending dollar value of expenditures, necessities/non-necessities, 2002 U.S. Consumer Expenditure Survey.

of interest using original documentation such as the code book, survey instrument or census form, or by consulting copies of earlier volumes of the same reference publication. Using that standardized approach to organize tables or charts of reference data facilitates users' collection efforts by maintaining consistency across sources. Table 1 above employs such an approach, presenting the expenditure categories in the standard order used in many BLS reports (U.S. Department of Labor 2004b). Having collected the data of interest to them, users can then organize those numbers to suit to their objectives, whether summarizing trends for a report or testing a hypothesis about relationships among variables.

Summary

Using appropriate organizing principles can significantly enhance the efficacy of a quantitative description or increase the accessibility of reference data. Readers of this article who would like to go further into the issues explored here may find it useful to refer to Miller (2004).

References

Duly, A. (2003). Consumer spending for necessities. *Monthly Labor Review,* **126**(5), 3. Available online at http://stats.bls.gov/opub/mlr/2003/05/art1full.pdf. Accessed June 2007.

Miller, J.E. (2004). *The Chicago Guide to Writing about Numbers.* The Chicago Guide to Writing, Editing, and Publishing. Chicago: University of Chicago Press.

U.S. Bureau of Labor Statistics (2004a). *Consumer Expenditure Survey, Diary Survey Form.* Available online at http://stats.bls.gov/cex/csx801p.pdf. Accessed June 2007.

U.S. Department of Labor, Bureau of Labor Statistics (2004b). *Consumer Expenditures in 2002.* Report 974. Available online at http://stats.bls.gov/cex/csxann02.pdf. Accessed June 2007.

Name: _____ Date: _____

Chapter 2 ■ Organizing Data in Tables and Charts: Different Criteria for Different Tasks

Questions for Discussion

1. In the introduction, Miller discusses the pros and cons of having figures integrated into the narrative of a document, as well as having them exist on their own so that readers can find the numbers they need with little written guidance. Consider each style. Which works better for your particular proposal? Why? Would your reader be able to understand the significance of your charts and graphs without any narrative guidance from you?

2. Many researchers choose to incorporate their charts and graphs directly into their narratives. How can the researcher introduce these text features in a way that provides just enough background information without making the charts and graphs seem superfluous?

3. Does your proposal more frequently discuss ordinal variables or nominal variables?

    a. If your proposal focuses mainly on ordinal variables, sketch out a few ideas for how you might be able to chart or graph this information based on Miller's guidelines on using rows, columns, and axes in clear sequences.

    b. If your proposal focuses mainly on nominal variables, the order in which you present your information may be a little less obvious. Create a plan for how this information could be presented in a way that seems logical and will be easy for the reader to follow.

4. Miller discusses both empirical ordering and theoretical grouping as viable options for creating figures. Look back at Figures 3 and 4 and then list the pros and cons of each technique. As a researcher, which technique do you prefer? Why?

5. Figure 4 is useful in that it presents the information in a way that is organized both theoretically and empirically. Would any of your research be best understood if it was organized in this manner? Using your own research, create a rough draft of a figure that is organized in this way. Then, have a classmate read it to see if it is clear. Discuss the strengths and weaknesses of your figure.

6. In what ways will you be more strategic about the presentation of your research after reading this piece? Will you focus more on simplifying your narratives so that your figures have a chance to shine? Will you better organize your figures so that they are easier to understand without a narrative introduction? Explain.

The Missing Link: The Lack of Citations and Copyright Notices in Multimedia Presentations

Stephanie Huffman

Abstract

Many of the projects and assignments we have our students complete for our classes include a multimedia presentation. Why are we not teaching our students how to cite their sources for these presentations? Writing style (APA, MLA, or Chicago) does not matter. Regardless of whether it is a paper or multimedia presentation students should always cite their sources, otherwise plagiarism is occurring. This is a skill we must teach and demand that our students take responsibility for when completing multimedia presentations. This article covers a brief overview of copyright law, provides helpful resources for students and teachers, and outlines a model that can be used in citing sources in multimedia presentations.

This model goes beyond the producer required credit slide to argue for the inclusion of "in product/text" citations for multimedia presentations.

Keywords: Copyright, Fair Use, Intellectual Property, Multimedia

As part of our course requirements, we offer and encourage students to integrate technology within their assignments. One of the fundamental techniques is the multi-media presentation. We are excited by their use of images, text, video, and audio as a means of expression. Yet, we allow or overlook the fact that often they do not give credit for the use of others' work within the multimedia presentation. We set and demand high standards for our students concerning the papers they submit for evaluation. We would be displeased with, and likely not accept, work that was not formatted or appropriately cited for others' works.

Our students are not alone. As part of our scholarly activity, we present our research at professional conferences and attend sessions for professional development. This is a vital part of sustained professional growth, as well as serving as an avenue for contributing to the overall body of knowledge in academia. In addition, we use multimedia presentations as a guide for our classroom lectures. Yet, the lack of citations and copyright notices is glaring and shocking. We can and must hold ourselves to a higher standard.

Why the Lack of Citations?

First, most do not understand that legally, regardless of the format used for expression or communication, credit must still be given to the authors/designers/photographers, etc., of works that are used as a foundation for professional presentations, classroom lectures, videos, teaching materials, and student work. Yes, we are made allowances under the *Copyright Fair Use Guidelines*, but *Fair Use* does not give us free reign. We must take responsibility. We must do everything within our power to ensure that proper credit is given.

Second, those faculty and students who do understand they should be citing sources do not know how to successfully accomplish this task or to what extent. There are numerous formatting guidelines for research papers and manuscripts (e.g., APA, MLA, Chicago), yet none of these publication manuals provide outlines or guidance in the realm of formatting "in product/text" citations for multimedia presentations. They do provide guidance in citing multimedia sources within a paper or manuscript and format of bibliographic citations listed on the reference page, works cited page, bibliography, etc. Scholars have written numerous articles about the necessity to cite sources when using these new media, the latest being the Code of Best Practices in Fair Use for Media Literacy published in November of 2008 in *Education Week*. "Whenever possible, educators should provide attribution for quoted materials, and of course they should use only what is necessary" (National Council of Teachers of English, 2008, p 11). Section 6.2 of, *The Fair Use Guidelines for Educational Multimedia* (1996), delineates the requirements for attribution and acknowledgments. Specifically, producers only require a credit slide for multimedia presentations. Should we not be doing more than this especially in regards to the text included within the multimedia presentation?

Therefore, the purpose of this article is twofold: 1) to provide some basic background information on intellectual property; and, 2) to share a guide/model for citing sources in a multimedia presentation; thus addressing the two major reasons for the lack of citations.

Intellectual Property

Products developed as a direct result of human activity are intellectual property. These products might include songs, designs, clothing, and inventions. Intellectual property refers to any intangible asset. "Intellectual property establishes how and when a person and society as a whole can benefit and profit from someone's creation" (Waxer & Baum, 2006, p 5). The treatment of tangible property versus intangible ideas can be difficult to understand. Notwithstanding a natural disaster, tangible property passes from owner to heir, unless sold. Intangible property cannot disappear. Property rights extend to the owner's heirs for decades after death. This contentious aspect of intangible property inspires argument and litigation as the law evolves in a constantly changing world.

The origins of intellectual property law are outlined in the United States Constitution, Article 1, Section 8, and Clause 8. "Congress has the power to promote the progress of science and useful arts, by securing for limited time to authors and inventors the exclusive right to their respective writings and discoveries" (Waxer & Baum, 2006, p. 6). There are seven categories of Intellectual Property. Copyright is the one most familiar and applicable to educators. Copyright law protects the expression of an idea but not the underlying idea itself. For example, subject matter is not protected, but the matter in which it is expressed is protected. There are eight main categories of copyrighted works: 1) literary works, 2) musical works, 3) dramatic works, 4) pantomimes and choreographic works, 5) pictorial, graphic, and sculptural works, 6) motion pictures and audiovisual works, 7) sound recordings, and 8) architectural works.

Copyright in most instances is the life of the author plus 70 years. Joint authorship, corporate authorship, old law copyright extensions, and the rights of copyright heirs are a few exceptions that could affect the length of the copyright. For these instances further examination of copyright law is recommended, but for most purposes only a basic understanding is needed. At one time, it was life plus 50 years, but that changed in 1998 when Congress enacted the Sonny Bono Copyright Extension Act (Underwood & Webb, 2006). A work enters public domain once the copyright lapses. The rights of the copyright owner are extended to five broad areas: 1) to reproduce the work, 2) to distribute the work publicly, 3) to make derivative works, 4) to display the work publicly, and to allow public performance of the work.

Fair Use

"Fair use is an essential balance to the wide range of rights that copyright law grants to copyright owners. Remember, even simple quoting can constitute an unlawful reproduction of the original work"

(Crews, 2004, p. 48). By simply citing our sources (giving the author credit and avoiding plagiarism), we are following fair use, although limits do apply. One must weigh four factors to determine if fair use is applied. For fair use to apply, the new work must be transformative, thus meaning the work is transformed into something new or of a new utility. For example, quoted text incorporated into a paper or pieces of mixed media put into a multimedia product for teaching purposes (Underwood & Webb, 2006). The second determining factor is nature. Nature refers to the characteristics of the work. Third, one must consider the amount of usage. Both quantity and quality define the amount of usage. The law does not outline an exact measure (quantity). The final factor is the potential impact on the market for, or value of, the original work; this directly links to the other three factors. The first three factors establish a baseline for the potential impact of the market place for the work. If the amount of the work used will influence the market value of the original work, then it is a copyright violation.

It is important to remember that copyright law is in constant flux, therefore, it is noted that the information previously outlined is a cursory treatment of copyright law and the Fair Use guidelines. It is recommended that every reader familiarize him or herself further with more detail. Listed below are excellent Web resources for information on fair use and copyright guidelines:

- Books, Periodicals, Music and Off-air Recordings http://www.musiclibraryassoc.org/copyright/
- Videotapes and Computer Software http://www.ifla.org/en/publications/the-ifla-position-on-copyright-in-the-digital-environment
- Visual Images, Distance Learning, and Multimedia http://www.uspto.gov/web/offices/dcom/olia/confu/conclu2.html
- Library of Congress: United States Copyright Office http://www.copyright.gov/
- Fair Use Guidelines for Educational Multi-media http://www.adec.edu/admin/papers/fair 10-17.html
- A Proposal for Educational Fair Use Guidelines for Digital Images http://www.utsystem.edu/ogc/intellectual-property/imagguid.htm
- Copyright and Fair Use in the Classroom http://www.umuc.edu/library/copy.shtml
- Copyright and Other Legal Information http://www.libraries.psu.edu/mtss/resources/copyright.html

Extending Accountability

As educational technology leaders we must first hold ourselves accountable for our work and second hold our students accountable for their work. Regardless of the vehicle with which our students or we choose to communicate, we must give respect to the work of others. Knowing the rules that govern copyright is just the beginning. The difficulty begins with explaining the importance of compliance to students who are lackadaisical in following any societal rule (Hoffman, 2001). So, why would they be concerned with copyright law? Extending accountability is essential to academic integrity, professionalism, and ethical behavior. Our expectations for students should be the same, as those we demand of ourselves. Educators need to be leaders, not followers in establishing best practices, holding themselves accountable, and extending that accountability to their students (NCTE, 2008).

As stated earlier the, *Fair Use Guidelines for Educational Multimedia* (1996), producers only require a credit slide for multimedia presentations. We should at least include a credit slide (reference slide) for our multimedia presentations and for those of our students. An argument can be made and should be made for extending accountability beyond this point. When requiring our students to write a paper or when developing a manuscript for publication, accountability is extended beyond the reference page. Within the body of the paper, "in text" citations are required and provide a *link* to copyrighted material listed on the reference page. These "in text-citations" distinguish the work of others from our work. When using photos, images, or figures created by others in a paper or manuscript a caption is required. Multimedia presentations have become extensions or substitutions (in some cases) to the term paper required of our students and for our research and manuscripts.

Why should these fundamental guidelines not be extended to the multimedia presentation? They should be. Otherwise, how are we distinguishing our work from the work of others within the presentation itself? Is plagiarism not occurring? Anyone might be accused of plagiarism if he or she only included a reference page for a paper and did not include in text-citations. As outlined by the, *Publication Manual of the American Psychological Association, 5th Edition*, "psychologists do not claim the words and ideas of another as their own; they give credit where credit is due. Quotation marks should be used to indicate the exact words of another. Each time you paraphrase another author, you will need to credit the source in the text" (American Psychological Association, 2001, p. 349). Ethical principals are imperative in ensuring the integrity of knowledge and to protect the intellectual property rights of others.

Thus, the main thrust for this article, which is to share a model for citing sources in multimedia presentations. The model goes beyond the mere producer requirement of a credit slide to include in-product/text citations, captions for images, figures, audio clips, and video clips, and an appendix slide for documenting free sources. There is a missing link between the content slides and the reference slide in multimedia presentations.

It should be noted that this model is specifically designed for multimedia presentations. It does not lend itself to other forms of multimedia. Although an argument can be made for the creation of models for the other various forms of multimedia. As was done in the past for written forms of communications, the links between the content of the product and the reference page should be included in order to remove all doubt as to the author of the ideas used to generate the product.

Huffman Multimedia Presentation Model for Citing Sources

This model was developed by reviewing the current literature on citing sources, applying the formatting and design principles used in Microsoft PowerPoint, and applying guidelines outlined in the, *Publication Manual of the American Psychological Association (APA)* (Huffman & Rickman, 2008). Unless the information included within the multimedia presentation is one's original work, then the following set of basic components should be included.

1. General Guidelines

    a. "Use only lawfully acquired copyrighted works or self created works" (Simpson, p. 10, 2005).
    b. All pictures, files, or text taken from the Internet must be from a free site, found in public domain, or authorized by a webmaster/author. APA recommends obtaining written permission for reuse (for both print and electronic form) from the copyright holder.
    c. One may not modify scanned images, video clips, or audio clips without permission (Walter, 1998). One must note all alteration in an appendix.
    d. Select a publication style to use as a guide for formatting citations (e.g., APA, MLA, Chicago).

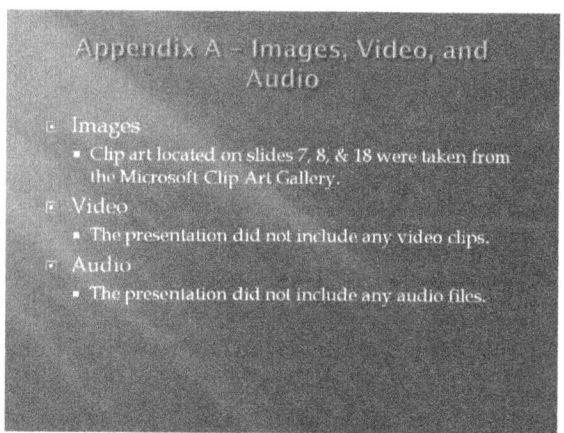

Figure 1 Appendix Slide from the Digital Responsibility presentation delivered by Stephanie Huffman and Wendy Rickman at the Southeast Regional Association of Teacher Educators Annual Conference in November of 2008.

2. Specific Formatting Guidelines
   a. The basic sequence of screens/slides is as follows: 1) title slide, 2) content slides, 3) reference slide, and 4) appendix.
   b. Place a copyright notice on the opening screen or slide (Walters, 1998). For example, "Notice: Certain materials are included under the Fair Use exemptions of U.S. copyright law, and have been prepared according to the Educational Multimedia Fair Use Guidelines and are restricted from further use."
   c. Acknowledge all sources used to create a screen or slide with a bibliographic citation, with an in product/text citation. Follow the rules outlined by the publication manual for specific format. The example demonstrates APA format for the in product/text citation.
   d. Single Column Layout
      i. If only one source is used for that screen or slide, then the citation is placed at the bottom of the slide aligned with the text. Placement of the citation in this location allows for maximum use of space on the screen/slide (see Figure 3).
      ii. If multiple sources are used for the content of the screen/slide, the citation is placed immediately following the text. If the text is directly quoted from the source, it is placed in quotation marks and a page number is included within the citation.
      iii. If the text is original (i.e., one's own thoughts & ideas), then no citation is necessary.

Figure 2 Title Slide from the Digital Responsibility presentation delivered by Stephanie Huffman and Wendy Rickman at the Southeast Regional Association of Teacher Educators Annual Conference in November of 2008.

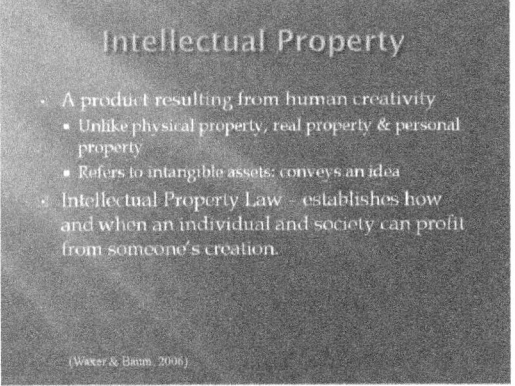

Figure 3 Intellectual Property Slide from the Digital Responsibility presentation delivered by Stephanie Huffman and Wendy Rickman at the Southeast Association of Teacher Educators Annual Conference in November of 2008.

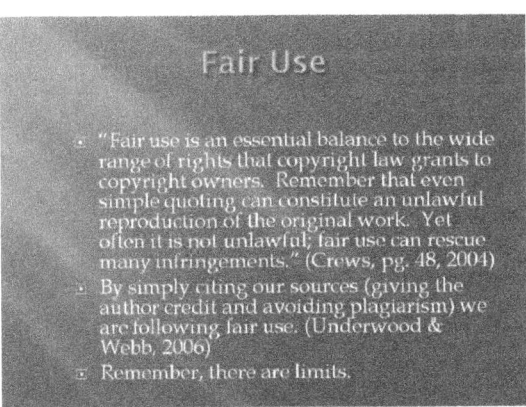

Figure 4 Fair Use Slide from the Digital Responsibility presentation delivered by Stephanie Huffman and Wendy Rickman at the Southeast Association of Teacher Educators Annual Conference in November of 2008.

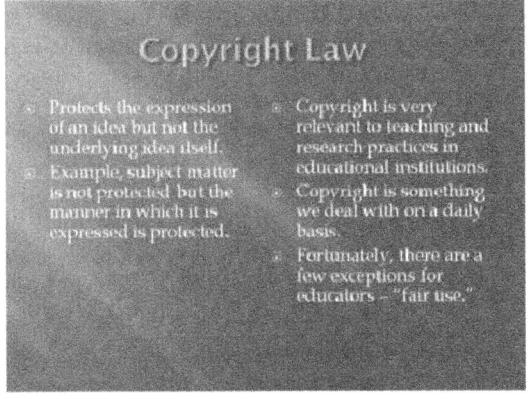

Figure 5 Copyright Law Slide from the Digital Responsibility presentation delivered by Stephanie Huffman and Wendy Rickman at the Southeast Association of Teacher Educators Annual Conference in November of 2008.

e. Multiple Column Screen/Slide Layout
   i. The same rules apply as outlined for single column layout.
   ii. Each column should be treated as a separate unit.
   iii. If only one source is used for the contents of the column, then the citation is placed at the bottom of the column aligned with the text.
   iv. If multiple sources are used for the content of the column, the citation is placed immediately following the text.
   v. If the text is quoted directly from the source, it is placed in quotation marks and a page number is included within the citation.
   vi. If the text is original, no citation is necessary.

f. Images (including tables and illustrations), Video, and Audio
   i. Images
      1. APA requires that a caption be created and that the author and copyright holder be acknowledged. "Any reproduced table (or figure) must be accompanied by a note at the bottom of the reprinted table (or in the figure caption) giving credit to original author and to the copyright holder" (American Psychological Association, 2001, p. 174).
      2. Due to limited space on a slide/screen, modifications to this rule are necessary. A brief caption is included along with an in product/text citation on the slide/screen in which the image appears. A full bibliographic citation is placed on the reference slide.
   ii. Video clips and Audio clips
      1. APA requires an in product/text citation and a full bibliographic citation on the reference page for papers and manuscripts. Because of the nature of multimedia presentations (icons used as placeholders for clips), this rule has been modified.
      2. Since the icon (placeholder for the clip) becomes an image, the same format discussed above should be utilized for giving credit to the author of the clips. A brief caption is included along with an in

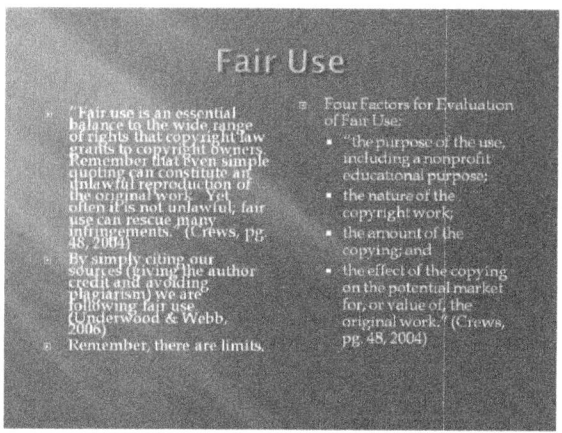

Figure 6 Fair Use Slide from the Digital Responsibility presentation delivered by Stephanie Huffman and Wendy Rickman at the Southeast Association of Teacher Educators Annual Conference in November of 2008.

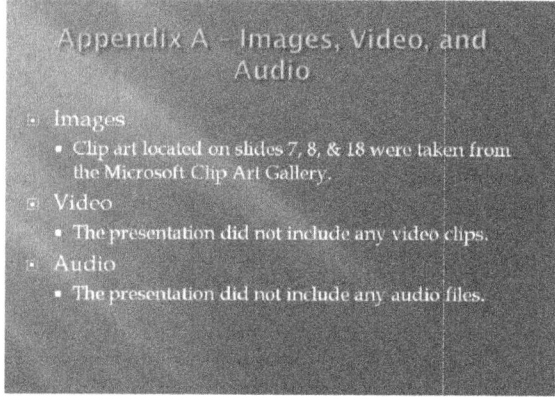

Figure 7 Appendix Slide (Version #2) from the Digital Responsibility presentation delivered by Stephanie Huffman and Wendy Rickman at the Southeast Association of Teacher Educators Annual Conference in November of 2008.

Figure 8 Image Slide from the Digital Responsibility presentation delivered by Stephanie Huffman and Wendy Rickman at the Southeast Association of Teacher Educators Annual Conference in November of 2008.

product/text citation on the slide/screen in which the audio or video appears. A full bibliographic citation is placed on the reference slide.

iii. Any image, video clip, or audio clip that is from a free source should be acknowledged by listing the source(s) in an appendix. This demonstrates a commitment to high ethical standards by documenting all sources. It also provides instructors with a way to check the integrity of the students' work with minimal effort.

iv. Any image, video clip, or audio clip that is not from a free source, should include a caption.

1. Due to space limitation, the caption should only include the title of the work. An abbreviated title can be used for works containing long titles.
2. The caption is place under the image, video icon, or audio icon, and should be aligned with the left most edge of the icon or image. The in product/text citation should be listed under the caption.
3. A caption is not included for any audio clip that plays in the background and/or is part of the time sequencing of the presentation. If taken from a free source, it should be listed in the appendix. If not taken from a free source, a full bibliographic citation should be included with the references.
4. A full bibliographic citation for all images, video, and audio should be included with the references.
    a. The following is an example of a bibliographic citation for both audio and video clips.
    b. For more examples, consult the APA manual.

g. References

i. Include a reference slide, works cited page, or a bibliography slide at the end of the presentation.
ii. For more examples, consult the APA manual.

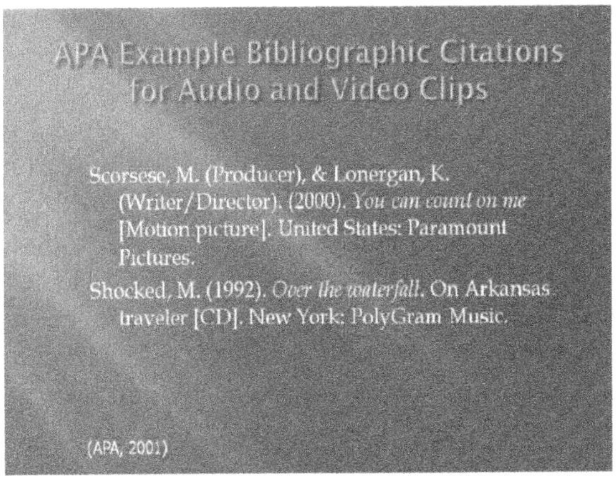

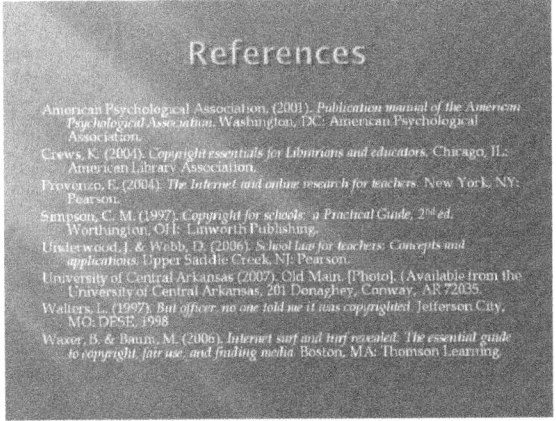

Figure 9 APA Slide from the Digital Responsibility presentation delivered by Stephanie Huffman and Wendy Rickman at the Southeast Association of Teacher Educators Annual Conference in November of 2008.

Figure 10 Reference Slide from the Digital Responsibility presentation delivered by Stephanie Huffman and Wendy Rickman at the Southeast Regional Association of Teacher Educators Annual Conference in November of 2008.

Conclusion

Technology has drastically changed the way in which we share ideas and information. Faculty and students have unparalleled access to all types and forms of information (text, images, sound, and video). This level of access combined with the simplicity in which people can publish their work, presents a new level of complexity to the relevance of copyright law (Provenzo, 2004). In creating multimedia products, faculty and students may use lawfully acquired copyrighted works as long as proper credit and citations are included in the multimedia product. Care should be used in downloading material from Internet sites. Faculty and students should be aware that some copyrighted works have been posted to the Internet without authorization of the copyright holder. Therefore, it is vital that they contact the primary source to get permission to use the material.

The Huffman Multimedia Presentation Model provides a structure for citing sources that goes beyond the producer requirement of a credit slide (outlined in the Fair Use Guidelines for Educational Multimedia). It establishes a set format for "in product/text" citation placement and for the essential components necessary to insure that the Fair Use Guidelines of Copyright Law are being followed. Without structure, links between sources cited on the reference screen/slide and actual content are missing. Whether paraphrasing or quoting an author directly, one must give credit to the source; otherwise, plagiarism is occurring (American Psychological Association, 2001).

Dr. Stephanie Huffman is an Associate Professor of Library Media and Information Technologies at the University of Central Arkansas. She has published research on technology planning and leadership, distance education, and information literacy.

References

American Psychological Association. (2001). Publication manual of the American Psychological Association. Washington, DC: American Psychological Association.

Crews, K. (2004). Copyright essentials for Librarians and educators. Chicago, IL: American Library Association.

Fair use guidelines for educational multimedia. (1996). Consortium of College and University Media Centers. Retrieved from http://www.adec.edu/admin/papers/fair10-17.html.

Hoffman, G. M. (2001). Copyright in cyberspace: questions and answers for librarians. NY: Neal-Schuman.

Huffman, S., & Rickman, W. (2008, November). Digital responsibility: Citing sources in multimedia presentations. Paper presentation for the 55th Annual Conference of the Southeastern Regional Association of Teacher Educators, Myrtle Beach, SC.

National Council of Teachers of English. (2008). Code of best practices in fair use for media literacy. Education Week, 1–20.

Provenzo, E. (2004). The Internet and online research for teachers. New York, NY: Pearson.

Simpson, C. M. (2005). Copyright for schools: a practical guide, 2nd ed. Worthington, OH: Linworth Publishing. Underwood, J. & Webb, D. (2006). School law for teachers: Concepts and applications. Upper Saddle Creek, NJ: Pearson.

University of Central Arkansas (2007). Old Main. [Photo]. (Available from the University of Central Arkansas, 201 Donaghey, Conway, AR 72035.)

Walters, L. (1997). But officer, no one told me it was copyrighted. Jefferson City, MO: DESE, 1998.

Waxer, B. & Baum, M. (2006). Internet surf and turf revealed: The essential guide to copyright, faire use, and finding media. Boston, MA: Thomson Learning.

Name: _____ Date: _____

Chapter 2 ■ The Missing Link: The Lack of Citations and Copyright Notices in Multimedia Presentations

Questions for Discussion

1. List the four characteristics of fair use.

    1.

    2.

    3.

    4.

    a. In what ways will you ensure that the work you do with your sources is transformative?

    b. Based on the requirements of the final proposal, how will you make sure that your use of sources is balanced and fair? How can you make sure that the research you've done is backed by your own analysis in order to reasonably present your own proposal?

2. Have you discovered any models of success (songs, designs, clothing, inventions) in your research that would need to be protected by the intellectual property law? If so, explain how you will be able to employ this paradigm to shape your own plan without violating this law.

3. As you compile a number of sources, how do you plan on holding yourself accountable for making sure that you are using them fairly? How will you regulate using your resources to *guide* your plan rather than fully *dictate* it?

4. Review the section titled "Huffman Multimedia Presentation Model for Citing Sources." Create a list of guidelines that could potentially be problematic for you. Then, jot down ideas for possible solutions to these problems. If you are stuck, reach out to a fellow classmate or your instructor for feedback.

5. Discuss the following terms with a partner or small group:

   a. Intellectual Property

   b. Fair Use

   c. Accountability

   d. Copyright

   e. Plagiarism

   Make sure that everyone is clear about the definitions of each term and how they pertain to the research being done in this class.

6. Are you aware of the penalties associated with plagiarism at your university? Familiarize yourself with your school's academic integrity policies. Be sure to also check the policies of the department that is offering your course. List the guidelines you find for submitting original, research-based papers. Be prepared to discuss this with the class.

The Cover Letter and Résumé

The Assignment

Prepare a cover letter and résumé in response to a specific, published job posting or advertisement. I recommend you use a posting in a newspaper or on the Internet so that you can offer a print copy. You must bring in a copy of the job listing for peer review day and hand it in with your final draft.

Unless your instructor chooses to set forth more specific guidelines, here is the assignment:

- Each document must be one page only (unless your instructor indicates otherwise).
- You must turn in the job announcement with your assignment or it is incomplete.
- These documents should be prepared according to standards discussed in class.
- They should be proofread closely so that there are no errors in either document.
- The assignment and any drafts discussed in class must be turned in according to the schedule set by your instructor. If you fail to turn in the assignment on time or if you fail to have a sufficient draft for peer revision, it will affect your grade for the assignment.

The job advertisement must accompany the other documents on the day of peer review, since without it peers and instructors cannot judge audience expectations. The résumé should be ordered in a way that best responds to the potential employer's needs, and the cover letter should offer significant details distinguishing the candidate and highlighting aspects of the résumé in a way that clearly responds to those needs. Normally, all qualifications, activities, and experiences are listed in reverse chronological order in the résumé. The cover letter should offer a high level of detail and should interpret the résumé for the potential employer.

I am always surprised by the level of error on the résumé, which ought to have absolutely no errors of syntax, grammar, consistency, or sense. Errors in consistency (in spacing, parallel form, layout, and capitalization) are especially prevalent. General sloppiness or failure to adhere to accepted principles (such as using active verbs) will definitely factor into your grade.

Sample Job Descriptions, Cover Letters, and Résumés

Jeremy Scardino

Job Posting: Three-Month Internship (June–August)

Interns for Green Industries will be responsible for the following:

Phase 1:

- Observe operations with regards to client hedge funds
- Sit in on meetings about operational risks associated with alternative assets

Phase 2:

- Support various platforms, including hedge fund seeding
- Check in with clients with regards to their accounts
- Learn from analysts about operational risks

Phase 3:

- Play a small role in meetings with partners about hedge funds and hedge fund service providers
- Conduct research on the hedge fund industry and reporting back to partners
- Analyze financial statements with the aide of a partner
- Present a culminating presentation on hedge fund industry trends

Qualifications:

- Interns should be in a current university business-related degree program and should have completed at least two years of classes
- Interns should live in the Central NJ area, since all duties will be performed from our New Brunswick, NJ office
- Interns should have strong verbal and written communication skills
- Interns should have at least a general knowledge of hedge funds and market analysis
- Interns should be able to keep up with a fast-paced work environment and to meet strict deadlines

Forward all application materials to:

Wesley Green, Esq.
President
Green Industries
123 Main Street
New Brunswick, New Jersey 08902

32 Evans Street
Metuchen, New Jersey 08840

January 27, 2016

Wesley Green, Esq.
President
Green Industries
123 Main Street
New Brunswick, New Jersey 08902

Re: Summer Internship—Green Industries

Dear Mr. Green,

I am highly interested in partaking in the Summer Analyst Program with Green Industries. Thanks to my professional network on LinkedIn, I was fortunate enough to hear about this opportunity from a fellow student of mine at Rutgers Business School, New Brunswick. I believe this program is perfectly tailored to what I'd like to accomplish this Summer: get my foot in the door at a prestigious financial firm and learn the ins and outs of sell side equity research so that I am more qualified when I graduate.

As a rising senior, I believe I possess all the necessary prerequisites to become a valuable asset to Morgan Stanley. Although I have tailored my undergraduate education to learning about financial analysis and the global markets, I think the most important trait I can offer is my deep-rooted interest in finance. Ever since my freshman year of high school, I have been looking forward to working on Wall Street, particularly as a researcher. To better prepare myself, I've minored in Environmental Business Economics in order to reinforce my understanding of the energy and utilities industries, which I would consider my niche industry. Furthermore, I have participated in the Bender Trust Project, which allows Rutgers students to get a taste of equity research by compiling a thorough report and making a presentation to alumni about the assigned industry and company.

Now that I have introduced myself, I hope I have conveyed my interest sufficiently to achieve my goal: to be considered for the Summer Analyst Internship Program at Green Industries. If you have any questions for me, please do not hesitate to call me at (732) 555-1234 or send me an email at 4567@rutgers.edu.

Sincerely,

Jeremy Scardino

Jeremy Scardino
Enclosure

Jeremy Scardino

32 Evans Street | Metuchen, New Jersey 08840
4567@rutgers.edu | (732) 555-1234

EDUCATION:

Rutgers University—Rutgers Business School (New Brunswick)—*Expected May 2017*
- B.S. in Accounting, Minor in Business & Technical Writing
- GPA: 3.2/4.0

HONORS:

Rutgers Undergraduate Research Writing Conference—*March 2015*
- Presented independent research to a panel of faculty, staff, and students.
- Proposed a change in the New Jersey Pinelands Commission's Comprehensive Management Plan.

Distributive Education Clubs of America (DECA)—*September 2011–May 2013*
- Placed 4th out of 200 students in the Accounting Applications Division of the 2012 New Jersey DECA State Finals.
- Received an award for Accounting Knowledge Excellence, 2012 NJ DECA State Career Development Conference.

WORK EXPERIENCE:

Plangere Writing Center—Rutgers University—*September 2014–Present*
Intern / Writing Tutor
- Tutor students (graduate and undergraduate) on advanced research and writing techniques using the Minimalist pedagogy.
- Presented tutoring methodologies to fellow interns at Writing Theory Symposiums.

LEADERSHIP:

Rutgers University Senate—*September 2013–May 2014*
Senator
- Represented the student body of Rutgers Business School—New Brunswick, serving as a liaison between the Senate and the business school's governing council.
- Member of the Instruction, Curricula and Advising Committee, contributing to the negotiation of various proposals affecting the staff, faculty, and students of Rutgers University.

Rutgers Business Governing Association (RBGA)—*September 2013–May 2014*
Assembly Member
- Voted on various requests for sponsorship/funding by student organizations affiliated with Rutgers Business School, and managed RBS apparel sales throughout the semester.
- Participated in the Junior Achievement program of Somerset County, NJ, teaching first-graders about the importance of businesses in our communities.

Robert Celentano

Job Title

Freelance Video Logger

Summary

Soccer Incorporated is seeking individuals in the Tri-State area to assist with the creation of and editing of videos with regards to our soccer program.

Description

Soccer Incorporated is seeking individuals who are willing to take notes on previously recorded video, capture new video, and edit video clips. This is done using our company's video system. You will look for highlights of each game and come up with relevant headlines to post on our social media sites. You will also be responsible for cutting out any video that is not relevant. Although this is your only responsibility, each video should take about 5 hours total, so it is not easy work. Since this is a freelance position, you may work from home most of the time. A few meetings may take place in our NYC headquarters and you will be expected to attend. You must be able to prove a strong Internet connection in order to qualify. Knowledge of Mac and PC is a plus. In order to continue the position, candidates must edit 2-3 videos per week and contribute at least one new post to our social media accounts. While there is a minimum, this position does not have maximum number of hours you can work. Please contact Mr. Michael Smith for more information: Msmith@soccerincorporated.com.

Qualifications

- Previous experience with video editing
- Previous film experience for sports-related videos
- Mac and PC knowledge
- Knowledge of current video-editing software
- Strong Internet connection and reliable computer
- In the Tri-State area & able to visit NYC on certain occasions
- Knowledge of social media such as Facebook, Twitter, etc.

Apply to:

Michael Smith
Human Resources Officer
Soccer Incorporated
230 First Avenue
New York, New York 10018

7 Elm Drive
Edison, New Jersey 08817

January 27, 2016

Michael Smith
Human Resources Officer
Soccer Incorporated
230 First Avenue
New York, New York 10018

Dear Mr. Smith,

I am writing to inform you that I would appreciate being considered for the Freelance Video Logger position that is currently being offered at Soccer Incorporated. It has come to my attention through searching for a position within the organization that I may be a proper fit. I currently write for *SB Nation* and their soccer blog, *Once a Metro*. Prior to being hired as a writer for the site, I started and solely operated my own soccer blog, *Bits and Bulls*. I believe that my past experiences of creating, writing, and operating a site single-handedly, and my present experiences of working in a setting with deadlines, editors, as a part of a well established sports website, will make me an asset to your organization.

Through starting my own soccer blog, I was offered an opportunity to work as a writer for *SB Nation*'s *Once a Metro*, which covers The New York Red Bulls. Aside from writing, I have also helped start a *YouTube* series for *Once a Metro*, created videos, and helped run the site's multiple social media accounts. Being a very active follower of multiple leagues in the world of soccer, I most certainly understand the sport in full. Regarding video content, I have a significant background in video editing, due to my work for *Once a Metro* as well as many videos I've created as a hobby. I have worked with various video editing programs, which I believe will assist me in being accurate and precise in the logging of broadcast files on the web interface. Additionally, I have received my Associates Degree in Computer Science from Raritan Valley Community College, and since then have transferred to Rutgers University where I will receive my Bachelor's Degree in Exercise Science/Sports Management.

I would very much enjoy getting a chance to speak to you more regarding this position and I thank you for your time and consideration. Please feel free to contact me with any questions via email at 1234@rutgers.edu or by phone at (908) 555-4567.

Sincerely,

Robert Celentano

Robert Celentano
Enclosure

Robert M. Celentano
1234@rutgers.edu | (908) 555-4567

Present	**Permanent**
1234 BPO Way	7 Elm Drive
Piscataway, NJ 08854	Edison, NJ 08817

Objective: Seeking to obtain the position of a Freelance Video Logger requiring the ability to accurately log broadcast files within a necessary timeframe.

Education:
Rutgers, The State University of New Jersey—School of Arts and Science
B.A., Exercise Science—Sports Management   May 2017

Raritan Valley Community College
A.S., Computer Science—GPA 3.7—Cum Laude   August 2015

Experience:
Writer—*SB Nation's Once a Metro*   April 2015–Present

- Write articles centralized on the New York Red Bulls
- Work with an editorial staff and meet deadlines
- Film and edit videos to be posted online
- Help run site's social media accounts, including Facebook, Twitter, Instagram, etc.
- DSLR photography for publishing

Writer and Founder - *Bits and Bulls*   February 2015–April 2015

- Built blog from scratch and grew followers purely through social media
- Produced original content for frequent publishing
- Wrote articles, created videos, and recorded audio podcasts concerning Major League Soccer content

Computer Skills:
Software: Microsoft Word, Microsoft PowerPoint, Microsoft Excel, Final Cut Pro, iMovie

Academic Honors:
- Phi Theta Kappa Honor Society Member   2015
- RVCC Galileo Scholar/Scholarship   2015
- President's List   Spring 2015
- Dean's List   Fall 2014

Name: _____ Date: _____

Chapter 3 ■ Cover Letter and Résumé Peer Review Workshop

Please fill out the following form for your partner. Feel free to write comments on the drafts as well.

Does the cover letter . . .
1. directly address the employer? _____ yes _____ no
2. respond to a specific, published job posting? _____ yes _____ no
3. explain why the job candidate is best suited to this job? _____ yes _____ no
4. include a high level of detail concerning the strengths of the job candidate? _____ yes _____ no
5. appear in full block form and include all six elements (return address, date, recipient's address, salutation, body, closing)? _____ yes _____ no

Is the cover letter . . .
1. signed? _____ yes _____ no
2. free of all grammatical and typographical errors? _____ yes _____ no
3. no more than one page in length, in 12 point Times New Roman font with one-inch margins? _____ yes _____ no

Does the résumé . . .
1. catch the attention of the reader? _____ yes _____ no
2. include specific, active language? _____ yes _____ no
3. list and describe relevant work and/or academic experience? _____ yes _____ no
4. list and describe relevant extracurricular interests and/or activities? _____ yes _____ no
5. list all experiences and/or activities in reverse chronological order?" _____ yes _____ no
6. provide appropriate contact information? _____ yes _____ no

Is the résumé . . .
1. visually appealing and appropriately formatted? _____ yes _____ no
2. free of all grammatical and typographical errors? _____ yes _____ no
3. no more than one page in length, in a professional font size and style? _____ yes _____ no

What parts of the drafts did you like the most?

What parts of the drafts need the most improvement?

Additional Comments/Suggestions:

Name: _____ Date: _____

Chapter 3 ■ Cover Letter and Résumé Peer Review Workshop

Please fill out the following form for your partner. Feel free to write comments on the drafts as well.

Does the cover letter . . .
1. directly address the employer? _____ yes _____ no
2. respond to a specific, published job posting? _____ yes _____ no
3. explain why the job candidate is best suited to this job? _____ yes _____ no
4. include a high level of detail concerning the strengths of the job candidate? _____ yes _____ no
5. appear in full block form and include all six elements (return address, date, recipient's address, salutation, body, closing)? _____ yes _____ no

Is the cover letter . . .
1. signed? _____ yes _____ no
2. free of all grammatical and typographical errors? _____ yes _____ no
3. no more than one page in length, in 12 point Times New Roman font with one-inch margins? _____ yes _____ no

Does the résumé . . .
1. catch the attention of the reader? _____ yes _____ no
2. include specific, active language? _____ yes _____ no
3. list and describe relevant work and/or academic experience? _____ yes _____ no
4. list and describe relevant extracurricular interests and/or activities? _____ yes _____ no
5. list all experiences and/or activities in reverse chronological order?" _____ yes _____ no
6. provide appropriate contact information? _____ yes _____ no

Is the résumé . . .
1. visually appealing and appropriately formatted? _____ yes _____ no
2. free of all grammatical and typographical errors? _____ yes _____ no
3. no more than one page in length, in a professional font size and style? _____ yes _____ no

What parts of the drafts did you like the most?

What parts of the drafts need the most improvement?

Additional Comments/Suggestions:

Name: _____ Date: _____

Chapter 3 ■ Cover Letter and Résumé Peer Review Workshop

Please fill out the following form for your partner. Feel free to write comments on the drafts as well.

Does the cover letter . . .
1. directly address the employer? _____ yes _____ no
2. respond to a specific, published job posting? _____ yes _____ no
3. explain why the job candidate is best suited to this job? _____ yes _____ no
4. include a high level of detail concerning the strengths of the job candidate? _____ yes _____ no
5. appear in full block form and include all six elements (return address, date, recipient's address, salutation, body, closing)? _____ yes _____ no

Is the cover letter . . .
1. signed? _____ yes _____ no
2. free of all grammatical and typographical errors? _____ yes _____ no
3. no more than one page in length, in 12 point Times New Roman font with one-inch margins? _____ yes _____ no

Does the résumé . . .
1. catch the attention of the reader? _____ yes _____ no
2. include specific, active language? _____ yes _____ no
3. list and describe relevant work and/or academic experience? _____ yes _____ no
4. list and describe relevant extracurricular interests and/or activities? _____ yes _____ no
5. list all experiences and/or activities in reverse chronological order?" _____ yes _____ no
6. provide appropriate contact information? _____ yes _____ no

Is the résumé . . .
1. visually appealing and appropriately formatted? _____ yes _____ no
2. free of all grammatical and typographical errors? _____ yes _____ no
3. no more than one page in length, in a professional font size and style? _____ yes _____ no

What parts of the drafts did you like the most?

What parts of the drafts need the most improvement?

Additional Comments/Suggestions:

Researching Your Topic

Research work is like any other work students encounter: a little basic knowledge makes the process more efficient. There are basically five things students need to know to be successful doing research for this course:

- When to use **primary** and **secondary** sources.
- How to judge among **scholarly, professional**, and **popular** publications.
- How to research **patrons, problems**, and **paradigms**.
- How to find **books, journal articles**, and other library resources.
- The proper way to cite sources according to **MLA style**.

These five aspects of research are covered in the paragraphs that follow.

Primary and Secondary Sources

How will you show that your topic is important and needs to be addressed? It will not be enough to rely on an emotional appeal or to expect people to take you at your word. Research will be required to demonstrate the nature and extent of the problem in a logical way. Your instructor may require primary research as well as secondary research, but knowing how and when to use them is important.

Primary Research

Primary research, sometimes called fieldwork, is data that you personally collect about the topic. Experiments, surveys, questionnaires, direct observations with note keeping, and interviews are typical examples of primary research. Data you collect in experiments, observations, and surveys can be presented in charts or graphs to quantify the problem. Questionnaires and interviews can be helpful when opinions are important.

Secondary Research

Even if you do collect your own research, you will need other research to interpret your data for others. That is why it is necessary to look at published sources. Secondary research is the term used to describe the search for published information, which you must take at secondhand. The value of secondary sources depends a lot on their credibility.

For your proposal, you might do both primary and secondary research to introduce the problem, but you must do secondary research for the literature review (or paradigm) that helps interpret the problem and explain your solution. Each proposal stands or falls on the quality of its research, and all need a solid foundation of published and authoritative research to support their claims. Without published sources you will be very hard pressed to develop a justification for your plan of action.

Scholarly, Professional, and Popular: Evaluating Secondary Sources

If there is one thing that students should learn in college, it is that not all information is equally valid or credible. When evaluating sources, students need to keep in mind the types of sources they are, since that will greatly affect the power they have to persuade the reader. Three terms are key: scholarly, professional, and popular.

Scholarly Sources

Scholarly sources are articles and research studies published in peer-reviewed journals or books. They show what scholars in a particular discipline are thinking about topics based on their research. In the scholarly journals, you will see that discussions reference accepted concepts and models. These readings can be difficult because the contributors to these journals use specialized vocabulary that someone outside of or fairly new to the discipline may not quickly comprehend. Realizing that these sources are the strongest authorities you will have for your proposal should help you persevere even when the reading is challenging. Scholarly sources are found in college and university libraries. Many journals are now in electronic form and accessible on the Web, but many are still only in print form. When you access your university library, you will see whether articles you need can be downloaded or whether you need to go to the library and photocopy or take notes on the information.

Professional Sources

Newsletters, journals, magazines, and websites that are used by the practitioners of a given profession or discipline are known as professional sources. They include up-to-date information about existing and new products, business applications, and commonplaces of the profession. You might find articles there about successful companies or methods written by respected people working in that field. These sources have some authority and can be excellent places to look for models of success. But because the writers of these publications often do not do research themselves and because they often do not take a critical perspective on their specialty or on companies in their industry (where these writers might be employed), professional sources are not considered quite as authoritative as scholarly sources. These publications can often be found in your university library or through Internet sources.

Popular Sources

Newspapers, magazines, and websites that are readily available to the public and written to a broad audience are generally called popular sources. While they are the easiest sources to find, they have the least value when authority is being established for a proposal that requests funding. Popular sources can, however, supplement the scholarly and professional sources and show how your topic is of general social interest. Many Internet sources would fall under the category of popular.

Based on this brief discussion of the three types of sources, you can see that often the more easily obtained the information is, the less authority it has. The most authoritative sources are generally written for a specialized audience. Recognize the category of the sources you use so you can judge how well they bolster your own authority. Each proposal stands or falls on the quality of its research, and all need a solid foundation of published and authoritative studies, theoretical works, and other documents.

Researching the Patron, Problem, and Paradigm

Often when students begin their research, they see their job as finding out as much as they can about the problem that they want to address. While this can be a good way to start your research, you need to recognize that finding information about the problem is only part of your task. You will also have to do research on funding sources (the patron) and ways of solving the problem (the paradigm). Each part of the project will require different types of research.

Patron

How will you find a funding source? And how will you pitch your project to them? You will have to do research to find the best patron for your project and to learn more about what interests them. Often this research is not directly cited in your paper, but it is among the most important in making your paper realistic.

Even if the organization that will be funding your project is the company you currently work for or the school you attend, you will still want to do some research to find out how your project fits with their mission and values. Look at your company website. Look at what is online about your school or about the specific department in your school you are going to ask for funding. How can you connect your project with the issues and problems that concern them?

If there are no local sources of funding for your project, you will need to do some research to see what organizations (including government agencies, private philanthropies, and corporations) share your interests. Here are three good methods for getting started finding a funding source:

Method 1: Go to the Library

University libraries have a wealth of print sources that can help you find funding. These sources are often more complete than sources you find on the Web, though they might not be as current or quick to browse. Ask the reference librarians for help getting started.

Method 2: Check Out Online Clearinghouses

There are a number of grant clearinghouse websites, where you can quickly access many groups that provide funding for projects. Some good websites to start your search for funding include the following:

The Foundation Center
http://foundationcenter.org/ and http://foundationcenter.org/findfunders/
This is the best clearinghouse for charity and private philanthropy information.

Catalogue of Federal Domestic Assistance
http://www.cfda.gov/
The official government clearinghouse for all types of funds.

Grants.gov
http://www.grants.gov/
A clearinghouse for different granting agencies of the U.S. government.

Community of Science
http://www.cos.com/
A clearinghouse for science-related projects.

National Science Foundation
http://www.nsf.gov/funding/
The NSF sponsors theoretical research in the sciences.

Environmental Protection Agency
http://www.epa.gov/epahome/grants.htm
The EPA sponsors environmental projects.

National Institutes of Health
http://grants1.nih.gov/grants/oer.htm
The NIH sponsors health and health education grants.

U.S. Department of Education
http://www.ed.gov/fund/landing.jhtml
A resource for educational projects.

Method 3: Browse the Web

Since most organizations who might fund your project probably have a website or are listed on the Web, a search engine, such as *Google,* is not a bad initial search tool. Try entering your keywords for your topic, perhaps along with the words "grants" or "funding," and you should at least get some hints about who is interested in your subject area. This method involves a lot of trial and error, and you are better off starting with Method 1 and Method 2. However, when looking for some initial guidance, doing a general Web search should at least give you a better sense of your topic and who is interested in it.

Problem

How can you prove that there is a problem? And how can you emphasize its importance? To make a good case, you will have to do some research on your topic with the goal of finding numbers or of defining your problem well enough to understand its scope.

Before you begin your research on the problem, it's a good idea to think about the specific information that would be useful to your case. Some questions to consider:

- What are the most important numbers needed to convince your patron that this problem is important to address? How can you quantify its scope and scale?
- Can you conduct some of this research yourself, or use research that you have already done? Or will you need to rely on secondary sources of research?
- In order to quantify the problem, what are your best sources of documented evidence? What secondary sources might have information that can help your case?
- Which groups or organizations might have already studied the problem? And where might they publish their findings?

If you can get good numbers, you will be able to make especially powerful visual aids.

When You Can't Find the Numbers You Need

- *Keep trying.* Often, especially with online research, key information is hidden behind the keywords that you haven't tried. For instance, say you are writing a project on making a community service project mandatory at a local high school. You need to find information about teens and community service or volunteering. A search in *Statistical Universe* using the keywords "teens" and "community service" or "volunteerism" will get you nowhere. The perfect graph for your project can only be found under "surveys—opinions and attitudes, by age." Start early and be persistent. Don't do your research when you are pressed for time.

- *Try extrapolating.* Often it is possible to take percentages from national studies and use them to make educated guesses as to how many people will be affected by an issue on a local level. In order for this to work well, your local population must be entirely typical with the rest of the larger area. For instance, if you absolutely can't find rates of smoking for your town, you could use state or local averages and then work out the equation. If 30 percent of people in New Jersey smoke, one might assume that 30 percent of people in Paterson smoke. However, if your local area is different in some significant way from the larger population, you should not rely on extrapolation.

  A town populated by a significant number of young families cannot be compared to a town with several senior citizen retirement villages. If you are reduced to documenting your local problem by extrapolating from national statistics, you must be honest about it and clearly show how you have arrived at the figures you are using.

- *Fill in the gaps with primary research.* Sometimes a problem is so new or so local that there is not a large amount of hard data to draw from. In that case, you will have to do some surveys or other primary research. Make sure that your surveys are legitimate and convincing. Your sample size must be large enough and varied enough to be representative. The fact that twenty of your friends say they dislike Economics 101 is not good evidence that a university should drop the course. As you survey, keep track of what day and time you did the survey, how many people responded, how many of each gender, age, and so on, depending upon the subject of the survey. You should also ask your survey questions in such a way that they will generate good statistical responses. If you conduct your surveys well and present them carefully, they can enhance your credibility. For example, which of the following two statements seems most convincing and why?

  - Fifty percent of the people I surveyed disliked Economics 101.
  - Out of 1,000 students, 50% stated that they ranked Economics 101 (on a scale of 1–10, 1 being the lowest) at 3 or below.

- *Use uncertainty to your advantage.* Sometimes a lack of knowledge is the best evidence you have that a problem exists. Scientists use uncertainty all the time in order to show that more research must be done. If you are writing a research proposal, you should use the lack of statistical information as part of your documentation of the problem. Be sure to discuss the possible dangers or lack of opportunities that result from "not knowing." Perhaps a central part of your project could be to gather data.

Paradigm

How do you support your claim that your plan is the best way to address the problem? A paradigm gives you that support. You should think of it as the research-based rationale for your plan. It authorizes your claims about the problem and justifies your methods.

If you are doing a scientific research project in any given field, your paradigm will derive from previous research. That previous research offers you both examples of practice (what experimental methods did they use?) and a way of understanding the results (how did the experiment support the hypothesis based on previous theory?) Defining your paradigm outside of the hard sciences is not as straightforward, because there is usually not as strong a consensus as there is in the sciences about which methods and theories are best. However, you can still use the model of the sciences to guide you in researching support for your plan.

You need to think of paradigms as ideally having two parts, along the scientific model: a **theoretical frame** and **models of success**. A model of success is an example of how others have successfully addressed the problem in some other context. A theoretical frame is a language for explaining how a certain solution will work.

Searching for a Theoretical Frame

Let's say that you wanted to take on the problem of crime on campus. To find research to justify a plan of action, you would want to find a theoretical frame and search for models of success. Both parts of your paradigm must be developed through the use of scholarly research.

If you were studying sociology or law enforcement, it would be logical for you to take on the problem of campus crime since your previous studies had already prepared you for the issue. You might already have an idea, in fact, of what theoretical frames might relate to the issue. If you don't, then at least you would know where to look to find out. You could talk to professors. You could look in your textbooks (especially in their bibliographies). Ultimately, though, you will need to do some research to see what others have written in journal articles and in books about ways of addressing the problem. That's where you will find your theoretical frame and the language you will need to explain it.

To address the problem of campus crime, you would want to look at what researchers have written in the areas of sociology or law enforcement (the fields that seem most applicable to your problem—though other fields might offer ideas as well). One theory of crime you might encounter in your reading is the "broken windows theory," which suggests that if you address small crimes (such as broken windows) you will be addressing the larger issue because, for one thing, small crimes and big crimes are committed by the same group of offenders.

Searching for Models of Success

If you wanted to address the problem of crime on campus, you would logically look at programs at other schools that helped to reduce crime. You would probably also want to look at towns and cities, since they are also potentially good models. You could look for these models in a number of ways.

- You might look in professional or popular sources, such as college journals or newspapers and magazines, which might have stories about successful crime stopping initiatives.
- You could look on the Web, where schools might have posted information about their programs (especially those that proved successful).
- You might ask experts in law enforcement who they look to for models, and then try to interview people involved with the programs they suggest.
- If you have already begun your theoretical research, you may have come across some examples in scholarly sources that you can then try to find out more about.

Once you found those models of success, you would want to repeat the research process to see what specific information you could turn up about how and why those programs worked. The more information you could turn up the better, since you will need that research to justify your own choices in constructing a plan.

Merging Theory and Practice

To construct a coherent project, you will need to merge theory and practice so that your theoretical frame explains the model of success you are using to justify your plan. A good example of this merging of theory and practice in the case of campus crime would be to use the model of the New York Police Department who made their city the safest in the nation by cracking down on low-level street crime (from petty theft to vandalism), following the logic of the broken windows theory. You could use the NYPD as your model and draw examples of good practice from them and explain them using the language of theory.

White Paper Assignment

A white paper is a document which describes a current problem. Your white paper will help you begin documenting and quantifying an actual problem in anticipation of the midterm letter. In addition, you will have the opportunity to present information in light of the needs of your chosen funding source.

The white paper should help you collate and organize information and test the viability of your topic. Pay close attention to the **scope** of your potential project. This is the time when you should be aware of your ability to fully address the problem identified. Upon further review, if the problem still requires additional narrowing or framing, this is the time to consider the possibilities. Your white paper should be brief (one to two pages) and include a significant amount of **fieldwork**. When drafting your white paper, consider whether a possible proposal does all of the following:

1. **Identifies with people**: Does the writer have a particular reader (or funding source) in mind? Does the writer's approach seem appropriate to the reader's concerns? Should the writer imagine a different reader for the idea or find out more about the reader's concerns? Does the project address the needs of a particular population? Might the interests of the reader differ from those of the population to be served? How so?

2. **Points to a problem**: Does the writer demonstrate a need for this proposal? Has he or she discussed a problem that could be researched and documented? How might the writer find out more about the problem? What sources of information might be helpful? What types of evidence would help illustrate the problem better?

3. **Faces complexity**: Is the idea of sufficient complexity to require a detailed proposal? If not, can you suggest ways to develop the project so that it would be adequately complex? Has the writer considered all the major problems here, or is there something he or she is avoiding?

4. **Suggests lines of research**: Does the topic lend itself to library research (a course requirement)? What other kinds of research should the writer consider? How might the writer support his or her claims about the problem suggested by the proposal?

5. **Positions the work within a paradigm**: Does the writer have a definite approach to the problem or issue? How might the writer position him or herself within a discipline or field of study in approaching the topic? What disciplines might be helpful? What research might the writer pursue in developing the paradigm?

6. **Demonstrates originality**: Is the specific work proposed at least somewhat original? Has this idea been tried before? What could make this idea more innovative? Are there other ways of approaching the problem?

7. **Stays within reach**: Is the proposed idea manageable? In other words, is the scope of the proposed work something that can be done well, given the time frame and resources? Is the student remaining within his/her reach, if not his/her grasp? Is the idea focused enough in terms of population, location, or issue? Is it something that could actually get done? Can you see this student actually taking on such a project now or being able to do so within the next few years?

Follow your instructor's directions about format and use of sources for this assignment.

Sample White Papers

What follows are two sample White Papers for prospective project proposals. The format and content of White Paper Assignment will vary greatly with each instructor's specific requirements. As you work through the proposal writing process in this text, you will follow the progression of these students' projects. In all of your assignments requiring cited research, be sure to follow the current MLA formatting guidelines. Consult your instructor for the most recent standards.

Clustering in the Pine Barrens

Jeremy Scardino
White Paper
February 13, 2016

Due to the stringent laws in place protecting the New Jersey Pine Barrens, property values have soared in the region over the past twenty years. Also in conjunction with the fact that New Jersey boasts the highest property taxes in the country, developers have increasingly sought to build housing developments rather than homes with several acres of land. For several reasons, the Pinelands Commission places restrictions on construction of these developments. One Pine Barrens town in particular, Buena Vista, is currently in the process of finalizing the agreement with the developer IMAJE LLC to build one such development, but has exposed a sort of loophole in the system. The effects that will be incurred if this project passes through the municipal government will endanger the health of the residents, and could cause physical and economic harm to over 2.3 million New Jerseyans.

One of the restrictions in place for all housing developments in the Pine Barrens is the requirement of an undeveloped area allotted for open space. Such housing developments are known as "clusters." Although the development in Buena Vista Township follows all zoning restrictions (it has the required open space), the homes are sprawled out in eight separate areas, and only 11 out of 97 properties will be adjacent to the open space. Some of the open space is not even close to the homes. While this restriction is primarily in place to prevent overdevelopment of the Pinelands, the open spaces also serve as dilution areas for septic systems. There is a clear problem, then, that the dilution areas are not contiguous with the homes. This problem is exacerbated by the hydrological nature of the Pine Barrens. The 16-trillion gallon aquifer that supplies some of the freshest drinking water in North America to millions of New Jerseyans is very shallow, and its soil is less than ideal for dilution. Because of the depth of the aquifer, large pumps cannot be used to extract the water. Therefore city water is not obtainable, which is why nearly all homes in the Pines have onsite wastewater treatment systems (septic tanks) along with individual wells. Bremer and Harter find the following, in terms of these systems:

> These are common in rural and semi-rural areas around the world; in the US, about 25–30% of households are served by a septic (onsite) wastewater treatment system, and many property owners also operate their own domestic well nearby. Site-specific conditions and local groundwater flow are often

ignored when installing septic systems and wells. In areas with small lots (thus high spatial septic system densities), shallow domestic wells are prone to contamination by septic system leachate. (Bremer and Harter 2453)

In addition to the shallowness of the Kirkwood-Cohansey aquifer, the soil composition in the Pine Barrens is also a contributing factor to contamination. The Pine Barrens derives its name from the fact that their soil (known as sugar sand to most residents) is extremely acidic and very low in nutrients, thus bad for agriculture. However, the soil is ideal for retaining water. New York politician and lawyer Matthew Titone explains, "Because the Pine Barrens' soils are highly porous, the region provides an excellent vessel for the storage and distribution of precipitation. Further, the precipitation that enters the system through the soil in the Pine Barrens radiates out to the north, south and east, feeding the entire aquifer and diluting the contaminants that may have entered the system from other sources." Because of the porousness of the soil, it is not very good for the dilution of contaminates. And if the Kirkwood-Cohansey aquifer is contaminated, it would take hundreds of years to cleanse itself. Furthermore, "Although septic tanks may remove a considerable amount of total suspended solids from household wastewater through settling ... septic system designs are based primarily upon soil percolation rates and hydraulic loadings, without consideration being given to the effectiveness of the soil in removing pollutants" (Huang). In layman's terms, the water that these homeowners will be drinking will be pumped out of the ground, which will be contaminated with their septic and everyone else's septic in the residential cluster. The result would be people getting very sick from drinking water contaminated with fecal coliforms (e coli) along with chemicals from their laundry detergents and cleaning products.

It is clear that IMAJE LLC's proposed development project would be serious problem to the buyers of these homes and also to those who live near this development. Since the development follows all zoning restrictions and has allocated the required amount of land to open space use, it is likely to be passed by Buena Vista Township. Over looked is the dangers of well poisoning and the destruction of New Jersey's main supply of water, which is becoming an increasingly expensive commodity. A plan to successfully avert environmental destruction could become the basis for future projects in the Pine Barrens and other fragile ecosystems in the United States.

Works Cited

Bremer, J. E. and Harter, T., "Domestic wells have high probability of pumping septic tank leachate." *Hydrol Earth Syst. Sci.*, 16, 2012, pp. 2453–2467.

Sherlock, Mark, et al. "Physical controls on septic leachate movement." *Hydrological Processes. Wiley InterScience*, 18 Apr. 2002. Web. 18 Feb. 2014

Titone, Matthew. "IN THE MATTER OF LONG ISLAND PINE BARRENS SOCIETY, INC." *Legal Information Institute*, 24 Nov. 1992. Web. 18 Feb. 2014.

Open Textbooks at Rutgers University

Robert Celentano
White Paper
February 13, 2016

    If one takes a look at Rutgers, The State University of New Jersey's New Brunswick 2015–2016 Tuition and Fees for full-time students, they may notice one very important cost left out in the annual spreadsheet: college textbooks. Students across the nation, but in this case Rutgers University students, are in a constant dilemma when it comes to purchasing the textbooks their classes so desperately require. According to College Board, "the average student spends $1,200 per year on textbooks and supplies" in which Rutgers University Senate and their Student Affairs Committee comment are, "as much as 39 percent of tuition and fees at a community college and 14 percent of tuition and fees at a four-year public institution" ("Response to Charge S-1402" 1). With students taking out loans simply to just pay for tuition and housing, textbooks are an area many look at to cut costs. The Government Accountability Office states that, "the cost of textbooks has risen 82 percent from 2002 to 2013" in which Rama Yousef comments, "With costs only going up, more students may decide to forgo buying textbooks altogether" (Yousef 1). Besides their practicality, the price of university textbooks is the issue at hand that needs to be resolved.

    It would be a bit ignorant of me if I were to think that I could solve the nation's problem right from the starting line, changing the prices of all textbooks at every university in the United States. That is why I believe Rutgers, the State University of New Jersey, specifically their New Brunswick campus, is a great stepping-stone for the country's issue at hand. Rather than this appearing as a self-serving project, Rutgers University is the largest, higher education institute in New Jersey. Furthermore, New Jersey is the most densely populated state in all of the country, making Rutgers University a vital institution in the overall process of changing the costs of college textbooks for the nation as a whole. Therefore, the population of Rutgers University New Brunswick will not only benefit from this project first hand, but will directly help benefit the universities across the country, as Rutgers will be a prime example of college textbooks done right.

    Rutgers, The State University of New Jersey would be one of the first institutions in the country to start to use open textbooks. But why would Rutgers University want to switch when they can make deals with publishing companies? "The return on investment figure used in regards to Tacoma Community College was calculated by dividing the total amount of student savings generated by the project by the total amount of money spent by the institution to develop and fund the project" (Senack 19). Senack also points out in his report, that full-time undergraduates would save $1.42 billion dollars a year (5). Therefore, Rutgers New Brunswick enrolls around 38,000 students. If we are to use the value given to us by College Board presented above, an average of $1,200 a year spent on textbooks per student, Rutgers New Brunswick students spend a year on average, $44.4 million on textbooks. If we were to implement the open textbook plan presented below, Rutgers University New Brunswick can start a chain reaction in bringing down the costs of higher education textbooks, keeping students happy by paying a lot less, and keeping themselves happy by allowing them to receive a larger portion of the $44.4 million that typically goes to publishers.

According to Ehtan Senack, "Used book markets, rental programs, and e-textbooks–are often heralded as the solution to high prices, but in reality, they only offer a temporary drop in student spending. One problem with these options is that they are consistently and successfully undermined by traditional publishers...publishers are able to limit the efficacy of these options and maintain their lock on the market" (7). Online textbooks are not the way to save money, they bring problems on their own, as Robert Stone and Lori Baker-Eveleth looked into electronic textbooks and came to the conclusion that, "As with any new technology adoption, its success or failure depends on numerous factors" (Stone 19). Those factors include areas such as ease of use, ease of obtaining, willingness to purchase an e-textbook, etc. Therefore, it is safe to say that e-textbooks are not a step in the right direction in terms of saving students money. "Open textbooks show an incredible return on investment. Where many financial aid programs deliver a dollar of savings for every dollar spent, the "return on investment" with open textbooks is exponential. At Tacoma Community College alone, students savings generated were more than 6 times the amount invested" (Senack 16). The ease of use of open textbooks is tremendous. For example, at the University of Minnesota's Open Textbook Library online (12 schools in network), one is able to view/download/and print all of their textbooks absolutely free.

Open Textbooks "are available free online, they are free to download, and print copies are available at $10-40, or approximately the cost of printing" (Senack 5). This plan will take some time for open textbooks to be completely interwoven into the University, and will begin by offering textbooks solely for introductory courses, eventually working their way up through 400 level classes. The first classes to have open textbooks in them, will be those introductory courses in which have the largest number of students registered for the class. As this of course will take time, Rutgers will then begin to start using the open textbooks, from the open textbook network, in their classrooms. While this is occurring, faculty may begin to contribute in writing as well as peer-reviewing the open textbook library. In our case, every member of the Rutgers University faculty who contributes in either writing textbooks or peer-reviewing them will be compensated. Sabbaticals will be offered based on the number of years at the University. "...The average cost of producing a book has decreased to $120,000 per book" (Hilton and Wiley 4) states John Levi Hilton and David Wiley, a price down from the original cost of $150,000 per book when Flat World Knowledge, at the time the article was written in 2011 an open textbook website, launched. Therefore, if a textbook costs around $120,000 from start to finish, we can determine how Rutgers will receive its return on investment. Using the $10-40 price tag of a printed open textbook from Senack, Rutgers can then take the median price of $25 a textbook, and multiply that by the average amount of students taking a specific course. For example, Expository Writing is a required class for all Rutgers University New Brunswick students to take. At 40,720 at Rutgers N.B., if 15 precent purchased the open textbook in print, the revenue would equal $152,700. This plan allows Rutgers University New Brunswick to not only make its students a lot happier as they pay less and less for textbooks, but allows them to basically, collect a return of investment as if it were a royalty check once the textbooks are created.

Works Cited

Hilton, John Levi, I., II, and David Wiley. "Open Access Textbooks and Financial Sustainability: A Case Study on Flat World Knowledge." *International Review of Research in Open and Distance Learning,* 12.5, 2011, ProQuest. 23 Sept. 2015.

Morris-Babb, Meredith, and Susie Henderson. "An Experiment In Open-Access Textbook Publishing: Changing The World One Textbook At A Time1." *Journal of Scholarly Publishing* 43.2, 2012. 23 Sept. 2015. pp. 148–155.

Rutgers University Senate. *Response to Charge S-1402, (Cost of Textbooks).* Student Affairs Committee, February 2015.

Senack, Ehtan. *Open Textbooks: The Billion-Dollar Solution.* The Student PIRGs, February 2015.

Stone, Robert W., and Lori Baker-Eveleth. "Students' Intentions to Purchase Electronic Textbooks." *Journal of Computing in Higher Education,* 25.1, 2013, pp. 27–47. ProQuest. Web. 20 Sept. 2015.

United States Congress. *Report to Congressional Committees, College Textbooks, Students Have Greater Access to Textbook Information.* U.S. Government Accountability Office. Web. 20 Sept. 2015.

Yousef, Rama. "Textbooks in Need of Reform, College Students Frustrated." *University Wire* Oct 31 2014. *ProQuest.* Web. 20 Sept. 2015.

Finding Books, Journal Articles, and Other Sources at the Library

Today there can never be the excuse that you "couldn't find any research" on something. You will see, in fact, that there is usually too much information on any topic. Just try a search on the Index called *Business Source Premier* at your university library. Enter keywords about your topic and you should find that there is lot of information out there (much of which is accessible online in full-text format). And if you try a search at *Google*, it is likely you will get too many hits to look through in a sitting. You must learn to be selective, have confidence in your ability to analyze what you read, and just simply get to work.

The only way to learn how to use at your university library or its home page is by using it. But if you have trouble getting started, there are tutorials online. Remember the reference librarians can be the best teachers of library skills; the library is their classroom, and you are their students. Show them what you have done; ask them questions; seek their advice whenever you get stuck looking for information. The more specific your question, the better the help you will receive.

If you can't locate a source at your university library, you can order any book or journal article through interlibrary loan, usually very quickly (no more than two weeks). If you start your research early, you should be able to get all the information you need. Be careful, however, to continue your research efforts while awaiting sources you have ordered. The deadline for completing an assignment will not change if your ordered source does not arrive on time or proves less than helpful.

Some Advice on Searching the Internet

You should never rely upon general Internet searching as your main source of information. Internet sources tend to be too simplified and too much driven by self-interest to serve as the basis for your research. You should always seek a wide variety of sources, using books for depth of coverage, peer-reviewed journals for thinking in your field, and periodicals for timely coverage of recent events. The Internet should be only a supplement to these sources. These suggestions are therefore intended to give you some ideas about using the Internet as an assistant rather than a crutch.

- Often web searches can help you most in developing a list of keywords that you can use later in searching through databases and books. Try putting quotes around specific phrases, like "binge drinking" rather than binge AND drinking, since this will help narrow your search to only sources that use those words together. Remember the basics of Boolean logic: use "and" to narrow and "or" to expand categories.

- An increasing number of statistical sources are available online. You can also use *Statistical Abstracts of the United States* and *Statistical Reference Index*, which are available in the reference section of most campus libraries. If you are seeking government statistics, check out "thomas," the government center for information at http://www.thomas.gov/. For New Jersey information, try http://www.state.nj.us/. For census information, go to http://www.census.gov/. If you were looking for statistics on campus crime (as in our example above), you would definitely need to visit the Office of Postsecondary Education's Campus Security Statistics Website at http://ope.ed.gov/security/.

- If you find a good website, see if it contains links to others or lists of references you can find in the library. Often, Web sources are abstracted versions of much better journal articles or books. Go to the original source!

A Brief Guide to Using MLA Style

The following guidelines are not intended to be all-inclusive but merely to help you avoid typical pitfalls in citation. For the purposes of this class, you should use citation style as given by the Modern Language Association. You will need to know MLA style for both in-text citation and your Works Cited page. The following are guidelines based on current MLA recommendations. For more information on the intricacies of MLA citation, consult the *MLA Handbook for Writers of Research Papers* (available in the reference section of all campus libraries). For the latest recommendations on electronic references, go to the frequently updated MLA website at <http://www.mla.org/>. The following examples of format are all based on those sources.

In-Text, Parenthetical Citation

MLA citation format tries to simplify references by eliminating footnotes and replacing them with short parenthetical citations that are elaborated in your Works Cited. The main purpose of in-text citation therefore is to link information in your text with entries on your Works Cited page. For that reason, you need to make the connection between citations and sources clear by using the same primary name in your text as the primary identifying reference in your Works Cited.

Unlike scientific citation formats, which emphasize author and date of publication, MLA emphasizes author and page number. The two pieces of information you should have in a textual reference are the last name of the author and the page number (if the text is paginated). Page references are especially important when you are using a direct or indirect quotation from the text. If you mention the author(s) in your sentence, then it is not essential to put the name(s) into your parenthetical citation. Two examples:

> According to James Q. Wilson and George Kelling, "at the community level, disorder and crime are usually inextricably linked, in a kind of developmental sequence" (33).

> According to the classic study of the "broken windows" phenomenon, disorder leads inevitably to crime (Wilson and Kelling 33)

In parenthetical or in-text citation with up to two authors, you should include both of the names; with three or more authors you should cite the primary author and indicate others with "et al." For example:

One author: (Jordan 98)

Two authors: (Jordan and Slinkoff 98)

Three or more: (Jordan et al. 78)

In-text citations for three or more authors would look like this:

> Jordan et al. found an increased cancer rate in overweight mice (78).

Sometimes page numbers are not available, especially when dealing with electronic sources. In this case, the MLA suggests that you use paragraph numbers for reference, especially when quoting. Otherwise, simply use the author's name in your parenthetical citation. And in the case of quoted material not spoken by the author, be sure to indicate that the line was quoted in (abbreviated "qtd. in") the source you used and was not an original citation. For example:

> The case of Abner Louima is the exception that proves the rule in Siegel's view: " 'the lesson of the 'broken windows' applies to cops as well as to criminals. With 'broken windows' you say, if you allow the small things to get out of hand, the big things will be worse'" (qtd. in Skelley 10). According to Siegel, the 70th precinct commander did not enforce rules vigorously, which allowed disorder and, eventually, criminality among his officers (Skelley).

If the source has no discernable author, then use the title (or the first few words of longer titles, followed by ellipses). And be sure to use the title for reference both parenthetically and in your works cited:

> *Parenthetical citation for unpaginated, non-authored source:*
> Safir's first action was to focus on the seemingly "trivial" crime of jumping subway turnstiles to avoid paying the fare ("Commissioner describes NYPD 'success story'").
>
> *Works Cited listing for unpaginated, non-authored web source:*
> "Commissioner describes NYPD 'success story.'" *Yale Bulletin and Calendar*, 28 Jan. 2000. Web. 3 March 2009.

Non-Accessible Sources

Since the whole purpose of including citations and references is to provide your reader with the means of using the same sources themselves for future research, you should consult with your instructor about which sources you can and cannot use on your Works Cited page. The MLA does offer style formats for citing e-mail messages, postings to a Listserv, and personal interviews. Original research that you have done to find information about your project (for example, survey results that you have gathered) should not be recorded on your Works Cited page, but should be explained clearly in your text.

> A survey of 45 Busch campus students conducted at the Busch Student Center on April 1, 2003, showed an overwhelming number avoided taking Friday classes.
>
> In an interview on January 12, 2003, Robert Spears, the Director of Parking and Transportation for the Rutgers, New Brunswick campus, discussed some of the problems that made additional parking spaces on College Avenue Campus impractical.
>
> In a March 10, 2003 e-mail response to my inquiries, Professor Dowling said that he thought student evaluations "put pressure on faculty to do the popular thing rather than the right thing" and therefore ought to be replaced by another system.

Your Works Cited Page

Your Works Cited page is just that: it reflects the works that you have actually used in your text, not works that you consulted for background information but did not use for reference. According to the latest guidelines, it should be double-spaced consistently throughout, with a hanging indent. You must list your sources in alphabetical order, either by the author's name or the title. If you have two or more sources by the same author, list them in alphabetical order by title and replace the author's name with "---." in the second entry. Do not number your entries on the page—alphabetical order and indentation will separate one entry from the next.

The following examples will give you some idea of format; for more complete information, consult with your instructor or the *MLA Handbook*.

A book:

> Jacobs, Jane. *The Death and Life of Great American Cities*. Random House, 1961.
>
> Wilson, William H. *The City Beautiful Movement*. Johns Hopkins UP, 1989.

A book with two or three authors:

> Wilson, James Q., and Richard Herrnstein. *Crime and Human Nature: The Definitive Study of the Causes of Crime*. Simon and Schuster, 1985.

A book chapter:

> Wilson, James Q., and George Kelling. "Broken windows: The police and neighborhood safety." *Thinking About Crime*, edited by J. Q. Wilson, Vintage, 1985.

Periodicals:

If the periodical is paginated continuously throughout the year, only the volume number is needed. If each issue begins with page 1, include the issue number after the volume number separated by a period. For example, for "volume 17, issue 4," use 17.4.

> Brown, Lawrence, and Wycoff, M.A. "Policing Houston: Reducing Fear and Improving Service." *Crime and Delinquency* 33.1, vol. 33, no. 1, 1987, pp. 71–89.

> Strecher, Victor. "Revising the Histories and Futures of Policing." *Police Forum*, vol. 1, no. 1, 1991, pp. 1–9.

Newspaper:

> Campbell, Geoffrey. "Crime Is Down All Over." *New York Times* 11 October 1997, late ed.: B14+.

Government documents and other reports:

> Federal Bureau of Investigation. *Crime in the United States, 2000*. U.S. Government Printing Office, 2001.

Web references:

Just as with print sources, web sources should be cited in the order of author, title, source. Differences arise because of the impermanence of web sources and the fact that many do not have clear authors or titles on their pages. The impermanence of web sources makes it necessary to add your date of access. In the case where there is no listed author, then use the title as your main listing, and only if there is no author or title should you merely list the source. In any case, be sure to list the actual article or page you are using, not simply the address of the website you accessed first. Do not expect your reader to be able to follow all of the links you followed to find the article.

> "Capitalism." World Book Online. Vers. 3.2.6. Nov. 2008. *World Book.* Web. 3 Dec. 2009.

> Muzzey, Elizabeth H. "Biochemical Reactions in Toddlers." *Journal of Northeastern Medicine* 36, 2001. Web. 17 Apr. 2009.

E-mail:

> Samson, Dolores. Message to the author. 3 May 2009.

> Samson, Dolores. "Re: Customer Service." 3 May 2009. Received by [author name].

Interview:

> Jorge, Eric. Personal interview. 1 May 2009.

> Sansevarius, Buran. Telephone interview. 7 Dec. 2008.

> Vandeen, Harry. Interview with Jon Stewart. *The Daily Show.* Comedy Central, 8 Aug. 2009.

Sample Annotated Bibliographies

An annotated bibliography is simply a preliminary Works Cited page to which notes or "annotations" have been added after each entry. The main information required would be a few sentences summing up what the source says and how it will be useful to your project. You might also want to say whether you will be using the source to quantify the problem or to set up the research paradigm for your project.

Clustering in the Pine Barrens

Jeremy Scardino
Annotated Bibliography
February 20, 2016

Works Cited

Atherholt, T.B., et al. "Coliform Bacteria In New Jersey Domestic Wells: Influence Of Geology, Laboratory, And Method." *Ground Water* vol. 51, no. 4, pp. 562–574. *Science Citation Index*. Web. 23 Feb. 2014.

In this article, Atherholt provides statistics and findings behind the mandatory testing of domestic wells, following the passage of the New Jersey Private Well Testing Act. From 50,800 domestic wells tested, significant data has been found that supports the claim that water pollution in the Pine Barrens is a major concern. According to the study, TC (total coliform) and FC (fecal coliform)/E. Coli was found 3.7 times more in the "unconsolidated strata of the Coastal Plain." In layman's terms, fecal leachate is found much for frequently in the loose sediments of the Pine Barrens than in the bedrock that can be found elsewhere in New Jersey. In addition, detection rates were higher in sedimentary rock (in South Jersey) than in igneous or metamorphic rock (North Jersey).

"Basic Information About Nitrate in Drinking Water." United States Environmental Protection Agency. Web. 22 Feb. 2014.

This webpage by the EPA focuses on nitrate contamination of drinking water. Like sodium, nitrate can come from fertilizer runoff, as well as from septic leakage. The effects of nitrate contamination are primarily focused on infants, and these effects can be deadly. Although uncommon, nitrate contamination in drinking water consumed by infants can lead to blue baby syndrome, a deadly heart disorder.

Bremer, J. E., and Harter, T. "Domestic wells have high probability of pumping septic tank leachate." Hydrol. *Earth Syst. Sci.*, 16, 2012, pp. 2453–2467.

The entry by Bremer and Harter discusses the prevalence of onsite wastewater treatment systems in the United States, along with domestic wells. Common in rural and suburban areas, about 25-30% of American households operate their own wastewater treatment systems (septic tanks), and many of these households also operate their own wells. Unfortunately, conditions that determine how well the septic system will filter throughout the property are ignored when these systems are installed. This is particularly important in the case of the proposed development in Buena Vista, because Bremer and Harter specifically point out the areas with small area lots and shallow domestic wells (which are the only option in the Pinelands) are prone to contamination to septic leachate, which can be very dangerous when these homes also operate their own wells.

"Clustering Gone Bad?" Pine Barrens, New Jersey Pinelands Protection. Web. 24 Feb. 2014.

This article from the New Jersey Pinelands Commission directly outlines the problem with the cluster development in Buena Vista. Although the proposed development follows all regulations as outline by the Commission, this is the first application for development in the Pinelands since the Comprehensive Management Plan was created, and has exposed a loophole in the said regulations. Although clusters are designed to preserve the Pinelands and create a sustainable drinking water environment, the layout of the proposed development will have very negative effects resulting from the placement of the required open space, which is not adjacent to the homes, and in some cases no where near the development. The result will ultimately be contaminated drinking water for those that occupy the homes.

Sherlock, Mark, et al. "Physical controls on septic leachate movement." *Hydrological Processes. Wiley InterScience*, 18 Apr. 2002. Web. 18 Feb. 2014.

Whereas the previous journal article applied to the proposal in terms of the planning of the development, this web article applies to the aspect of the environmental concerns of septic systems in the Pine Barrens. Although no mention is specifically made to the Pine Barrens, the information helps to explain why the Pinelands are less than ideal for soil percolation. The article first describes the functions of a septic system, and how it distributes effluent (liquid waste) into the soil. Although these systems remove a good amount of solids from household wastewater, they are not as good at reducing biochemical oxygen demand and nitrogen that is harmful to the environment. Once again, the article makes mention to how developers of these systems do not take into consideration the effectiveness of the soil in removing pollutants. As we will see in the next source, the Pine Barrens' soil is very ineffective in filtering contaminants, and furthermore exacerbates the distribution of contaminants throughout the Kirkwood-Cohansey aquifer.

"Sodium Chloride in Private Drinking Wells." University of Massachusetts—Amherst Center for Agriculture. United States Environmental Protection Agency, 1 June 2007. Web. 22 Feb. 2014.

While the previous articles have focused on well water contaminants from septic systems, this article focuses on sodium chloride contamination from outside the property and from the well itself. Three aspects relate to the development in Buena Vista: contamination from road salt, fertilizers, and water softeners. The development sits on the edge of a heavily used road in Buena Vista, Weymouth Road. Sodium chloride can contaminate wells from its uses on roads during the winter months. In addition, Buena Vista and the surrounding area is a farming area, which can contribute to contamination from fertilizers. Finally, sodium contamination can come from water softeners, which are present on just about all domestic wells. The effects of this are not as serious as the contamination of well water from coliform, but can cause problems for those on low sodium diets, and more so for infants whose kidneys are not developed enough to handle high levels of sodium (which can result in kidney failure).

Taylor, James. "Evaluating Groundwater Nitrates from On-Lot Septic Systems, a Guidance

Model for Land Planning in Pennsylvania." *Taylor Geo Services.* Web. 22 Feb. 2014.

This article essentially corroborates the Pinelands Commissions' concerns about water contamination in the Buena Vista development, while using examples from cluster developments in Pennsylvania. It also explains the source of and dangers associated with nitrate contamination.

Titone, Matthew. "IN THE MATTER OF LONG ISLAND PINE BARRENS SOCIETY,

INC." *Legal Information Institute,* 24 Nov. 1992. Web. 18 Feb. 2014.

Matthew Titone, a member of the New York State Assembly's 61st District, explains the very real negative effects of water pollution in the Pine Barrens of Long Island. Although across the Hudson River, the ecological state of the Pine Barrens is identical to those in New Jersey. Titone explains how the aquifer under the Pine Barrens serves as an excellent vessel for the storage and distribution of precipitation to the north, south, and east. He explains that the soil in the Pinelands is very permeable, thus not capable of filtering pollutants. Corroborated by several studies, he concludes that if the aquifer were to be contaminated, it would take centuries if not thousands of years for the groundwater to return to acceptable quality. Therefore, if contaminated, the results would essentially be irreversible.

Open Textbooks at Rutgers University

Robert Celentano
Annotated Bibliography
February 20, 2016

Works Cited

Hilton, John, and Carol Laman. "One College's Use Of An Open Psychology Textbook."

Open Learning, vol. 27, no. 3, 2012, pp. 265–272. *Academic Search Premier*. Web. 25

Sept. 2015.

John Hilton and Carol Laman specifically looked at a community college in Houston, Texas and their use of an open textbook in psychology. Hilton and Laman clearly show the advantages to using open textbooks when they say, "First, all students have access to a book, regardless of their ability to pay. Second, all students have access to that book before the first day and throughout the semester…Third, because faculty members are able to make adaptations to the text, they are able to include all of the department-identified key terms and objectives within the text…Fourth, there are inherent advantages to digital texts… Finally, faculty can be selective about which supplemental materials to use and can post them on internal websites or learning management systems" (6). I plan on using the information provided by Hilton and Laman in the paradigm of the assignment, as it shows many of the advantages to using open textbooks, as well as a real-world example of open textbooks in action.

Hilton, John Levi, I.,II, and David Wiley. "Open Access Textbooks and Financial Sustain-

ability: A Case Study on Flat World Knowledge." *International Review of Research in*

Open and Distance Learning, vol. 12, no. 5, 2011. *ProQuest*. Web. 23 Sept. 2015.

John Levi Hilton and David Wiley bring forth the company, "Flat World Knowledge" and their attempt on the open textbook market. For those unfamiliar, "FWK" as it is often abbreviated to, was a publisher who offered people ability to download open textbooks free of charge from their website. Yet since late 2012, three years after launching, the company started charging for its textbooks due to financial issues. The journal article written by Hilton and Wiley dive into the world of open textbooks, using FWK as a source of information, to help shed light on the costs and other aspects concerning open textbooks. "…The average cost of producing a book has decreased to $120,000 per book" (4). I believe Hilton and Wiley's article may be very useful in the plan of my paper, as it gives recent and real world data concerning aspects associated with open textbooks.

Morris-Babb, Meredith, and Susie Henderson. "An Experiment In Open-Access Textbook Publishing: Changing The World One Textbook At A Time." *Journal Of Scholarly Publishing,* vol, 43, no. 2, 2012, pp. 148–155. *Academic Search Premier.* Web. 23 Sept. 2015.

Morris-Babb and Henderson provide a plethora of information regarding open textbooks. Their work provides real world statistics to the table with multiple examples of open textbooks being integrating into current colleges and universities across the country. "At the University of Florida (UF), the provost offered all deans up to $30,000 of seed money for faculty who wanted to write an OA text" (5). Data such as this is paramount to creating a plan regarding open textbooks. I intend to use their data and research in order to help prove that open textbooks can be beneficial for students, Rutgers University, and their faculty. Most likely, I will be using their research in the plan of my paper, but their work is so well done, I can easily see myself using it almost anywhere. Though specifically, the plan, patron, and paradigm are probably the most likely.

Petrides, Lisa, et al. "Open Textbook Adoption And Use: Implications For Teachers And Learners." *Open Learning,* vol. 26, no. 1, 2011, pp. 39–49. *Academic Search Premier.* Web. 25 Sept. 2015.

Lisa Petrides along with the four other authors who contributed in this journal article, take a different look at the world of open textbooks. Rather than strictly looking at the price and the savings they can bring, they look at how open textbooks may provide educational information that quite possibly may be a greater asset to teachers as well as students. At the end of their scholarly journal article, they conclude, "This research has revealed that, while cost savings and ease of use initially attracted both faculty and students to adopt open textbooks and use them to facilitate existing teaching and learning practices, opportunities nonetheless exist for engaging and building upon open textbook use to increase interactivity and enhance teaching and learning for users" (9). This gives another advantage to the open textbook system. Though I am focusing mainly, if not exclusively on the prices of college textbooks, this gives a new outlook and shows that open textbooks have the potential to surpass their traditional counterparts in both price and information. I plan to use this information in either helping persuade the patron or prove in the paradigm, that open textbooks are the correct solution to college textbook prices.

Rutgers University Senate. *Response to Charge S-1402, (Cost of Textbooks).* Student Affairs Committee, February 2015. Web. 20 Sept. 2015.

The Rutgers University Senate report brings forth the issue of the costs of textbooks and possible was in which the school could go about solving that problem. This report brings home the countrywide problem, right down to our local university, presenting the problem in a more narrow focus. The University Senate makes a remarkable statistical point in that "as much as 39 percent of tuition and fees at a community college and 14 percent of tuition and fees at a four-year public institution" (1). This data shows us that textbook prices truly are a problem and are not just statements made from students. It proves to us that a serious issue is at hand that is in need of resolving. Therefore, I plan on using the Senate's report mainly in the problem of the paper. They do a tremendous job in clearly stating that there is something wrong with the costs of textbooks and provide ways in which Rutgers University may be able to solve them, yet do not provide any concrete steps the university has taken.

Senack, Ehtan. *Open Textbooks: The Billion-Dollar Solution.* The Student PIRGs, February

    2015. Web. 20 Sept. 2015.

According to Ethan Senack, open textbooks are the countrywide solution to the major problem of college textbook prices. Senack uses five schools across the country as proof throughout his work, that open textbooks can not only save students money, but also bring in a revenue to the universities that are implementing open textbook systems themselves. Senack shows us that "…a student saves $128 per course, when their traditionally published textbook is replaced with an open textbook" (5), an important figure when calculating the amount of money a student could be saving if he/she were to use open textbooks completely throughout their academic careers. Ethan Senack's work is one of the strongest sources of information out right now in my opinion, and I plan to use his work throughout the paradigm as well as the plan. His data collected will be very valuable in stating why open textbooks are the best option available, over traditional publisher owned print as well as publisher owned e-textbooks. This data will also be very useful in helping construct a plan for Rutgers University New Brunswick, using the strong points made in the report, and weeding out the weak ones.

Stone, Robert W., and Lori Baker-Eveleth. "Students' Intentions to Purchase Electronic

    Textbooks." *Journal of Computing in Higher Education,* vol. 25, no. 1, 2013, pp. 27–47.

    ProQuest. Web. 20 Sept. 2015.

Robert Stone and Lori Baker-Eveleth explore the reasons in which students may possible lean towards purchasing electronic textbooks over traditional print copies. Their work looks to see if students are looking to save money, even if it means sacrificing convenience. Their research shows that e-textbooks are a step in the right direction, but also shows that e-textbook prices really aren't saving students much money at all. This is because e-textbooks are still owned by publishers, rather than being under an open license. According to Stone and Baker-Eveleth, "As with any new technology adoption, its success or failure depends on numerous factors" (19). At the conclusion of their work, they seem to concede a bit in saying that e-textbooks quite possibly could fail, which tells that they are certainly not a completely proven solution. This will be quite useful in the paradigm, as it sheds light on the fact that e-textbooks are not foolproof solutions to the problem at hand.

United States. Congress. *Report to Congressional Committees, College Textbooks, Students Have Greater Access to Textbook Information.* U.S. Government Accountability Office. Web. 20 Sept. 2015.

The report done by the United States Government Accountability Office provides in-depth information on the different ways in which students may access textbook information. They make quite the statement when they say, "Based on GAO's review of a nationally representative sample of schools, an estimated 81 percent provided fall 2012 textbook information online, and stakeholders GAO interviewed said implementation costs were manageable and students have benefited from increased transparency" (2). This shows that online textbook information is not a problem for schools across the nation. If one applies this to the world of open textbooks, one can only assume that implementation and costs would only be less expensive, as it shows many schools already have some form of textbook information presence online plus the fact that open textbooks are cheaper than traditional ones. I plan on using this information in the paradigm in order to show that open textbooks are the correct solution to overall problem, even over traditional e-textbooks.

Yousef, Rama. "Textbooks in Need of Reform, College Students Frustrated." *University Wire*, 31 Oct 2014. *ProQuest.* Web. 20 Sept. 2015.

Rama Yousef's comments on the world of textbooks provide a quick look at the nation's problem at hand. Yousef makes a strong point in saying, "With costs only going up, more students may decide to forgo buying textbooks altogether" (1). This comment sheds light, as well as gives a fresh outlook, on college textbooks, focusing on something other than strictly the price. His article may be the shortest of the works cited in my paper, though it provides quotes as well as comments that are useful in help explaining the overall issue. I plan to use his work as a reference and stepping-stone to other sources such as the Government Accountability Office in the problem.

Name: _____ Date: _____

Chapter 4 ▪ Annotated Bibliography Peer Review Workshop

Please fill out the following form for your partner. Feel free to write comments on the draft as well.

1. Is the document clearly labeled as a list of Works Cited at the top of the page? _____ yes _____ no

2. Does the document contain a minimum of six sources? _____ yes _____ no

3. Are there various types of sources represented (books to develop a theoretical framework, scholarly journals for detailed models, etc.)? _____ yes _____ no

4. Are at least 50 percent of the references cited from scholarly sources? _____ yes _____ no

5. Is the document formatted in proper MLA citation style (alphabetized, indented after first line, publication elements ordered correctly, etc.)? _____ yes _____ no

6. Is the document correctly spaced, in 12 point Times New Roman type, with one-inch margins? _____ yes _____ no

7. Is each entry annotated and detailed in describing how the corresponding source would be useful to the plan? _____ yes _____ no

8. Is each annotation 100–150 words in length, single-spaced, and presented in a clear, readable form? _____ yes _____ no

9. Do the bibliographic entries suggest a theoretical framework for the plan? _____ yes _____ no

10. Do the bibliographic entries include models of success appropriate to the plan? _____ yes _____ no

11. Based upon the entries, is there evidence of a recognizable paradigm (or rationale) for the plan? _____ yes _____ no

12. Is the document free of errors in grammar, usage and/or sentence structure? _____ yes _____ no

What is the one part of the draft you liked the most?

What is the one part of the draft that needs the most improvement?

Additional Comments/Suggestions:

Name: _____ Date: _____

Chapter 4 ■ Annotated Bibliography Peer Review Workshop

Please fill out the following form for your partner. Feel free to write comments on the draft as well.

1. Is the document clearly labeled as a list of Works Cited at the top of the page? _____ yes _____ no
2. Does the document contain a minimum of six sources? _____ yes _____ no
3. Are there various types of sources represented (books to develop a theoretical framework, scholarly journals for detailed models, etc.)? _____ yes _____ no
4. Are at least 50 percent of the references cited from scholarly sources? _____ yes _____ no
5. Is the document formatted in proper MLA citation style (alphabetized, indented after first line, publication elements ordered correctly, etc.)? _____ yes _____ no
6. Is the document correctly spaced, in 12 point Times New Roman type, with one-inch margins? _____ yes _____ no
7. Is each entry annotated and detailed in describing how the corresponding source would be useful to the plan? _____ yes _____ no
8. Is each annotation 100–150 words in length, single-spaced, and presented in a clear, readable form? _____ yes _____ no
9. Do the bibliographic entries suggest a theoretical framework for the plan? _____ yes _____ no
10. Do the bibliographic entries include models of success appropriate to the plan? _____ yes _____ no
11. Based upon the entries, is there evidence of a recognizable paradigm (or rationale) for the plan? _____ yes _____ no
12. Is the document free of errors in grammar, usage and/or sentence structure? _____ yes _____ no

What is the one part of the draft you liked the most?

What is the one part of the draft that needs the most improvement?

Additional Comments/Suggestions:

Name: _____ Date: _____

Chapter 4 ■ Annotated Bibliography Peer Review Workshop

Please fill out the following form for your partner. Feel free to write comments on the draft as well.

1. Is the document clearly labeled as a list of Works Cited at the top of the page? _____ yes _____ no
2. Does the document contain a minimum of six sources? _____ yes _____ no
3. Are there various types of sources represented (books to develop a theoretical framework, scholarly journals for detailed models, etc.)? _____ yes _____ no
4. Are at least 50 percent of the references cited from scholarly sources? _____ yes _____ no
5. Is the document formatted in proper MLA citation style (alphabetized, indented after first line, publication elements ordered correctly, etc.)? _____ yes _____ no
6. Is the document correctly spaced, in 12 point Times New Roman type, with one-inch margins? _____ yes _____ no
7. Is each entry annotated and detailed in describing how the corresponding source would be useful to the plan? _____ yes _____ no
8. Is each annotation 100–150 words in length, single-spaced, and presented in a clear, readable form? _____ yes _____ no
9. Do the bibliographic entries suggest a theoretical framework for the plan? _____ yes _____ no
10. Do the bibliographic entries include models of success appropriate to the plan? _____ yes _____ no
11. Based upon the entries, is there evidence of a recognizable paradigm (or rationale) for the plan? _____ yes _____ no
12. Is the document free of errors in grammar, usage and/or sentence structure? _____ yes _____ no

What is the one part of the draft you liked the most?

What is the one part of the draft that needs the most improvement?

Additional Comments/Suggestions:

The Initial Sales Letter

The Assignment

Write a four- to five-page business letter or memo, single-spaced, not including the list of works cited, that accomplishes the following:

- Represents the initial correspondence to your patron
- Addresses a specific person by name
- Explains a current problem
- Explains at least some of your initial research toward a solution (your paradigm)
- Cites your research clearly (according to MLA Style)
- Gives a sense of your plan of action and associated costs
- Closes with an invitation to your oral presentation
- Appends a list of works cited of at least eight sources, cited in MLA Style (remember, though, that at least ten sources are required for the project proposal)

The initial sales letter should be written as a **letter of persuasion,** and as such it carries the added burden of addressing a particular reader and using some of the means of persuasion available to you for appealing to him or her (with special attention to rational or logical appeals).

Requirements

This assignment will be graded according to how well it does the following:

- Adheres to proper letter or memo format
- Discusses, documents, and quantifies the problem
- Highlights the reader's concerns about that topic
- Cites specific facts and examples from your research
- Briefly proposes a plan and provides a rationale for it

- Convinces your reader to hear more
- Provides a list of works cited in MLA Style
- Is proofread for errors and appearance

Purpose

The initial sales letter serves the following purposes:

- As a draft of the project proposal, it provides you an opportunity to organize your research toward a practical goal and to begin presenting your information clearly.
- As an evaluative tool, it allows you to receive feedback on your work thus far, so you can have a sense of where you stand with your proposal and in the class.
- As an exercise in persuasive writing, it gives you practice in the most valuable form of professional correspondence.

Typical Pitfalls and Problems

Students typically go wrong with this assignment in the following ways:

- They do not address a specific person capable of funding the project.
- They fail to provide evidence of the problem or trend they seek to address.
- They fail to explicitly cite their research.
- They assert things without evidence.
- They fail to attach a list of works cited.
- They use insufficient or inappropriate sources.
- They are poorly proofread for errors and appearance.

Some General Advice, or "14 Steps to a Strong Sales Letter"

You have already gained some practice in writing the letter of persuasion when you wrote the cover letter with your résumé. Here you are also making a sales pitch, but in a much more detailed way. There are fourteen things you will want to consider as you write it. Obviously, each situation should dictate the type of approach you take. Also, these ideas should not limit your creativity. Remember that the audience should always direct your approach. Who will read your letter? What are your reader's concerns and interests? How can you appeal to this reader most powerfully? How can you explain your evidence? The answers to these questions should guide the way you write the sales letter, and they will always vary from situation to situation. What follows, generally speaking, are fourteen essential elements to a persuasive sales letter:

1. **Know your audience.**

    Knowing your audience will require some preliminary primary research, or fieldwork. If you are responding to a specific request for a proposal (commonly called an RFP), then you will know some of what your audience expects. You will usually be addressing someone you do not know very well at all. Find out what you can. What is the corporate culture like at your reader's organization? What is their motto or corporate philosophy? What image do they project in their advertising? What recent endeavors have they undertaken? What problems are they facing? What is their competition up to? Find out about your reader's general interests so that you can know better how they might fit with your idea. What specific benefits can the individual or organization you plan to address gain from solving the problem or responding to the trend you are considering?

2. **Get the right name, and get the name right.**

   Address your letter to a specific person. How many times have you seen a letter that opens, "Dear Sir or Madam"? Does that inspire much interest in you? Not only is a letter addressed to a specific person bound to generate a more positive response, it will more certainly be read—and it will more likely be read by that specific person capable of making a decision on your project. (The success of annoying ads like Publisher's Clearinghouse is due in no small way to the appearance of personal interest: even the most cynical readers are unconsciously and unavoidably flattered by the fact that Publisher's Clearinghouse knows their name.)

   How do you find out the person to whom you should address the letter?

   This is another one of those "legwork" things, but fortunately these days it doesn't require any walking around: usually a simple telephone call or a "visit" to the company website is all you need. This is part of the fieldwork, or primary research, discussed in Chapter Four.

   When in doubt, just ask! Call up the company and ask a receptionist. Talk to a few people—maybe even speak to the person you plan to address (that will give you a better sense of his or her style and will provide a good introduction to your letter). Just ask, and be nice about it. Who would handle the sort of project you have in mind? What department? What person in that department?

   Once you know who you should address, find out how you should address that person. How do you spell his or her name? For purposes of the oral presentation, you will want to know how it is pronounced. Does he or she have a title? Does she prefer Ms., Mrs., or Dr.? Is there a middle initial? A Jr., Sr., or Roman numeral? Find out.

3. **"Dear" is never wrong as an address.**

   "Dear" is the expected mode of address. Though you may have struggled in personal correspondence over whether or not to write "Dear" to your reader, in business correspondence it is simply a standard formality.

4. **Make a strong first impression.**

   How you open your letter will depend upon the specific audience and the specific appeal you want to make. If you know the addressee, you will likely want to remind him or her of that fact and allude to your most recent or most positive interaction. If you don't know the addressee personally, you'll have to be more creative. You can rarely go wrong by trying to open with a confident and definitive statement, and you should open emphatically whenever possible. Point to the problem or need you seek to address, or state the sort of vision you will provide in responding to this need. Get this person to read further.

5. **Show that you identify with your reader's concerns.**

   Explicitly state what you know about your audience's interest in the idea you will propose or the problem you seek to solve. Explain why this person is the most appropriate addressee. Show that you can see things from the reader's perspective, and that you see the proposal as a win-win situation. Your funding source will want to know what is in it for them.

6. **Specify and quantify the problem or need you seek to address.**

   If you can quantify the problem, you can show its magnitude and importance. Alternately, you might give an anecdote or example that helps highlight the importance of this problem to your audience.

7. **Get to the point.**

    There are some cases where you may wish to enigmatically string your reader along before revealing your specific project. Usually, though, readers in business don't have time to read a mystery novel. So don't keep your reader waiting too long for your discussion of how you intend to solve the problem or respond to the recent trend you have identified. If you offer a deal, be up front about it. What are you offering? What do you want in return? Give your reader a forecast of what to expect.

8. **Provide evidence and examples.**

    This is the key to a successful letter for this course. You must cite your research. You must also show that you can use the information you have collected to construct an effective argument for action. You might say that it requires putting information into action. Evidence is always logically persuasive.

9. **Activate your reader's imagination.**

    Invite your reader to engage with your idea, perhaps by using rhetorical questions. Get your reader to participate in your text.

10. **Encourage empathy.**

    Now that you have shown your reader that you see things from his or her perspective, start to turn the tables a bit. Get the reader to identify with your reasons for being involved in this project, and present your reasons in the best light possible. If your ethos is key to your appeal, you may consider highlighting it earlier in your letter.

11. **Close with a call to specific action and further contact.**

    Make sure that the reader sees this as a pressing need, with a deadline for action. For the purposes of your sales letter for the class, you must invite your reader to hear your presentation, listing the specific date, time, and location.

12. **Make contact easy.**

    It is always a good idea to provide a way for your reader to contact you easily, either by phone or e-mail. Don't forget to put that down, usually in the last paragraph—especially if it isn't clearly printed on the stationery you use.

13. **Sign off "Sincerely."**

    Don't get fancy with the closing address, unless it is especially appropriate to offer "Best wishes." Like "Dear" at the outset, "Sincerely" is the standard close.

14. **Follow up and be persistent.**

    Many times you will discover that your letter has languished in the wrong department or that a busy addressee has failed to take any action because the letter has gotten buried under more pressing work. Follow up your letter after a reasonable interval, perhaps with a phone call or another method of contact. Don't give up.

Sample Initial Sales Letters

The sample papers that follow are rather typical of the work that students turn in at this point in the proposal writing process. Generally, they are competent samples. However, in line with the chronology of assignments, they all need to be improved to make them more coherent and turn them into fully developed projects.

Since the Six P's represent the process of writing the proposal, in order, it is not surprising that most initial sales letters do a good job of identifying an appropriate patron to fund the project, defining a population to be served, and trying to understand the problem they want to address, but that they also might be rather vague about their paradigm and the plan. Of course, the price can never be definitive until the plan is sufficiently detailed. Some vagueness is natural, but the better assignments will still suggest a more coherent sense of project and will do more not only to describe a paradigm but also to show how that paradigm informs the plan. Since each element of the plan must be justified by published research, you can't possibly have all of the parts of your plan in place until you have identified and integrated all of your sources. However, in the initial sales letter all of the Six P's must be represented in some way.

The following papers are representative examples of student submissions. They are intended for discussion purposes only and should not necessarily be taken as models of strong work.

Jeremy Scardino
32 Evans Street
Metuchen, New Jersey 08840

March 1, 2016

Rick Bracaliello, Zoning Officer
Buena Vista Township
890 Harding Highway
PO Box 605
Buena, New Jersey 08310

Re: Imaje LLC Development

Dear Mr. Bracaliello,

The development being proposed along 9th Street in Buena Vista, while seemingly a benefit for the community, has serious implications that could result in health risks to the residents of these homes. With research corroborated by the Pinelands Commission, it is clear that the proposed development will cause significant damage to the surrounding area's water supply, which could be overlooked in the face of financial gain.

As a recent graduate of Buena Regional High School, and like many of the residents of the surrounding area, I am concerned about maintaining the fragile ecosystem of the Pine Barrens. I am also happy to see development in the area, which will bring tax revenue to the township and spur economic activity. However, although the proposed development follows all restrictions of the Pinelands Commissions' Comprehensive Management Plan, the construction of this development will not be beneficial to the community nor to the integrity of the Pine Barrens. To explain the problem in detail, it is necessary to first outline Imaje LLC's compliance with the CMP.

Pinelands Commission Compliance

The mission of the Pinelands Commission's Comprehensive Management Plan (CMP) is to "preserve, protect, and enhance the overall ecological values of the Pinelands, including its large forested areas, its essential character, and its potential to recover from disturbance" ("Clustering Gone Bad?"). To promote these criteria, The Pinelands Commission adopted new amendments to the CMP in 2009 to make clustering of such housing developments mandatory. As such, housing developments must allot a certain amount of land to open-space and must be permanently restricted from further development. Ira Mendelsohn's development adheres to these restrictions, but has exposed somewhat of a loophole in the CMP.

Simply by looking at the map of the proposed lots, a problem is identifiable: most of the homes are not near the open-space, and the open-space is not contiguous across the extent of the cluster. Whereas most of the homes are situated on 9th Street, with a smaller subdivision near Jackson Road, much of the deed-restricted land is adjacent to 11th Street. One might ask, "Why does it matter where the land is being protected as long as it is being protected?" Many would agree with this claim, but there are environmental factors have been overlooked. The primary reasoning behind clustering is based off the soil composition in the Pine Barrens.

Soil Composition in the Pine Barrens

As you may know, the Pine Barrens takes its name from the soil, commonly referred to as "sugar sand," that can be found under the layers of pine needles in South Jersey. Due to its acidic nature, very few plants can thrive in this environment and therefore the Pinelands are not optimal for agriculture uses, which is how the term was coined. However, the soil is good for something: holding water. New York politician and attorney Matthew Titone explains, "Because the Pine Barrens' soils are highly porous, the region provides an excellent vessel for the storage and distribution of precipitation" (Titone). The nature of the soil in the Pine Barrens works well in conjunction with the water aquifer that serves New Jersey. But the porous soil that allows for excellent water distribution can exacerbate contamination. Matthew Titone continues with the following:

> Unfortunately, the same characteristics that make the Central Pine Barrens an ideal source of recharge also make it especially vulnerable to the risk of pollution, since its permeable soil is not readily capable of filtering or degrading contaminants. As is indicated by at least one study, once the deep recharge system in this area becomes contaminated, it would take centuries to flush it sufficiently to return it to clean groundwater quality. Thus, as a practical matter, contamination would be irreversible. (Titone)

Although pollutants can come from any number of sources, the issue most prevalent with Imaje LLC's development is contamination from septic systems. There are several types of contaminants that come from septic leachate, but the focus should be directed to fecal coliform (E. coli). In a study performed by Atherholt, it was found that such contamination levels of fecal coliform are significantly higher in the Pine Barrens. According to the study, TC (total coliform) and FC (fecal coliform)/E. Coli was found 3.7 times more in the "unconsolidated strata of the Coastal Plain" (Atherholt). In layman's terms, fecal leachate is found much for frequently in the loose sediments of the Pine Barrens rather than in the bedrock that can be found elsewhere in New Jersey. In addition, detection rates were higher in sedimentary rock (in South Jersey) than in igneous or metamorphic rock (North Jersey). This is the primary reasoning behind the Pinelands Commission's amendment to its Comprehensive Management Plan concerning the clustering of developments, as will now be discussed.

Clustering to Prevent Contamination

I will now refer back to the question I posed earlier: "Why does it matter where the land is being protected as long as it is being protected?" From the standpoint of protecting the Pinelands from development, having the open-space spread out (not contiguous) may actually be beneficial, as it would prevent the further construction of large developments and commercial properties. But this is not the chief concern behind why the Pinelands Commission requires clustering.

As previously discussed, the soil of the Pine Barrens is not effective in removing contaminants from water. Therefore, where on-site septic treatment facilities are being used, the leachate that is dispersed from the septic system can cause more contamination to nearby wells. Knowing this, looking at the plan for Imaje LLC's development can bring about the realization of danger.

Most of the lots in Ira Mendelsohn's proposed development do not even come close to bordering the designated open-space. The main concern is the lack of a sizeable area for the 97 septic systems to dilute. Because on-site septic systems are accompanied by a private well, there is an imminent reality that the residents of these homes will have highly contaminated drinking water. The problem with a lack of dilution area is not new to developers, as this report from Taylor Geo Services explains:

> When lots are clustered into high density subdivisions, nitrates from septic systems, lawn fertilizers or historic land use can concentrate in the shallow groundwater at levels exceeding safe drinking water standards. Once in the groundwater, nitrates are mobile and fairly recalcitrant and tend to persist for long periods of time, sometimes migrating great distances down-gradient from the source. Dilution from infiltrating groundwater recharge is the primary attenuation process for nitrates; so that providing sufficient lot or open space acreage to allow offsetting groundwater recharge for each septic system is essential to maintain water quality. (Taylor)

This report concerns the problems incurred in Pennsylvania, but again the issue is exacerbated by the soil conditions prevalent in the Pine Barrens. The effects of contaminated drinking water will now be discussed, as this is where the problem really manifests itself.

Well Contamination

The two contaminants that are the most dangerous to inhabitants of the proposed development are fecal coliform and nitrate, both of which can leachate from septic systems. First, let's focus on fecal coliform contamination.

Fecal coliform is a type of bacteria that is present in our intestines that helps with digestion. But the specific bacterium that can cause significant physical harm is Escherichia coli (E. coli). Adults who experience E. coli infections usually become very ill, although without medical attention the bacteria is dangerous enough to result in death. In children, E. coli contamination can be much more serious. "In some people, particularly children under 5 years of age and the elderly, the infection can also cause a complication called hemolytic uremic syndrome, in which the red blood cells are destroyed and the kidneys fail ... Blood transfusions and kidney dialysis are often required" ("Basic Information about E. coli O157:H7 in Drinking Water").

Another concern for contamination is nitrates, which are also found in septic systems. Like E. coli, the health effects are serious, but death can be averted with hospitalization. Infants are by far the most susceptible to illness from nitrate contamination. "Infants below six months who drink water containing nitrate in excess of the maximum contaminant level (MCL) could become seriously ill and, if untreated, may die. Symptoms include shortness of breath and blue baby syndrome" ("Basic Information About Nitrate In Drinking Water"). Obviously, both nitrate and fecal contamination are very serious, and should be the main focus when assessing the problem at hand.

Environmental Contamination

In addition to the contamination of private wells used by residents of the proposed developments, due to the ability of the Pine Barrens' soil to transport water (and contaminants along with it), Ira Mendelsohn's development would contribute to further pollution of the Pinelands surrounding Buena Vista. The Pinelands Commission has already assessed the possible contamination of nearby homes and environments for several endangered species. "The 74 conventional septic systems, in theory, will have the benefit of the open space for dilution, but this open space does not surround the homes portion of the development. For the 59 home cluster portion the dilution area is about a half a mile to the north with ground water flow to the south of the development cluster" ("Clustering Gone Bad?"). So even if the open-spaces were contiguous, they are located in the wrong area for the dilution of septic leachate, and therefore do not contribute to diluting contaminants. The homes surrounding the development will also experience water contamination.

Financial Concerns

Now that the hazards have been addressed, if that isn't enough to stop the proposal, I should address the financial backlash that will result from the development. Rather than being shortsighted, the planning board of Buena Vista Township should realize the worst-case scenario: that these health hazards could potentially lead to lawsuits, bankrupting the municipal government. Even if this doesn't happen, the likelihood is high that expensive maintenance to septic systems and individual wells will be necessary. The cost of such repairs could cause homeowners to not be able to afford their mortgages, causing foreclosures. These scenarios are all circumstantial, and therefore the costs cannot be estimated because there is no guarantee that these events will occur. One thing that is going to be required, however, is the existence of a homeowner's association. As the Pinelands Commission explains, "Homeowners will have to belong and pay into a homeowners association responsible for maintaining all the storm water measures and protecting the open space . . . requiring storm water system maintenance, no tree removal, and limiting the accessory uses to each lot" ("Clustering Gone Bad?").

The Solution

To mitigate this problem, Buena Vista Township needs to take action by rejecting Ira Mendelsohn and Imaje LLC's proposal for the development along 9th Street in Buena Vista. In addition, the Township needs to support further amendments to the legislation behind the Pinelands Commission's Comprehensive Management Plan. The planning board may see this as an expense (a loss of potential income), but because the potential liabilities associated with this project are so high, I believe rejecting the proposal would actually prevent the loss of township funds rather than be a cost to the city. If rejected, Ira Mendelsohn will still have the opportunity to construct a development that would not harm its residents, nearby homes, nor the millions of people who consume the water that travels under the Pine Barrens

Before closing, I would like to personally thank you for taking the time to read this letter. I believe the information presented should be of great concern to you. If my letter has done its job, I hope you will consider attending a presentation of this proposal on April 7 at 11:30 AM, at the Rutgers—New Brunswick campus, Murray Hall 105. Please don't hesitate to contact me if you have any concerns or additional questions at (732) 555-1234 or at 4567@rutgers.edu. Once again, I thank you for your concern for the residents of Buena Vista Township and for the sustainable future of the New Jersey Pine Barrens.

Sincerely,

Jeremy Scardino

Jeremy Scardino

Works Cited

Atherholt, T. B., et al. "Coliform Bacteria In New Jersey Domestic Wells: Influence of Geology, Laboratory, And Method." *Ground Water*, vol. 51, no. 4, pp. 562–574. *Science Citation Index*. 23 Feb. 2014.

"Basic Information about E. coli O157:H7 in Drinking Water." *Drinking Water Contaminants*. United States Environmental Protection Agency, 19 June 2013, http://water.epa.gov/drink/contaminants/basicinformation/ecoli.cfm.

"Basic Information About Nitrate in Drinking Water." United States Environmental Protection Agency. 22 Feb. 2014.

Bremer, J. E., and T. Harter. "Domestic wells have high probability of pumping septic tank leachate," Hydrol. *Earth Syst. Sci.*, vol. 16, 2012, pp. 2453–2467.

"Clustering Gone Bad?" *Pine Barrens, New Jersey Pinelands Protection*. 24 Feb. 2014, http://www.pinelandsalliance.org/protection/hotissues/development/clusterbuenavista.

"Human Health." United States Environmental Protection Agency, 1 March 2014, http://water.epa.gov/drink/info/well/health.cfm.

Taylor, James. "Evaluating Groundwater Nitrates from On-Lot Septic Systems, a Guidance Model for Land Planning in Pennsylvania." *Taylor Geo Services*. 22 Feb. 2014, http://www.taylorgeoservices.com/papers/nitratereport.PDF.

Titone, Matthew. "In the Matter of Long Island Pine Barres Society...," Legal Information Institute, 24 Nov. 1992, http://www.law.cornell.edu/nyctap/I92_0227.htm

7 Elm Drive
Edison, New Jersey 08817

March 1, 2016

Chris Scherer
Director
Office of New Program Initiatives and Digital Learning
77 Hamilton Street, Suite 201B
New Brunswick, New Jersey 08901

Re: Implementing an Open Textbook System for Rutgers Students

Dear Mr. Scherer:

The Office of New Program Initiatives and Digital Learning, and more specifically their Creative Works Project, aim at helping create strategies for proposed educational projects in which can better Rutgers University as a whole. I believe an open textbook system is an option as well as the solution to the current day dilemma of college textbook prices in which I feel needs to be considered and addressed for Rutgers University. Open textbooks provide students with faculty written work, in which is free to download online as well as inexpensive to purchase in print. Specifically, the flagship campus of New Brunswick, can be the cornerstone of the revolution behind changing not only how students purchase textbooks, but the way in which they are created. John Hilton and Carol Laman illustrate some of the reasons why open textbooks are beneficial in saying that, "…because faculty members are able to make adaptations to the text, they are able to include all of the department-identified key terms and objectives within the text…faculty can be selective about which supplemental materials to use and can post them on internal websites or learning management systems" (270). Other than strictly their in-class benefits, open textbooks support a strong return on investment for the University while providing students with the least expensive way of purchasing their textbooks. With that said, the price for this system to be implemented at Rutgers University – New Brunswick, in an initial start-up of five introductory courses will be $600,000.

The Issue At Hand

If one takes a look at Rutgers, The State University of New Jersey's New Brunswick 2015-2016 Tuition and Fees for full-time students, they may notice one very important cost left out in the annual spreadsheet: college textbooks. Students across the nation, but in this case Rutgers University students, are in a constant dilemma when it comes to purchasing the textbooks their classes require. According to College Board, "the average student spends $1,200 per year on textbooks and supplies" (qtd. in Student Affairs Committee 1). Rutgers University Senate and their Student Affairs Committee comment on this that, "as much as 39% of tuition and fees at a community college and 14% of tuition and fees at a four-year public institution" (1). With students taking out loans simply to just pay for tuition and housing, textbooks are an area many look at to cut costs. The Government Accountability Office states that, "the cost of textbooks has risen 82 percent from 2002 to 2013" (qtd. in Yousef 1) to which Rama Yousef comments, "With costs only going up, more students may decide to forgo buying textbooks altogether" (1). Besides their practicality, the price of university textbooks is the issue at hand that needs to be resolved.

The Reason Behind Rutgers

It would be a bit ignorant of me if I were to think that I could solve the nation's problem right from the starting line, changing the prices of all textbooks at every university in the United States. That is why Rutgers, the State University of New Jersey, specifically their New Brunswick campus, is a great stepping-stone for the country's issue at hand. Rather than this appearing as a self-serving project, Rutgers University is the largest, higher education institute in New Jersey. Furthermore, New Jersey is the most densely populated state in all of the country, making Rutgers University a vital institution in the overall process of changing the costs of college textbooks for the nation as a whole. Therefore, the population of Rutgers University—New Brunswick will not only benefit from this project first hand, but will directly help benefit the universities across the country, as Rutgers will be a prime example of college textbooks done right.

Rutgers, The State University of New Jersey would be one of the first institutions in the country to start to use open textbooks. But why would Rutgers University want to switch when they can make deals with publishing companies? "The return on investment figure used in regards to Tacoma Community College was calculated by dividing the total amount of student savings generated by the project by the total amount of money spent by the institution to develop and fund the project" (Senack 19). Senack also points out in his report, that full-time undergraduates would save $1.42 billion dollars a year (5). Therefore, Rutgers New Brunswick enrolls around 38,000 students. If we are to use the value given to us by College Board presented above, an average of $1,200 a year spent on textbooks per student, Rutgers New Brunswick students spend a year on average, $44.4 million on textbooks (qtd. in Student Affairs Committee 1). If we were to implement the open textbook plan presented below, Rutgers University - New Brunswick can start a chain reaction in bringing down the costs of higher education textbooks, keeping students happy by paying a lot less, and keeping themselves happy by allowing them to receive a larger portion of the $44.4 million that typically goes to publishers.

The Correct Solution to the Problem

Open textbooks are of course, not the only solution to the issue of college textbook prices; yet, they are the best option. "Used book markets, rental programs, and e-textbooks – are often heralded as the solution to high prices, but in reality, they only offer a temporary drop in student spending. One problem with these options is that they are consistently and successfully undermined by traditional publishers...publishers are able to limit the efficacy of these options and maintain their lock on the market" (Senack 7). Online textbooks are not the way to save money; they bring numerous problems on their own as Robert Stone and Lori Baker-Eveleth, who support the adoption of electronic textbooks, closed their article to say, "As with any new technology adoption, its success or failure depends on numerous factors" (45). Those factors include areas such as ease of use, ease of obtaining, willingness to purchase an e-textbook, etc. Therefore, it is safe to say that e-textbooks are not a step in the right direction in terms of saving students' money. In fact, they are merely just another way for publishers to reach more and more students, while giving the public the idea that "cheaper textbooks" are available to them.

On the other end of the spectrum, open textbooks take the positives from e-textbooks while removing the negative of large publishing companies. What I mean by this is that e-textbooks do have some positive qualities. These include the ability for students to carry all of their textbooks on one device, widespread access for all to obtain, and easy implementation for universities and their faculties. Due to publishing companies however, e-textbooks still carry a heavy price tag. Open textbooks use these positives of e-textbooks to their advantage and by removing publishers from the picture, are able to offer these textbooks online for free.

With this aspect of "free" however, many may wonder how universities are able to make a profit from using an open textbook system. "Open textbooks show an incredible return on investment. Where many financial aid programs deliver a dollar of savings for every dollar spent, the "return on investment" with open textbooks is exponential. At Tacoma Community College alone, students savings generated were more than 6 times the amount invested" (Senack 16). Continuing with this train of thought, Ethan Senack also mentions that, "...potential savings per student when a course is transitioned from a traditional textbook to an open textbook have hovered between $95 - $115...It is worth noting that even at $100 average savings per course, calculations of national impact would still land over $1 billion" (19). From this, one is able to see that college textbooks clearly are not a small market. With that in mind, Rutgers has an opportunity to take part in a larger portion of that market, one in which is traditionally controlled by publishers.

Open textbooks provide students as well as faculty members multiple benefits in and out of the classroom. "...While cost savings and ease of use initially attracted both faculty and students to adopt open textbooks and use them to facilitate existing teaching and learning practices, opportunities nonetheless exist for engaging and building upon open textbook use to increase interactivity and enhance teaching and learning for users" (Petrides 47). This shows us again, that open textbooks have benefits other than just their initial price saving interests. "First, all students have access to a book, regardless of their ability to pay. Second, all students have access to that book before the first day and throughout the semester...there are inherent advantages to digital texts" (Hilton and Laman 270). By allowing students the opportunity to download their textbook free of charge anytime throughout the semester, many problems are avoided. With that, even if students do not own devices capable of downloading these textbooks, open textbooks provide inexpensive print editions as well. Open textbooks are the future, and Rutgers University can make them the present.

We Are Not Alone
The ease of use of open textbooks is tremendous. For example, at the University of Minnesota's Open Textbook Library online, one is able to view/download/and print all of their textbooks absolutely free, without even being a student of their university (*open.umn.edu*). Schools listed on their website in the open textbook network include: The University of Arizona, The Ohio State University, Oregon State University, Purdue University, The University of Oklahoma, and more (*open.umn.edu*). Alongside this network, five colleges/universities have started implementing an open textbook system into their schools: University of Massachusetts, Kansas State University, Tacoma Community College, University of Minnesota, and the University of Maryland (Senack 18). This shows us that Rutgers University is not alone in their implementation and adoption of open textbooks. They will in fact however, be the first higher education institution to do so in New Jersey, one of the most expensive states to live in the country.

Initial Plan

To begin, one must understand what open textbooks are, as well as their benefits of use. To tell you what they are not, they are not textbooks written and therefore owned by publishing companies. They are not expensive for students to buy. Simply, they are not what publishers want. "Open textbooks are faculty-written, peer-reviewed textbooks that are published under an open license – meaning that they are available free online, they are free to download, and print copies are available at $10-40, or approximately the cost of printing...a student saves $128 per course, when their traditionally published textbook is replaced with an open textbook" (Senack 5). In order to begin the implementation of open textbooks, Rutgers University may begin to cut its ties with any publishing deals they have already made. This plan will take some time for open textbooks to be completely interwoven into the University, and should begin by offering textbooks solely for introductory courses, eventually working their way up through 400 level classes. The first classes to have open textbooks in them will be those introductory courses in which have the largest number of students registered for the class. For example, Expository Writing, Introduction to Chemistry, Introduction to Biology, etc. The official five courses will be determined upon these guidelines. As this of course will take time, Rutgers will then begin to start using the open textbooks, from the open textbook network, such as the University of Minnesota's Open Textbook Library presented above, in their classrooms (*open.umn.edu*). While this is occurring, Rutgers faculty may begin to contribute in writing as well as peer-reviewing the open textbook library. In our case, every member of the Rutgers University faculty who contributes in either writing textbooks or peer-reviewing them will be compensated. This is part of where the initial implementation costs are used. "The state of Ohio created challenge grants to award up to $50,000 to authors or author teams to create a textbook for open-access use. At the University of Florida (UF), the provost offered all deans up to $30,000 of seed money for faculty who wanted to write an OA text" (Morris-Babb and Henderson 152).

Rutgers University - New Brunswick can then look to start to receive their return on investment as students start to save money. According to John Levi Hilton and David Wiley, "... The average cost of producing a book has decreased to $120,000 per book" (21). This is a price down from the original cost of $150,000 per book when Flat World Knowledge, at the time the article was written in 2011 an open textbook website, launched. Though, because Flat World Knowledge is a company, rather than a school, its cost of creating open textbooks varies a bit differently. According to Hilton and Wiley, Flat World Knowledge spent on average $20,000 a textbook on simply peer-reviewing (21). This $20,000 per textbook will therefore be what is available for faculty members to earn, divided based on their contributions. So forth, if a textbook costs around $120,000 from start to finish, we can determine how Rutgers will receive its return on investment. Using the $10-40 price tag of a printed open textbook from Senack (5), Rutgers can then take the median price of $25 a textbook and multiply that by the average amount of students taking a specific course. For example, Expository Writing is a required class for all Rutgers University - New Brunswick students to take. There are 40,720 students enrolled there. If every student who went through this class his or her freshman year and purchased the open textbook in print, the revenue would be $1,018,000. Of course, not every student will purchase the print copy, and many will choose to download it for free as they are entitled to. So, if 15% of the students enrolled at Rutgers New Brunswick were to purchase the textbook in print (nearly 6,108 students), the revenue would equal $152,700, a profit of around $32,700. It is to be noted that this is simply just one class, one textbook, and one example of how Rutgers will receive its return on investment.

Again, this process will begin with five select introductory courses (100 level). After the initial implementation of five open textbooks in five introductory classes, Rutgers University - New Brunswick will review the revenue generated by this system. Upon observation that the system deems positive results, Rutgers will continue to build its open textbook library, specifically with introductory courses. In the long run, Rutgers will move on from all 100 level courses, to

200 and so forth. Eventually, classes of higher levels (300/400) will begin to use open textbooks as they become available. This overall, will bring textbook prices down as a whole. The plan illustrated allows Rutgers University - New Brunswick to not only make its students a lot happier as they pay less and less for textbooks, but allows them to basically, collect a return on investment as if it were a royalty check once the textbooks are created.

I would like to thank you for taking the time to review what I have presented today. I encourage you to look over the plan, and see if it fits what Rutgers University is looking for from its Creative Works Project. I am poised to believe that Rutgers University can gain a significant return on investment by working with students, rather than working against them. I would also like to invite you as well as your staff to my oral presentation of this proposal on Tuesday, March 1 at 3:20 p.m., at the Piscataway Campus in Tillett Hall 105. Please feel free to contact me via email at 1234@rutgers.edu or by telephone at (908) 555-4567 anytime before or after the presentation. I greatly appreciate your time and look forward to meeting with you.

Sincerely,

Robert Celentano

Robert Celentano

Works Cited

Hilton, John, and Carol Laman. "One College's Use Of An Open Psychology Textbook." *Open Learning*, vol. 27, no. 3, 2012, pp. 265–272. *Academic Search Premier*. 25 Sept. 2015.

Hilton, John Levi, I., II, and David Wiley. "Open Access Textbooks and Financial Sustainability: A Case Study on Flat World Knowledge." *International Review of Research in Open and Distance Learning*, vol. 12, no. 5, 2011. *ProQuest*. 23 Sept. 2015.

Morris-Babb, Meredith, and Susie Henderson. "An Experiment In Open-Access Textbook Publishing: Changing The World One Textbook At A Time." *Journal of Scholarly Publishing*, vol. 43, no. 2, 2012, pp. 148–155. *Academic Search Premier*. 23 Sept. 2015.

Petrides, Lisa, et al. "Open Textbook Adoption And Use: Implications For Teachers and Learners." *Open Learning*, vol. 26, no. 1, 2011, pp. 39–49. *Academic Search Premier*. 25 Sept. 2015.

Rutgers University Senate. *Response to Charge S-1402, (Cost of Textbooks)*. Student Affairs Committee, February 2015. 20 Sept. 2015.

"Search the Library." *Open Textbook Library*. 04 Oct. 2015.

Senack, Ethan. *Open Textbooks: The Billion-Dollar Solution*. The Student PIRGs, February 2015. 20 Sept. 2015.

Stone, Robert W., and Lori Baker-Eveleth. "Students' Intentions to Purchase Electronic Textbooks." *Journal of Computing in Higher Education*, vol. 25, no. 1, 2013, pp. 27–47. *ProQuest*. 20 Sept. 2015.

United States Congress. *Report to Congressional Committees, College Textbooks, Students Have Greater Access to Textbook Information*, 2013. GAO. U.S. Government Accountability Office. 20 Sept. 2015.

Yousef, Rama. "Textbooks in Need of Reform, College Students Frustrated." *University Wire*, 31 Oct. 2014. *ProQuest*. 20 Sept. 2015.

Name: _____ Date: _____

Chapter 5 ■ Initial Sales Letter Peer Review Workshop

Please fill out the following form for your partner. Feel free to write comments on the draft as well.

Does the document . . .

1. directly address the funding source? _____yes _____no
2. catch the attention of the reader? _____yes _____no
3. discuss why the reader is appropriate? _____yes _____no
4. include specific and descriptive headings to help guide the reader? _____yes _____no
5. express a clear command of population and problem? _____yes _____no
6. adequately *define* and *document* a problem for a specific location and population? _____yes _____no
7. appropriately *quantify* the problem? _____yes _____no
8. argue in a way that would *appeal* to the audience? _____yes _____no
9. refer to specific *evidence*? _____yes _____no
10. offer *examples* and/or *details* from sources? _____yes _____no
11. cite each source in-text according to MLA format? _____yes _____no
12. describe a particular *paradigm*? _____yes _____no
13. offer a researched *rationale* for the plan? _____yes _____no
14. present a plan which follows logically from the *research*? _____yes _____no
15. include the *suggestion* of a budget? _____yes _____no
16. invite the reader to his/her presentation (including date, time, and location)? _____yes _____no
17. include a list of *Works Cited* prepared according to MLA standards with a minimum of eight published sources and at least 50% cited from scholarly work? _____yes _____no
18. appear in full block form and include all six elements (return address, date, recipient's address, salutation, body, closing)? _____yes _____no

Is the document . . .

1. signed? _____yes _____ no

2. free of all grammatical and typographical errors? _____yes _____ no

3. four to five pages in length, not including the Works Cited page(s), in 12 point Times New Roman font with one-inch margins? _____yes _____ no

What parts of the draft do you like the most?

What parts of the draft need the most improvement?

Additional Comments/Suggestions:

Name: _____ Date: _____

Chapter 5 ■ Initial Sales Letter Peer Review Workshop

Please fill out the following form for your partner. Feel free to write comments on the draft as well.

Does the document . . .

1. directly address the funding source? _____yes _____no
2. catch the attention of the reader? _____yes _____no
3. discuss why the reader is appropriate? _____yes _____no
4. include specific and descriptive headings to help guide the reader? _____yes _____no
5. express a clear command of population and problem? _____yes _____no
6. adequately *define* and *document* a problem for a specific location and population? _____yes _____no
7. appropriately *quantify* the problem? _____yes _____no
8. argue in a way that would *appeal* to the audience? _____yes _____no
9. refer to specific *evidence*? _____yes _____no
10. offer *examples* and/or *details* from sources? _____yes _____no
11. cite each source in-text according to MLA format? _____yes _____no
12. describe a particular *paradigm*? _____yes _____no
13. offer a researched *rationale* for the plan? _____yes _____no
14. present a plan which follows logically from the *research*? _____yes _____no
15. include the *suggestion* of a budget? _____yes _____no
16. invite the reader to his/her presentation (including date, time, and location)? _____yes _____no
17. include a list of *Works Cited* prepared according to MLA standards with a minimum of eight published sources and at least 50% cited from scholarly work? _____yes _____no
18. appear in full block form and include all six elements (return address, date, recipient's address, salutation, body, closing)? _____yes _____no

Is the document...

1. signed? _____yes _____ no

2. free of all grammatical and typographical errors? _____yes _____ no

3. four to five pages in length, not including the Works Cited page(s), in 12 point Times New Roman font with one-inch margins? _____yes _____ no

What parts of the draft do you like the most?

What parts of the draft need the most improvement?

Additional Comments/Suggestions:

Name: _____ Date: _____

Chapter 5 ■ Initial Sales Letter Peer Review Workshop

Please fill out the following form for your partner. Feel free to write comments on the draft as well.

Does the document . . .

1. directly address the funding source? _____yes _____no
2. catch the attention of the reader? _____yes _____no
3. discuss why the reader is appropriate? _____yes _____no
4. include specific and descriptive headings to help guide the reader? _____yes _____no
5. express a clear command of population and problem? _____yes _____no
6. adequately *define* and *document* a problem for a specific location and population? _____yes _____no
7. appropriately *quantify* the problem? _____yes _____no
8. argue in a way that would *appeal* to the audience? _____yes _____no
9. refer to specific *evidence*? _____yes _____no
10. offer *examples* and/or *details* from sources? _____yes _____no
11. cite each source in-text according to MLA format? _____yes _____no
12. describe a particular *paradigm*? _____yes _____no
13. offer a researched *rationale* for the plan? _____yes _____no
14. present a plan which follows logically from the *research*? _____yes _____no
15. include the *suggestion* of a budget? _____yes _____no
16. invite the reader to his/her presentation (including date, time, and location)? _____yes _____no
17. include a list of *Works Cited* prepared according to MLA standards with a minimum of eight published sources and at least 50% cited from scholarly work? _____yes _____no
18. appear in full block form and include all six elements (return address, date, recipient's address, salutation, body, closing)? _____yes _____no

Is the document . . .

1. signed? _____yes _____ no

2. free of all grammatical and typographical errors? _____yes _____ no

3. four to five pages in length, not including the Works Cited page(s), in 12 point Times New Roman font with one-inch margins? _____yes _____ no

What parts of the draft do you like the most?

What parts of the draft need the most improvement?

Additional Comments/Suggestions:

The Oral Presentation

Chapter 6

The Assignment

The oral presentation is a ten- to fifteen-minute spoken proposal addressed to your patron (i.e., the person or people who might fund your idea). The ten- to fifteen-minute parameter does not include time spent setting up and breaking down the materials. This limit also does not include the time required for questions from the audience. This is a formal presentation, and you must use visual aids to help convey information clearly and effectively. The point of the presentation is to make a leadership statement for a specific audience that puts information into action by proposing a research-justified solution to a well-defined problem.

The oral presentation is both a useful step in the process of developing your project and a unique assignment for which you will receive a grade. It therefore serves two, sometimes competing, purposes:

- As an "oral draft" of the proposal project, it's an opportunity to rehearse your audience-awareness, to organize your research, to develop your plan, and to get feedback from the class and the instructor on how to improve your project. A significant amount of your grade will be based on how well you have researched your topic and how well prepared you are to put together the project proposal.

- As an exercise in public speaking, it's a chance to practice the arts of oral persuasion. Part of your grade will be based on how well you perform as a speaker.

While instructors will generally focus their grades and their remarks on the strength of your content, offering advice on revision, they will also take notice of your form and poise. Usually, those students who have the strongest content do best overall.

The basic parts of the presentation are laid out in the sections that follow. I suggest that you carefully read over the advice offered here, especially if this is the first time you have ever spoken before a group.

The Basic Parts of the Presentation

Every presentation will have to take its own form, based on the situation and the topic. If you are addressing a potentially resistant audience, for example, you may have to begin by winning them over or addressing possible objections they might have to your idea. Therefore, you should recognize that you cannot always adhere to a single form for the talk, and the outline below may have to be adapted to your particular needs.

As part of the drafting process of your proposal, the oral presentation gives you a chance to firm up your project and work out all of the parts. You should therefore keep in mind the Six P's of the project proposal: patron, population, problem, paradigm, plan, and price. Each of the Six P's should be represented in your presentation. Your talk should suggest the basic form of the project proposal and should do these nine basic things:

1. Announce your topic with a "title slide," which should display your name and the title of your talk. This corresponds to your title page in your proposal.
2. Begin by addressing your specific audience, explaining why they should be interested in your project. This corresponds to the letter of transmittal in the project proposal, where you address the Patron.
3. Give your audience some sense of how you'll proceed, perhaps with an outline, or presentation agenda. This corresponds to the table of contents in the project proposal. This could be presented on a slide, in a handout, or both.
4. Define the problem and try to quantify it in some way. This corresponds to your introduction section of the project proposal, where you will generally lay out the Problem.
5. Present your research, being sure to cite sources in the proper format. This will correspond to the research or literature review section of the project proposal, which is where you develop your Paradigm.
6. Describe your plan of action. This corresponds to your plan or procedures section, where you set forth the Plan.
7. Tell us about your budget and explain the Price.
8. Close with a call to action, which might correspond to your discussion section of the project proposal.
9. Along the way, be sure to use visual graphic aids, just as you will in your project proposal.

The two main differences, then, between the oral presentation and the project proposal is (1) that the oral is spoken and (2) that it is missing a list of works cited. You must, however, cite any published material used in your presentation.

How to Prepare

As with all assignments, you will have to prepare in the ways that have worked for you in the past. But here is some advice if you don't know where to start:

- **Research your imagined audience.** Who do you imagine might come to your talk? What is their degree of prestige and power? What level of knowledge or technical sophistication do they possess? What are their names? Many people like to begin their talk by welcoming the people in the imagined audience and thanking some of them by name for coming. This could appear on the title slide, as well. The more specifically you can imagine your audience the better your talk will be.

- **Plan ahead.** You can't wait until the last minute to prepare for a talk, and the sooner you start the better. The most important things to work on ahead of time are your visual aids, especially any visual graphic aids you want to use, such as PowerPoint slides, video, and/or audio. The sooner you begin putting your materials in order, the more secure you will feel about the presentation itself.

- **Focus your talk around key points or examples.** Remember that you can't cover everything in your talk, but you will be able to cover the major points of your argument and the chief examples that support you (which you should be able to discuss in detail). If you can establish these points on paper, you will be able to focus your work.

- **Prepare an outline.** You will definitely want to prepare an outline for yourself, and you likely will want to provide your audience with an outline as well so they can follow you more easily. As you outline, pay attention to the logic and flow of your talk.

- **Develop solid visual graphic aids.** Remember one rule of thumb: if it can be represented visually, then it should be. You should have at least three visual graphic aids (visual representations of numerical information), but if your talk will cover technical information or you will be referencing numerical information you may need to use more than that. These should be effective and useful to your talk.

- **You might prepare notecards for details.** You shouldn't read your talk, but you may need to write some things down for reference. You may want to use notecards to remember numbers, names, and key details you want to cover. Number your notecards so you can keep them in order, and try to key them to your outline for easy use.

- **Know your information and examples so you can talk about them freely.** One of the best ways to prepare for the talk is just to read over your research so that you know your topic well. If you can talk about your key examples off the cuff, then you will do fine. This skill will prove to be vital in the question-and-answer part of the presentation.

- **Rehearse the talk out loud.** The key to preparing any fine performance is a dress rehearsal. Practice in front of the mirror or, better, in front of a friend. Time your talk to make sure it will not run over 15 minutes (you will be surprised how easy that is to do), and so you have a better sense of time management. If you are especially nervous about speaking in a classroom, rehearse your talk in an actual classroom.

- **Get some sleep the night before.** A good night's sleep may be the best preparation for any situation where you will be the center of attention.

- **Double-check everything.** Make a checklist for yourself. Are your slides in order? Do you have your notecards? Make sure you have everything covered. Arrive early to test and set up any equipment you plan to use.

- **Back up all software.** You can't afford delays due to fumbling with technology. Most likely, you won't get an opportunity to reschedule your presentation.

The Question of Delivery

Delivery is all about ethos. Do we believe you? Do you impress us? Do you know what you are talking about? Like the way you package and present your project proposal, the way you present your information will go a long way toward keeping their interest and attention. Here is some general advice on delivery:

- **Dress the part.** Students always ask, "Do we have to dress up for our presentation?" I usually respond, "It depends on your imagined audience." If you research your patron properly, you will know what they expect. You should definitely wear clothes that are appropriate to the context. If you want to make a good impression, it's generally a good idea to break out some of your better clothes. Sweatpants will not reflect well on you in any situation. For men, a tie is always best, but an outfit you would wear on a casual Friday at an office job might do. For women, any outfit you would wear to an office job should be sufficient. Ask your instructor for specific guidelines.

- **Create the context.** Clothes are only part of setting the stage for your talk. You will also want to indicate your imagined audience and acknowledge their interests whenever possible. Highlight the fact that you know your imagined audience well and make sure that you keep them in mind throughout.

- **Use a tone appropriate to your imagined audience.** One way of keeping the audience in mind is by using the same language and tone that you'd use if they really were in the room.

- **Enunciate and speak clearly.** This doesn't always mean speaking loudly, but you should speak clearly enough so that everyone can hear you.

- **Make eye contact.** Try to make eye contact with everyone in the room at some point during your talk.

- **Don't rely too much on notes.** Organize your presentation around an outline and use notecards, but *do not write out or read the presentation*. In other words: speak it, don't read it. You should know your information well enough at this point to be able to speak with confidence and knowledge using only an outline and visual aids to support and guide you. If you need to write down facts, figures, names, or an outline, use notecards because they are relatively unobtrusive. Try not to put too much between yourself and the audience . . . and NEVER read the slides to your audience.

- **Project energy and "sell" your idea.** If I have one major criticism of student presentations, it's that they rarely give off much energy. Imagine that you are really asking someone for money. You have to sell them on your plan. Turn any nervousness you have about the talk into energy and put a little bit of performance into your presentation. It will count for a lot with your audience and will keep them interested.

- **Ignore distractions and mistakes.** Everyone slips up here and there. Don't draw attention to mistakes, but move on so that both you and your audience can leave them behind.

- **Move for emphasis only—don't pace.** Everyone has tics and idiosyncratic actions that come out when they speak before a group. One person I know always holds a cup of water between himself and the audience as a sort of shield. Odd tics are usually an unconscious way of defending yourself from the people you're addressing. Pacing, for example, presents your viewers with a moving target so they can't hit you if they start to throw vegetables or bricks. Try to recognize these actions ahead of time and work through them. You have nothing to fear from your listeners, so try generally to stand still. Just don't stand in front of the screen too often or you'll be blocking people's view of your visual aids.

- **Be careful with humor.** Many guides to giving oral presentations will tell you to begin with a joke to loosen up your audience. What if you're talking about an especially serious topic? Use humor in moderation and only where appropriate.

Advice on Using PowerPoint Slides

Since most students rely almost exclusively on PowerPoint, or some other commercially-available presentation software, for their visual aids, here is some advice on preparing and using them:

- **Begin with a title slide**. Be sure to have a title slide that sets the stage for your talk and introduces yourself and your topic. It also helps to make a good first impression—especially if it is well prepared. The title slide, like a title page, should display your title, your name, and your organization. Welcome your patron and make him/her/them comfortable. Use white space, graphics, color, or design elements that are consistent with your other slides to make it attractive.

- **Use a slide for each section of your talk.** Each section of your talk—or even every topic you cover—should have its own slide. This way you can mark the turns in your argument by changing the visual image, and you can help guide your audience through each part.

- **Have one theme per slide.** Remember not to crowd too much information onto each slide. It's best to just try to cover one theme on each one. Be wary of **text-heavy** slides.

- **Give each one a header (and number them if it helps you).** Each of your slides should have its own head line or header, indicating the topic it covers. You might want these headers to correspond to the outline you presented earlier to make your talk easier to follow. Headers should have a consistent style and form and should give a good idea of what you'll cover in that section of your talk.

- **Be sure to cite sources on charts, graphs, paraphrases, or quotes.** Each visual graphic aid that uses information derived from a source should have a "source" reference at the bottom, fully visible to your audience.

- **Use large letters and a clear font.** Remember that your slides have to be seen in the back of the room as well as the front. Make them as clear and as large as possible, yet strive for an attractive appearance.

- **Maintain a consistent font and style**. All of your slides should have the same font and if you use a border it should be the same on each one. Often it is less important to follow any rule than it is to be consistent in the styles you choose. Such consistency helps to project a sense of unity to your presentation.

- **Try a unifying border or logo**. To help further project that image of unity, you can use a logo or border on each slide. This is especially useful when you are representing a company, where you may want to have your company logo or a border with colors or a style consistent with your company image.

- **Jazz it up with color if you can**. There is no question that people are impressed by color, and your presentation will stand out more if you use color in your slides and in your visual aids.

- **Strive for active voice.** Use active voice forms in your slides whenever possible, just as in all professional writing.

- **Put numbers in a visual graphic form**. A picture is not always worth a thousand words, but it will usually keep you from using a thousand words to say the same thing. If a number or an idea or a definition or a procedure can be illustrated, it probably should be.

- **Let the audience absorb each slide.** Too often students don't leave their slides up long enough, often because they are hurrying through the presentation. Try to manage your time well and use a slide for each section of your talk, leaving each one on the screen until you raise a new topic.

- **Point to your slides for reference.** Draw your audience's attention to key aspects of your slides by interacting with them. You can do this in several ways—on screen, with the mouse, with a shadow, or with a light pen.

Some PowerPoint Slide "Don'ts"

- **Don't use all caps.** Studies show that people can distinguish words and parts of sentences more easily if you use both lowercase and capital letters. Readers also perceive text written in all capital letters as shouting.

- **Don't put too much information on each slide, or use long sentences, because viewers cannot absorb it all.** Try to put no more than short phrases on each slide, and don't overcrowd them. If you find yourself putting a lot of information on a slide, then likely you need to break that information up to fit on several.

- **Don't use characters smaller than 20 point.** Remember that the people in the back of the room will have trouble with small text.

- **Don't violate the rule of parallel form.** Each slide should have information that fits together in such a way that you can list it using phrases in parallel form. This helps the audience to see connections and to organize information.

- **Don't be inconsistent in capitalizing words.** In fact, don't be inconsistent about anything.

- **Don't forget to proofread for typos**. Typos on a presentation slide are like an unzipped fly: they destroy your ethos and make you look silly.

Final Words of Advice

Recognize that it's normal to be nervous.

Most people feel a bit nervous whenever they have to speak before an audience, especially the first few times they have to do so. Remember that this is normal. If fears persist, though, here are a few thoughts that might help you get past your fears:

- Remember that you know more about your topic than anyone in the room. Just try to make yourself clear and you will automatically have something to offer the audience.

- Your listeners take your nervousness for granted. In fact, since most student listeners are not used to giving presentations themselves, they expect everyone to be nervous and will either overlook or identify with your situation.

- This might be the friendliest audience you will ever face. As fellow students, your listeners are on your side and generally want to give you high marks: I often notice that student reviewers generally see the most positive aspects of individual talks and tend to overlook problems (even after I have urged them to offer critical comments).

- Recognize that if this is your first talk it is a necessary rite of passage. The more practice you have giving presentations, the easier they will get and the less nervous you will feel each time.

- Turn fear into motivation. Nervousness can be a spur to greater preparation. Fear is not necessarily a negative thing, but the way you respond to it has to be positive. One common negative response to fear is procrastination, which is merely avoidance behavior (a variation on running away). The best response to fear is work, which can only help you in developing your project and bolstering your confidence in your subject knowledge.

If you still have worries or fears, talk them over with your professor or with friends. The more you face your fears, the better off you'll be in the long run.

Don't talk down to your audience, but challenge them to follow.

The biggest mistake that students make in presenting a technical subject is trying to get their audiences "up to speed" by giving lots of background information, usually in the form of textbook knowledge, before they begin the presentation itself. Excessive background information should not be presented at the start, for several reasons:

- It destroys the fiction you are trying to create that you are speaking to a knowledgeable audience. Right away, you have confused your listeners as to who your audience really is. Chronologically speaking, your audience has read your initial sales letter and are there to hear more.

- It sets the wrong tone, making your audience feel like they are being talked down to by a schoolmaster. Treat your audience as equals and they will prick up their ears in order to become equal to your conception of them.

- It underestimates your audience's intelligence. Because you are speaking to a college-educated audience, most of your listeners will already possess much of the basic knowledge needed to follow your talk. There may even be some audience members as expert as yourself in your field of study. Listeners will feel insulted by your explanations of "osmosis," for example, and will tune you out. Challenge them to tune in instead.

- It wastes time that you will need to present your idea. Remember that you only have a maximum of 15 minutes to give your talk. How can you present everything you learned about your topic in such a short time? You can't, so don't try.

- It mistakenly tries to anticipate questions that are best left to the question-and-answer period. Remember, if someone in the audience doesn't understand something they can always ask about it afterward. And what question is easier for you to handle than the most basic questions where you get to show off the breadth of your knowledge?

- It will not make sense in the abstract. Because information is never useful except in context, audiences have a very difficult time understanding definitions, explanations, or lessons offered in report form apart from the flow of argument.

- It is unnecessary. If a presentation is organized logically, your audience will follow your argument even if they do not understand all of the details. If you feel it is necessary to explain certain technical ideas, remember that it is much more useful to offer such explanations briefly in the context of your argument (or in the question period after) than it is to give them ahead of time. Just do your thing with confidence and your audience will be impressed, especially if they don't understand all the details.

Logic should govern above all.

This point was brought home to me once while listening to a student presentation on training co-op students to use proper care and technique in recording information in the field so as to comply with government regulations. Basically, these students were making many small mistakes (such as recording temperatures in Fahrenheit instead of Centigrade) that were destroying the integrity of whole projects. What could be more understandable? Yet the speaker began by presenting "background information" about the types of studies the students were doing and the specific data they were collecting. By the time she had finished offering that long explanation, she had to rush through her plan to train these students in better data-collecting techniques. As one reviewer in the audience noted, "I had no idea what she was talking about until she said that these students were using felt-tipped pens on rainy days to write down information." Basically, the audience did not need to know what was being written down with that felt-tip pen to understand that such pens posed a problem in the field.

State your argument up front; don't keep your audience in the dark.

You will never have your audience's attention more than you do at the outset of your talk. So tell them as much as you can up front. Someone once said that the best advice for giving a talk is to do three things: "One: tell your audience what you're going to say; two: say it; and three: tell them what you said." While following that advice literally will lead you to an overly formulaic presentation, it does suggest the importance of leading your audience clearly through your argument with all of the forecasting statements and signposts you can muster. As I suggest above, one of the easiest ways of helping your audience to follow your talk is to provide an outline at the outset and then use slides to signal your transitions (just as you should use strong topic sentences to signal your transitions at the opening of a new paragraph in writing).

Focus on your evidence.

The most important aspect of the presentation is that you show that you have the evidence and research to support your assertions. Just as you would do in a written form, be sure to cite your sources. Name the authorities who inform your paradigm. Name the sources for all statistical data you cite. Name the authors of studies or experiments that you reference. Describe examples or models you reference in specific detail. Emphasize that there is a wide array of evidence to support you in your claims.

Illustrate your budget with a pie chart.

As part of your plan, you must include a budget, since it is one of your imagined audience's biggest concerns. Since this is one place you will always have numbers to work with, why not use a nice pie chart or other visual aid to sum up your budget? A pie chart is most appropriate because it lets you enumerate both the total and the parts.

Close with a polished call to action.

The closing of your presentation should sum up the plan you have in mind and urge your audience to act upon it. Hence the content of your close should focus on what needs to be done, and it should take a form that tries to influence your audience to act. Use whatever rhetorical powers you can muster to get them to listen. Listeners tend to remember best what comes at the beginning and at the end of a presentation more than anything in between. Therefore, in the same way you should strive to make a good first impression, you should close your talk with words that reflect well upon you as a speaker and offer up the "take home" message of your talk in a memorable way. Some speakers actually write out their closing words in order to polish and hone their form and tone. A strong close also signals clearly the end of your talk and lets the audience know it is time to applaud.

Using Presentation Software to Develop a Presentation

You are required to use visual aids in your presentation, including at least three visual graphic aids (such as graphs or charts). There are a number of computer programs that can help you put together a coherent slide show that combines words and images. One of these programs, PowerPoint, offers both the graph-making abilities of Excel and the text-making abilities of Word while giving you powerful tools for keeping your slides consistent in layout and design.

What to Include on Your Slides

Do not try to put everything you want to say on your slides or you will overwhelm your audience with information. Instead, your slides should emphasize the major points and primary evidence that you want your audience to remember. Focus your presentation slides around key points or examples. Ideally, you should try to limit each slide's content to four to five bulleted points (never more than seven) that are about five words each (the sound bite version of your talk). This way your audience will be able to focus on what you are saying rather than focusing on reading the slides.

Because writing and presenting is an active decision-making process, you want to control the content-making process so that your presentation best suits your audience's needs. A design template may offer you a professional-looking presentation. However, these templates are somewhat generic and are usually recognized by business professionals, so you might consider creating your own template.

Creating a Title Slide

You should begin your presentation with a title slide that sets the stage for your talk and introduces you and your topic. A good title slide will also help you make a good first impression. The title slide, like a title page, should display your title, your name, and your organization. This is also a good opportunity to welcome your patron. Use white space, graphics, color, or design elements that are consistent with your other slides to make it attractive.

Organizing the Rest of Your Presentation

Before you select the blank slides for the rest of your presentation, think about the logical progression of your talk. You might find the Six P's a useful basic outlining tool, moving in order through Patron (why did you choose this audience?), Population (who needs help?), Problem (what evidence do you have of a problem?), Paradigm (what research informs your solution?), Plan (how will your course of action be implemented?), and Price (how much will it cost?). Try to chunk major ideas together on each slide, outlining your talk so that the audience can remember its most important points and understand the parts of your argument. For each section, ask yourself what the key ideas are and develop bullet points to represent each one. Spend some time thinking about what visual graphic aids will be the most powerful in persuading your audience. You should especially try to use visual graphic aids to help quantify the problem, since a picture can be a powerful persuader early on in your talk.

Inserting Tables

Tables are used to show a large amount of numerical data in a small space. They provide more information than a graph with less visual impact. Because of the way they organize information into vertical columns and horizontal rows, tables also permit easy comparison of figures. Be sure to use concise, descriptive table titles and column headings. In addition, arrange the rows of the table in a logical order. When putting dollar amounts into tables, be sure the decimals are aligned for easy addition or subtraction.

Inserting and Editing Graphs

Before you make a graph, think about the information you want to convey. Draw a picture by hand and think about whether there is room for text on the page as well. You can choose several different graphing options, including bar graphs, pie graphs, line graphs, and even bubble graphs. Select the graph that is best suited to conveying your data. For instance, line charts are generally used to show changes in data over a period of time and to emphasize trends. Bar charts compare the magnitude of items, either at a specific time or over a period of time. Pie charts compare parts that make up the whole. With pie charts, you should start at the 12 o'clock position with the largest unit and work around in descending order. Whatever chart you choose, be sure to keep it simple. Your goal is to focus the reader's attention on the data in the chart rather than on the chart itself. In addition, you will want to label all charts as figures and assign them consecutive numbers that are separate from table numbers. This way if your audience has a question about a specific image later, they can refer to it by name and number.

Using Photos and Graphics

The "power" of programs such as PowerPoint comes from the way it allows you to seamlessly integrate text and images. Images can be a powerful support for your message, though they can also distract from what you want to say if they are not well chosen. Ideally, you will want to develop your own original images to use in your presentation. Sometimes, however, sourced graphics and images can be useful.

Making a Master Slide

You can also make any graphic or photo into a background for all of your slides. Sometimes it is hard to see text against an image background. However, if the image is well chosen or especially appropriate to your topic it can help you to create an original background that breaks from the familiar generic backgrounds that most presenters use. Also, there are ways to make a background image fade into the background so that your text and support graphics can take center stage.

Adding Text

Once you have the basic visual layout of your talk, you can add your text. Remember to keep your slides consistent and uncluttered. Keep in mind that you, and not your slides, are delivering your presentation. Develop slides that will help you achieve your independent goals, in support of your proposal.

Graphic Aids Assignment

Visual aids are an important part of both your oral presentation and your project proposal. They can provoke an immediate response in your audience in a way that a paragraph of statistics may not. In preparation for your oral presentation, bring in at least three visual aids with written commentary.

For the purposes of this assignment, these three visual graphic aids should be taken from popular sources, such as newspapers or magazines, or printed out from online sources (e.g., *Google* images). They could be ones that you are considering using for your oral presentation and project proposal, but they could also just be interesting examples of graphics. Please do not bring in pictures or photographs for this particular assignment: I would much rather have you find images which are visual representations of statistical information, as in charts, tables, graphs, and so on. You may find certain graphics that you find misleading, or would like to show the class possible "sneaky" tactics used by the presenters. To help you develop good, informative, attractive visual aids, we will look at your examples and some others in a peer review/class presentation session.

Sample Oral Presentation Slides

You are being provided with actual student samples of this assignment. To help see the continuity among assignments, these presentations match the initial sales letters from the previous chapter. These are representative samples that we see at this point in the proposal writing process and have both strong and weak points.

Jeremy Scardino

Slide 1

Protecting the New Jersey Pine Barrens

Slide 2

The Problem:

- A proposed housing development in rural South Jersey has exposed an inadequacy in the legislation regarding cluster developments in the Pine Barrens
- Due to conditions present in the Pine Barrens, water contamination would be prevalent in the development and surrounding area
- Pollution in the area would be a major health hazard, and would eventually spread throughout the entire aquifer, destroying natural habitats

Slide 3

I. How is this different in the Pine Barrens
II. What is a cluster development?
III. Background on septic systems and wells
IV. Effects of contamination

Slide 4

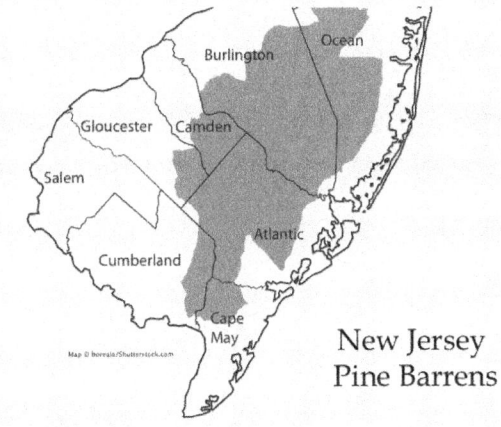

New Jersey Pine Barrens

Slide 5

The Pine Barrens

- Shallow aquifer and rural environment prevents use of city sewer systems
- Unique soil is less than ideal for filtering contaminants

Slide 6

Kirkwood-Cohansey Aquifer

- Source of drinking water for over **3 million** New Jerseyans
- Holds **17 trillion** gallons of water
- Aquifer's shallowness accelerates the spread of contamination

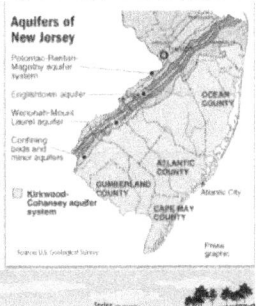

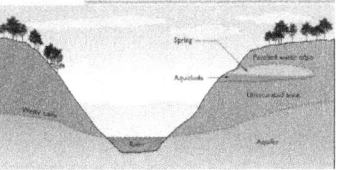

Slide 7

Berlin Well

Slide 8

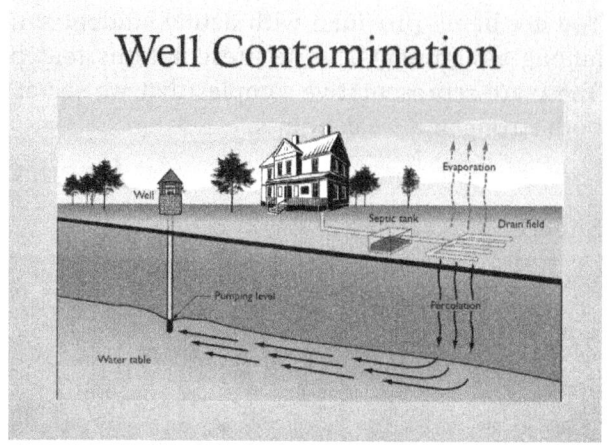

Well Contamination

Slide 9

Slide 10

Soil Composition

- Highly acidic (pH: 3-5)
- Highly porous
- Does not filter contaminants through percolation

Slide 11

Cluster Developments

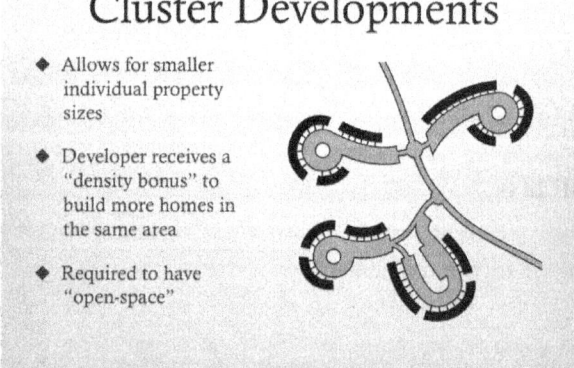

- Allows for smaller individual property sizes
- Developer receives a "density bonus" to build more homes in the same area
- Required to have "open-space"

Slide 12

Cluster Developments

Parcel Size	FOREST AND RURAL DEVELPOPMENT AREA CLUSTERING BONUS Permitted Residential Density			
	3.2-4.99 acres per unit	5.0-9.99 acres per unit	10-24.99 acres per unit	≥25 acres per unit
<50 acres	0	0	0	0
50-99.99 Acres	+10%	+15%	+20%	+25%
100-149.99 acres	+15%	+20%	+25%	+30%
≥150 acres	+20%	+25%	+30%	+40%

260 acres ÷ 81 homes = 3.209 acres/unit
81 x 20% = 16 additional homes
Total 97 homes

Slide 13

Cluster Developments

- Open-space is permanently deed restricted from further development
- Protects the Pine Barrens by creating more preserved land

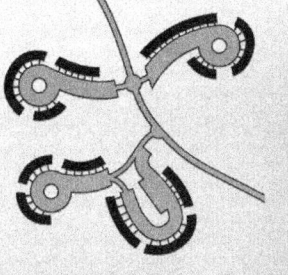

Slide 14

IMAJE LLC Development

- 97 Single-family homes
- First proposed development since amendments to CMP
- Northwestern open-space lot is a half mile north of 59 home portion
- Ground water flow to the South

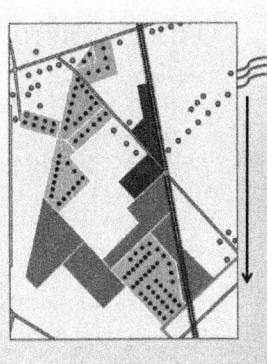

Slide 15

E. coli O157:H7

- E. coli is naturally found in the intestines of humans and animals
- Facilitates the breakdown of fecal coliform in septic tanks
- This strain, if ingested, can lead to dysentery, organ failure (esp. kidneys), and death

Slide 16

Blue Baby Syndrome

- (Methemoglobinemia)
- Infants are at a much higher risk of complications from excessive nitrate intake

Slide 17

IMAJE LLC Development

- Consistent with Pinelands CMP
- Development has passed preliminary approval and is awaiting township approval

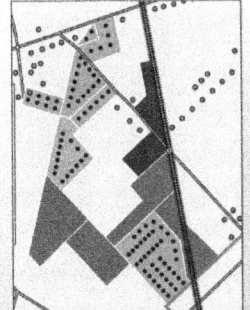

Slide 18

Pinelands Commission Compliance

- § 7.50-5.19 (c) :
- "Clustering of residential development on parcels located within the Forest Areas and Rural Development Areas shall be required whenever two or more units are proposed as part of a residential development…" – CMP
- "The parcel on which clustering is proposed must contain only contiguous lands. There is no requirement that all of the open space be contiguous…"

  – Paul Leakan, Pinelands Commission Communications Officer

Slide 19

The Problem:
- The Pinelands Commissions' Comprehensive Management Plan does not mandate that land designated as open-space in cluster developments be either contiguous or in proximity to the homes

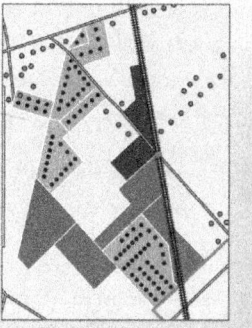

Slide 20

The Plan:
① Reject Ira Mendelsohn's proposed development in Buena Vista Township

② Support amending the Comprehensive Management Plan to require that open space be within a certain proximity to all homes within a cluster development
  - Have an environmental site assessment performed on the property in Buena Vista Township

Slide 21

The Price:
- 260 acres
- Undeveloped land
- ~$4,000
- Environmental Justice Small Grants Program

Slide 22

Robert Celentano

Slide 1

Slide 2

Slide 3

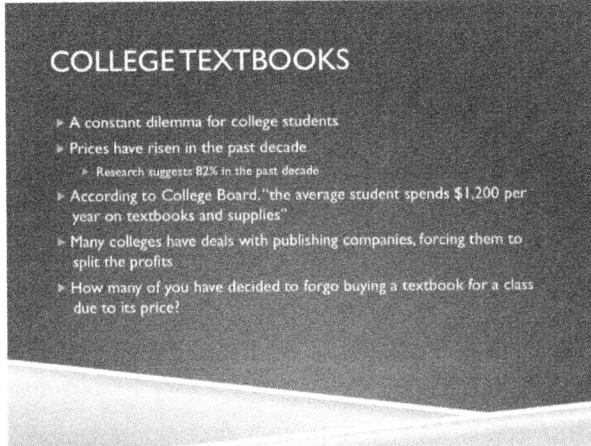

Slide 4

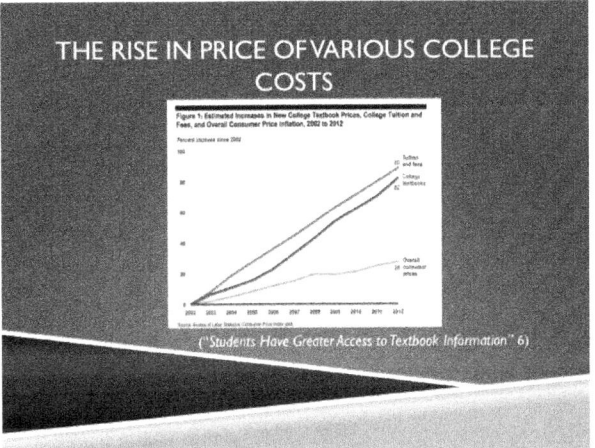

Slide 5

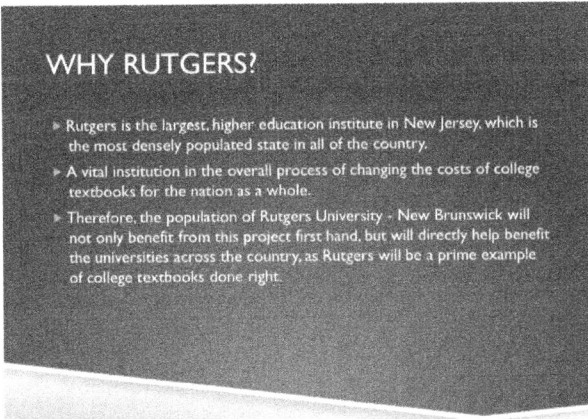

Slide 6

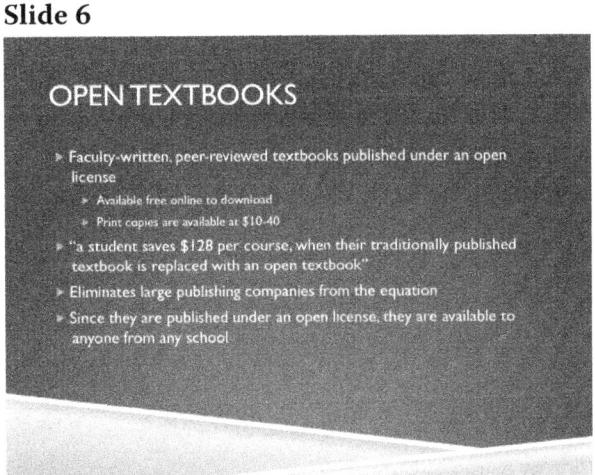

Slide 7

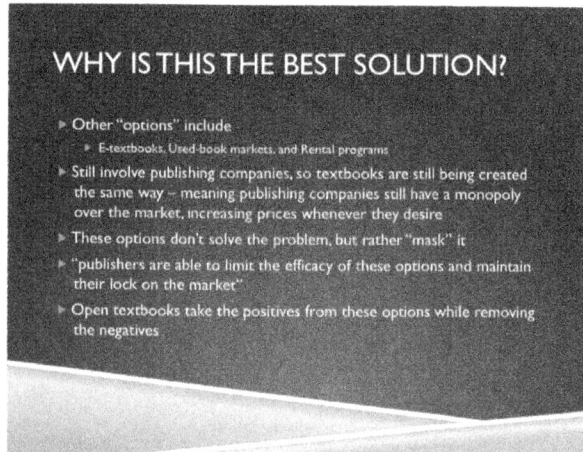

Slide 8

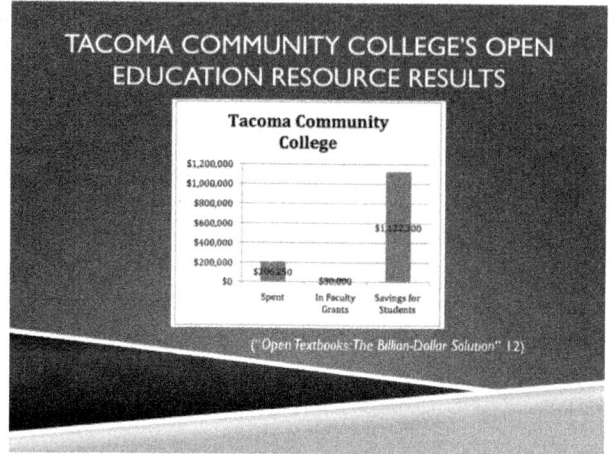

Slide 9

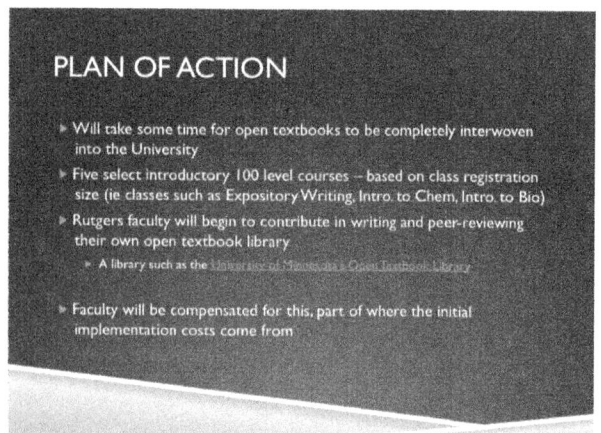

Slide 10

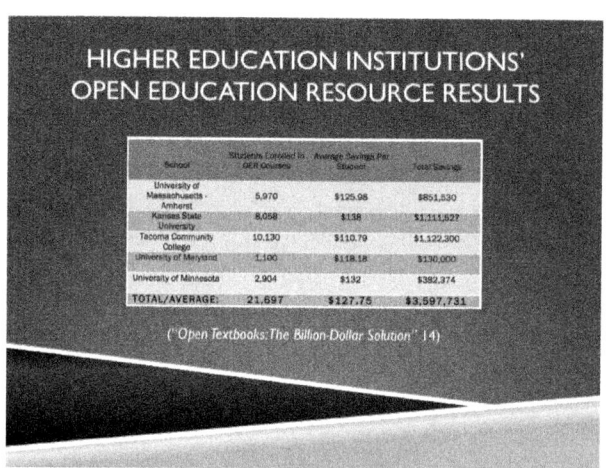

Slide 11

Slide 12

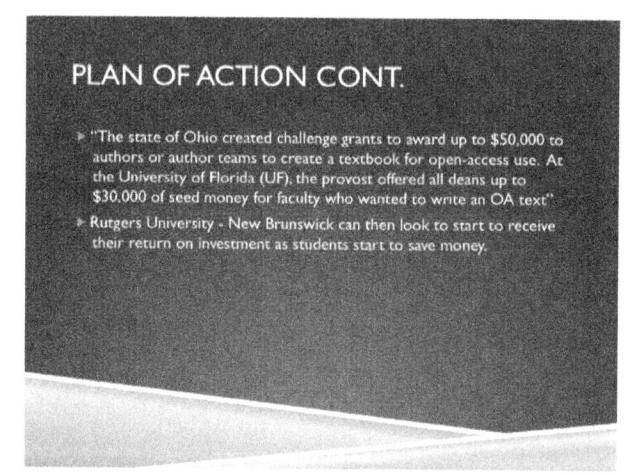

Slide 13

A LOOK AT THE FIGURES

- Flat World Knowledge was an open textbook company in 2011, spent on average $20,000 on peer-reviewing, averaging $120,000 a textbook
  - This money spent per textbook will be what is available for faculty members to earn, divided based on their contributions
- Yet since Rutgers University New Brunswick is a school, rather than a company, many costs can be lowered or simply not needed. This reduces the $120,000 average found by Flat World Knowledge dramatically.
- This allows Rutgers to offer its faculty attractive compensations.
- From these numbers, we can determine how Rutgers will receive its return on investment

Slide 14

A LOOK AT THE FIGURES CONT.

- Using the $10-40 price tag from earlier, we will take the median of 25$ a textbook (print) and multiply that by the average amount of students taking a specific course
- For example, Expository Writing is a required class for all Rutgers University - New Brunswick students to take. There are 40,720 students enrolled there. If every student who went through this class their freshman year purchased in print, the revenue would be $1,018,000.
- If just 15% of the students enrolled at Rutgers New Brunswick were to purchase the textbook in print (nearly 6,108 students), the revenue would equal $152,700.

Slide 15

A LOOK AT THE FIGURES CONT.

- Budget per Open Textbook:
- Writing (Faculty Compensation) - $20,000
- Peer-Reviewing (Faculty Compensation) - $15,000
- Design, Illustrations, Art - $15,000
- Production - $25,000

- Total = $75,000

- Total Initial Implementation Costs for Five Courses = $375,000

Slide 16

ANY QUESTIONS? THANK YOU!

Chapter 6 ■ The Oral Presentation

Name: _____ Date: _____

Chapter 6 ■ Oral Presentation Evaluation

1. **Audience**: How well did the speaker address the funding source?
   1   2   3   4   5   6   7   8   9   10
2. **Eye Contact**: How well did the speaker acknowledge and address those actually present?
   1   2   3   4   5   6   7   8   9   10
3. **Delivery**: How were the speaker's volume, enunciation, posture, appearance, and body language?
   1   2   3   4   5   6   7   8   9   10
4. **Evidence**: Did the speaker support claims, give examples, reference facts, and cite sources?
   1   2   3   4   5   6   7   8   9   10
5. **Organization**: Was the presentation easy to follow? Were all Six P's represented, in the correct order?
   1   2   3   4   5   6   7   8   9   10
6. **Visual Aids**: Were there sufficient, attractive, and useful visual graphic aids?
   1   2   3   4   5   6   7   8   9   10
7. **Preparation**: Did the presentation show careful planning, good time management, and smooth transitions?
   1   2   3   4   5   6   7   8   9   10
8. **Questions**: Did the speaker demonstrate knowledge, confidence, courtesy, and interest?
   1   2   3   4   5   6   7   8   9   10

Additional Comments/Suggestions

The Project Proposal

Chapter 7

The Assignment

The project proposal is the final draft of the project you have worked on all term. Like the oral presentation, it should be a leadership statement that puts information into action by proposing a research-justified solution to a well-defined problem. Unlike the presentation, though, it must adhere to a specific format, which is presented below and illustrated in the sample papers that follow. The guidelines for preparing this document may not conform to those of your workplace or those requested for specific grant applications you might be considering. These guidelines, though, should be readily adaptable to any real-world submission. We encourage you to revise your final project for submission in your workplace or in your future graduate work, but for the time being focus on fulfilling the requirements in this chapter. Please consult with your instructor if there are any discrepancies between the parameters presented here and the instructions included in a published Request for Proposals.

Remember that the heart of the proposal is a problem, paradigm, and plan that work together to create a unified concept. The paradigm should grow organically out of the way you define the problem, and the plan you present should be clearly rationalized by the paradigm. If you unify and focus your argument, you will be able to present a well-organized and logical paper.

The final draft of the project proposal must be from 15 to 20 pages inclusive, single-spaced (though your Works Cited should be double-spaced in keeping with MLA guidelines). You should also be sure to do the following:

- Strive for a consistent professional tone throughout.
- Number your pages clearly.
- Provide coherence to your paper using rhetorical, design, and signposting strategies.
- Use clearly distinguished headings and subheads to help guide your reader through the parts of each section.
- When appropriate, use bullets or numbers to list items for easy comprehension.
- Label and number all graphs and figures for easy reference.
- Unify your paper with a consistent typography and style.

- Polish your writing for style and emphasis.
- Proofread for errors in spelling, grammar, and syntax.

The Parts of the Proposal

The formal aspects of the project proposal help you to present your overall argument in a way that is useful for your reader. There are fourteen parts of the project proposal, most of which should be labeled and presented in order (with the exception of visual graphic aids, which should ideally be incorporated into the body of the paper with individual titles):

1. Cover Letter—generally one full page (not numbered or titled)
2. Title Page—one page (not numbered)
3. Abstract—one page (Roman numeral i)
4. Table of Contents—one page (Roman numeral ii)
5. Table of Figures—one page (Roman numeral iii)
6. Executive Summary—one to two pages (Roman numerals iv–v)
7. Introduction—generally two or more pages (Arabic numeral 1+)
8. Literature Review—generally two or more pages (or Research)
9. Plan—generally one to two pages (or Procedures)
10. Budget
11. Discussion (perhaps including an Evaluation Plan)
12. Works Cited
13. Visual Aids (or Figures)—incorporated into the text when possible
14. Appendix (if necessary)

1. Cover Letter

Like the cover letter that accompanied your résumé, this letter of transmittal is intended to explain and interpret the attached document. It should explain why the reader has received your proposal, and it should try to persuade the reader to examine it closely, offering details about the content intended to interest or intrigue him or her. This letter of transmittal should respond to the situation of reading and answer the reader's likely questions: "Why is this on my desk?" and "Why should I read this when I have a dozen other things to do?"

The transmittal letter can take the form of a letter (for a reader outside of your organization) or memo (for a reader within your organization). While an increasing number of transmittals are written in e-mail form, where the proposal is usually an attached file, we ask that you adhere to the traditional paper forms for the purposes of this course.

If it is a letter, it should follow the full block style, in which all of the elements are flush with the left margin in this order:

1. Return address (your name and address)
2. Date (for the purposes of the class, use the due date of the project proposal)
3. Recipient's address (including name, title, organization, and business address)

4. Salutation ("Dear" plus formal address and name)

5. Body (see discussion below)

6. Closing ("Sincerely") and signature

If you are using the letterhead of a specific organization, you will not need to include your address. If the cover letter is prepared as a memo, then it should be written on company stationery (or facsimile) and prepared in memo form:

1. To: (addressee's full name)

2. From: (your full name and handwritten initials)

3. Date: (today's date)

4. Subject: (a line indicating your proposal topic)

5. Body: (see discussion below)

Many of the rules for writing the cover letter to accompany your résumé apply here. Since your imagined reader probably attended your presentation (or at least you created a context where he or she was imagined in the room), you may want to begin by reminding the reader of that event, explaining that this is the full version of that proposal. Whether or not you have met your reader before, begin by explaining why you sent him or her your proposal and why it should be of interest. Emphasize what you know about the reader's interests and highlight the principal ways in which this proposal matches those interests.

The central paragraph (or central two paragraphs) should offer an overview of the project, highlighting salient details about the problem, paradigm, and plan. Again, point to those aspects of your project most likely to interest your reader.

The final paragraph should invite further contact, offering the most convenient way for the reader to get in touch with you (perhaps by phone or e-mail).

2. Title Page

The page should include the following information:

- Project title
- Submitted by: Your full name and title (or position)
- Submitted to: Your addressee's full name, title, and business address
- Date

You should also indicate somewhere near the bottom of the page the course for which this paper was prepared, your instructor's name, and any class information requested by your instructor. (This way if your paper gets lost it won't end up on the desk of the imagined audience but will have a chance of being returned.)

The title of your project should be carefully chosen and crafted for maximum communication in the shortest space. It is one of the first things the reader sees of your proposal, and it will become the means of referencing it to others. The more communicative power it has, the more effective it will be. Strive to be both clear and memorable. Remember that you can use a two-part title, especially if you want to give your project a catchy title followed by a more technically specific one.

There are many ways to design the title page, and you should do what looks and works best for your specific project. Use white space, color, and other page elements to design an attractive image that is consistent with the document design as a whole. You might want to use graphics or pictorial lettering to highlight your topic.

3. Abstract

The abstract should be clearly labeled as an "abstract" at the top of the page and should be no more than one or two paragraphs in length. The purpose of the abstract is to tell busy people (or their secretaries) how to file your report. It should be written from a disinterested perspective, providing a balanced view of the project idea as though written by an outside party. Usually it is written in the third person or uses passive voice to avoid naming the agent. For the purposes of this class, you should write a relatively long, informative abstract that includes details about your overall argument and covers elements of the problem, paradigm, and plan (in that order). Be sure to indicate your rationale and what specific action you want to take. Aim to be maximally communicative within minimal space—generally between 150 and 300 words.

4. Table of Contents

Clearly label and design your table of contents for easy use. Recognize that the table of contents has two main uses: it helps readers locate the information that interests them most (this is especially true of longer proposals) and it gives your reader an overview of the project and its parts. You should list all parts of the project listed above (excluding the cover letter, title page, and visual aids), along with any important subheads. Number the front matter (abstract, table of contents, table of figures, and executive summary) with small Roman numerals (i, ii, iii) and then use Arabic numbers (1, 2, 3) beginning with the introduction section. Use whatever design elements you can to help make the information clear and usable—indenting subheads, using ellipses to link section names and page numbers, and aligning all related parts. You may want to use dot leaders to align the elements of your table. The style and font should be consistent with the design throughout your document.

You can work up a table by carefully laying out the items in it, but many word processing programs, such as Microsoft Word, will generate a table for you.

5. Table of Figures

If your table of contents is short, you might include your table of figures (clearly labeled) on the same page. Otherwise, it should occupy its own page. Ideally, each figure and illustration you use should have a number for easy reference. List the number and title of each figure along with the page on which it appears. Again, dot leaders may be helpful for proper alignment.

6. Executive Summary

The executive summary should be clearly labeled. This is usually the last thing you write, but it is often the first (and sometimes only) thing that your audience will read closely. It is a "miniature" or condensed version of the paper itself written for busy executives (hence the name). Basically, the executive summary presents your whole argument, *in the order of the paper itself,* with key details and evidence, all in only 10 percent of the space of the whole paper (generally no more than two pages for a twenty-page proposal). A reader should be able to understand your entire project (including problem, paradigm, and plan) after having only read these two pages. Generally, you should cite critical evidence and sources here, but you should not include illustrations. Unlike the abstract, which is intended for description only, the executive summary can contain persuasive language.

In writing some parts of the proposal you may feel like you are repeating yourself. To an objective reader of the entire document, there may seem to be an element of redundancy. However, you should recognize that while you may present the same information several times in different parts of the proposals, each part is intended, in a sense, for a different reader. This part is written for the busy executive. The body of this document is written for the (perhaps same) executive who has time for a closer examination of your ideas.

7. Introduction

There are two purposes for the introduction: to present information about the problem you will address and to forecast your overall argument. Here is where you will want to offer all the information you have on the problem you seek to address. You should try to define and quantify the problem, as well as offer images that help clarify and emphasize the key aspects of it. Focus on those aspects of the problem that will most interest your reader, and suggest by the way you examine or define the problem a direction for approaching it. Close the introduction with a forecasting statement giving your reader a sense of your argument to follow and providing a transition to the next part.

8. Literature Review (or Research)

This is the section in which you present, analyze, and integrate your paradigm research into your proposal. The literature review section should open with some reference to the problem (especially by way of transition from the introduction), but it should focus mostly on the justification for your project. The research you present should explain why you will approach the problem in a particular way; it should also provide a unified rationale for the specific plan of action you describe in your plan. Thus the paradigm is essential for unifying your paper because it shows how the plan of action you will propose is a logical approach to the problem you have defined. Remember, there are two sides to paradigms—they are represented by **theory** and by **models of success**. These elements work together to provide justification for your specific course of action.

While each of you will have to explore research in a way unique to your topic, all of you should strive to show that you are not merely asserting your approach to the problem based on opinion, politics, or personal view, but that there is a consensus of opinion or a well-documented trend or development that supports your idea. You will want to discuss theories that form the basis for your assertion that the plan you have in mind will be effective—offering evidence and authority to show that your plan is responding to a body of knowledge in a particular field. If you are planning experimental work that grows out of a well-established scientific paradigm, you should review the tradition of work in the field that you are building on in your research. You will also discuss examples of similar or related projects you are using as models, focusing on the procedures and plans that worked in those instances and emphasizing the positive results achieved. Remember that the main purpose of the research is to justify your plan of action. Thus, if you plan to educate people about a specific environmental issue, you will likely want to focus more on an effective way (or paradigm) of educating people than you will on that environmental issue (though you will need research on that as well).

One of the purposes of the literature review is to establish your authority, which will stand or fall based on the quality of the research you cite. By demonstrating your command over recognized or paradigmatic research, you show that you have the knowledge and expertise to make valid recommendations. You should strive to find the most useful and authoritative research whenever possible, and you should discuss published research (ideally, research that has been subjected to peer review). Many projects will, however, call for a wide range of research sources, including articles, books, Internet sources, published government statistics, interviews, surveys, field studies, calculations, and experimental results. You should do your best to evaluate sources and use only the most solid in building your literature review. To use low-quality materials in constructing your paper is equivalent to using low-quality materials in building a house, and your product will be evaluated and graded accordingly.

9. Plan (or Procedures)

The plan should be as specific as possible and should follow logically from your research. How it is presented will depend upon the specific project you have in mind. If you are proposing a workplace project, you might focus on how your idea will be implemented (perhaps providing a flowchart or time line). If you are proposing to do an experiment, you should lay out the specific procedures you will use. If you are building something, you will want to describe how it will be built and provide diagrams. You might wish to reference research to support the specific choices you are making, though the literature review section should provide the bulk of your rationale.

10. Budget

The budget should list everything you will need for your project, from salaries to supplies. Some items may require explanation, which you should provide here as well. You should arrange the cost of your budget items in aligned accountant's columns to make your addition clear.

11. Discussion (or Evaluation Plan)

Generally your paper should conclude by summing up your project and making a final pitch for its value. If you are proposing a project whose results can be tested in some way, then you should also offer an evaluation plan.

12. Works Cited

This section should list all sources of information cited in your paper in alphabetical order. The list of Works Cited should be prepared according to MLA style, covered in the MLA Style Guide in Chapter Four. For those who want extra guidance, you might consult *The MLA Handbook,* which is available in the reference section of any campus library.

13. Visual Aids (or Figures)

You should have at least three graphic aids that are visual representations of numerical information. These might include graphs, tables, charts, or maps. In addition to these three, you may include drawings, photographs, flowcharts, maps, organization charts, Gantt charts, time lines, diagrams, or floor plans. Each visual graphic aid should be numbered (e.g., Figure 1, Figure 2, etc.) and should have a title. If the graphic is based on information from a source, then you should have a citation line at the bottom (i.e., Source: Alvarez 26). If you can incorporate your graphics into the body of the paper, do so. If you cannot incorporate your graphics, then include them at the end in an appendix or interpaginate them directly following the first reference to them.

14. Appendix (optional)

If you have other information that doesn't exactly fit into your text, you could include it as an appendix (which is literally appended to the end of your document). For example, if you cite a map or chart which is too big to be incorporated into the body of your text, you could label it as Appendix A. Be sure to list it under Appendices in your table of contents, and refer to it in the text (i.e., See Appendix A, p. 20).

Sample Project Proposals

What follows are typical samples of student work, as with the previous assignments, presented for illustrative purposes. This section is included to generate discussion, provide the opportunity for objective critique, and facilitate practicing of conscientious peer review. These project proposals are not provided to represent a particular grade or to distinguish between passing and failing work. As with all representative examples, these papers have a variety of strong and weak moments. We encourage you to utilize the course grading criteria to attempt to situate these papers, with the guidance of your instructor. Hopefully, as you prepare to revise your work, this experience will help you to identify the usual moments of achievement, as well as areas that would benefit from improvement.

For the purposes of this book, some editorial modifications were made to these student samples. As mentioned earlier, when developing your project proposals, the "title page," "abstract," "table of contents," and "table of figures" will normally appear on separate pages. In addition, each subsequent section will begin on a new page. Consult your instructor for specific formatting guidelines.

Jeremy Scardino
32 Evans Street
Metuchen, New Jersey 08840

May 5, 2016

Rick Bracaliello, Zoning Officer
Buena Vista Township
890 Harding Highway, PO Box 605
Buena, New Jersey 08310

Re: Imaje LLC Development Proposal

Dear Mr. Bracaliello,

First of all, I would like to thank you for attending my presentation at Rutgers University. The development being proposed by Ira Mendelsohn in Buena Vista Township will have devastating effects on the community and its surrounding water supply. As a resident of the nearby area, I appreciate your concern for the protection of the Pine Barrens and its inhabitants.

As mentioned in the presentation, the problem with Ira Mendelsohn's development stems from the proximity of open-space to the homes in the cluster development. Due to this, the 97 traditional on-site septic treatment systems will not have sufficient area to dilute. In addition, the area that has been designated as open space will not serve as a dilution area because of, (a) its location, and (b), the underground flow of water in the Kirkwood-Cohansey aquifer, which provides over 3 million people with their drinking water. Further contamination of this vital water supply would be extremely hazardous in the short run, and in the long run could be devastating both New Jersey's ecosystem and economic well-being.

Whereas my previous letter focused on the problems with the proposed development, I now wish to focus primarily on how we can fix this problem in Buena Vista, along with the rest of the Pine Barrens communities. This plan not only includes rejecting the proposal (as it currently stands), but also making amendments to New Jersey's legislation regarding the Pine Barrens: the Pinelands Commissions' Comprehensive Management Plan.

I appreciate your time and dedication to this cause. Once again, if there are any questions or concerns I have not answered, feel free to contact me at (732) 555-1234 or 4567@rutgers.edu.

Sincerely,

Jeremy Scardino

Jeremy Scardino

Preventing Contamination of the Kirkwood-Cohansey Aquifer

A proposal to promote the sustainability of life in the New Jersey Pine Barrens

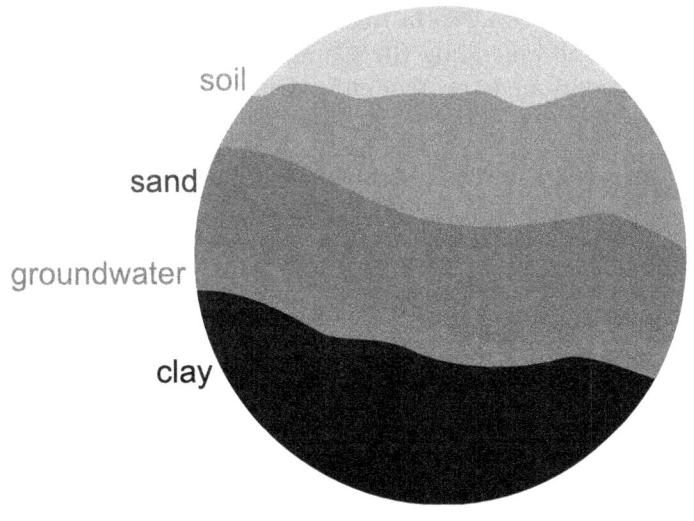

©N-2-s/Shutterstock.com

Submitted by:
Jeremy Scardino

Submitted to:
Rick Bracaliello
Zoning Officer
Buena Vista Township
890 Harding Highway, PO Box 605
Buena, New Jersey 08310

May 5, 2016

Prepared for:
Writing for Business and the Professions
Professor Robert Smith

Abstract

This is a research-supported proposal that outlines an apparent inadequacy in the New Jersey Pinelands Commission's Comprehensive Management Plan (CMP). The CMP is the legislation that determines the zoning policies in the Pine Barrens. One development in particular, the first since the last amendment of the CMP, has exposed the inadequacy in the legislation. The Pinelands Commission has approved the development, and if approved by the township, the development will bring about an environmental hazard that threatens the residents of the development and those of its surrounding area.

Included is the sufficient background information necessary to understand why housing developments are of especial concern in the Pine Barrens. By making an example of this particular development and amending the Comprehensive Management Plan, the Pinelands Commission can continue to protect our nation's first National Reserve.

Table of Contents

Abstract 220

Table of Contents 220

Table of Figures 220

Executive Summary 221

Introduction. 222

    The Problem 222

    Effects of Contamination. 223

    Why It Is Important to Act Now 224

Literature Review 225

Plan 227

Budget. 228

Discussion 229

Table of Figures

Figure 1. 223

Figure 2. 226

Figure 3. 227

Executive Summary

The problem concerning on-site septic treatment in high-density neighborhoods has been known for some time now. However, in the unique ecosystem of the New Jersey Pine Barrens, this problem is exacerbated by several contributing factors. One particular development, proposed by Ira Mendelsohn and IMAJE LLC, poses a serious threat to its residents, the Pine Barrens' ecosystem, and the three million New Jersey residents who drink from the Kirkwood-Cohansey aquifer. To avoid an environmental hazard, it is necessary that Buena Vista Township rejects this proposal, and more importantly, that the Pinelands Commission's Comprehensive Management Plan be amended. This is necessary to promote the sustainability of life in the Pine Barrens

What comes to mind when most people think of water pollution is industrial and agricultural pollution. Factories' disposal of harsh chemicals, along with farms' use of fertilizers and pesticides are a major contributor to contamination. However, "nonpoint source (NPS) pollution remains the Nation's largest source of water quality problems," which includes pollution from faulty septic systems (Nonpoint Source Pollution). However, site-specific conditions can cause septic systems to pollute the environment even when they are functioning perfectly. This type of contamination will be the concern of this proposal, and therefore it is necessary to discuss why septic systems are the only sewage treatment option available in this area.

For two reasons, almost all homes in the Pine Barrens use both an on-site septic treatment facility (septic system) and a domestic well. The primary reason is because the aquifer is too shallow in the Pine Barrens to allow large-scale pumping. The second reason is that the Pine Barrens are very rural, and therefore city sewer systems would not be cost effective to implement.

Septic systems are used in urban areas around the country, but conditions prevalent in the Pine Barrens make them a potential polluter. The soil in the Pine Barrens is highly permeable, and therefore isn't capable of filtering or degrading contaminants (Titone). Unlike most aquifers, the Kirkwood-Cohansey is exceptional at storing water but is highly vulnerable to contamination due to its porous soil and shallow aquifer.

Exacerbating this problem is the fact that the Pinelands Commission (a division of the New Jersey Department of Environmental Protection) requires the "clustering" of properties in housing developments. A cluster development is essentially a housing development with designated open space to protect the Pine Barrens from over-development. In locations where city sewer systems aren't available, the open space also serves to facilitate the dilution of waste- and groundwater. While the development in Buena Vista Township follows all regulations of the Pinelands Commissions' Comprehensive Management Plan, most of the land that has been designated as open-space will be ineffective for dilution. There are two basic problems with the development, the southernmost sub-development in particular. First, its open-space is located a half mile away from the homes in the development. Additionally, the water flow under the housing development is to the south, and the open-space is to the north (Clustering Gone Bad?). Clearly, the open-space is too far away to serve as a dilution area for the homes in the southernmost development, and even if it was in proximity to the homes, waste- and ground-water would not flow into this dilution area. Still, the development has been approved by the Pinelands Commission and is waiting approval from Buena Vista Township.

This lack of regulation for developers puts the residents of these homes and the residents of nearby homes at great risk. In addition to the residents of Buena Vista Township, the entire New Jersey Coastal Plain is in danger. According to the Environmental Protection Agency, the waters in the Kirkwood-Cohansey "are hydrologically inter-connected such that they respond collectively as an interrelated aquifer system ... If the aquifer were to become contaminated, exposure of the persons served by the system would constitute a significant hazard to public health" (Coastal Plain Aquifer).

The effects of contaminated drinking water include E. coli infections, which can be potentially deadly to children. Also, newborns are highly susceptible to blue baby syndrome, which if untreated, is also a terminal illness.

To protect the residents of Buena Vista and those who draw from the Kirkwood-Cohansey aquifer, the first step is to reject the proposed development in Buena Vista Township. The second step is to amend the Comprehensive Management Plan to require open-space in cluster developments to be within a certain required proximity to the homes in the development (when those developments are not supplied with city sewer systems or a septic treatment facility that is deemed harmless to the water supply). In order to do this, a site assessment will be performed on the land under the proposed development to justify the claims made in the proposal. Doing so would be a necessary step to keep New Jersey a habitat that is sustainable for both humans and the unique species that inhabit the Pine Barrens.

Introduction

The mission of the New Jersey Pinelands Commission, a division of the New Jersey Department of Environmental Protection, is to "preserve, protect, and enhance the overall ecological values of the Pinelands, including its large forested areas, its essential character, and its potential to recover from disturbance" (Clustering Gone Bad?). This organization, which regulates land use in the Pine Barrens, first issued its Comprehensive Management Plan in 1981, shortly after the Pine Barrens became the first U.S. National Reserve.

The Comprehensive Management Plan (CMP) was amended in 2008 to require "the clustering of developments within the Forest and Rural Development Areas" (Comprehensive Management Plan). In short, these developments require a certain percentage of land to be dedicated to open- space. This land becomes permanently deed restricted, preventing the land from further development. But in rural Pine Barrens towns where there is no city sewer system, this open space is necessary to serve as a dilution area for septic systems.

The Problem

In 2009, Ira Mendelsohn and IMAJE LLC received a Certificate of Filing from the Pinelands Commission. This document verifies that the development is in full compliance with the CMP, and is ready for approval by the township in which the development resides. This development is the first proposed in either the Forest or Rural Development Areas since the amendments to the CMP, and has exposed an apparent inadequacy in the legislation.

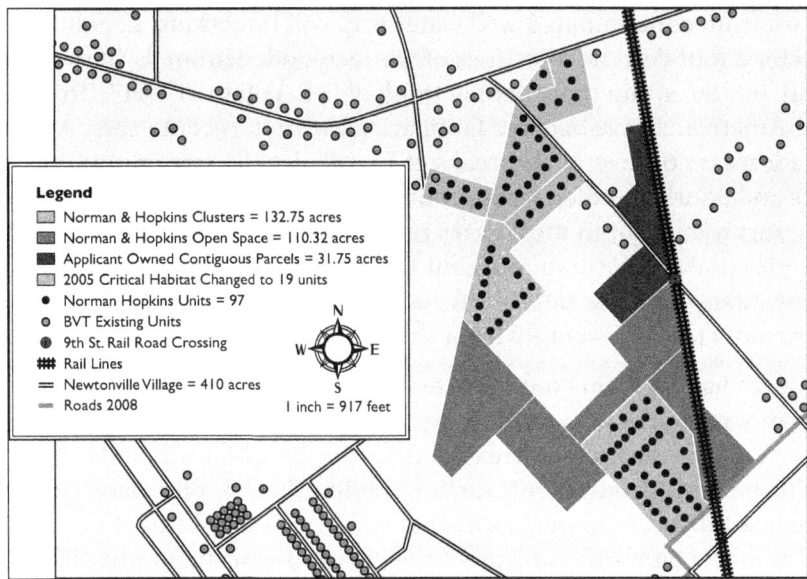

Figure 1—Source: Pinelands Protection Alliance

The problem with Ira Mendelsohn's development is identifiable just by looking at the map of the proposed development (Figure 1): In both sub-developments (highlighted in red), there are homes that are nowhere near the open-space (highlighted in green). There are only a handful of homes out of the 97 planned that will border the open-space. In addition, the open-space dedicated for the southernmost sub-development is located a half mile to the north, while water flow in the area is travelling to the south (Clustering Gone Bad?). Therefore, almost none of the homes in the development would have a sufficient dilution area for their septic systems.

Effects of Contamination

Water contamination is of greater concern in areas that use septic systems rather than city sewers. Whereas city water is sent to a filtration center to be constantly monitored and tested, homeowners with domestic wells are responsible for maintaining their own clean water. Law does not require that domestic wells be tested for contamination, simply because it would be too great an expense for both the homeowner and the state.

Since the general, overarching problem here is water contamination, it should be made clear the three effects it will have: (1) the contamination will pose serious, possibly fatal health risks to those who live in the development and the surrounding area, (2) the contamination will quickly spread throughout the aquifer, contributing to the decaying purity of our water supply, and (3), water contamination will drive out the species that are specific to the New Jersey Pine Barrens, destroying its unique ecosystem.

It is hard to determine exactly which species of plants and animals will be harmed by the contamination, but any change in the Pine Barrens' ecology will create a domino effect of harm to the ecosystem. It is much easier, on the other hand, to predict the effects that will concern the families who occupy the proposed homes and those in the surrounding area, which is where the immediate focus should be directed.

The first hazard from contaminated well water is E. coli infections. E. coli is a naturally occurring bacteria found in the intestines of warm-blooded animals (Basic Information About E. Coli), but the strain most people think of is E. coli O157–H7. This particular strain is what Americans have become familiarized with in recent years. As consumers, we have been made aware of several outbreaks of E. coli, usually stemming from ill-prepared beef products and poorly handled farm products. With proper medical treatment, E. coli infections are survivable, but in most cases require long hospital stays and sometimes invasive surgeries (Basic Information About E. Coli). As with most illnesses, the effects experienced by infants and the elderly alike are much more serious, and therefore, these age groups are more prone to fatality from the infection.

The second health hazard from contaminated well water is increased nitrate. "Infants below the age of six months who drink water containing nitrate in excess of the MCL could become seriously ill, and if untreated, may die. Symptoms include shortness of breath and blue baby syndrome" (Nitrate in Drinking Water). Blue baby syndrome is a relatively rare heart disorder in newborns that can be deadly. While it can be transmitted genetically, it is most commonly a result of the environment the mother has been exposed to while carrying the child. Blue baby syndrome results from a heart defect called tetralogy of fallot, which results in a lack of oxygen in the blood. Infants who have this defect go through "tet spells," where their extremities swell up at the tips, signaling a lack of blood flow. These tet spells cause brain damage, and if not treated, will eventually cause death.

Why It Is Important To Act Now

Due to the current economic climate, in particular the housing market, Ira Mendelsohn is stalling the approval process until it is more feasible to build. But when the economy comes back in full force, the decision to approve this development is entirely in the hands of the zoning department of Buena Vista Township. Unless this problem is brought to their attention, they will have no reason to reject the development.

When contamination occurs, the development's residents will face a great expense to fix their wells and have their septic systems redesigned, although there is no obvious solution to create an efficient system in a housing development with such high density. If uncorrected, there will be a significant health hazard to the development and its surrounding area.

Therefore, it is important to bring this to the attention of not only the Buena Vista Township Planning Board, but also to the Pinelands Commission, and within a timely fashion. With the research supporting this problem, it should be very feasible to prevent further contamination of New Jersey's water supply.

To sum the problem up briefly, water contamination resulting from domestic septic systems is a major problem in the Pine Barrens. Due to its rural nature, city sewer systems are largely unavailable in Pine Barrens towns. Additionally, on-site septic systems do not work as efficiently in the Pine Barrens because the soil there is highly porous, and does not filter contaminants as they travel to the water table (percolation). Contaminants quickly spread throughout the aquifer, which provides drinking water for three million New Jersey residents.

These factors are not taken into consideration by the laws that govern how cluster developments are designed. Therefore, the same scenario could occur in any rural Pine Barrens town. If the Kirkwood-Cohansey aquifer were to be contaminated, New Jersey would have an environmental and economic catastrophe on its hands.

Literature Review

"Clustering Gone Bad?"—NJ Pinelands Protection Alliance

This article, published by the New Jersey Pinelands Protection Alliance (a nonprofit organization) is the only publicized information specifically regarding the development in Buena Vista Township. The reason the Buena Vista Township Planning Board hasn't realized this problem is that "The IMAJE LLC, - Ira Mendelsohn application, located in Buena Vista's Rural Development Area, is the first application for a cluster development that PPA is aware of since these new cluster rules took effect" (Clustering Gone Bad?). Being the first development proposed in the Forest/Rural Areas since clustering was made mandatory, the township will not be aware of the inadequacy of the law unless it is directly presented to them.

The article also provides a basic understanding of how contamination would spread: "The 74 conventional septic systems, in theory, will have the benefit of the open space for dilution, but this open space does not surround the homes portion of the development. For the 59 home cluster portion the dilution area is about a half a mile to the north with ground water flow to the south of the development cluster" (Clustering Gone Bad?).

This is where the inconsistency occurs in the Comprehensive Management Plan. The CMP only mandates the minimum size of the allotted space, but makes no mention to the minimum distance the open-space can be from the homes in the development. Although the individual housing units will be large enough to accommodate a septic system and domestic well, the open-space (dilution area) is a half-mile to the north and the contaminants will travel to the south. For these reasons, water contamination is imminent.

Domestic Wells Have High Probability of Pumping Septic Tank Leachate—Hydrology and Earth Systems Science Journal

Ira Mendelsohn's development wouldn't raise any red flags if septic systems weren't necessary. But because Buena Vista is a very rural area, and due to the makeup of the Kirkwood-Cohansey aquifer, city sewer systems are not available. Therefore it is necessary to understand the basics of how a septic system works, which is illustrated in Figure 2. Effluent from the home travels to a small tank where sewage is stored and decomposed by bacteria. Liquid effluent is piped into the leach field, where it is further treated by bacteria in the soil. The liquid percolates (travels through the porous soil) to the water table. Usually a reasonable distance from the leach field is the domestic well, which draws from the water table, filters the water (as best as it can), and pumps into the house.

But whereas city sewer systems discard of waste and provide water, septic systems only discard waste. "About 25–30% of households are served by a septic (onsite) wastewater treatment system, and many property owners also operate their own domestic well nearby" (Domestic Wells). Almost all homes in the Pine Barrens follow this model. But, "In areas with small lots (thus high spatial septic system densities), shallow domestic wells are prone to contamination by septic system leachate" (Domestic Wells). Therefore, this is a special concern in housing developments. The nature of the aquifer, the soil in the Pine Barrens, and also the lack of open- space near one of the developments in Ira Mendelsohn's proposal exacerbate this problem.

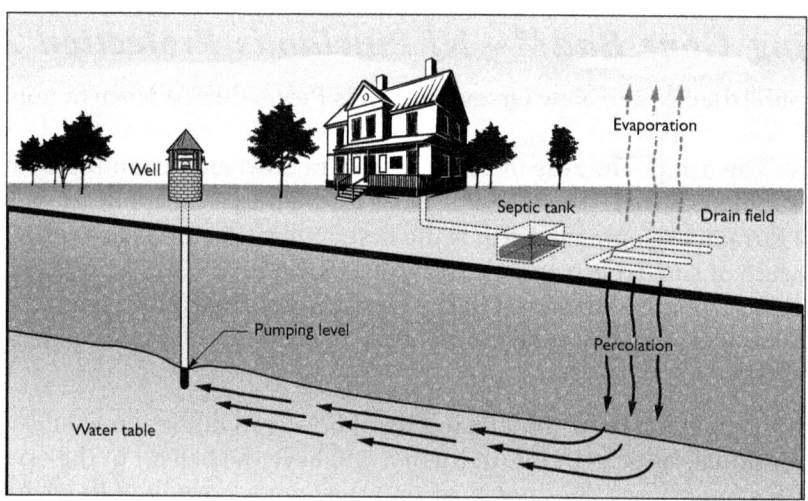

Figure 2—Source: "Septic Systems: Part One"

Pinelands Soil Background— The State of New Jersey

The Pine Barrens derives its name from the sandy soil that lies underneath the years' worth of pine needles that we find on the ground. Because the soil is so acidic, almost no crops can be grown there, which is why the area was never desirable to live in, and thus has remained mostly uninhabited. Because of its fine and granular composition, the soil is considered porous, meaning liquids can travel unimpeded through the ground and into the aquifer. As a result, only the following can be concluded:

> Pollutants, like large quantities of water soluble chemicals in liquid form, are able to move quickly through the sandy soil to the water table just as easily as it is for water to flow through a sieve. It is important to remember this when determining the amount of chemicals that may safely be used on both agricultural and residential land, as well as the suitability of on-site disposal of wastewater with the standard septic tank. Without careful planning, it would be easy for pollutants to reach the water table and harm the water supply. (Pinelands Soil Background)

These contaminants travel rather quickly to the water table (part of the aquifer) where wells collect water for consumption. And because of the composition of the Kirkwood-Cohansey aquifer that lies beneath the Pine Barrens, contamination would spread quickly and take thousands of years to recover.

New Jersey Coastal Plain Aquifer—EPA

The New Jersey Coastal Plain spans from Sandy Hook to Cape May and is home to the Kirkwood-Cohansey Aquifer. "The New Jersey Coastal Plain Area depends upon the under-lying Coastal Plain Aquifer System for seventy-five percent (75%) or more of its drinking water to serve 3 million people" (Coastal Plain Aquifer). For this reason, it is of the utmost importance to protect the Pine Barrens to prevent contamination of the aquifer. "The New Jersey Coastal Plain Aquifer System is susceptible to contamination across several interfaces. In the outcrop areas, the water table conditions and the highly permeable nature of the soil ... facilitate the movement of contaminants from the land surface into the system. Significant pollution sources include septic tanks" (Coastal Plain Aquifer). Therefore, not only does soil in the Pine Barrens contribute to pollution, but also the Kirkwood-Cohansey aquifer's makeup expedites the spread of contamination throughout the Coastal Plain. If the aquifer were eventually deemed unsafe for human consumption, there really would be no alternative source to turn to.

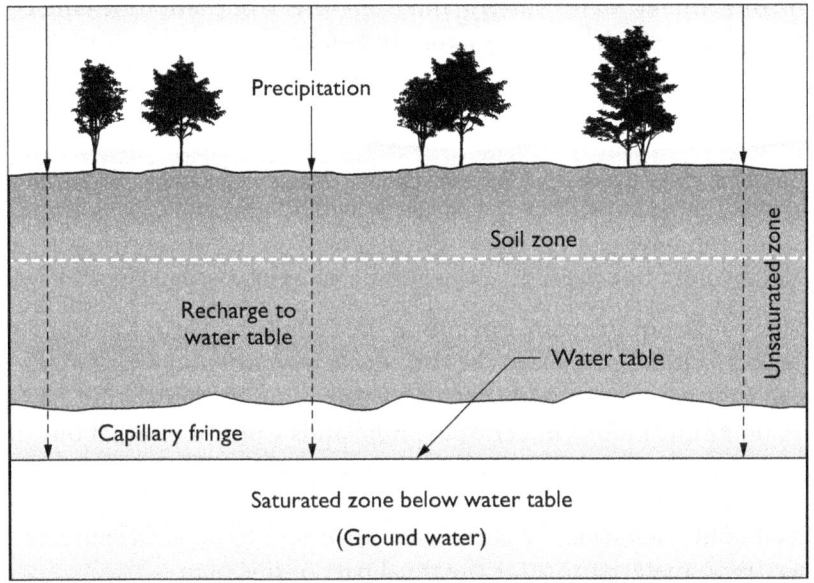

Figure 3

Plan

The plan to prevent contamination of the Kirkwood-Cohansey aquifer is relatively simple and very feasible. The cost of implementing the plan will be extremely low in relation to the costs that would be incurred if this problem were not addressed.

The first part of the plan is to have an environmental site assessment performed on the land that Ira Mendelsohn has proposed his development on. Although the research in this proposal should be enough to convince the Buena Vista Township Planning Board and the Pinelands Commission that contamination would be imminent, corroboration from a team of environmental consultants would be a worthwhile investment.

The second step is for the Buena Vista Township Planning Board to reject Ira Mendelsohn's proposed development. From the conclusions drawn in this proposal, it should be clear that this development would cause serious health and financial implications to the residents of the proposed homes and those of the existing homes in the area.

The final and most important part of the plan is to amend the Pinelands Commission's Comprehensive Management Plan. The existing regulations regarding cluster developments in the Forest and Rural Development Areas needs to be revised to require that open-space be within a certain proximity to the homes it serves as a dilution area for. Since Ira Mendelsohn's development is the first to be proposed in one of these areas since the legislation was last amended, it should serve as an example of the inadequacy of the law. It is in the interest of the Pinelands Commission to prevent contamination before the problem exposes itself in the form of

If enacted, this plan could potentially save New Jersey from a health, environmental, and financial disaster. At the very least, it would save the residents of Buena Vista Township from contaminants in their water supply, and therefore save them thousands of dollars on very expensive repairs to their septic systems and wells.

Budget

As aforementioned, this plan will be extremely feasible financially. Rejecting Ira Mendelsohn's development would cost nothing, although the Township may see this as a loss of potential income. But in reality, it would be an avoidance of major liability.

Regarding the third part of the plan, amending the Comprehensive Management Plan has no foreseeable cost. Although it may take time away from the members of the Pinelands Commission, there are no associated costs with amending the legislation. When I asked Paul Leakan (Communications Officer of the Pinelands Commission) about this, he confirmed that "when the Commission decides to amend the CMP, the Commission staff drafts the amendments and ensures compliance with all state rulemaking requirements. There is no need to hire additional engineers or attorneys to do so." (Paul Leakan). Therefore, there is no material cost for the third part of this plan.

The only part of the plan that would involve any foreseeable costs is the environmental assessment. But even this cost is very reasonable. For a 260-acre parcel of undeveloped land, according to the CEO of Resource Controls (an environmental consulting agency), it would cost approximately "$2,500 to $3,500 for undeveloped land, depending on many variables" (Atwood). It is difficult to get an exact number for this expenditure, but a rough estimate should not exceed $4,500.

To pay for this plan, an application would be submitted for the EPA's Environmental Justice Small Grants Program. This program has given out over $24 million to individuals and organizations since 1990. The serious implications of this problem should yield a grant from the EPA, since it is corroborated by their research. Even if this grant is not attained, there are countless other environmental grant programs that could be applied for.

Discussion

The New Jersey Pine Barrens is a "last frontier" of sorts in New Jersey. Unfortunately, many people think that New Jersey is all highways and power plants; you don't see the natural habitats unless you really go looking for them. The Pine Barrens is by far the largest natural habitat in New Jersey and arguably the most scenic. It is home to many endangered species, and is a very unique ecosystem that needs to be preserved.

In addition, the Pine Barrens needs to be protected to ensure that New Jersey's water supply isn't contaminated. This was one of the primary reasons that it became the first U.S. National Reserve. Due to environmental factors present in this unique ecosystem, the aquifer (where we get our drinking water from) is at an elevated risk of contamination.

Unfortunately, New Jersey's industrial nature has taken its toll on what has, historically, been some of the purest water in the country. However, since the 1980s, federal legislation has worked to prevent pollution from industrial sources. But the largest contributor to water pollution today is nonpoint source pollution. This category of pollution comes from many different sources, including septic systems.

All septic systems release pollutants into the ground, but because of the soil composition in the Pine Barrens, there is a much higher risk for contamination from septic sludge. And because of the nature of the aquifer and the rural environment of the Pine Barrens, septic systems are the only available means of managing effluent.

This problem becomes a major concern when building high-density housing developments, such as the one proposed by Ira Mendelsohn in Buena Vista Township. The surrounding area will feel the effects of contamination from this development. In addition to the health hazards, there will be significant financial loss for homeowners who experience well contamination.

These problems can be alleviated with minimal cost, but it is up to the Buena Vista Township Planning Board to reject the proposal. Furthermore, it is up to the Pinelands Commission to enact legislation to prevent such water contamination in the Pine Barrens, so that more neighborhoods are not affected. If the Pinelands Commission does not do so, water contamination will lead to the end of sustainable life in the Pine Barrens.

Works Cited

Atwood, Robert. Personal Interview. 24 April 2014.

"Basic Information about E. Coli O157:H7 in Drinking Water." *Basic Information About E. Coli O157:H7 in Drinking Water.* Environmental Protection Agency, 19 June 2013.

"Basic Information about Nitrate in Drinking Water." *Basic Information about Nitrate in Drinking Water.* Environmental Protection Agency, 5 Feb. 2014.

Bremer, J. E., and T. Harter. "Domestic Wells Have High Probability of Pumping Septic Leachate." *Hydrology and Earth System Sciences Discussion.* Hydrology and Earth System Sciences,

"Clustering Gone Bad?" *Pine Barrens, New Jersey Pinelands Protection.* Pinelands Protection Alliance,

Leakan, Paul. Personal Interview. 17 April 2014.

"New Jersey Coastal Plain Aquifer New Jersey Coastal Plain Aquifer." *EPA.* Environmental Protection Agency, 10 May 2010.

"Nonpoint Source Pollution: The Nation's Largest Water Quality Problem." *Water: Outreach & Communication.* Environmental Protection Agency, 22 Aug. 2012.

"Pinelands Soil Background." *Pinelands Soil Background.* New Jersey Pinelands Commission,

"Septic Systems: Part One." *Buying Property for Homesteading.* Going Slowly, 9 Sept. 2011.

Titone, Matthew. "IN THE MATTER OF LONG ISLAND PINE BARRENS SOCIETY…" Legal Information Institute, 24 Nov. 1992.

United States. New Jersey Pinelands Commission. *Pinelands Comprehensive Management Plan.* 2012.

Robert Celentano
7 Elm Drive
Edison, New Jersey 08817

May 1, 2016

Chris Scherer, Director
Office of New Program Initiatives and Digital Learning
77 Hamilton Street, Suite 201B
New Brunswick, New Jersey 08901

Re: Implementing an Open Textbook System at Rutgers University—New Brunswick

Dear Mr. Scherer:

The Office of New Program Initiatives and Digital Learning, and their Creative Works Project has assisted in creating, supporting, and turning new educational program ideas into a reality. The department has been able to integrate such programs into the University's system seamlessly, showing it is able to solve problems plagued in and around the college's campus. College textbooks are one of those issues that are harming students as well as Rutgers University as a whole. Open textbooks will allow for a way that students can have access to the textbooks their classes require, free of cost, as well as allow Rutgers to gain a return on investment that is worthwhile for the University.

Rutgers New Brunswick students have been suffering from the prices of college textbooks due to the high costs assigned by publishing companies. Research shows that students are overpaying for college textbooks due to monopolies these publishing companies have. These monopolies force colleges to deals with the publishing companies, or else be left without the information they hold. Open textbooks are written and peer-reviewed by faculty and placed under an open license. This allows students to have the ability and choice to either download the textbooks free of charge, or purchase a low-cost print copy. As students start to save money, Rutgers University can look to start to receive their return on investment. Rutgers can begin this process by implementing open textbooks into five select introductory one hundred level courses, ones that have the largest number of students registered. Upon observation that the system in five classes deems positive results, Rutgers will continue to build its open textbook library.

Rutgers students must have this available to them in order to help cut costs while on the college pathway. The Creative Works Project aims at helping create strategies for new educational projects, and open textbooks are needed for both students and the University of Rutgers. If you have any questions, please feel free to call 908-555-4567 or email me at 1234@rutgers.edu. I appreciate and thank you for your time.

Sincerely,

Robert Celentano

Robert Celentano

Implementing an Open Textbook System to Rutgers University—New Brunswick

©vasabii/Shutterstock.com

Submitted by:
Robert Celentano

Submitted to:
Chris Scherer
Director
Office of New Program Initiatives and Digital Learning
77 Hamilton Street, Suite 201B
New Brunswick, New Jersey 08901

May 1, 2016

Prepared for:
Writing for Business and the Professions
Professor Janice Pennington

Abstract

The price of textbooks on college campuses has risen over the past decade or so. Rutgers University New Brunswick has experienced this price increase first hand, from making deals with publishing companies to having to offer custom edition textbooks for some classes due to their size. Therefore, these elements contribute to students having to pay more for the material their classes require, as well as require Rutgers to split the sales of the textbooks that they sell. Textbooks under an open license provide students with the choice and availability to download their textbooks free of cost online as well as purchase a print copy for around the same price as a meal for two. These textbooks are written and peer-reviewed by faculty members, so the profits of the print copies go almost entirely to the Universities themselves. This eliminates the middlemen publishing companies from the equation, providing students an inexpensive way to access the content needed for their classes as well as allows schools to garner a return on investment. The Theory of Reasoned Action speaks about our beliefs leading us to combat the norms of others, and together, both influence our behavior. This can be applied to Rutgers by wanting to go towards an open textbook system rather than selling textbooks the traditional way through large publishing companies. The University applies this theory as Rutgers took a step towards open textbooks through Scholarly Open Access at Rutgers, or SOAR. The next step is for Rutgers to implement a pilot system of open textbooks into their classes.

In order to properly and seamlessly interweave these textbooks under an open license into an institution such as Rutgers University New Brunswick, five introductory courses will begin the implementation process. These select courses will be five, one hundred level courses, determined based upon class registration size. Once the textbooks are written and reviewed by faculty members, they will be compensated, which is partially where some of the funds for the project will go. These textbooks will then be made available for the classes chosen. This will allow for the largest amount of students to begin to use these textbooks as well as give the largest sample size results at the least expensive price for the University. If the first five courses return positive results, such as a positive return on investment and well liked by a majority of students, the system will be further reviewed and seek to be implemented greater into the University.

Table of Contents

Abstract	232
Table of Figures	234
Executive Summary	234
Introduction	236
Literature Review	239
Plan	243
Budget	246
Discussion and Evaluation	249
Works Cited	250

Tables of Figures

    Figure 1: Estimated Increases in New College Textbook Prices 237

    Figure 2: College Textbook Prices Are Only Rising 238

    Figure 3: Tacoma Community College Student Savings 242

    Figure 4: Various Schools' Students' Savings 243

Executive Summary

College textbooks are a problem not only for students every semester, but a problem for the universities that sell them. Students across the country spend hundreds of dollars year after year purchasing expensive texts that are usually used for no longer than a semester's worth. The Universities, which sell these textbooks, are not the source of this problem of high costs however. Large publishing companies that create these textbooks are. These publishing companies have a monopoly over the textbook market and therefore technically force colleges into "big money deals" with them in order for their students to have the material needed for their classes. Rutgers University – New Brunswick is the largest higher education institution in New Jersey, the most densely populated state in the whole country. Combining these two aspects, many may wonder how Rutgers University can help change the way that one purchases college textbooks? More importantly, however, what needs to be changed in order for college textbook prices to go down?

The correct solution to this problem is open textbooks. Open textbooks offer faculty written and peer-reviewed textbooks under an open license. This open license allows anyone, students included, to download these textbooks free of charge online, or purchase the textbooks in print for around the cost of a meal for two. Since faculty members write these textbooks, the information inside these textbooks are extremely well coordinated to the classes in which students are registered. This also allows for faculty members to "tweak" the information inside these textbooks and use the parts which they believe are the most beneficial to their classes. Simply, open textbooks are highly editable allowing for a wide range of versatility. This combination of extremely low print copy costs, free e-textbook costs, and a wide range of benefits inside the classroom make open textbooks the number one option for solving the nation's crisis of college textbook costs.

Open textbooks therefore do not only change the price tags on college textbooks significantly, but completely change the way they are created. Large publishing companies are completely eliminated from the equation, allowing for universities to gain all the profits. Open textbooks therefore provide an immense return on investment. Besides benefiting students as well as the University as a whole, open textbooks have benefits for faculty members, too. These benefits come in the form of monetary compensation and an increased control of what is being taught in their classes. By allowing faculty members the opportunity to be compensated for writing as well as peer-reviewing open textbooks, they are not only able to receive these monetary benefits but be able to include the information they know to be vital in their classes. Also by allowing this, faculty members have the opportunity to earn large sums of monetary compensation for their work. This aspect is one of the initial implementation costs for the University, but is a win-win situation. The University will see a return in profits from students purchasing print copies and faculty members will be paid upfront for their work. These monetary compensations can be in the tens of thousands for faculty members, giving an extremely high incentive for them to participate. With all these benefits one may ask, what are the other options other than open textbooks?

Other options besides open textbooks include used textbook markets, e-textbooks, and lease/rental programs. Used textbooks simply offer the same textbooks for an extremely small drop in price. Used textbooks also are simply, not new. This means that online codes needed for classes that are included with new textbooks must be purchased separately, textbooks very well may have physical issues including torn pages, highlights, water damage, or completely missing pages, and the latest editions may not be offered or are in limited supply as used editions. Rental programs follow the same train of thought and still involve publishing companies, disallowing Universities to make a majority of the profits. In terms of e-textbooks, they offer problems for students such as ease of use and ease of obtaining. E-textbooks are not saving students any money either and still include publishing companies.

The Theory of Reasoned Action "predicts behavioral intention, a compromise between stopping at attitude predictions and actually predicting behavior" ("*Theory of Reasoned Action*"). This theory has been worked towards by Rutgers University with programs such as SOAR, or Scholarly Open Access at Rutgers. As their site explains, "SOAR gathers, and makes available globally via the Internet, scholarly articles deposited by Rutgers faculty, doctoral students, and postdoctoral scholars" ("*Scholarly Open Access at Rutgers*"). While SOAR is different than open textbooks for undergraduate students, it exemplifies the Theory of Reasoned Action by moving one step closer to open resources and one step away from traditional databases, proving that Rutgers University is willing to combat the norms represented by other universities.

In terms of open textbooks, they have proved to be successful in the universities across the country that have implemented them in one-way or another. These universities have also seen large results, saving students a combined millions of dollars. According to research, "A student saves $128 per course, when their traditionally published textbook is replaced with an open textbook" (Senack 5). Therefore, students actually end up saving money each time their classes switch to using open textbooks. Open textbooks are surely the right solution to the problem. How may Rutgers implement a system of open textbooks into their University?

The first classes to have open textbooks in them will be those introductory courses that have the largest number of students registered for the class, likely to be the most profitable for Rutgers. Rutgers may begin to use open textbooks by offering them in the initial implementation for the introductory courses, Expository Writing, Introduction to Chemistry, Calculus I, Introduction to Sociology and Introduction to Biology. Open textbooks will then eventually work their way up through higher-level classes. Rutgers will then start to use the open textbooks, from the open textbook network, such as the University of Minnesota's Open Textbook Library online, in their classrooms. While this is happening, Rutgers faculty may begin to contribute in writing as well as peer-reviewing Rutgers University's open textbook library. In our case, every member of the Rutgers University faculty who contributes in either writing textbooks or peer-reviewing them will be compensated. This pilot process will begin with five select introductory courses (100 level) and will take place over a full academic year. After this implementation of five open textbooks in five introductory classes, Rutgers University will review the revenue generated by this system. Upon observation that the system deems positive results, Rutgers will continue to build its textbook library, specifically with introductory courses.

With an implementation cost of $525,000 and the help that you and your team bring to the table, Rutgers University—New Brunswick can help change not only how college textbooks are priced, but the way that they are created. The University will make a profit by selling print editions of the textbooks to students. Though there is an option for students to download the texts for free, many will choose to pay for low-cost print editions. Pricing them more reasonably than they currently are, students will be inclined to purchases textbooks. If Rutgers can sell printed copies to a very small percentage of students, around 15% or so, they can see a worthwhile return on investment. The higher the percentage of students that pay for the print editions, the more profit Rutgers will make. This profit will not only help pay for faculty compensation but for future open textbook endeavors if the University so chooses. Rutgers University will be the turning point for the nation. We can bring down the costs of higher education textbooks, keeping students happy by paying a lot less, and keeping the University happy by receiving a large return on investment, potentially millions.

Introduction

If one takes a look at Rutgers, The State University of New Jersey's New Brunswick 2015-2016 Tuition and Fees for full-time students, one may notice a very important cost left out in the annual spreadsheet: college textbooks. Students across the nation, but in this case Rutgers University students, are in a constant dilemma when it comes to purchasing the textbooks their classes require. College Board states that, "the average student spends $1,200 per year on textbooks and supplies" (qtd. in Student Affairs Committee 1). Rutgers University Senate and their Student Affairs Committee evaluate this price tag as being, "as much as 39% of tuition and fees at a community college and 14% of tuition and fees at a four-year public institution" (1). With students taking out loans simply to just pay for tuition and housing, textbooks are an area many look at to cut costs. Regardless of their practicality, the price of university textbooks is the issue at hand that needs to be resolved.

The Government Accountability Office states that, "the cost of textbooks has risen 82 percent from 2002 to 2013" (qtd. in Yousef 1) to which Rama Yousef comments, "With costs only going up, more students may decide to forgo buying textbooks altogether" (1).

Figure 1: Estimated Increases in New College Textbook Prices

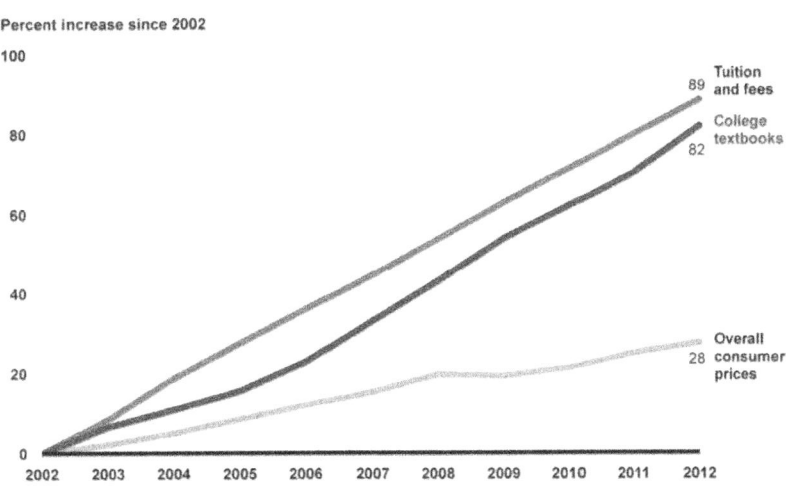

(Source: "Students Have Greater Access to Textbook Information" 6)

The United States Government Accountability Office (GAO) presented a graphic visual aid from the Bureau of Labor Statistics' Consumer Price Index that showed the rise in price of various costs associated with college. Those costs included tuition and fees as well as college textbooks followed by comparing them to overall consumer prices. The very important key element from this is the college textbooks rise in costs from 2002 to 2012. From this, one can visualize truly how much college textbook prices haven risen in a decade and can further conclude that they will only continue to rise unless someone does something about it. Due to the fact that large publishing companies holding a monopoly are running the current market for college textbooks, their price tags are only going to continue to rise. Using open textbooks will of course provide a more financially affordable way for students to learn.

It is not just common knowledge that students forgo purchase of college textbooks either. According to Professor Doug Ward of the University of Kansas, "Surveys have found that two-thirds to three-quarters of college students refused to buy textbooks because costs were too high and many instructors used only a few chapters...Many alter their class schedules based on the price of textbooks" (Ward). This goes on to show that college textbook prices therefore affect students' ability to learn. By pricing textbooks at so high of a cost, students must go without the material their classes require, altering the education a university is attempting to provide. So forth, charging expensive prices for textbooks impacts students negatively as they are put at a disadvantage by not owning the material.

The problem therefore arises that college textbooks are too expensive. What causes this? Research suggests that, "One suspected cause of increased prices is that there are fewer textbook publishers due to consolidations in the publishing industry... Publishers have large fixed costs in printing as well as a need for editors and reviewers" (Silver, Stevens, and Clow 2). This shows that publishing companies are to blame for such high costs in the world of college textbooks. Is this because of the authors wanting more money, or is there another reason behind this rise in cost? "Textbook publishers have been accused of using tactics that actually increase the cost of textbooks...Authors also pressure textbook publishers to lower the price. Because the author is paid a percentage of the revenue, his or her income is maximized when more books are sold at a lower price" (2). There are two items that we can take from this. First, the tactics that Silver, Stevens, and Clow are referring to include areas such as creating online codes as well as any other supplemental material classes can require so that publishers can increase costs. Second, authors are not to blame for the expensive costs of college textbooks. They are, in fact, the ones who wish prices to be lower. Silver, Stevens, and Clow continue to speak on this, paraphrasing Robert Carbaugh and Koushik Ghosh's 2005 study "Are College Textbooks Priced Fairly?" to say, "Publishers are more interested in profits and desire a higher price to maximize the difference between revenue and costs" (2). So forth, one may find it appropriate to say that the reason college textbook prices are the way they are, are entirely due to the publishing companies that create them.

In an article earlier this year by Ben Popken of NBC News, he cited the Bureau of Labor Statistics (BLS) and found that college textbook prices have risen over 1000% percent since 1977. This article goes on to speak about how some college textbooks have risen to over $400 for certain books, but more importantly includes a very interesting visual that showcases once again, truly how much the price has risen for textbooks.

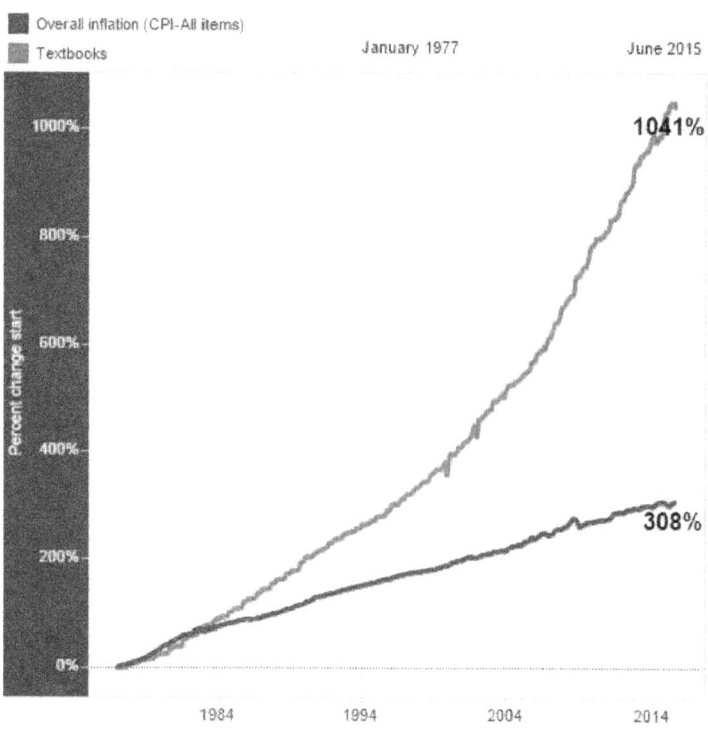

Figure 2: College Textbook Prices Are Only Rising

(Source: "College Textbook Prices Have Risen 1,041 Percent Since 1977.")

This graphic complements Figure 1 nicely, as both show the sure increase in costs of textbooks. The advantage and difference presented in Figure 2 above, is it dates back almost four decades and is continued to more current day. This, plus the fact that it provides data comparing to overall inflation, helps prove that textbook prices are not simply just complaints by students, but can be statistically backed by research. Therefore it has been established that college textbook prices are a problem. But the question still remains: Why Rutgers?

It would be a bit ignorant of me if I were to think that I could solve the nation's problem right from the starting line, changing the prices of all textbooks at every university in the United States. That is why Rutgers, the State University of New Jersey, specifically their New Brunswick campus, is a great stepping-stone for the country's issue at hand. Rather than this appearing as a self-serving project, Rutgers University is the largest, higher education institute in New Jersey. Furthermore, New Jersey is the most densely populated state in all of the country, making Rutgers University a vital institution in the overall process of changing the costs of college textbooks for the nation as a whole. Therefore, Rutgers University—New Brunswick will not only benefit from this project first hand, but will directly help benefit universities across the country, as Rutgers will be a prime example of open access to educational materials.

This open access to educational materials is the solution to the nation's problem. These open access materials are better wise known as open textbooks, or open license textbooks. These materials offer faculty written, peer-reviewed open license textbooks that are free for anyone to download or purchase in print in-expensively. Open textbooks prove to be the solution and best option for solving college textbook prices for Rutgers University—New Brunswick and eventually, the nation as a whole.

Literature Review

Rutgers University—New Brunswick must deal with the price of college textbooks in a way that not only changes the price tag listed for students, but the way that textbooks are created. This in turn creates a long term, lasting effect on the way that college textbooks are produced in the future as well as sold. The best option as well as the solution to this problem comes in the form of open licensed textbooks.

Open textbooks are therefore the topic behind the solution to college textbook prices, but what is the theory? The Theory of Reasoned Action can be best described by "our attitudes lead us to do one thing but the relevant norms suggest we should do something else, both factors influence our behavioral intent" ("*Theory of Reasoned Action*"). An example of this theory would be Rutgers University wanting to combat the way that college textbooks are created through open textbooks, but the norms represented by other universities across the country are to go through traditional publishing companies. Rutgers has taken this theory and contributed it towards a model through their SOAR resources, or Scholarly Open Access at Rutgers. Rutgers describes SOAR as "the repository website/portal where authors can deposit their scholarly works and discover the open access publications of other Rutgers faculty and graduate students" (*"Scholarly Open Access at Rutgers"*). While SOAR is not typically used by or for undergraduate students, it does provide a place where Rutgers faculty and graduate students can upload their work for open use by anyone. Though SOAR is different than open textbooks for undergraduate students, it is a major step for the University in terms of open access resources. SOAR helps illustrate the Theory of Reasoned Action by the University beginning to shift its mindset on how resources are used as well as distributed, moving one step farther away from a traditional database mentality.

Open textbooks provide students as well as faculty members multiple benefits in and out of the classroom. As research suggests, "Opportunities nonetheless exist for engaging and building upon open textbook use to increase interactivity and enhance teaching and learning for users" (Petrides et al. 47). This shows us again, that open textbooks have benefits other than just their initial price saving interests. John Hilton and Carol Laman make a good point in saying, "These textbooks are part of a larger subset of open educational resources; educational resources that are freely available and licensed in such a way as to promote reuse and remix" (266). This "reuse and remix" is an interesting phrase. The first, reuse, meaning that educational materials not only be put to use by one class at one university, but that these educational materials can be used by any university. The second, remix, allows faculty members from universities across the country to be able to use the same textbook, yet in different ways. What this means is that these educational materials allow for versatility so that any class at any school can have the ability to alter the information inside and be used to their liking. John Hilton and Carol Laman then begin to speak on other benefits of open textbooks in saying, "First, all students have access to a book, regardless of their ability to pay. Second, all students have access to that book before the first day and throughout the semester…there are inherent advantages to digital texts" (270). By allowing students the opportunity to download their textbook free of charge anytime throughout the semester, many problems are avoided. With that, even if students do not own devices capable of downloading these textbooks, open textbooks provide inexpensive print editions as well. On the other hand, open textbooks "are available free online, they are free to download, and print copies are available at $10-40, or approximately the cost of printing" (Senack 5). Open textbooks are the future, and Rutgers University can make them the present.

Open textbooks, are of course, not the only solution to the issue of college textbook prices; yet, they are the best option. Yet what are the other options available to Rutgers University? There seem to be quite a few, but there happens to be a large distinction between the following options and the solution behind open textbooks. Ethan Senack talks about used book markets, rental programs, and e-textbooks saying they, "only offer a temporary drop in student spending. One problem with these options is that they are consistently and successfully undermined by traditional publishers…publishers are able to limit the efficacy of these options and maintain their lock on the market" (7). Used textbook markets simply provide students with textbooks at a slightly lesser cost. This may slightly affect one part of the problem, the price of college textbooks, yet still involves the publishing companies of today, the how behind the way in which textbooks are created.

Online textbooks are not the correct way to save money either; they bring numerous problems on their own as Robert Stone and Lori Baker-Eveleth, who support the adoption of electronic textbooks, closed their article saying, "As with any new technology adoption, its success or failure depends on numerous factors" (45). Those factors include areas such as ease of use, ease of accessing, willingness to purchase an e-textbook, etc. Therefore, it is safe to say that e-textbooks are not a step in the right direction in terms of saving students' money. In fact, they are merely just another way for publishers to reach more and more students to make more and more money, while giving the public the idea that "cheaper textbooks" are available to them. According to research, e-textbooks actually have a higher net-cost than a traditional textbook. This research suggests, "the etextbook cost on average (is) exactly the same as a new hard copy of the same title bought and sold back to the bookstore...[and] twice as much as a used hard copy of the same title bought and sold back to the bookstore" (qtd. in Bossaller and Kammer 69). Therefore, e-textbooks are not saving students as much money as previously thought.

On the other end of the spectrum, open textbooks take the positives from e-textbooks while removing the negative of large publishing companies. What I mean by this is that e-textbooks do have some positive qualities. These include the ability for students to carry all of their textbooks on one device, widespread access for all to obtain, and easy implementation for universities and their faculties. Due to publishing companies, however, e-textbooks still carry a heavy price tag. Open textbooks use these positives of e-textbooks to their advantage and, by removing publishers from the picture, are able to offer these textbooks online for free.

With this aspect of "free" however, many may wonder how universities are able to make a profit from using an open textbook system. Open textbooks in fact show a return on investment that interests many universities across the country. As Ethan Senack says, "Where many financial aid programs deliver a dollar of savings for every dollar spent, the 'return on investment' with open textbooks is exponential. At Tacoma Community College alone, students savings generated were more than 6 times the amount invested" (16). Continuing with this train of thought, he also mentions that, "...potential savings per student when a course is transitioned from a traditional textbook to an open textbook have hovered between $95 - $115...even at $100 average savings per course, calculations of national impact would still land over $1 billion" (19). From this, one is able to see that college textbooks clearly are not a small market. With that in mind, Rutgers has an opportunity to take part in a larger portion of that market financially, one that is traditionally controlled by publishers. What does this larger portion of that market really mean, however, to Rutgers?

Rutgers, The State University of New Jersey would be one of the first institutions in the country to start to use open textbooks. But why would Rutgers University want to switch when they can make deals with publishing companies? As Ethan Senack puts it, "The return on investment figure used in regards to Tacoma Community College was calculated by dividing the total amount of student savings generated by the project by the total amount of money spent by the institution to develop and fund the project" (19). Senack also points out in his report, that full-time undergraduates would save $1.42 billion dollars a year (5). Rutgers New Brunswick enrolls around 38,000 students. If we are to use the value given to us by College Board presented above, an average of $1,200 a year spent on textbooks per student, Rutgers New Brunswick students spend a year on average, $44.4 million on textbooks (qtd. in Student Affairs Committee 1). If we were to implement the open textbook plan presented below, Rutgers University - New Brunswick can start a chain reaction in bringing down the costs of higher education textbooks, keeping students happy by paying a lot less, and keeping themselves happy by allowing them to receive a larger portion of the $44.4 million that typically goes to publishers.

The ease of use of open textbooks is tremendous. For example, at the University of Minnesota's Open Textbook Library online, one is able to view, download, and print all of their textbooks free of charge, without even being a student of their university. Schools listed on Minnesota's website in the open textbook network include: The University of Arizona, The Ohio State University, Oregon State University, Purdue University, The University of Oklahoma, and more. Alongside this network, five colleges/universities have started implementing an open textbook system into their schools: University of Massachusetts, Kansas State University, Tacoma Community College, University of Minnesota, and the University of Maryland (Senack 18). This shows us that Rutgers University is not alone in their implementation and adoption of open textbooks.

Figure 3: Tacoma Community College Student Savings

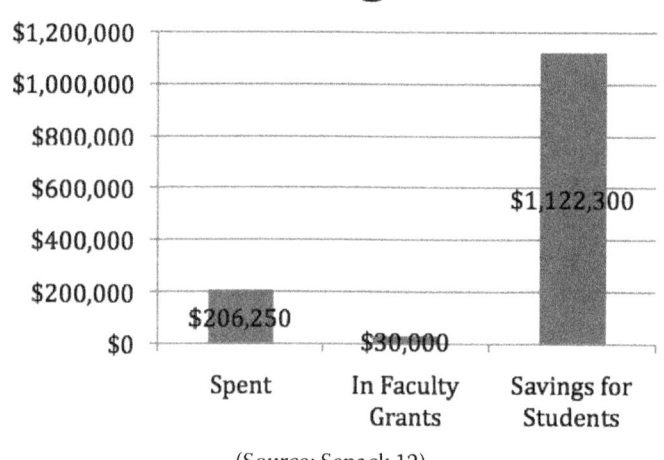

(Source: Senack 12)

Ethan Senack uses Tacoma Community College as one of the main higher education institutions in his argument for open textbooks. A key element within this graphic visual aid is the difference between the money spent by the school and the amount of money therefore saved by students. Figure 3 shows that even community colleges are able to successfully implement open textbooks into their education system. Typically, four-year institutions have more capital than community colleges. Therefore, Rutgers University can not only save students more money, but also assume a lower risk due to its high capital. Ethan Senack introduces this GVA by saying, "Since its launch, the OER Project has reached more than 10,000 students at Tacoma Community College, generating more than $1.1 million dollars in student savings" (12). This therefore can help reinforce the savings available for students. Another school has benefited from open textbooks, and Rutgers can too.

Figure 4: Various Schools' Students' Savings

School	Students Enrolled in OER Courses	Average Savings Per Student	Total Savings
University of Massachusetts - Amherst	5,970	$125.98	$851,530
Kansas State University	8,058	$138	$1,111,527
Tacoma Community College	10,130	$110.79	$1,122,300
University of Maryland	1,100	$118.18	$130,000
University of Minnesota	2,904	$132	$382,374
TOTAL/AVERAGE:	21,697	$127.75	$3,597,731

(Source: Senack 14)

Furthermore, Ethan Senack uses other schools' data, including Tacoma Community College, in order to show the benefits of open textbooks. The subject of this figure is to highlight some of the higher education institutions across the country that implemented in one way or another using open textbooks in their schools. A key element here would be Kansas State University, who averaged saving the most per student. This, along with the other four schools, totaled over three million dollars in savings, showing that open textbooks really can benefit students. Ethan Senack uses this figure and states, "From this information, we can predict that when a traditional print textbook for an introductory level course is replaced with OER and open textbooks, a student saves approximately $128 per course, per semester" (14). This gives us a real-world number that we can work with in order to help calculate potential savings for Rutgers University—New Brunswick students.

Therefore, open textbooks are indeed the correct solution to the problem of college textbooks and their prices. The question still remains, however, how do we implement a system into Rutgers University—New Brunswick?

Plan

To begin to answer the question of how to implement a system into Rutgers University – New Brunswick, one must understand what open textbooks are, as well as their benefits. To tell one what they are not, they are not textbooks written and therefore owned by publishing companies. They are not expensive for students to buy. Simply, they are not what publishers want. To help explain what open textbooks are exactly, "Open textbooks are faculty-written, peer-reviewed textbooks that are published under an open license" (Senack 5). In order to begin the implementation of open textbooks, Rutgers University will begin to cut its ties with any publishing deals they have already made. This plan will take some time for open textbooks to be completely interwoven into the University, and should begin by offering textbooks solely for introductory courses, eventually working their way up through 400 level classes. The first classes to have open textbooks in them will be those introductory courses that have the largest number of students registered for the class. The five courses that will be used for the initial implementation of open textbooks will be Expository Writing, Introduction to Chemistry, Calculus I, Introduction to Sociology, and Introduction to Biology. This is because they will likely be the most profitable for Rutgers University due to their number of sections available to students and class sizes. As this will take time, Rutgers will then begin to start using the open textbooks, from the open textbook network, such as the University of Minnesota's Open Textbook Library online presented above, in their classrooms. While this is occurring, Rutgers faculty may begin to contribute in writing as well as peer-reviewing the open textbook library.

In our case, every member of the Rutgers University faculty who contributes in either writing textbooks or peer-reviewing them will be compensated. First, one must know how faculty members are funded in order to do their work. This is part of how the initial implementation costs have been used at other institutions: "The state of Ohio created challenge grants to award up to $50,000 to authors or author teams to create a textbook for open-access use. At the University of Florida (UF), the provost offered all deans up to $30,000 of seed money for faculty who wanted to write an OA text" (Morris-Babb and Henderson 152). Morris-Babb and Henderson continue this train of thought to speak on how university authors who create these academic texts can be funded by the universities who employ them. As Morris-Babb and Henderson explain, at the University of Florida, specifically their Mathematics department and Calculus courses, faculty members grew tired of the very similar $215 textbooks released every so often (153). So, they set out to create an open textbook for their classes. Morris-Babb and Henderson continue by saying, "The money was split between two faculty members, Dr. Sergei Shabanov and Dr. Miklos Bona, both of whom had received the UF Teacher of the Year awards" in order to start the project (153). As Morris-Babb and Henderson explain, after partnering with WebAssign and Integrated Book Technologies (IBT), these two faculty members were able to lower the subscription costs for students on WebAssign from $75 to $25 as well as find a way for students to pay for the print versions of these open textbooks through IBT (154). One may also wonder how Rutgers will be paid for open textbooks in print, and IBT had a solution for that as well. As explained in the article, "The student places the order, paying with either PayPal or other forms of credit, and a professionally printed paperback book ships within twenty-four to forty-eight hours" (154). Therefore, only one question remains in terms of faculty members. How are they to be compensated?

The compensation for each faculty member will be determined on a textbook per textbook basis. In the case of this initial implementation process of five courses, five textbooks must be created. Seth Bergman shows that there is anywhere from one to up to five different types of authors per open textbook; including primary authors, co-authors, secondary authors, contributors, as well as minor contributors (5). For example, Bergmann states that a co-author is someone responsible for the "submission and acceptance of at least one complete chapter" where as a contributor is someone who contributes a "submission and acceptance of at least one chapter section, three figures, diagrams, sample problems, etc." (5). These guidelines must then be developed for Rutgers. Therefore, a primary author will be granted a majority of the money available for compensation based on his/her majority of the work being done. Therefore, writing and peer-reviewing must be separate in terms of compensation. An example of this would be there being one author of the open textbook. In this scenario, that one author would be entitled to 100% of the compensation available for the writing aspect of the textbook. If there were two authors, the percentage of the work submitted by each must be determined. If author A submitted 3 chapters and author B submitted 1, author A would therefore be entitled to 75% of the money and author B would be entitled to 25%. These percentages will be based on the amount of page numbers submitted rather than chapters, as some chapters are shorter than others. The same train of thought goes for peer-reviewing compensation. If one faculty member peer-reviewing 90 pages and another 10, the former would be entitled to 90% of the money and the latter would be entitled to 10%. These percentages will then be multiplied by the total amount in each category, whether writing or peer-reviewing compensation. Again, these compensatory figures between writing and peer-reviewing are kept separate.

To continue, Rutgers University - New Brunswick can then look to start to receive their return on investment as students start to save money and purchase print copies of textbooks. According to research, "Student Public Interest Research Group (Student PIRG) found that 75% of students prefer a printed textbook over a digital textbook, and 60% would buy a low cost print copy even if a digital book were free" (qtd. in Bossaller and Kammer 69). This 60% is a vital percentage in determining the profits for open textbooks. Furthermore, John Levi Hilton and David Wiley state that, "...The average cost of producing a book has decreased to $120,000 per book" (21). This is a price down from the original cost of $150,000 per book when Flat World Knowledge, at the time the article was written in 2011 an open textbook website, launched. Though, because Flat World Knowledge is a company, rather than a school, its cost of creating open textbooks varies a bit differently. According to Hilton and Wiley, Flat World Knowledge spent on average $20,000 a textbook on simply peer-reviewing (21). This $20,000 per textbook will therefore be what is available for faculty members to earn, divided based on their contributions. So forth, once determined how much Rutgers University will have to spend in order to create an open textbook from start to finish, one can determine how Rutgers much Rutgers will profit per open textbook created. Using the $10-40 price tag of a printed open textbook from Senack (5), Rutgers can then take the median price of $25 a textbook in this example, and multiply that by the number of students taking a specific course. For example, Expository Writing is a required class for all Rutgers University - New Brunswick students to take. According to Rutgers University, there are 40,720 students enrolled there ("*Facts and Figures*"). If every student who went through this class his or her freshman year and purchased the open textbook in print, the revenue would be $1,018,000. Of course, not every student will purchase the print copy, and many will choose to download it for free as they are entitled to; but as said above, it is to be argued that many will not. So, if 60% of the students enrolled at Rutgers New Brunswick were to purchase the textbook in print (24,432 students), the revenue would equal $610,800 if the book were priced at $25. It is to be noted that this is simply just one class, one textbook, and one example of how Rutgers will receive its return on investment. Rutgers can then determine what price of each textbook will sway students to purchase the print copy over the free download. The lower the cost, the more students will purchase. The higher the cost, the more profit Rutgers will make on each textbook. This fine line between having a low-cost inclining students to purchase, but a high enough margin for Rutgers to make a worthwhile return on investment is how Rutgers can calculate profits per textbook. Once Rutgers can determine that happy medium, such as the $25 price tag, they will have successfully implemented a profitable open textbook system.

Again, this pilot process will begin with five select introductory courses (100 level) and will take place over a full academic year. After the initial implementation of five open textbooks in five introductory classes, Rutgers University - New Brunswick will review the revenue generated by this system. Upon observation that the system deems positive results, Rutgers will continue to build its open textbook library, specifically with introductory courses. In the long run, Rutgers will move on from all 100 level courses, to 200 and so forth. Eventually, classes of higher levels (300/400) will begin to use open textbooks as they become available. This overall, will bring textbook prices down as a whole. The plan illustrated allows Rutgers University - New Brunswick to not only make its students a lot happier as they pay less and less for textbooks, but allows them to collect a return on investment. This is because faculty members will have already been compensated for their work from the initial implementation costs, so no royalties are given to university authors, thus allowing for the university to reap the profits. Rutgers University – New Brunswick can gain a significant return on investment by working with students, rather than working against them. One last question remains however, what are the costs to make this plan into a reality?

Budget

Open licensed textbooks may be available free for students, provide faculty members with the chance to be compensated, and for Rutgers University—New Brunswick to make a worthwhile profit, but an initial investment for this system to be implemented correctly is needed. The reason that you are the one I am seeking funding is due to the fact that your team is able to take proposed educational projects and create strategies that can better Rutgers University as a whole. The costs in order to make this plan into a reality are listed below:

Seed Money	$30,000
Production	$25,000
Writing (Faculty Compensation)	$20,000
Peer-Reviewing (Faculty Compensation)	$15,000
In-Text Illustrations	$15,000
Mason Gross School of the Arts Undergraduate Student Textbook Cover Artistry/Email Creation	$0
Software	$0
Ten Project Interns	$0
Total	$105,000
Total Initial Implementation Costs for Five Courses	$525,000

Three figures above are based upon Flat World Knowledge, from a study called "*Open Access Textbooks and Financial Sustainability: A Case Study on Flat World Knowledge*" by John Hilton III and David Wiley. Those figures are Writing, Peer-Reviewing, and Production costs. Since Flat World Knowledge is a company, rather than a school, its cost of creating open textbooks varies a bit differently; so many aspects in terms of the budget will be divergent. In this case, their costs are actually a lot more expensive than what Rutgers University—New Brunswick's will be. This is due to the fact that Rutgers can forgo many aspects that are typically needed by a company. Flat World Knowledge spent on average $120,000 per open textbook created (Hilton and Wiley 21). After reviewing what drove costs up for Flat World Knowledge, one is able to view the areas that Rutgers can cut for themselves. For example, alternate versions of textbooks, listed at $15,000, instructor ancillaries at $15,000, and student ancillaries at $15,000 (21). This amounts to $45,000 per textbook that Rutgers can eliminate from the equation. Alternate versions of the textbook include versions such as audio or handheld according to Flat World Knowledge, which Rutgers does not need to pursue in creating (21). Instructor and student ancillaries are not needed as well, as faculty members will be the ones who will be doing the necessary work in order for the textbooks to be created, and the resources they will need are already available to Rutgers University.

The validation for the writing and peer-reviewing go back to what was said about Rutgers being a school, rather than a company. These two figures in the budget are ones that are entirely up to Rutgers because they are compensatory. Therefore, its faculty members will be enticed to create these open textbooks due to the $35,000 compensation available for each textbook. If compensation for these two categories was too low, faculty members may as well choose to create traditional textbooks rather than open textbooks. If compensation is too high, Rutgers could begin to diminish its profit margin. According to Hilton and Wiley, Flat World Knowledge found that, "The cost to acquire one faculty member under this model was over $2,500, and on average that faculty member's course delivered about $225 in gross profit" (21). This goes to show that faculty members currently are valuable in the process of creating open textbooks. Flat World Knowledge originally had authoring fees (writing) listed for $15,000 and peer reviewing for $20,000 (21). Due to what John Hilton III and David Wiley had to say about how much a faculty member costs to acquire, I have switched the costs between writing and peer reviewing, as they are essential components to this project. This $35,000 is then available to faculty members for each textbook created. This therefore generates a very desirable amount of money for faculty members to make, on top of their regular salaries from the institution of Rutgers University – New Brunswick; but at the same time allows for a realistic profit margin. This profit margin was shown in the Expository Writing example. The compensation per faculty member therefore will be based on a percentage system. The more pages one writes or peer-reviews, the more money he/she is entitled to.

The production price is a fairly standard industry cost. As there is no longer a "big money" publisher involved, where manufacturing is taken care of, Rutgers University assumes the costs of producing the textbooks. Flat World Knowledge tells us that production costs include areas such as XML (Extensible Markup Language), proofing, and quality assurance (21). $25,000 is a realistic price based upon this.

Faculty members need money in order to create open textbooks. Following the example of the University of Florida, $30,000 is an adequate amount for faculty members to make open textbooks (Morris-Babb and Henderson 152). Morris-Babb and Henderson state that this seed money was, "split between two faculty members, Dr. Sergei Shabanov and Dr. Miklos Bona" (153). Being that the textbook that these two faculty members were creating were for Calculus, one of the classes that is part of the initial five for this pilot process, $30,000 is to be considered a reasonable amount in terms of seed money.

In-text illustrations are another aspect needed in textbooks. These illustrations help explain material in the text provided by the author. Research Associate Tony Bates tells us that, "designing for an open textbook requires specialist knowledge...I would suspect though one would need a minimum of $10,000 to cover the graphics design, probably more, in order to work in the way that is needed" ("*The Cost of Developing an Open Textbook: $80,000–$130,000*"). Therefore, provided on his web article is a minimum cost of $10,000 but an average of $15,000 for "instructional design" ("*The Cost of Developing an Open Textbook: $80,000–$130,000*"). In order for Rutgers to be sure they do not undervalue the costs associated with in-text illustrations, it would be smart to use the average cost of $15,000.

Aside from in-text illustrations, cover art is still needed for the print and digital copies of the textbooks. For this, undergraduate students from the Mason Gross School of the Arts will have the opportunity to have their work featured on these textbooks. This comes at zero monetary gain for the students, but proves to be a strong piece to be included in their art portfolios. Visual art students specifically, may submit their artwork via email to RUOpenTextProject@rutgers.edu for consideration. It is to be noted this email address is created free of charge. Five designs will be chosen, respectfully one for each course in the initial implementation process. Students must include their name, RU ID, desired textbook, and attached artwork in the email. Students whose artwork is chosen will be emailed within three weeks of submission. Faculty who create the textbooks will choose which artwork they want featured.

In order to create these open textbooks, certain software is needed. For example, Morris-Babb and Henderson tell us that at the University of Florida, the calculus open textbook was, "written in LaTeX, a mathematics program" (153). After researching software possibly needed by faculty for creating open textbooks, software charges will equal $0. Faculty members may use Apache OpenOffice, as their site describes itself as an, "open-source office software suite for word processing, spreadsheets, presentations, databases, and more" for the majority of their work ("*Open Office*"). Programs such LaTeX and Eclipse are also free of charge, allowing for faculty members to create these open textbooks on software that is of no cost to the University.

Ten project interns will be hired by Rutgers University to work with the faculty members who are creating the open textbooks. They will specifically help with the day-to-day operations and provide assistance to faculty members. For every open textbook being created, two interns will be assigned. These interns will also help manage the email account. These are unpaid internships.

Resources needed for Rutgers faculty can be either purchased with the seed money given to them or already be available for free. As Morris-Babb and Henderson stated, "Using their lecture notes as the basis for the text and mining three different calculus books already in the Orange Grove Repository open-access textbook collection for their problems and examples, Shabanov and Bona wrote the text during the summer of 2010" (153). Between Rutgers databases, libraries, and the school's many connections, faculty members do not need to worry about getting the resources that help create textbooks. If a resource does cost money, their seed money will contribute to that.

The total cost for the initial implementation of open textbooks for five courses is $525,000. With each textbook priced at $105,000, Rutgers University is below the average $120,000 per textbook established by Flat World Knowledge (Hilton and Wiley 21). This price is also well within the price margin found by Tony Bates that was between $80,000 and $130,000 ("*The Cost of Developing an Open Textbook: $80,000–$130,000*").

Discussion and Evaluation Plan

The return on investment for Rutgers University goes far beyond the monetary gains associated with implementing an open textbook system into the school. Students are guaranteed to be happier as well as less stressed by not having to worry about high costs of college textbooks. Faculty members have an opportunity to make tens of thousands of dollars in compensation for writing and peer-reviewing these texts. Lastly, the University itself has the chance to invest and create a steady stream of income without having to make deals with publishing companies. Rutgers can change the way that college textbooks are priced and even more importantly, created. Rutgers can be the cornerstone of the revolution of open textbooks and make a positive effect on the nation as a whole. I ask you to speak with your team to see that open textbooks can become a reality at Rutgers and that the future vision detailed can be turned into the present.

If Rutgers was to see that the pilot academic year was successful and garnered the university an impressive amount of profit, they may look to bring open textbooks to more than just the initial five classes. The next classes to have open textbooks would be five more introductory level courses. The exact courses would again be determined based on class registration size and therefore provide a chronological context of the way that classes would be chosen to have open textbooks created for them. As open textbooks would take time to once again be created for new classes, Rutgers would use textbooks from online libraries from other universities while creating their own textbooks for these five new classes. Once the textbooks are completed, they would be implemented for an academic year. The results would determine if yet another five (or more) classes would be a value for Rutgers. It is to be noted that classes that yield positive feedback from the University would continue to use the open textbooks until the material within them becomes outdated. This entire process continues for as long as Rutgers sees positive monetary results for the university.

In the case that Rutgers does not see value in the initial five classes after the first year of use of open textbooks, Rutgers may choose to abandon the project. Rutgers then has two options. The first is to continue printing for the five classes using open textbooks, but not create any new textbooks for other classes. This would be done in order to try and make more money from the project. Since the textbooks will have already been completed, the only costs Rutgers would endure would be printing them. This is a safe plan of action, as Rutgers will have the ability to simply create revenue and make a profit off of the price of selling print copies to students. In my opinion, this is the better option of the two, as Rutgers will have the textbooks in their library and their only cost would be printing. The second option is to completely stop the use of open textbooks, and not print any copies for students. This will entirely erase the project, earning no revenue but instead, wiping Rutgers free from open textbooks as a whole. In both situations however, Rutgers has the option to go back to traditional ways of selling college textbooks. To conclude, open textbooks offer a fairly safe investment opportunity with the potential of benefiting multiple groups of people at Rutgers University—New Brunswick.

Works Cited

Bates, Tony. "*The Cost of Developing an Open Textbook: $80,000–$130,000.*" 8 June 2015.

Bergman, Seth. "Open Source Textbooks: A Paradigm Derived From Open Source Software." *Publishing Research Quarterly*, vol. 30, no. 1, 2014, pp. 1–10. *Academic Search Premier*.

Bossaller, Jenny, and Jenna Kammer. "Faculty Views On Etextbooks: A Narrative Study." *College Teaching*, vol. 62, no. 2, 2014, pp. 68–75. *Academic Search Premier*. 9 Nov. 2015.

Facts and Figures. Rutgers University, 29 Nov. 2015.

Hilton, John, and Carol Laman. "One College's Use Of An Open Psychology Textbook." *Open Learning*, vol. 27, no. 3, 2012, pp. 265–272. *Academic Search Premier*. 25 Sept. 2015.

Hilton, John, and David Wiley. "Open Access Textbooks and Financial Sustainability: A Case Study on Flat World Knowledge." *International Review of Research in Open and Distance Learning*, vol. 12, no. 5, 2011, *ProQuest*. 23 Sept. 2015.

Morris-Babb, Meredith, and Susie Henderson. "An Experiment in Open-Access Textbook Publishing: Changing the World One Textbook at a Time." *Journal of Scholarly Publishing*, vol. 43, no. 2, 2012, pp. 148–155. *Academic Search Premier*. 23 Sept. 2015.

Open Office. Apache, 2010.

Petrides, Lisa, et al. "Open Textbook Adoption and use: Implications for Teachers and Learners." *Open Learning*, vol. 26, no. 1, 2011, pp. 39–49. *Academic Search Premier*. 25 Sept. 2015.

Popken, Ben. "College Textbook Prices Have Risen 1,041 Percent Since 1977." *NBC News*. 6 Aug. 2015.

Rutgers University Senate. *Response to Charge S-1402, (Cost of Textbooks)*. Student Affairs Committee, February 2015.

Scholarly Open Access at Rutgers. Rutgers University, 2015.

"Search the Library." *Open Textbook Library*.

Senack, Ethan. *Open Textbooks: The Billion-Dollar Solution*. The Student PIRGs, February 2015.

Silver, Lawrence S., Robert E. Stevens, and Kenneth E. Clow. "Marketing Professors' Perspectives On The Cost Of College Textbooks: A Pilot Study." *Journal of Education for Business,* vol. 87, no. 1, 2012, pp. 1–6. *Academic Search Premier*. 4 Nov. 2015.

Stone, Robert W., and Lori Baker-Eveleth. "Students' Intentions to Purchase Electronic Textbooks." *Journal of Computing in Higher Education*, vol. 25, no. 1, 2013, pp. 27–47. *ProQuest*. 20 Sept. 2015.

Theory of Reasoned Action. Communication Institute for Online Scholarship,

United States. Congress. *Report to Congressional Committees, College Textbooks, Students Have Greater Access to Textbook Information*. U.S. Government Accountability Office.

Ward, Doug. "Why You Ought To Think Twice Before Assigning A Pricey Textbook." *Chronicle of Higher Education*, vol. 62, no. 2, 2015, pp. 14. *Academic Search Premier*. 4 Nov. 2015.

Yousef, Rama. "Textbooks in Need of Reform, College Students Frustrated." *University Wire*, 31 Oct 2014. *ProQuest*. 20 Sept. 2015.

Name: _____ Date: _____

Chapter 7 ■ Project Proposal Peer Review Workshop I

Please fill out the following form for your partner. Feel free to write comments on the draft as well.

Cover Letter and Title Page

Does the cover letter . . .

1. directly address the funding source? ____yes ____no
2. explain why the reader has received this proposal? ____yes ____no
3. persuade the reader to examine this plan closely? ____yes ____no
4. offer details about the content of the plan? ____yes ____no
5. appear in full block form and include all six elements
   (return address, date, recipient's address, salutation, body, closing)? ____yes ____no

Is the cover letter . . .

1. signed? ____yes ____no
2. free of all grammatical and typographical errors? ____yes ____no

Does the title page . . .

1. include all five elements (project title, name of sender, name of recipient, date, return information)? ____yes ____no
2. catch the attention of the reader? ____yes ____no
3. have a title appropriate to the plan? ____yes ____no

Is the title page . . .

1. visually appealing? ____yes ____no
2. free of all grammatical and typographical errors? ____yes ____no

What parts of the drafts did you like the most?

What parts of the drafts need the most improvement?

Abstract

1. Is the document clearly labeled as an "Abstract" at the top of the page? _____ yes _____ no
2. Is the document written from a third-person perspective? _____ yes _____ no
3. Does the document provide a balanced view of the project idea? _____ yes _____ no
4. Does the document cover elements of the problem, paradigm, and plan (in that order)? _____ yes _____ no
5. Does the document indicate a specific course of action? _____ yes _____ no
6. Is the document between 150 and 300 words and no longer than two paragraphs in length? _____ yes _____ no
7. Is the document single-spaced, in 12 point Times New Roman type? _____ yes _____ no
8. Is the document free of errors in grammar, usage, and/or sentence structure? _____ yes _____ no
9. Is the document presented in a clear, readable form? _____ yes _____ no
10. Would this document encourage me to read this plan? _____ yes _____ no

What is the one part of the draft you liked the most?

What is the one part of the draft that needs the most improvement?

Table of Contents and Table of Figures

1. Are these documents clearly labeled and presented in a logical and readable form? _____ yes _____ no
2. Are these documents free of errors in grammar, spacing, and punctuation? _____ yes _____ no

Additional Comments/Suggestions:

Name: _____ Date: _____

Chapter 7 ■ Project Proposal Peer Review Workshop I

Please fill out the following form for your partner. Feel free to write comments on the draft as well.

Cover Letter and Title Page

Does the cover letter . . .

1. directly address the funding source? _____yes _____no
2. explain why the reader has received this proposal? _____yes _____no
3. persuade the reader to examine this plan closely? _____yes _____no
4. offer details about the content of the plan? _____yes _____no
5. appear in full block form and include all six elements
   (return address, date, recipient's address, salutation, body, closing)? _____yes _____no

Is the cover letter . . .

1. signed? _____yes _____no
2. free of all grammatical and typographical errors? _____yes _____no

Does the title page . . .

1. include all five elements (project title, name of sender, name of recipient, date, return information)? _____yes _____no
2. catch the attention of the reader? _____yes _____no
3. have a title appropriate to the plan? _____yes _____no

Is the title page . . .

1. visually appealing? _____yes _____no
2. free of all grammatical and typographical errors? _____yes _____no

What parts of the drafts did you like the most?

What parts of the drafts need the most improvement?

Chapter 7 ■ Project Proposal Peer Review Workshop I   255

Abstract

1. Is the document clearly labeled as an "Abstract" at the top of the page? _____ yes _____ no
2. Is the document written from a third-person perspective? _____ yes _____ no
3. Does the document provide a balanced view of the project idea? _____ yes _____ no
4. Does the document cover elements of the problem, paradigm, and plan (in that order)? _____ yes _____ no
5. Does the document indicate a specific course of action? _____ yes _____ no
6. Is the document between 150 and 300 words and no longer than two paragraphs in length? _____ yes _____ no
7. Is the document single-spaced, in 12 point Times New Roman type? _____ yes _____ no
8. Is the document free of errors in grammar, usage, and/or sentence structure? _____ yes _____ no
9. Is the document presented in a clear, readable form? _____ yes _____ no
10. Would this document encourage me to read this plan? _____ yes _____ no

What is the one part of the draft you liked the most?

What is the one part of the draft that needs the most improvement?

Table of Contents and Table of Figures

1. Are these documents clearly labeled and presented in a logical and readable form? _____ yes _____ no
2. Are these documents free of errors in grammar, spacing, and punctuation? _____ yes _____ no

Additional Comments/Suggestions:

Name: _____ Date: _____

Chapter 7 ■ Project Proposal Peer Review Workshop I

Please fill out the following form for your partner. Feel free to write comments on the draft as well.

Cover Letter and Title Page

Does the cover letter . . .

1. directly address the funding source? ____yes ____no
2. explain why the reader has received this proposal? ____yes ____no
3. persuade the reader to examine this plan closely? ____yes ____no
4. offer details about the content of the plan? ____yes ____no
5. appear in full block form and include all six elements
   (return address, date, recipient's address, salutation, body, closing)? ____yes ____no

Is the cover letter . . .

1. signed? ____yes ____no
2. free of all grammatical and typographical errors? ____yes ____no

Does the title page . . .

1. include all five elements (project title, name of sender, name of recipient, date, return information)? ____yes ____no
2. catch the attention of the reader? ____yes ____no
3. have a title appropriate to the plan? ____yes ____no

Is the title page . . .

1. visually appealing? ____yes ____no
2. free of all grammatical and typographical errors? ____yes ____no

What parts of the drafts did you like the most?

What parts of the drafts need the most improvement?

Abstract

1. Is the document clearly labeled as an "Abstract" at the top of the page? _____ yes _____ no
2. Is the document written from a third-person perspective? _____ yes _____ no
3. Does the document provide a balanced view of the project idea? _____ yes _____ no
4. Does the document cover elements of the problem, paradigm, and plan (in that order)? _____ yes _____ no
5. Does the document indicate a specific course of action? _____ yes _____ no
6. Is the document between 150 and 300 words and no longer than two paragraphs in length? _____ yes _____ no
7. Is the document single-spaced, in 12 point Times New Roman type? _____ yes _____ no
8. Is the document free of errors in grammar, usage, and/or sentence structure? _____ yes _____ no
9. Is the document presented in a clear, readable form? _____ yes _____ no
10. Would this document encourage me to read this plan? _____ yes _____ no

What is the one part of the draft you liked the most?

What is the one part of the draft that needs the most improvement?

Table of Contents and Table of Figures

1. Are these documents clearly labeled and presented in a logical and readable form? _____ yes _____ no
2. Are these documents free of errors in grammar, spacing, and punctuation? _____ yes _____ no

Additional Comments/Suggestions:

Name: _____ Date: _____

Chapter 7 ■ Project Proposal Peer Review Workshop II

Please fill out the following form for your partner. Feel free to write comments on the drafts as well.

Executive Summary

1. Is the document clearly labeled as an "Executive Summary" at the top of the page? _____ yes _____ no
2. Is the document within the two-page guideline? _____ yes _____ no
3. Does the document follow the order of the full proposal? _____ yes _____ no
4. Does the document provide key details and evidence? _____ yes _____ no
5. Does the document use persuasive language? _____ yes _____ no
6. Is all source material cited appropriately in MLA format? _____ yes _____ no
7. Is the document single-spaced, in 12 point Times New Roman type? _____ yes _____ no
8. Is the document free of errors in grammar, usage and/or sentence structure? _____ yes _____ no
9. Is the document presented in a clear, readable form? _____ yes _____ no
10. Would this document encourage someone to read the full plan? _____ yes _____ no

Which part of the draft did you like the most?

Which part of the draft needs the most improvement?

Additional Comments/Suggestions:

Name: _____ Date: _____

Chapter 7 ▪ Project Proposal Peer Review Workshop II

Please fill out the following form for your partner. Feel free to write comments on the drafts as well.

Executive Summary

1. Is the document clearly labeled as an "Executive Summary" at the top of the page? _____ yes _____ no
2. Is the document within the two-page guideline? _____ yes _____ no
3. Does the document follow the order of the full proposal? _____ yes _____ no
4. Does the document provide key details and evidence? _____ yes _____ no
5. Does the document use persuasive language? _____ yes _____ no
6. Is all source material cited appropriately in MLA format? _____ yes _____ no
7. Is the document single-spaced, in 12 point Times New Roman type? _____ yes _____ no
8. Is the document free of errors in grammar, usage and/or sentence structure? _____ yes _____ no
9. Is the document presented in a clear, readable form? _____ yes _____ no
10. Would this document encourage someone to read the full plan? _____ yes _____ no

Which part of the draft did you like the most?

Which part of the draft needs the most improvement?

Additional Comments/Suggestions:

Name: _____ Date: _____

Chapter 7 ■ Project Proposal Peer Review Workshop II

Please fill out the following form for your partner. Feel free to write comments on the drafts as well.

Executive Summary

1. Is the document clearly labeled as an "Executive Summary" at the top of the page? _____ yes _____ no
2. Is the document within the two-page guideline? _____ yes _____ no
3. Does the document follow the order of the full proposal? _____ yes _____ no
4. Does the document provide key details and evidence? _____ yes _____ no
5. Does the document use persuasive language? _____ yes _____ no
6. Is all source material cited appropriately in MLA format? _____ yes _____ no
7. Is the document single-spaced, in 12 point Times New Roman type? _____ yes _____ no
8. Is the document free of errors in grammar, usage and/or sentence structure? _____ yes _____ no
9. Is the document presented in a clear, readable form? _____ yes _____ no
10. Would this document encourage someone to read the full plan? _____ yes _____ no

Which part of the draft did you like the most?

Which part of the draft needs the most improvement?

Additional Comments/Suggestions:

Name: _____ Date: _____

Chapter 7 ■ Project Proposal Peer Review Workshop III

Please fill out the following form for your partner. Feel free to write comments on the draft as well.

Introduction and Literature Review

Does the introduction . . .

1. attempt to define and quantify the problem? _____yes _____no
2. include visuals that help clarify and emphasize the key aspects of the problem? _____yes _____no
3. focus on the aspects of the problem that would most interest the reader? _____yes _____no
4. suggest a direction for approaching the problem? _____yes _____no
5. close with a forecasting statement giving the reader a sense of the argument to follow and providing a transition to the next section? _____yes _____no

Is the introduction . . .

1. single-spaced, in 12 point Times New Roman font? _____yes _____no
2. free of all grammatical and typographical errors? _____yes _____no

Does the literature review . . .

1. open with a reference to the problem? _____yes _____no
2. focus on the paradigm of the project? _____yes _____no
3. explain why the problem will be approached in a particular way? _____yes _____no
4. provide a unified rationale for the specific plan of action? _____yes _____no
5. show how the plan of action proposed is a logical approach to the problem defined? _____yes _____no
6. include the most useful and authoritative sources (especially those subject to peer review)? _____yes _____no

Is the literature review . . .

1. single-spaced, in 12 point Times New Roman font? _____yes _____no
2. free of all grammatical and typographical errors? _____yes _____no

What parts of the drafts did you like the most?

What parts of the drafts need the most improvement?

Additional Comments/Suggestions:

Name: _____   Date: _____

Chapter 7 ■ Project Proposal Peer Review Workshop III

Please fill out the following form for your partner. Feel free to write comments on the draft as well.

Introduction and Literature Review

Does the introduction . . .

1. attempt to define and quantify the problem? _____yes _____no
2. include visuals that help clarify and emphasize the key aspects of the problem? _____yes _____no
3. focus on the aspects of the problem that would most interest the reader? _____yes _____no
4. suggest a direction for approaching the problem? _____yes _____no
5. close with a forecasting statement giving the reader a sense of the argument to follow and providing a transition to the next section? _____yes _____no

Is the introduction . . .

1. single-spaced, in 12 point Times New Roman font? _____yes _____no
2. free of all grammatical and typographical errors? _____yes _____no

Does the literature review . . .

1. open with a reference to the problem? _____yes _____no
2. focus on the paradigm of the project? _____yes _____no
3. explain why the problem will be approached in a particular way? _____yes _____no
4. provide a unified rationale for the specific plan of action? _____yes _____no
5. show how the plan of action proposed is a logical approach to the problem defined? _____yes _____no
6. include the most useful and authoritative sources (especially those subject to peer review)? _____yes _____no

Is the literature review . . .

1. single-spaced, in 12 point Times New Roman font? _____yes _____no
2. free of all grammatical and typographical errors? _____yes _____no

What parts of the drafts did you like the most?

What parts of the drafts need the most improvement?

Additional Comments/Suggestions:

Name: _____ Date: _____

Chapter 7 ■ Project Proposal Peer Review Workshop III

Please fill out the following form for your partner. Feel free to write comments on the draft as well.

Introduction and Literature Review

Does the introduction . . .

1. attempt to define and quantify the problem? _____yes _____no
2. include visuals that help clarify and emphasize the key aspects of the problem? _____yes _____no
3. focus on the aspects of the problem that would most interest the reader? _____yes _____no
4. suggest a direction for approaching the problem? _____yes _____no
5. close with a forecasting statement giving the reader a sense of the argument to follow and providing a transition to the next section? _____yes _____no

Is the introduction . . .

1. single-spaced, in 12 point Times New Roman font? _____yes _____no
2. free of all grammatical and typographical errors? _____yes _____no

Does the literature review . . .

1. open with a reference to the problem? _____yes _____no
2. focus on the paradigm of the project? _____yes _____no
3. explain why the problem will be approached in a particular way? _____yes _____no
4. provide a unified rationale for the specific plan of action? _____yes _____no
5. show how the plan of action proposed is a logical approach to the problem defined? _____yes _____no
6. include the most useful and authoritative sources (especially those subject to peer review)? _____yes _____no

Is the literature review . . .

1. single-spaced, in 12 point Times New Roman font? _____yes _____no
2. free of all grammatical and typographical errors? _____yes _____no

What parts of the drafts did you like the most?

What parts of the drafts need the most improvement?

Additional Comments/Suggestions:

Name: _____ Date: _____

Chapter 7 ■ Project Proposal Peer Review Workshop IV

Please fill out the following form for your partner. Feel free to write comments on the draft as well.

Plan, Budget, and Discussion

Does the plan . . .

    1. transition logically from the research?   ____yes ____no
    2. focus on how the idea will be implemented?   ____yes ____no
    3. reference research to support the writer's choices?   ____yes ____no
    4. present information clearly?   ____yes ____no
    5. consider all possibilities in justifying its recommendations?   ____yes ____no

Is the plan . . .

    1. organized logically?   ____yes ____no
    2. free of unanswered questions or areas of confusion?   ____yes ____no
    3. single-spaced, in 12 point Times New Roman font?   ____yes ____no
    4. free of all grammatical and typographical errors?   ____yes ____no

Does the budget . . .

    1. list everything needed for the project?   ____yes ____no
    2. explain items that may be unfamiliar to the reader?   ____yes ____no

Is the budget . . .

    1. arranged in aligned accountant's columns?   ____yes ____no
    2. single-spaced, in 12 point Times New Roman font?   ____yes ____no
    3. free of all mathematical, grammatical, and typographical errors?   ____yes ____no

Does the discussion . . .

    1. conclude by summing up the project?   ____yes ____no
    2. make a final pitch for the value of the project?   ____yes ____no
    3. offer an evaluation plan for testing the results?   ____yes ____no

Is the discussion . . .

    1. single-spaced, in 12 point Times New Roman font?   ____yes ____no
    2. free of all grammatical and typographical errors?   ____yes ____no

Which parts of the drafts did you like the most?

Which parts of the drafts need the most improvement?

Works Cited

1. Is the document clearly labeled as a list of Works Cited at the top of the page? _____ yes _____ no
2. Does the document contain a minimum of ten published sources? _____ yes _____ no
3. Are there various types of sources represented (books to develop a theoretical framework, scholarly journals for detailed models, etc.)? _____ yes _____ no
4. Are at least 50% of the references cited from scholarly sources? _____ yes _____ no
5. Is the document formatted in proper MLA citation style (alphabetized, indented after first line, publication elements ordered correctly, etc.)? _____ yes _____ no
6. Is the document correctly spaced, in 12 point Times New Roman type, with one-inch margins? _____ yes _____ no
7. Is the document free of errors in grammar, punctuation, and capitalization? _____ yes _____ no

Additional Comments/Suggestions:

Name: _____ Date: _____

Chapter 7 ■ Project Proposal Peer Review Workshop IV

Please fill out the following form for your partner. Feel free to write comments on the draft as well.

Plan, Budget, and Discussion

Does the plan . . .

1. transition logically from the research?   _____yes _____no
2. focus on how the idea will be implemented?   _____yes _____no
3. reference research to support the writer's choices?   _____yes _____no
4. present information clearly?   _____yes _____no
5. consider all possibilities in justifying its recommendations?   _____yes _____no

Is the plan . . .

1. organized logically?   _____yes _____no
2. free of unanswered questions or areas of confusion?   _____yes _____no
3. single-spaced, in 12 point Times New Roman font?   _____yes _____no
4. free of all grammatical and typographical errors?   _____yes _____no

Does the budget . . .

1. list everything needed for the project?   _____yes _____no
2. explain items that may be unfamiliar to the reader?   _____yes _____no

Is the budget . . .

1. arranged in aligned accountant's columns?   _____yes _____no
2. single-spaced, in 12 point Times New Roman font?   _____yes _____no
3. free of all mathematical, grammatical, and typographical errors?   _____yes _____no

Does the discussion . . .

1. conclude by summing up the project?   _____yes _____no
2. make a final pitch for the value of the project?   _____yes _____no
3. offer an evaluation plan for testing the results?   _____yes _____no

Is the discussion . . .

1. single-spaced, in 12 point Times New Roman font?   _____yes _____no
2. free of all grammatical and typographical errors?   _____yes _____no

Which parts of the drafts did you like the most?

Which parts of the drafts need the most improvement?

Works Cited

1. Is the document clearly labeled as a list of Works Cited at the top of the page? _____ yes _____ no
2. Does the document contain a minimum of ten published sources? _____ yes _____ no
3. Are there various types of sources represented (books to develop a theoretical framework, scholarly journals for detailed models, etc.)? _____ yes _____ no
4. Are at least 50% of the references cited from scholarly sources? _____ yes _____ no
5. Is the document formatted in proper MLA citation style (alphabetized, indented after first line, publication elements ordered correctly, etc.)? _____ yes _____ no
6. Is the document correctly spaced, in 12 point Times New Roman type, with one-inch margins? _____ yes _____ no
7. Is the document free of errors in grammar, punctuation, and capitalization? _____ yes _____ no

Additional Comments/Suggestions:

Name: _____ Date: _____

Chapter 7 ■ Project Proposal Peer Review Workshop IV

Please fill out the following form for your partner. Feel free to write comments on the draft as well.

Plan, Budget, and Discussion

Does the plan . . .

1. transition logically from the research? _____yes _____no
2. focus on how the idea will be implemented? _____yes _____no
3. reference research to support the writer's choices? _____yes _____no
4. present information clearly? _____yes _____no
5. consider all possibilities in justifying its recommendations? _____yes _____no

Is the plan . . .

1. organized logically? _____yes _____no
2. free of unanswered questions or areas of confusion? _____yes _____no
3. single-spaced, in 12 point Times New Roman font? _____yes _____no
4. free of all grammatical and typographical errors? _____yes _____no

Does the budget . . .

1. list everything needed for the project? _____yes _____no
2. explain items that may be unfamiliar to the reader? _____yes _____no

Is the budget . . .

1. arranged in aligned accountant's columns? _____yes _____no
2. single-spaced, in 12 point Times New Roman font? _____yes _____no
3. free of all mathematical, grammatical, and typographical errors? _____yes _____no

Does the discussion . . .

1. conclude by summing up the project? _____yes _____no
2. make a final pitch for the value of the project? _____yes _____no
3. offer an evaluation plan for testing the results? _____yes _____no

Is the discussion . . .

1. single-spaced, in 12 point Times New Roman font? _____yes _____no
2. free of all grammatical and typographical errors? _____yes _____no

Which parts of the drafts did you like the most?

Which parts of the drafts need the most improvement?

Works Cited

1. Is the document clearly labeled as a list of Works Cited at the top of the page? _____ yes _____ no

2. Does the document contain a minimum of ten published sources? _____ yes _____ no

3. Are there various types of sources represented (books to develop a theoretical framework, scholarly journals for detailed models, etc.)? _____ yes _____ no

4. Are at least 50% of the references cited from scholarly sources? _____ yes _____ no

5. Is the document formatted in proper MLA citation style (alphabetized, indented after first line, publication elements ordered correctly, etc.)? _____ yes _____ no

6. Is the document correctly spaced, in 12 point Times New Roman type, with one-inch margins? _____ yes _____ no

7. Is the document free of errors in grammar, punctuation, and capitalization? _____ yes _____ no

Additional Comments/Suggestions:

Name: _____ Course: _____ Semester: _____

Chapter 7 ■ Project Proposal Evaluation

1. The proposal includes all necessary sections and is within the page-length requirement.
   1   2   3   4   5   6   7   8   9   10

2. The proposal strives to persuade (and address the needs of) its audience.
   1   2   3   4   5   6   7   8   9   10

3. The proposal clearly defines and quantifies a viable problem, using published research and fieldwork.
   1   2   3   4   5   6   7   8   9   10

4. The proposal attempts a challenging and/or original task.
   1   2   3   4   5   6   7   8   9   10

5. The proposal is based upon relevant and/or innovative scholarly research.
   1   2   3   4   5   6   7   8   9   10

6. The Works Cited page includes the required number of sources and is presented in MLA format.
   1   2   3   4   5   6   7   8   9   10

7. The research is organized into a clearly and carefully delineated paradigm.
   1   2   3   4   5   6   7   8   9   10

8. The plan of action follows logically from the research and is specifically described to the audience.
   1   2   3   4   5   6   7   8   9   10

9. The proposal places sources in logical relation to each other and to the project as a whole.
   1   2   3   4   5   6   7   8   9   10

10. The proposal is fully justified by the published research.
    1   2   3   4   5   6   7   8   9   10

11. The proposal engages possible complications suggested by the research or the plan.
    1   2   3   4   5   6   7   8   9   10

12. The transitions and headings help guide the reader through the project.

    1 2 3 4 5 6 7 8 9 10

13. The visuals are appropriate and effective at conveying information to the reader.

    1 2 3 4 5 6 7 8 9 10

14. The writing is fluent and virtually error-free.

    1 2 3 4 5 6 7 8 9 10

15. The proposal exhibits an overall attractive appearance and visually appealing design.

    1 2 3 4 5 6 7 8 9 10

Index

A

Abstract, 214
  sample, 220, 233
Action, in six Ps, 5–6
Active voice, 195
Addictions, 19
Annotated bibliography, 155
  peer review workshop, 163, 165, 167
Annotation, 155
Appendix, 216
The Aquarian Conspiracy, 18
Arford, Tammi, 75, 90
  "'I'm Ambivalent about It': The Dilemmas of PowerPoint" discussion questions, 91–92
  "'I'm Ambivalent about It': The Dilemmas of PowerPoint" reading, 75–87
Assumptions, 19
Attire, 193–194
Audience, 170–171, 192, 196
  in PowerPoint presentation, 195
  researching, 192

B

Background information, excessive, 197
Banking crisis, and CLS pedagogy, 58–59
Barker, Joel Arthur, *vii*, 15, 17
  Defining a Paradigm discussion questions, 23-24
  Defining a Paradigm reading, 17–21
Benchmark, 3
Book, as source, 152, 154–155
Border, 195
Brand, Stewart, 25

Budget, 4, 216
  sample, 228, 246–249
Business school pedagogy, 52–53
Business Source Premier, 6, 152
Business strategy, 37

C

Call to action, 198
Chart, 107, 195
Citations
  Huffman multimedia presentation model, 118–121
  "The Missing Link: The Lack of Citations and Copyright Notices in Multimedia Presentations" essay, 115–122
  MLA style, 153–155
  in PowerPoint, 195
Closing, letter, 172, 213
Collinson, David, 15, 49, 72
  "Teaching Leadership Critically: New Directions for Leadership Pedagogy" discussion questions, 73–74
  "Teaching Leadership Critically: New Directions for Leadership Pedagogy" reading, 49–67
Color, 195
Common sense, 19
Complexity, 145
Compulsions, 19
Conventional wisdom, 19
Copyright, "The Missing Link: The Lack of Citations and Copyright Notices in Multimedia Presentations" essay, 115–122

Conventions, 19
Corporate social responsibility, 42
Cover letter, 125, 126, 127, 130
    peer review workshop, 133, 135
    in proposal, 212–213
Culture, 15, 39
Customs, 19

D

Darwinian theory, 36
Data
    collecting, 139
    "Organizing Data in Tables and Charts: Different Criteria for Different Tasks" essay, 107–111
Data organization, 107
Decision making, and knowledge, 1
Defining a Paradigm, vii, 17–21
Delivery, 193–194
    and attire, 193–194
    context of, 194
    enunciation in, 194
    eye contact, 194
    humor in, 194
    movement during, 194
    "sell" your idea, 194
    tone in, 194
Dennett, Mary, 25
Diagrams, 216
Disciplinary matrix, 3
Discussion, 216
    sample, 229, 249
Doctrine, 19
Dogma, 19
Drawings, 216
Drucker, Peter, 1

E

Economism and humanism, 34–44
Email, 155
Empathy, 172
Enunciation, 194
Essays, 17–124. *see also* Readings/essays
Evaluation plan, 216
Evidence, 172
Examples, in letter, 172
Executive summary, 214, 214–215
    sample, 221–222, 234–236
Exemplar, 3
Eye contact, 194

F

Fair use, 116–117
Fellowship, 61–63
Ferguson, Marilyn, 18
Fieldwork, *viii*, 139, 145
Figures list, sample, 220, 234
Figures, table of, 214
First impression, 171
"The 5 R's: An Emerging Bold Standard for Conducting Relevant Research in a Changing World", 93–104
Floor plans, 216
Flowcharts, 216
Follow-up, 172
Font, 195
Forests of paradigms, 19
Frames of reference, 19

G

Gantt charts, 216
Glasglow, Russell E., 93
    "The 5 R's: An Emerging Bold Standard for Conducting Relevant Research in a Changing World" discussion questions, 105–106
    "The 5 R's: An Emerging Bold Standard for Conducting Relevant Research in a Changing World" reading, 93–104
Google, 142, 152
Google images, 200
Governance, 37–38
Government documents, 155
Graphics, 193, 195, 199
Graphs, 195, 199
    editing, 199

H

Habits, 19
Handicraft, 25
Harmon, Willis, 17
Healthcare, and research, 93
Hill, Andrea, 15, 75, 90
    "'I'm Ambivalent about It': The Dilemmas of PowerPoint" discussion questions, 91–92
    "'I'm Ambivalent about It': The Dilemmas of PowerPoint" reading, 75–87
Huffman, Stephanie, 15, 115
    "The Missing Link: The Lack of Citations and Copyright Notices in Multimedia Presentations" discussion questions, 123–124

"The Missing Link: The Lack of Citations and Copyright Notices in Multimedia Presentations" reading, 115–122
Huffman multimedia presentation model, 118–121
"Humanism in Business—Towards a Paradigm Shift?", 33–44
Humor, 194
Hypothesis, 3

I

Ideology, 19
Imagined audience, 192
"I'm Ambivalent about It: The Dilemmas of PowerPoint", 75–87
An Incomplete Guide to the Future, 17
Inhibitions, 19
Initial sales letter, 167, 169–184. see also Sales letter
Intellectual property, 116
Interdependence, of six Ps, 4–5
Internet, 125
Internet search, 152
Internet sources, 140, 152
Interview, 155
Introduction, 215
  sample, 222, 236–239

J

Job advertisement, 125
Job description, 126, 129
Job search, 125–131. see also Cover letter; Resume
Journal, as source, 140, 152

K

Kelly, Kevin, 27
Kessler, Rodger S., 93
  "The 5 R's: An Emerging Bold Standard for Conducting Relevant Research in a Changing World" discussion questions, 105–106
  "The 5 R's: An Emerging Bold Standard for Conducting Relevant Research in a Changing World" reading, 93–104
Key points, 193
Klesges, Lisa M., 93
  "The 5 R's: An Emerging Bold Standard for Conducting Relevant Research in a Changing World" discussion questions, 105–106

  "The 5 R's: An Emerging Bold Standard for Conducting Relevant Research in a Changing World" reading, 93–104
Knowledge, in decision making, 1
Knowledge, lack of, 143
Knowledge society, 1
Knowledge workers, 1
Kuhn, Thomas, *vii*, 3, 15, 17, 18, 20, 21

L

Lawrence, Paul R., 15
  "Humanism in Business—Towards a Paradigm Shift?" discussion questions, 47–48
  "Humanism in Business—Towards a Paradigm Shift?" reading, 33–46
Leadership, 15, 38–39, 49
  "Teaching Leadership Critically: New Directions for Leadership Pedagogy" essay, 49–72
Leadership romanticism, 54
Letter. see Cover letter
Letter of persuasion, 169
Library research, 141
Literature review, 215
  purpose, 215
  sample, 225, 239–243
Logic, 195
Logo, 195
Lubitow, Amy, 75, 90
  "'I'm Ambivalent about It': The Dilemmas of PowerPoint" discussion questions, 91–92
  "'I'm Ambivalent about It': The Dilemmas of PowerPoint" reading, 75–90

M

Magazine, 140
"Making It," 25–30
Manageability, of idea, 145
Management theory, 15
Maps, 216
Master slide, 200
Megatrends, 19
Methodology, 19
Miller, Jane E., 15, 107
  "Organizing Data in Tables and Charts: Different Criteria for Different Tasks" discussion questions, 113–114
  "Organizing Data in Tables and Charts: Different Criteria for Different Tasks" reading, 107–111

Mind-set, 19
"The Missing Link: The Lack of Citations and Copyright Notices in Multimedia Presentations, 115–122
MLA Handbook for Writers of Research Papers, 153, 216
MLA style. *see* Modern Language Association (MLA) style
Model, 19
Models of success, 143, 144
Modern Language Association (MLA) style, 153–155
   annotated bibliographies, 155
   non-accessible sources, 154
   in-text citation, 153–154
   works cited page, 154–155
Morozov, Evgeny, 15, 21, 25
   "Making It" discussion questions, 31–32
   "Making It" reading, 25–30
Multimedia presentations, "The Missing Link: The Lack of Citations and Copyright Notices in Multimedia Presentations" essay, 115–122

N

Naisbitt, John, 19, 20
Nerves, during presentation, 196
New Sense Bulletin, 18
Newsletter, 140
Newspaper, 125, 155
Newspaper exercise, 7
Non-accessible sources, 154
Normal science, 15
Notecards, 193

O

Online clearinghouses, 141–142
Online resources, 141–142
Oral draft, 191
Oral presentation, 191–207
   advice for, 196–198
   assignment, 191
   and audience, 196–197
   basic parts of, 192
   delivery of, 193–194
   evaluation form, 209
   and logic, 197
   and nerves, 196
   and PowerPoint, 194–196
   preparing for, 192–193
   and presentation software, 198–200
   vs. project proposal, 192
   sample slides, 201–207
   visual aids, 200
Organization charts, 216
Organization of presentation, 199
"Organizing Data in Tables and Charts: Different Criteria for Different Tasks," 107–111
Originality, 145
Outline, 193

P

Paradigm, 15
   defined, 18
   Defining a Paradigm essay, 17–21
   and research, 143
Paradigm, as part of proposal, *vii*, 3, 5, 11, 13, 143
Paradigm-based plan, 2
Paradigm shift, 15, 19, 20, 21
   "Humanism in Business—Towards a Paradigm Shift?" essay, 33–46
Paradigm shifter, 21
Parallel form rule, 196
Paraphrase, 195
Parenthetical citation, 152–153
Partners, 4
Parts, of proposal
   abstract, 214
   appendix, 216
   budget, 216
   cover letter, 212–213
   discussion, 216
   executive summary, 214
   figures, 214
   introduction, 215
   literature review/research, 215
   plan, 215–216
   table of contents, 214
   title page, 213
   visual aids, 216
   works cited, 216
Patron, and research, 141–142
Patron, as part of proposal, 1, 2, 5, 11, 13
Patterns, 19
Peek, C. J., 15, 93
   "The 5 R's: An Emerging Bold Standard for Conducting Relevant Research in a Changing World" discussion questions, 105–106
   "The 5 R's: An Emerging Bold Standard for Conducting Relevant Research in a Changing World" reading, 93–104

Peer-reviewed publication, 140
Periodical, 155
Persistence, 172
Persuasion, 140, 169
Photos, 199, 216
Pie chart, 198
Pirson, Michael A., 15, 33
    "Humanism in Business—Towards a Paradigm Shift?" discussion questions, 47–48
    "Humanism in Business—Towards a Paradigm Shift?" reading, 33–46
Plan, 215–216
    sample, 227–228, 243–246
Plan, as part of proposal, 3–4, 5, 11, 13, 215–216
Point, getting to, 172
Politics, 4
Popular publication, 139
Population, as part of proposal, 2, 5, 11, 13
PowerPoint
    active voice, 195
    advice on using, 194–195
    and audience, 195
    and background information, 197
    citations in, 195
    color in, 195
    "Don'ts" in, 196
    "Don'ts" on, 196
    font, 195
    headers, 195
    "'I'm Ambivalent about It': The Dilemmas of PowerPoint" essay, 75–90
    sample slides, 201–207
    themes, 195
    title slide, 194–195
    and visual aids, 199, 200
PowerPoint dilemmas, 75
Powers of the Mind, 17
Prejudices, 19
Preparation, 193
Presentation, 191–200. *see also* Oral presentation
Presentation software, 198–200
    graphics, 199
    graphs, 199
    master slide, 200
    organizing presentation, 199
    photos, 199
    tables, 199
    text, 200
    title slide, 199
    what to include, 198

Price, as part of proposal, 4, 5, 11, 13, 216
Principles, 19
Primary source, 139, 140, 143
Problem, and research, 142
Problem, as part of proposal, 2–3, 5, 11, 13, 142
Problem solving model, 3
Procedure, 215–216
Professional publication, 139
Project proposal, 1–6, 211–278
    abstract, 214
    appendix, 216
    assignment, 211–212
    budget, 216
    cover letter, 212–213
    discussion, 216
    evaluation form, 277–278
    evaluation plan, 216
    executive summary, 214
    figures, 216
    interdependence of six Ps, 4–5
    introduction, 215
    literature review/research, 215
    vs. oral presentation, 192
    paradigm, 2, 3
    and partners, 4
    patron, 1, 2
    peer review workshop, 253–276
    plan, 3–4
    plan/procedures, 215–216
    and politics, 4
    population, 1, 2
    price, 4
    problem, 2–3
    sample project proposals, 217, 218–251
    samples of, 216
    six P formula in, 1–4
    six Ps in action, 5–6
    table of contents, 214
    table of figures, 214
    title page, 213
    visual aids, 216
    "why" questions in, 1
    works cited page, 216
Project scope, 145
Proposal, 1–6. *see also* Project proposal
Protocol, 19
Purcell, E. Peyton, 93
    "The 5 R's: An Emerging Bold Standard for Conducting Relevant Research in a Changing World" discussion questions, 105–106

"The 5 R's: An Emerging Bold Standard for Conducting Relevant Research in a Changing World" reading, 93–104

Q
Quantify, problem, 3
Quote, 195

R
Reader, identifying with, 171
Readings/essays, 15–16, 17–124
    "The 5 R's: An Emerging Bold Standard for Conducting Relevant Research in a Changing World," 93–104, 105–106
    Defining a Paradigm, 17–21, 23–24
    "Humanism in Business—Towards a Paradigm Shift?," 33–46, 47–48
    "'I'm Ambivalent about It': The Dilemmas of PowerPoint," 75–90, 91–92
    "Making It," 25–30, 31–32
    "The Missing Link: The Lack of Citations and Copyright Notices in Multimedia Presentations," 115–122, 123–124
    "Organizing Data in Tables and Charts: Different Criteria for Different Tasks," 107–111
    "Organizing Data in Tables and Charts: Different Criteria for Different Tasks," 113–114
    "Teaching Leadership Critically: New Directions for Leadership Pedagogy," 49–72, 73–74
Rehearsal, 193
Relationship marketing, 6
Request for Proposal (RFP), 170, 211
Research, 139–167
    "The 5 R's: An Emerging Bold Standard for Conducting Relevant Research in a Changing World" essay, 93–104
    annotated bibliographies, 155–161, 163, 165, 167
    book sources, 152
    Internet sources, 152
    journal sources, 152
    library sources, 152
    MLA style, 153–155
    paradigm, 143
    patron, 141–142
    primary sources, 139
    problem, 142–143
    secondary, 139–141
    success models search, 144
    theoretical frame search, 144
    theory and practice merge, 144
    white paper assignment, 145
    white paper samples, 146–151
Research, and project, 5
Research-based rationale, 3
Resume, 125, 126, 128, 131
    peer review workshop, 133, 135
Revision, 5, 211
Rituals, 19
Ross, Denman W., 25
Routines, 19

S
Sales letter, 169–184
    14 steps to a strong sales letter, 170–172
    assignment, 169
    letter of persuasion, 169
    peer review workshop, 185–190
    pitfalls and problems, 170
    purpose, 170
    requirements, 169–170
    sample letters, 173, 174–184
Salutation, 171, 213
Scale of problem, 142
Scholarly publication, 139
Scientific practice, 17
Secondary source, 139–140
    popular, 140–141
    professional, 140
    scholarly, 140
Six P formula (Six Ps), *vii*
    in action, 5–6
    interdependence of, 4–5
    newspaper exercise, 7
    and oral presentation, 192
    other considerations in, 4
    paradigm, 2, 3
    and partners, 4
    patron, 1, 2
    plan, 3–4
    and politics, 4
    population, 2
    price, 4
    problem, 2–3
    and sales letters, 173
Six Ps exercise, 9, 11, 13
Smith, Adam, 17
Smollin, Leandra M., 75, 75–90, 90
    "'I'm Ambivalent about It': The Dilemmas of PowerPoint" discussion questions, 91–92

"'I'm Ambivalent about It': The Dilemmas of PowerPoint" reading, 75–90
Social entrepreneurship, 42–44
Societal system, 39–40
Software, 198–200
Standards, 19
Stanford Research Institute, 17
Stange, Kurt C., 93
    "The 5 R's: An Emerging Bold Standard for Conducting Relevant Research in a Changing World" discussion questions, 105–106
    "The 5 R's: An Emerging Bold Standard for Conducting Relevant Research in a Changing World" reading, 93–104
Statistical Abstracts of the United States, 152
Statistical Reference Index, 152
The Structure of Scientific Revolutions, vii, 17, 20
Success models, and research, 144
Superstitions, 19

T

Table of contents, 214
    sample, 220, 234
Tables, 107, 199
Target marketing, 6
"Teaching Leadership Critically: New Directions for Leadership Pedagogy," 49–67
In-text citation, 152–153
Text-heavy slide, 195
Text, in presentation software, 200
Theme, 195
Theoretical frame, 143, 144
Theoretical question, 2
Theory, 19
Theory and practice, 144
Time lines, 216
Title page, 213
Title slide, 192, 194–195, 199
Tone, 194
Topic research, 139–167. *see also* Research
Tourish, Dennis, 15, 49, 72
    "Teaching Leadership Critically: New Directions for Leadership Pedagogy" discussion questions, 73–74
    "Teaching Leadership Critically: New Directions for Leadership Pedagogy" reading, 49–67
Traditions, 19

U

Uncertainty, 143

V

Values, 19, 41
Virtual community, 6
Visual aids, 193, 195, 200, 214, 216
Voice, 195

W

Web browsing, 142
Web references, 155
Website, 140
Website research, 142
White paper, 145–151
    checklist, 145
    and fieldwork, 145
    project scope, 145
    samples, 146–151
White space, 199
Whole Earth Catalog, 25, 26, 27
Works cited
    book, 154
    book chapter, 155
    book with two or three authors, 154
    email, 155
    examples, 156
    government documents, 155
    interview, 155
    newspaper, 155
    periodicals, 155
    in project proposal, 216
    web references, 155
Works cited page, 154–155, 216
    sample, 230, 250–251

CPSIA information can be obtained
at www.ICGtesting.com
Printed in the USA
LVOW02s1800050517
533337LV00004B/7/P